# COMMON MARKET LAW OF COMPETITION

1

AUSTRALIA
The Law Book Company Ltd.
Sydney : Melbourne : Brisbane

GREAT BRITAIN
Sweet & Maxwell Ltd.
London

INDIA
N. M. Tripathi Private Ltd.
Bombay

ISRAEL
Steimatzky's Agency Ltd.
Jerusalem : Tel Aviv : Haifa

MALAYSIA : SINGAPORE : BRUNEI
Malayan Law Journal (Pte.) Ltd.
Singapore

NEW ZEALAND
Sweet & Maxwell (N.Z.) Ltd.
Wellington

PAKISTAN
Pakistan Law House
Karachi

U.S.A. AND CANADA
Matthew Bender & Co. Inc.
New York

# Common Market Law of Competition

By

**CHRISTOPHER BELLAMY**, M.A. (Oxon.)
*of the Middle Temple and Gray's Inn;*
*and of the South Eastern Circuit, Barrister*

and

**GRAHAM D. CHILD**, M.A, (Oxon.)
*Solicitor of the Supreme Court*

Consultant Editor
**JEREMY LEVER**, M.A. (Oxon.)
*One of Her Majesty's Counsel;*
*Fellow of All Souls College, Oxford*

*LONDON*
SWEET & MAXWELL

*NEW YORK*
MATTHEW BENDER

1973

*Published in Great Britain by*
*Sweet & Maxwell Ltd. of*
*11 New Fetter Lane, London*
*Published in the U.S.A. by*
*Matthew Bender & Co. Inc. of*
*235 East 45th Street,*
*New York, New York 10017*
*Printed in Great Britain*
*by Eyre & Spottiswoode Ltd,*
*Thanet Press, Margate, Kent*

SBN Hardback 421 17930 9

Library of Congress Catalog Card No. 73-80039

# PREFACE

Since January 1, 1973 the common market rules on competition
have formed part of the domestic law of the United Kingdom.
The law and practice governing competition in the EEC is to be
found not only in the relevant Treaty provisions but also in a
substantial number of Regulations, decisions of the European
Court of Justice and decisions and other pronouncements by the
Commission of the European Communities. This diffuse body of
legislation and case law is often unfamiliar, and at times
inaccessible, to those who now have to deal for the first time with
the many practical problems that arise. In this work we attempt
to explain the general principles of the Community rules from
a practical point of view and to illustrate those general principles
by reference to the available decisions. We hope we may contribute a little to assist those who have to grapple with the
mysteries of " categories of decisions by associations of undertakings," " absolute territorial protection," " parallel imports "
and the like.

One general point must be made. Although this work is
entitled " Common Market Law of Competition," we deal almost
entirely with the European Economic Community. Under
pressure of time we have omitted detailed discussion of the
relevant provisions of the Treaty establishing the European Coal
and Steel Community. For the same reason we have been able
to deal only in outline with Article 90 of the EEC Treaty and
the relevant rules on competition relating to Agriculture and
Transport within the Community.

We must also draw attention to two matters in relation to
the sources used in this book. First, it is Continental practice, in
systems in which learned jurists play a greater part than the
common law allows, to cite the works of distinguished authors as
authority for the propositions advanced in the text. It is also the
practice to draw the reader's attention to those authors who take
a contrary view. We regret that it has not been possible for us
to follow this practice. For linguistic and geographical reasons
many relevant works of scholarship have not been available to us.

Accordingly, the authors cited in this work form a small, and highly selective, number of those who have published, or will shortly publish, works in English. For the most part the works cited are Deringer, *The Competition Law of the European Economic Community* (1968), published by CCH; Oberdorfer, Gleiss and Hirsch, *Common Market Cartel Law* (2nd ed. 1971), published by Commerce Clearing House (CCH); Mégret, Waelbroeck and others, *Le droit de la Communauté Economique Européenne*, published by Editions de l'Université de Bruxelles (1972); and, finally, a more general work, Mathijsen, *A Guide to European Community Law* (1972), published by Sweet & Maxwell. Where we have referred to these authorities, we apologise to others who hold similar or contrary views but whose works it has not been possible for us to cite.

Secondly, it must be emphasised that although the translations of the relevant Regulations used in this work are those supplied by H.M.S.O. in *European Communities Secondary Legislation* (1972) (except for Regulations 2591/72 and 2779/72), those translations do not represent authentic texts of Community Regulations. No authentic texts of Regulations were available on January 1, 1973, despite their immediate impact upon the rights and duties of very many persons in the acceding states as from that date. Similarly, the translations into English of decisions of the Court of Justice of the European Communities (the European Court) and of decisions and announcements of the Commission of the European Communities (the Commission) used and referred to in this work are in no way official translations.

Where decisions of the Commission prior to January 1, 1973 have been reported in the *Common Market Law Reports* the relevant report in that (unofficial) series has been cited; but references have also been given to the appropriate issue of the French edition of the *Official Journal of the European Communities*. Citations from the *Common Market Law Reports* have also been given in respect of decisions of the European Court, where such decisions have been reported in that series. Reports of European Court decisions are also to be found in the *Recueil de la Jurisprudence de la Cour* (Recueil), the official series in French, the *Common Market Reporter* (CMR) and the *Common Market Law Review* (C.M.L.Rev.), references to all of which are included in the *Table of Decisions*. Both the Recueil and the CMR reports contain the arguments of the parties, while the *Common Market Law Review* reports usually include helpful annotations of the more important cases. However, where difficulties arise in respect of decisions of the European Court or the Commission, reference should always be made to an authentic text in one of the original official languages. Happily, the relevant provisions of the Treaties which are cited have been drawn from authentic pre-accession texts (Cmnd. 4862–4864).

There are many people to whom we must express our gratitude for the assistance we have received in the course of preparing this work. First and foremost, our thanks are due to Jeremy Lever, Q.C., our consultant editor, who undertook the onerous task of reading each successive draft of the manuscript. His knowledge, ready help and constructive criticism has not only been an invaluable contribution to this work, but was also a source of great encouragement to us both throughout its preparation. We are also very grateful to Mr. John Swift, Barrister, who wrote the whole of Chapter 7 which deals with Article 86 of the EEC Treaty. We much regret that he was not able to play the full part in the authorship of this book which was originally envisaged. We must also express our thanks to Mr. Willy Alexander, of the Hague Bar, who collaborated closely with this project in its early stages. Most unfortunately, pressure of time prevented the continuance of this collaboration but we have derived very great assistance from Mr. Alexander's insight and wide experience in relation to EEC matters. Much of Chapter 8, which concerns exclusive dealing agreements, was written with his help and guidance. His own work, *The EEC Rules of Competition*, is published in English by Kluwer-Harrap.

Many others have also read parts of the manuscript and have made helpful comments upon it. First, there are many senior members of the staff of the European Commission. These include Herr J. Thiesing, Legal Adviser, and Dr. N. Koch, Dr. Spormann, Dr. Stoever, Dr. Benini and Dr. Schroeter, all of the Directorate-General for Competition. To each of these we are most grateful. As far as the United Kingdom is concerned, we have been assisted by illuminating comments from Mr. Antony Graham-Dixon, Barrister; Dr. Valentine Korah, Reader in English law, University of London (who kindly read the whole manuscript); Professor

# PREFACE

A. G. Guest, Professor of English law, University of London;
and Mr. David Gibbins, Barrister. We have also received help
and encouragement from Mr. Floris Vogelaar and Mr. Colin
McFadyean, Mr. Maurice Firth and Mr. Paul Egerton-Vernon,
Solicitors, and from many others. Of course, we make it clear
that the errors that remain are entirely our own, and are in no
way attributable to those who have assisted us.

We must also thank all those who have helped to overcome the
considerable typing and administrative problems which preparation of this work has posed. We are particularly grateful to
Miss Elizabeth Strickland, Mrs. Barbara Thexton, Mrs. D. Lane
and Miss Kathy Fullick. In addition we were assisted in the task
of proof reading by Philip Bretherton, Philip Bovey, Dinah
Cartwright, Alasdair Gordon, David Hughes, Andrew Laidlaw,
Malcolm Nicholson, Marie Powell, David Stevens and Paul
Walker. We would also like to thank Sidney and Ian Jefferys
for the help they have given.

Finally we would like to express our thanks to Messrs.
Sweet & Maxwell, who have published this work with efficiency
and speed.

The law is stated as at March 10, 1973. However only brief
reference has been possible to the decision of the European Court
in *Europemballage Corporation and Continental Can Co. Inc.* v.
*E.C. Commission*, and to certain decisions of the Commission, the
text of which was either unavailable, or available only shortly
before, that date. However, particular account has been taken
of the decision of the European Court in *Brasserie de Haecht*
(*No. 2*), February 6, 1973, which relates to the civil validity of
agreements falling within Article 85. That case illustrates, first,
that the Court is prepared to depart from its own recently
delivered previous decisions (*e.g. Bilger*); and, secondly, that it
may do so without explaining the reasoning which leads it to
overrule or distinguish those previous decisions. Many English
lawyers will find such a judicial approach unfamiliar.

C.W.B.  
Gray's Inn Chambers  
Gray's Inn.

G.D.C.  
35 Basinghall Street  
London, E.C.2.

# CONTENTS

[ ix ]

# CONTENTS

CONTENTS

[ xi ]

# TABLE OF TREATIES

# TABLE OF REGULATIONS

# TABLES OF DECISIONS

[ xvii ]

DECISIONS OF THE COMMISSION OF THE EUROPEAN COMMUNITIES UNDER
ARTICLES 85–90 OF THE EEC TREATY[1]

---

[1] Including several other announcements relating to individual cases.

PARA

PARA

CHAPTER 1

# COMPETITION IN THE EUROPEAN COMMUNITIES

## 1. IN GENERAL

### (a) *The EEC*

**101**    **The European Economic Community.**   Article 2 of the Treaty
establishing the European Economic Community [1] provides that
" The Community shall have as its task, by establishing a common market and progressively approximating the economic
policies of Member States, to promote throughout the Community a harmonious development of economic activities, a
continuous and balanced expansion, an increase in stability, an
accelerated raising of the standard of living and closer relations
between the States belonging to it." Article 3 of the Treaty sets
out, in broad terms, the activities to be carried on by the Treaty
for the purposes of achieving the objectives of Article 2. These
activities are directed towards the two main aims of the Community: the establishment of a common market and the
approximation of the economic policies of Member States. The
tasks set out in Article 3 which are directed primarily towards the
establishment of a common market include the elimination, as
between Member States, of customs duties and of quantitative
restrictions on the import and export of goods and of all other
measures having equivalent effect; the establishment of a common

[1] The Treaty Establishing the European Economic Community (Cmnd. 4864)
has been amended by: the Treaty of April 8, 1965 establishing a Single Council
and a Single Commission of the European Communities (the Merger Treaty);
the Treaty of April 22, 1970 amending Certain Budgetary Provisions of the
Treaties establishing the European Communities and of the Treaty establishing
a Single Council and a Single Commission of the European Communities (the
Budgetary Treaty); and by the Treaty Concerning the Accession of the Kingdom
of Denmark, Ireland, the Kingdom of Norway and the United Kingdom of
Great Britain and Northern Ireland to the European Economic Community
and the European Atomic Energy Community, and Decision of the Council of
the European Communities Concerning the Accession of the said States to the
European Coal and Steel Community (the Accession Treaty). This latter Treaty
contains the Act Concerning the Conditions of Accession and the Adjustments
to the Treaty, and entered into force on January 1, 1973 (see Cmnd. 4862—I and
II) for a consolidated version of the Treaty as amended: see *Sweet & Maxwell's
European Community Treaties* (1972).

[ 1 ]

customs tariff and of a common commercial policy towards third countries; the abolition, as between Member States, of obstacles to freedom of movement for persons, services and capital; and the adoption of common policies in the spheres of agriculture and transport. The detailed provisions governing the implementation of these tasks are set out in Part 2 of the Treaty which is entitled, appropriately, " The Foundations of the Community." [2] Part 3 of the Treaty, which is entitled, " Policy of the Community," contains provisions which are essentially complementary to those contained in Part 2. These include provisions relating to the co-ordination of the economic policies of Member States [3]; the harmonisation of national laws [4]; the creation of a European Social Fund [5] and a European Investment Bank [6]; and the association of overseas countries and territories. [7] For present purposes the most important of the provisions of Part 3 of the Treaty are those entitled " Rules on Competition," which are contained in Articles 85–94 of the Treaty. These Rules regulate the competitive activities of undertakings and certain economic activities of Member States.

**102**   **Purpose of the rules on competition.** Through the implementation of the fundamental rules set out in Part 2 of the Treaty, including in particular the rules relating to the free movement of goods, services, persons and capital throughout the common market, the Community aims to establish not merely a free trade area but a full economic and customs union between the Member States. However, the reproduction of the conditions of a national market on a Community scale may be jeopardised if the operation of that market is distorted, not by customs barriers, but by the individual economic policies of Member States or by private barriers to trade erected by undertakings. As the Commission of the European Communities (" the Commission ") has said, [8]

---

[2] See: Free Movement of Goods, Arts. 9–11; the Customs Union, Arts. 12–29; Elimination of Quantitative Restrictions between States, Arts. 30–37; Agriculture, Arts. 38–47; The Free Movement of Persons, Services and Capital, Arts. 48–73; Transport, Arts. 74–84.
[3] Arts. 103–116.
[4] Arts. 95–102.
[5] Arts. 117–128.
[6] Arts. 129–130.
[7] Arts. 131–136.
[8] 5th General Report of the Activities of the EEC (1971).

" The creation and development of this unified market would be difficult if not impossible if while conventional trade barriers among the Six were being speedily reduced, other obstacles, less visible but equally restrictive, were allowed to persist.  These may arise from Member States applying different economic and fiscal regulations, or systems of State aid, or from the abuse of dominant positions on the part of private firms or from agreements to restrict competition among them."

**103**    Hence, the Treaty makes provision for rules on competition which prevent the dismantled barriers to inter-State trade being re-erected through the unilateral economic activities of States or the private activities of undertakings.  At the same time, the rules on competition have a dynamic role.  As the Commission's First Report on Competition Policy puts it [9]:

" Competition is the best incentive for economic activity since it guarantees to its participants the widest possible freedom of action.  An active competition policy based upon the treaty provisions facilitates the continual adaptation of the demand and supply structures to technical evolution; thanks to the implementation of a system of decentralised decision-making, a constantly improved efficiency can be obtained from undertakings; this is the basic condition for a continuous raising of the standard of living and employment opportunities within the Member States of the Community.  When so understood, competition policy is an essential instrument to ensure a high degree of satisfaction of private and collective requirements."

**104**    **The rules on competition.**  Accordingly, Article 3 (*f*) of the Treaty provides that the activities of the Community shall include " the institution of a system ensuring that competition in the common market is not distorted."  The implementation of this system is achieved under Articles 85–94 of the Treaty. Articles 85–90 contain the Rules on competition applicable to undertakings.  Article 91 regulates dumping practices within the common market.  Articles 92–94 regulate aids granted by Member States in so far as those aids distort or threaten to distort competition in a way which affects inter-State trade.

[9] First Report on Competition Policy (1972), p. 11.

**105**   **Rules on competition applying to undertakings.**   This book is
concerned primarily with the rules on competition applying to
undertakings, and particularly with Article 85 and Article 86 of
the Treaty.   Broadly, Article 85 [10] prohibits as incompatible with
the common market agreements between undertakings, decisions
by associations of undertakings, or concerted practices which may
affect trade between Member States and which have as their
object or effect the prevention, restriction or distortion of competition within the common market.   Article 86 [11] prohibits any
abuse by one or more undertakings of a dominant position within
the common market or a substantial part of it, in so far as that
abuse affects trade between Member States.   Articles 87–90 of the
Treaty contain supplementary and ancillary provisions.[12]   As has
been seen, the rules on competition applying to undertakings are
only one part of the complex Community system which is designed
to break down national barriers and create a unified domestic
market, where conditions of free competition prevail.   Hence,
when considering any particular problem arising under this part
of the Treaty, it is important to see Articles 85–90 in their context
as part of the overall system for the establishment of the Community.   This is particularly so for two reasons.   First, because
the decisions of the Commission and of the Court of
Justice of the European Communities (" the European Court ")
relating to the application of Articles 85–90 are strongly influenced by the need to consider the fundamental principles and
objectives of the Community.   Secondly, in any particular case
other provisions of the Treaty may be relevant to a problem
arising under the rules on competition, *e.g.*: the provisions
relating to the free movement of goods.[13]

### (b) *The ECSC*

**106**   **The European Coal and Steel Community.**   The Treaty establishing the European Coal and Steel Community,[14] set up a
common market for coal and steel, the operation of which

[10] *Post,* §§ 201 *et seq.* and §§ 301 *et seq.*
[11] *Post,* §§ 701 *et seq.*
[12] *Post,* §§ 116 *et seq.*
[13] See *e.g.* the exercise of industrial property rights in relation to provisions
governing the free movement of goods: *post,* §§ 901 *et seq.*
[14] The Treaty Establishing the European Coal and Steel Community (Cmnd. 4863)
has been amended by the instruments set out in note 1, *supra.* (See particularly
Cmnd. 4862, I and II.)

continues to be governed by the provisions of that Treaty and not
by the provisions of the Treaty Establishing the European
Economic Community.  Article 4(*d*) of the ECSC Treaty provides
that within the coal and steel Community shall be abolished and
prohibited " restrictive practices which tend towards the sharing
or exploiting of markets."  This general prohibition is imple-
mented more fully under Articles 65 and 66 of the Treaty.  Article
65 (1) provides that all agreements between undertakings,
decisions by associations of undertakings and concerted practices
tending directly or indirectly to prevent, restrict or distort normal
competition within the common market shall be prohibited.
Under Article 65 (2), the Commission [15] has power to authorise
certain specialisation, joint buying or joint selling agreements, or
agreements strictly analagous thereto.  Article 65 (4) provides
that all agreements and decisions prohibited under Article 65 (1)
shall be automatically void; and that the Commission has sole
jurisdiction to rule whether any such agreement or decision is
compatible with Article 65.  Article 65 (3) and Article 65 (5)
contain ancillary provisions relating to enforcement.  Article 66
gives the Commission wide powers to control mergers taking
place within the coal and steel Community.  A more detailed
appraisal of the rules relating to competition within the ECSC is
at present outside the scope of this work.[16]

## 2.  THE EEC RULES ON COMPETITION: SOURCES

### (a) *The Structure of the Community*

**107**    **The organisation of the EEC.**  Before dealing with the
sources of the EEC rules on competition, it is convenient to
summarise the main organisational structure of the EEC.  Article
4 of the Treaty provides that the tasks entrusted to the Community
shall be carried out by (a) an Assembly (b) a Council (c) a
Commission and (d) a Court of Justice.

[15] Formerly the High Authority—see Art. 9 of the Merger Treaty.
[16] The relevant Directives and Decisions of the High Authority and the Commission relating to administrative matters are set out in *European Communities
Secondary Legislation*, Part 4, H.M.S.O. pp. 103 *et seq.;* Some Decisions relating
to the application of Article 65 (2) are printed in *Common Market Law Reports*,
*e.g.* at [1968] C.M.L.R. 91; [1970] C.M.L.R. 503; [1972] C.M.L.R. D105–D111;
others are to be found in the relevant issues of the *Official Journal*.  See also
Art. 156 of the Act of Accession. And see *post*, §150, note 15.

**108**    **The Assembly.** The Assembly,[17] generally known as the
European Parliament, is attended by delegations from each
Member State, nominated by the respective national Parliaments.
Broadly speaking, the powers of the European Parliament are
only advisory and consultative, although it has limited super-
visory powers over the Commission. In the present context, the
only such power of importance is the right to obtain from the
Commission oral or written answers to questions put to it by the
European Parliament or by its members.[18]

**109**    **The Council.** The Council [19] consists of one delegate from
the government of each Member State. Its main task is to ensure
co-ordination of the general economic policies of the Member
States. The Council is the body which takes the major economic
and political decisions about Community policy. In practice,
the Council is the Community's principal legislator, although in
many cases it can only act on a proposal from the Commission.[20]
Under Article 87 of the Treaty, the Council is charged with the
duty, acting on a proposal from the Commission and after
consulting the Assembly, of adopting appropriate regulations or
directives to implement the principles of Articles 85 and 86 of the
Treaty.

**110**    **The Commission.** The European Commission [21] is the administrative body charged with ensuring that the provisions of the
Treaty are applied and observed. In particular, it is responsible
for executing the decisions of the Council and for putting forward
opinions or recommendations on matters dealt with in the
Treaty, where the Treaty so provides or where the Commission
considers it necessary. In accordance with the Treaty, it also has
power to take its own decisions and to participate in the shaping
of measures by the Council (who may frequently only act on a
proposal by the Commission).[22] Finally, it may exercise powers
conferred on it by the Council to implement the rules laid down by

[17] Arts. 137–144 of the Treaty.
[18] Art. 140.
[19] Arts. 145–154.
[20] *e.g.* under Arts. 21, 43, 44, 49, 54, 63, 69, 75 and 87 of the Treaty.
[21] Art. 155 of the EEC Treaty; Arts. 10–18 of the Merger Treaty.
[22] Note 20, *supra.*

the latter.[23] The Commission itself consists of thirteen members,[24] nominated by the Member governments and supported by a staff of over 5,000 which is, in effect, the civil service of the Community. The Commission is of central importance in the Community law on competition. Under Regulations made by the Council, it is charged with enforcing the provisions of the Treaty, with administering the system set up under those Regulations, and with bringing an end to infringements. Its decisions and other public pronouncements are of great importance in laying down the general principles upon which it proposes to act.[25] The part of the Commission principally concerned with Articles 85 and 86 is the Directorate-General of Competition which has a total staff of about 150.

**111** **The European Court.** The Court of Justice [26] of the European Communities, which sits at Luxembourg, consists of nine judges, assisted by four Advocates-General. [27] For present purposes, the Court is important in two respects. First, under Article 173 of the Treaty, an appeal lies to the Court against a decision of the Commission on grounds of lack of competence, infringement of an essential procedural requirement, infringement of the Treaty or any rule of law relating to its application, or misuse of powers (détournement de pouvoir). In respect of appeals against decisions of the Commission imposing penalties, the Court has a wider jurisdiction. [28] Secondly, under Article 177 of the Treaty, the Court has jurisdiction to give preliminary rulings concerning, *inter alia*, the interpretation of the Treaty. Where such a question arises in the course of domestic litigation, a national court of a Member State may, and a national court of final resort must, request the European Court to give a ruling thereon. The decisions of the European Court both on appeals from the Commission's decisions and on requests for preliminary

[23] Art. 155.
[24] Merger Treaty, Art. 10 (1); Accession Act, Art. 15 provides for fourteen members, but now reduced to thirteen by the non-accession of Norway.
[25] *Post,* §§ 132 *et seq.*
[26] Arts. 164–188; see also the Statute of the Court of Justice annexed as a Protocol to the Treaty.
[27] Under Arts. 165–166, as amended by Arts. 17–18 of the Act of Accession, there were to have been eleven judges and three Advocates-General. Following the non-accession of Norway it is understood that there will be nine judges, one of the existing judges stepping down to become a fourth Advocate-General.
[28] Art. 172 of the Treaty; and see Reg. 17, Art. 17.

rulings from national courts have provided valuable guidance for the interpretation of the Community rules on competition.[29]

## (b) *The Provisions of the Treaty*

**112**    **Articles 85 and 86.**    This work is primarily concerned with Articles 85 and 86 of the Treaty, the full text of which is set out in Appendix I.    Articles 85 and 86 are " directly applicable " provisions; that is to say, from January 1, 1973, they become part of the domestic law of the United Kingdom conferring rights and duties upon individuals.    The prohibitions imposed by those Articles require no prior decision of the Commission or of any other authority before taking effect; their application to undertakings is direct and immediate.[30]

**113**    **Article 85.**    Article 85 (1) [31] prohibits all agreements between undertakings, or decisions by associations of undertakings and concerted practices which may affect trade between Member States and which have as their object or effect the prevention, restriction or distortion of competition within the common market.    Article 85 (2) [32] provides that any agreements or decisions prohibited under Article 85 (1) shall be automatically void.    Article 85 (3) [33] provides in effect that agreements, decisions or concerted practices (or categories thereof) may be exempted from the prohibition of Article 85 (1) where they contribute to improving the production or distribution of goods, or to promoting technical or economic progress; provided that they also allow consumers a fair share of the resulting benefit, only impose restrictions indispensable to achieving those objectives and do not permit the elimination of competition.    The essential, and to British lawyers unfamiliar, feature of Article 85 is that its application in any given case depends upon the economic aims or effects of transactions entered into between undertakings.

[29] *Post*, §§ 136 *et seq.*
[30] See Reg. 17, Art. 1; *Bosch* v. *de Geus* (13/61) [1962] C.M.L.R. 1; European Communities Act, 1972, s. 2.
[31] §§ 201 *et seq., post.*
[32] §§ 401 *et seq., post.*
[33] §§ 601 *et seq., post.*

**114**    **Article 85 must be treated as a whole.** It must also be emphasised from the outset that the three parts of Article 85 are closely interrelated. From this one particularly important consequence follows. Contrary to the express words of the Treaty, certain agreements which fall within Article 85 (1) are *not* to be treated as void while there is a possibility that they may be exempted under Article 85 (3). The European Court has said [34] that the structure of Article 85 of the Treaty is characterised by the formulation of a prohibition (Article 85 (1)) and the consequences attached thereto (Article 85 (2)), subject to the power to grant exemptions (Article 85 (3)). Thus a given agreement or some of its clauses are automatically void only if the agreement comes within paragraph 1 of Article 85 and cannot qualify for application of the provisions of Artilce 85 (3)." Under Regulation 17 of the Council ("Regulation 17"), which is the principal Regulation providing machinery for the implementation and enforcement of Article 85, the Commission is empowered to grant exemptions under Article 85 (3) in respect of agreements duly notified to it for the purpose of obtaining such an exemption. [35] Certain other agreements do not require to be notified to the Commission at all. [36] Where an agreement has been duly notified to the Commission, or is not required to be notified, the parties may be able to enforce the agreement pending the Commissions' decision under Article 85 (3). But this doctrine, which is known as "provisional validity", applies only to agreements already in existence at the date of entry into force of Regulation 17.[37]

**115**    **Article 86.** Article 86 [38] provides that an abuse by one or more undertakings of a dominant position within the common market or in a substantial part of it shall be prohibited as incompatible with the common market in so far as it may affect trade between Member States. Whereas Article 85 (1) strikes at various

---

[34] In *Portelange* v. *Smith Corona International* (10/69) 15 Recueil 309; noted at 7 C.M.L.Rev. 234; CMR 8075; but see now *Brasserie de Haecht* (*No. 2*) (48/72), February 6, 1973.

[35] Arts. 4–7 and 25 of Reg. 17; see also Arts. 8 and 9 (1) of Reg. 17. *Post,* §§ 501 *et seq.*

[36] Art. 4 (2) of Reg. 17. *Post* §§ 413, 528 *et seq.*

[37] For the meaning of " provisional validity " see *post,* §§ 401 *et seq.* especially §§ 410 *et seq., post.* For notification see §§ 501 *et seq., post.* For exemption under Art. 85 (3) see §§ 601 *et seq., post.* For the Commission's powers of surveillance and enforcement (including the power to fine) see §§ 1201 *et seq., post.*

[38] *Post,* §§ 701 *et seq.*

forms of co-operation, Article 86 strikes at abusive conduct, not primarily characterised by any agreement, decision or concerted practice between undertakings. As with Article 85, the prohibition of Article 86 takes immediate effect as from January 1, 1973 in the domestic law of the United Kingdom.[39] Unlike Article 85 there is no provision for exemption from the prohibition. Hitherto the activities of the Community in respect of Article 86 have been limited; but they may be expected to increase.[40]

**116**   **Article 87.**   Article 87 gives the Council, acting on a proposal from the Commission and after consulting the European Parliament, the duty to adopt appropriate regulations [41] or directives [42] to give effect to the principles set out in Articles 85 and 86. In particular under Article 87 such regulations and directives are to be designed to ensure compliance with the prohibitions of Article 85 (1) and Article 86 and to make provision for fines and other penalty payments; to lay down detailed rules for the application of Article 85 (3); and to make provision for certain other matters including the scope of Articles 85 and 86 in various branches of the economy, the respective functions of the Commission and the European Court, and the relationship between national laws and Community laws. Hitherto the Council has made several Regulations under the provisions of Article 87, the most important of which is Regulation 17, the principal Regulation providing for the administration and enforcement of Articles 85 and 86.[43]

**117**   **Article 88.**   Article 88 of the Treaty provided transitional provisions relating to the enforcement of Articles 85 and 86 by authorities of Member States until the date of entry into force of measures taken under Article 87. Under Regulation 17 the enforcement of these Articles is almost entirely in the hands of the Commission.[44]

**118**   **Article 89.**   Article 89 charges the Commission with the duty of ensuring the application of the principles of Articles 85 and 86.

[39] Reg. 17, Art. 1; European Communities Act 1972.
[40] First Report on Competition Policy, paras 81 *et seq.*
[41] See *post*, § 121.
[42] See Art. 189 of the Treaty.
[43] *Post*, § 122.
[44] See Art. 9 of Reg. 17. See also § 1220, *post.*

This Article is primarily a transitional provision empowering the Commission to investigate cases of suspected infringement, and to take the measures required to bring such infringement to an end. The procedure which the Commission must follow before finding that Articles 85 and 86 are infringed, and the measures to be taken to bring those infringements to an end are now fully set out in Regulation 17 and the regulations made thereunder.[45]

**119**    **Article 90.** Any detailed discussion of the provisions of Article 90 lies, at present, outside the scope of this work.[46] In brief, Article 90 (1) provides that the Member States are under a duty neither to enact nor to maintain in force any measure in respect of public undertakings or undertakings "to which Member States grant special or exclusive rights " which is contrary to Article 7 or Articles 85–94 of the Treaty. Article 7 of the Treaty prohibits any discrimination on the grounds of nationality. Articles 91–94 lay down detailed provisions relating to State aids and dumping practices. In essence, the purpose of Article 90 is to ensure that the rules on competition apply equally to the public sector of the economy. Article 90 (2) provides that undertakings entrusted with the operation of services " of general economic interest " or " having the character of a revenue producing monopoly " are subject to such rules in so far as the application thereof " does not obstruct the performance in law or fact of the particular tasks assigned to them." [47] The extent of this limited exception is not at present clear; but Article 90 (2) also provides that the development of trade must not be affected to such an extent as would be contrary to the interests of the Community.[48] Under Article 90 (3) the Commission is under a duty to enforce Article 90 by addressing appropriate decisions or directives [49] to Member States. When considering Article 90, reference should also be made to Article 37 of the Treaty which relates to State trading monopolies.

[45] *Post*, §§ 121 *et seq.*; Art. 89 remains important in sectors where implementing regulations do not apply, now only sea and air transport. See Council Reg. 141 and § 131, *post*.
[46] For an extensive treatment see Deringer, *The Competition Law of the European Economic Community* (1968), paras 801 *et seq.*
[47] See *Re Gema*, J.O. 1971 L134/15; [1971] C.M.L.R. D35.
[48] And see (10/71) *Ministère Public Luxembourgeois* v. *Müller*, 17 Rec. 723; 9 C.M.L.Rev. 1972, 481.
[49] See Art. 189.

**120    Other provisions of the Treaty.**  As has been seen, Articles 85–90 must always be considered in their context in the Treaty as a whole.  In dealing with any given problem, therefore, other provisions may be relevant.  This is particularly so in respect of Articles 2, 3, 5, 6 and 7 which occur in Part One of the Treaty under the Title " Principles."  Those Articles relate to the purposes and tasks of the Community (Arts. 2 and 3); to the duty of Member States to take all appropriate measures to achieve the Community's objectives and to refrain from measures likely to jeopardise their objectives (Art. 5); to the duty of Member States to co-ordinate their economic policies (Art. 6); and finally, in Article 7, to the prohibition of any discrimination on the grounds of nationality.  Other provisions of the Treaty which are important include the provisions relating to the free movement of goods (Arts. 9–37, especially Arts. 30–36 [50]), those relating to dumping and State aids (Arts. 91–94), those relating to tax provisions (Arts. 95–99) and to the approximation of laws (Arts. 100–102).

(c) *The Regulations of the Council and the Commission*

**121    In general.**  Under Article 189 of the Treaty, regulations made by the Council or the Commission have general application.  They are binding in their entirety and directly applicable in all Member States.  Article 87 empowers the Council to make implementing regulations in respect of Articles 85 and 86.  It has exercised this power to make three principal Regulations (Regs. 17, 19/65 and 2821/71) which Regulations have empowered the Commission to make subordinate regulations implementing further the Regulations made by the Council.  In chronological order, the principal Regulations hitherto made by the Council and the Commission are as follows.

**122    Regulation 17.**  Regulation 17 [51] was the first Regulation implementing Articles 85 and 86 and came into force on March 13, 1962.  Article 1 of that Regulation provides, generally speaking, that the prohibitions of Articles 85 and 86 take direct effect without any prior decisions being required. [52]  The remaining provisions of the Regulation may conveniently be divided into

---

[50] See particularly *post*, §§ 912 *et seq.*
[51] As amended by Reg. 59, Reg. 118/63, Reg. 2822/71 and by The Act of Accession, Annex I.
[52] See § 401, *post*.

two broad parts, those relating to applications by undertakings to the Commission, either for exemption under Article 85 (3) or for a declaration known as a " negative clearance "; and those relating to the Commission's general powers of enforcing the provisions of Articles 85 and 86.

**123**     **Notification and negative clearance.** Under Regulation 17 two procedures are available to undertakings whose agreements, decisions or concerted practices fall, or may fall, within Article 85 (1). First, the agreement may be notified to the Commission for the purpose of obtaining an individual exemption under Article 85 (3).[53] The provisions relating to notification are Articles 4–7 and Article 25 of Regulation 17.[54] Article 25 provides transitional provisions in respect of Accession agreements (*i.e.* agreements already in existence on January 1, 1973 and falling within the Treaty solely as a result of Accession).[55] Such agreements require to be notified before June 30, 1973.[56] Notification gives the parties certain temporary advantages— relief from fines, and in some cases, " provisional validity " of the agreement.[57] A second procedure is provided under Article 2 of Regulation 17, whereby the parties may apply for a declaration by the Commission that, on the basis of the facts in its possession, there are no grounds under Article 85 (1) [58] for action on its part in respect of the agreement, *i.e.* that the agreement falls outside the Treaty altogether. A declaration to this effect is known as a negative clearance.[59] Application for negative clearance, however, does not carry the same temporary advantages as a notification for exemption under Article 85 (3).[60] Such an application should therefore always be combined with a notification for the purposes of Article 85 (3), a course which can conveniently

---

[53] For exemption under Art. 85 (3) see §§ 601 *et seq., post.*
[54] *Post,* §§ 501 *et seq.*
[55] See § 207, *post* and §§ 517 *et seq., post.*
[56] Art. 25 of Reg. 17.
[57] See *post,* §§ 504-507 *et seq.;* and see §§ 410 *et seq., post.*
[58] Or Art. 86; see §§ 701 *et seq., post.*
[59] Technically, an exemption under Art. 85 (3) is a "declaration of inapplicability," which is given where Art. 85 (1) is applicable to the agreement, but may be declared inapplicable under Art. 85 (3). " Negative clearance " is a declaration that Art. 85 (1) does not apply at all.
[60] See §§ 501-503, *post.*

be followed by filling up both parts of the Form A/B upon which both applications for negative clearance and notification have to be made.[61]

**124** **Other provisions of Regulation 17.** Broadly, the other important provisions of Regulation 17 are as follows. Under Article 9 (2) the Commission has power to apply Articles 85 and 86. Under Article 9 (1) the Commission has sole power to grant exemption under Article 85 (3).[62] Under Article 3 the Commission may, by means of a decision, require the termination of infringements.[63] In exercising this power it may act on its own initiative, or on a complaint by a Member State or by individuals with a legitimate interest. Under Article 15 (2) the Commission has wide powers to impose fines of up to one million units of account [63a] in respect of infringements of the Treaty or breaches of the provisions of Regulation 17.[64] Under Article 16 the Commission may enforce its decisions through periodic penalty payments.[65] Articles 11–14 give the Commission authority to require information, to make inquiries into sections of the economy and to carry out investigations into undertakings either by itself or through the authorities of Member States. Other provisions of Regulation 16 relate to further liaison with the authorities of Member States, to review by the Court of Justice, to hearings, to professional secrecy, to the publication of decisions and to other ancillary matters[67].

**125** **Regulation 27.** Regulation 27 [68] (as amended by Reg. 1133/68) sets out the procedure for making applications for negative clearance and for notifying agreements for the purposes of obtaining exemption under Article 85 (3), including the form to be used (Form A/B) and other relevant details.

**126** **Regulation 99/63.**[69] This Regulation makes detailed provision for the procedure at hearings of the parties and other interested

---

[61] See §§ 503 and 534 *et seq., post.*
[62] *Post,* §§ 601 *et seq.*
[63] *Post,* §§ 1202 *et seq.*
[63a] Or a sum in excess thereof up to 10 per cent of turnover in the preceding business year.
[64] *Post,* §§ 1205 *et seq.* For other powers to impose fines see Art. 15 (1), *post,* §§ 535, 1219.
[65] *Post,* §§ 1204, 1219.
[66] *Post,* §§ 1213 *et seq.*     [67] *Post,* §§ 1221 *et seq.*
[68] *Post,* §§ 534 *et seq.*     [69] *Post,* §§ 1221 *et seq.*

persons which the Commission must hold before reaching a decision under Regulation 17.

127    **Regulation 19/65.**  Regulation 19/65[70] made by the Council, empowers the Commission to exempt under Article 85 (3), by means of a regulation, certain categories of agreements, decisions and concerted practices.  Such an exemption is known as " a block exemption."  Under this Regulation the Commission may so exempt certain exclusive dealing agreements and certain agreements relating to industrial property rights.  Hitherto the Commission has not exercised its powers in relation to the latter agreements.

128    **Regulation 67/67.**[71]  Regulation 67/67 was made by the Commission in pursuance of the powers conferred upon it under Regulation 19/65.  It provides a block exemption in respect of those exclusive dealing agreements which satisfy the criteria therein set out.  Such agreements no longer require notification.

129    **Regulation 2821/71.**  This Regulation, also made by the Council, empowers the Commission to exempt under Article 85 (3) by way of Regulation, certain categories of standardisation, research and development and specialisation agreements.  On December 21, 1972 the Commission made a Regulation relating to the block exemption of a limited class of specialisation agreements. [72]

130    **Draft Regulations.**  Regulations are published in draft form before being enacted by the Council or the Commission. At present a draft has been published of a Regulation of the Council relating to the limitation of actions.[73]  Such draft Regulations are of no legal force until they have been finally enacted.

131    **Other Regulations.**  Finally, mention should be made of certain other Regulations the discussion of which at present falls outside the scope of this work.  Under Regulation 26, Articles

[70] As amended by Act of Accession, Annex I.
[71] As amended by Act of Accession, Annex I, and by Reg. 2591/72; *post,* §§ 818 *et seq.*
[72] Reg. 2779/72, J.O. 1972 L292/23. *Post,* §§ 1023 *et seq.*
[73] *Post,* § 1211.

85–90 of the Treaty apply to agreements, decisions and practices relating to the production of and trade in certain agricultural and fishery products,[74] which prior to July 1, 1962 fell outside those provisions.[75] Such agreements, etc. are now governed by the provisions of Regulation 17. However, Article 2 of Regulation 26 contains important exceptions to the application of Article 85 (1) in favour of domestic marketing organisations. Articles 3 and 4 of that Regulation relate to dumping practices and subsidies. Further, under Regulation 1017/68, the provisions of Regulation 17 were made applicable to transport by rail, road and inland waterway, which had previously been exempted from the provisions of Regulation 17 under Council Regulation 141.[76] Generally speaking, Regulation 1017/68 prohibits restrictive practices in relation to transport in terms similar to those of Articles 85 and 86. Exceptions are made in favour of certain technical agreements,[77] and in favour of arrangements made by groups of small and medium sized undertakings,[78] which do not require notification. Other agreements may obtain exemption from the provisions of Regulation 1017/68 by way of a procedure analogous to the obtaining of an exemption under Article 85 (3).[79] For this purpose notification of the relevant agreement is required.[80] Regulation 1017/68 also contains enforcement and other ancillary provisions broadly akin to those found in Regulation 17.[81] Regulations 1629/69 and 1630/69 contain provisions further implementing those of Regulation 1017/68. Hitherto the Commission has taken no decisions under Regulation 1017/68.

### (d) Decisions and other Pronouncements of the Commission

**132    In general.** The Commission is the primary source of Community competition law. Within the broad framework of Articles 85 and 86 and Regulation 17 it is the Commission's task to administer the competition rules of the Treaty. Partly because of the wide terms in which Articles 85 and 86 are couched, and

[74] As listed in Annex II to the Treaty.
[75] Under Art. 42 of the Treaty.
[76] Sea and air transport are still outside the provisions of this Regulation, but the Commission is examining cross-channel ferries under Art. 89 of the Treaty. See Parliamentary Question 360/72 (M. Vredeling), J.O. 1972 C125/11.
[77] Art. 3 of Reg. 1017/68.                 [78] Art. 4 of Reg. 1017/68.
[79] Art. 6 of Reg. 1017/68.                 [80] Art. 12 of Reg. 1017/68.
[81] Arts. 7–31 of Reg. 1017/68.  See also Treaty of Accession, Annex VII/IV.

partly because of the limited nature of the review of the Commission's decisions by the European Court, the Commission has been left free to determine a competition policy for the European Community. Its decisions,[82] although having legal effect, are often an expression of that policy. Similarly, the Commission's policy is to be seen in its other announcements and notices.[83] Broadly, the Commission regards the first task of the Community rules on competition to be the removal of private barriers which hinder the development of inter-State trade.[84] These barriers are erected particularly by agreements which have as their object or effect the division of the common market along national boundaries, including agreements which perpetuate or hinder the abolition of separate national markets within the Community. At the same time, there is a positive aspect to the Commission's competition policy. It has consistently encouraged collaboration between small and medium sized firms, and it has promoted other forms of co-operation which lead to better and more rational use of resources.[85] This positive aspect is also seen in the Commission's decisions and its other pronouncements.

**133    The Commission's decisions.**    A decision of the Commission is binding in its entirety to those to whom it is addressed.[86] Decisions of the Commission are published in the *Official Journal of the European Communities.* The decisions of the Commission fall broadly into three categories: (i) decisions imposing fines in respect of infringements; (ii) decisions granting negative clearance; and (iii) decisions granting or refusing exemption under Article 85 (3). Decisions imposing fines are as yet few in number, but such decisions clearly show that undertakings which infringe the Treaty may face severe financial penalties.[87] The decisions on negative clearance have defined some of the circumstances in which Article 85 (1) has no operation. The decisions in relation to the application of Article 85 (3) illustrate the implementation of the Commission's policy of breaking down national barriers while encouraging agreements which bring positive benefits.[88]

[82] *Post,* § 133.
[83] *Post,* §§ 134–135.
[84] See generally, First Report on Competition Policy, Introduction.
[85] See *e.g.* The Notice relating to Agreements of Minor Importance, App. 13, *post;* Notice on Co-operation Agreements, App. 12, *post.* And see §§ 601 *et seq., post.*
[86] Art. 189 of the Treaty.
[87] *Post,* §§ 1201 *et seq.*
[88] *Post,* §§ 601 *et seq.*

**134** **The Commission's Notices.** In addition to decisions, the Commission issues Notices from time to time which provide guidance for undertakings and indicate the Commission's view on various matters relating to Article 85. It must be emphasised that these Notices only provide general guidelines and do not purport to lay down definitive principles appropriate to every situation. In certain respects subsequent decisions of the Commission have sometimes taken a divergent view from that suggested by the relevant Notice.[89] The Notices, while helpful, must therefore be treated with a due degree of caution. They are at present four in number,[90] as follows: 1. Notice concerning contracts made with exclusive commercial agents (December 24, 1962) 2. Notice on Patent Licensing Agreements (December 24, 1962) 3. Notice on Co-operation Agreements (July 28, 1968) 4. Notice concerning Agreements of Minor Importance (May 27, 1970).

**135** **Other pronouncements by the Commission.** Guidance as to the Commission's views on particular matters can be obtained from a number of other official and semi-official pronouncements. Most important is the recently published First Report on Competition Policy, annexed to the Fifth General Report on the activities of the Communities.[91] This report surveys the Commission's activity under Articles 85 and 86 since the introduction of Regulation 17, and it gives helpful indications as to the Commission's general policy and as to its attitude in respect of various undecided matters. Next, there is the Commission's " Guide Pratique " (Practical Guide),[92] first issued in 1962 as a manual for firms. Unfortunately, the Guide Pratique has never been brought up to date and in some respects it is now unreliable in view of subsequent decisions by the Commission and the European Court.[93] Other useful sources of information may be summarised as follows. First are notices under Article 19 of Regulation 17, under which the Commission publishes the gist of a notification and invite comments upon it from third parties

[89] *e.g. Re Henkel-Colgate*, J.O. 1972 L14/14; §§ 1106 *et seq., post.*
[90] *Post*, Appendices 10–13.
[91] Available from the EC Information Office, 23, Chesham St., London S.W.1.
[92] Guide Pratique concernant les articles 85 et 86 du traité instituant la CEE et leurs reglements d'application. Ref. No. 8062/1/IX/1962/5.
[93] See *e.g.* § 528, *post.*

prior to giving a decision. Such notices indicate the broad terms of the agreement and are published when the Commission proposes to give a favourable decision in respect of it.[94]  Next, press releases and reports published in the *Bulletin of the European Communities* often give helpful guidance.  These deal particularly with matters where agreement has been reached between the parties and the Commission and hence no more formal decision or pronouncement is necessary.  Finally the Commission's written answers to questions put to it by Members of the European Assembly [95] give general indications of the Commission's views on particular matters.

### (e) *Decisions of the European Court of Justice and National Courts*

**136    The European Court.**  The decisions of the European Court under Articles 173 and 177 of the Treaty are of fundamental importance in the interpretation of Community competition law. Decisions under Article 173, which relates to appeals from decisions of the Commission, are concerned only with whether the Commission has reached its decision in accordance with a proper interpretation of the Treaty and the procedural and other requirements of " natural justice " set out in Article 173.  The Court is not concerned to substitute its own economic judgments for those of the Commission.[96]  In the case of decisions imposing fines, however, the Court has unlimited jurisdiction as to fact and law, and may reduce, confirm or increase the penalty imposed by the Commission.[97]  By contrast, in the case of judgments under Article 177 of the Treaty, the Court is not primarily concerned with the facts of the case.  Here the Court has been asked by a national court to give an interpretative ruling in relation to a matter of Community law that has arisen in the course of national domestic litigation.  In such cases the European Court is very careful not to appear to be determining questions of fact or questions of national law, which are a matter solely for the national court.  Its function is rather to lay down, in the abstract, the principles of Community law to be applied to the

[94] § 1225, *post.*
[95] *Ante*, § 108.
[96] *Consten & Grundig* v. *EEC Commission* (56/64, 58/64) [1966] C.M.L.R. 418, 477.
[97] Art. 172 of the Treaty; Art. 17 of Reg. 17.

[ 19 ]

case in question. Inevitably, the judgments of the Court under Article 177 are often couched in very general terms. None the less, the Court has delivered a series of wide ranging judgments under Article 177 which have done much to promote the integration of the common market, often at the expense of national laws which tended to perpetuate territorial restrictions.[98]   The Court is also assisted by an Advocate-General, who summarises the arguments of the parties and makes his own submissions to the Court in a role akin to that of an *amicus curiae*. Such submissions often contain useful summaries of the relevant principles and authorities.

**137**   **National courts.** In the course of national litigation, disputes between undertakings concerning Article 85 come before national courts. The decisions of such courts occasionally provide some guidance as to the approach adopted by other jurisdictions, but they should be used with caution. Very often the court's decisions are closely concerned with the particular provisions of national law which are appropriate to the case and they are arrived at by a different procedure and a different judicial approach to that commonly found in England. Moreover, it must be borne in mind that such decisions are likely to be unreliable in the light of subsequent statements of principle laid down by the European Court.

**138**   **Text book writers.** In reaching their decisions, national courts upon the continent of Europe tend to place more reliance upon the writings of jurists and other persons of authority than is customary in common law jurisdictions. Few of such writings are available in the English language; a brief and necessarily highly selective reference to important works will be found in the Preface.

### 3. COMMUNITY LAW AND NATIONAL LAW
#### (a) *The Effect of Community Law on National Laws*

**139**   **In general.** In the realm of competition within the EEC two main questions arise in relation to Community law and national

---

[98] See in particular, *Consten & Grundig* v. *EEC Commission*, note 96, *supra; Sirena* (40/70) [1971] C.M.L.R. 260; *post*, § 908; *Deutsche Grammophon* (78/70) [1971] C.M.L.R. 631, *post*, §§ 912, *et seq.*

law.  The first question is how far undertakings may rely upon
or exercise rights conferred upon them by national laws when the
exercise of those rights is likely to prevent, restrict or distort
competition within the common market and affect trade between
Member States.  This question raises fundamental issues as to
the status of Community law.  It will be seen that Community
law severely restricts the rights available to undertakings where
the exercise of those rights would hinder the objectives of the
Treaty.  The second question is how far national restrictive
practices legislation continues to be applicable in circumstances
where the provisions of the Treaty also apply.  This latter
question is dealt with in the next subsection.

**140      Superiority of Community law.** Briefly, the Community
Treaties establish an independent legal order, which is capable
of creating obligations and rights affecting not only the governments of Member States but also individuals within those States.
Those provisions of the Treaties which directly confer such rights
and duties on individuals are known as " self executing " provisions.[99]  Such provisions take precedence, under Community
law, over the domestic law of a Member State.  This procedure
has been recognised by the European Court [1] and by several
decisions of national courts.[2]  The effect of sections 2 (1) and
3 (1) of the European Communities Act 1972, is to import the
above principles into United Kingdom law.  Section 2 (1) of that
Act provides that " all such rights, powers, liabilities, obligations
and restrictions from time to time created or arising by or under
the Treaties, as in accordance with the Treaties are without further
enactment to be given legal effect or used in the United Kingdom
shall be recognised and available in law, and be enforced, allowed
and followed accordingly."  Section 3 (1) further provides that
any question as to the meaning or effect of any of the Treaties shall
be treated as a question of law and if not referred to the European
Court, be for determination as such in accordance with the
principles laid down by and any relevant decision of the European
Court.

[99] As to " self executing " provisions, see Bebr's articles in (1970) 19 I.C.L.Q. 257
and (1971) 34 M.L.R. 481.
[1] *e.g. Van gend en Loos* (26/62) [1963] C.M.L.R. 105; *Costa* v. *Enel* (6/64) [1964]
C.M.L.R. 425; *Molkerei-Zentrale, etc.* (28/67) [1968] C.M.L.R. 187.
[2] *e.g.* in Belgium in *Fromagerie Franco-Suisse " Le Ski,"* Cour de Cassation,
May 27, 1971, [1972] C.M.L.R. 330; 86 *Journal de Tribuneaux*, 460.

**141** **Conflict with national laws.** It follows from the superiority of
Community law over national law in the case of " self executing "
provisions of the Treaty, and from sections 2 and 3 (1) of the
European Communities Act 1972, that in certain circumstances
the exercise of rights conferred under British law may be unlawful
under the Treaty. Consequently those rights may not be relied
on before English courts. The circumstances in which this may
arise may be illustrated by past decisions of the European Court
and national courts. For example, prominent among the " self
executing " provisions of the Treaty is Article 85. Under Community law, Article 85 takes precedence over national laws where
such laws come into conflict with it. In several judgments the
European Court, in applying Article 85, has seriously restricted
the power of individuals to exercise rights conferred under
national law, where to exercise those rights would defeat the
objectives of the Treaty. In the case of industrial property rights,
for example, it has been held that where the right to exercise
a trademark derives from an agreement (*e.g.* a trademark licence
or an assignment) Article 85 may be infringed where the right is
exercised to prevent imports from another Member State—
notwithstanding that such exercise of the right would be perfectly
lawful under domestic law.[3] Again, the Court has in effect held
that where an exclusive dealing agreement in France falls under
Article 85 (1), an exclusive distributor in France cannot rely on
the French law of unfair competition (which permits the distributor to sue third parties who do not respect his exclusive rights)
in order to prevent imports of the relevant goods entering France
from another Member State.[4] More recently, the European
Court's ruling has prevented an undertaking in Germany from
relying on a German copyright law where the giving of effect to
rights under that law would prevent certain imports into Germany
and contravene the provisions relating to the free movement of
goods in Articles 30–36 of the Treaty.[5] In the British context,
circumstances in which the lawful exercise of rights conferred
under national law will be contrary to the provisions of the

---

[3] *Consten & Grundig* v. *EEC Commission* (56/64, 58/64) [1968] C.M.L.R. 418;
*Sirena* (40/70) [1971] C.M.L.R. 260.
[4] *Béguelin* (22/71) [1972] C.M.L.R. 81.
[5] *Deutsche-Grammophon* (78/70) [1971] C.M.L.R. 631. For subsequent proceedings before the German Court, following the European Court's ruling, see
[1972] C.M.L.R. 107.

Treaty are most likely to arise in connection with licensing agreements to which Article 85 is applicable.

### (b) *National Laws on Restrictive Practices*
**(i) Relevant provisions of British law**

**142**    **In general.**   When considering agreements or situations which are governed by the provisions of the Treaty of Rome, it is also necessary to consider the application of British domestic law relating to restrictive practices.   In this context, the basic principle to be observed is that British law may apply in any given circumstances notwithstanding that Article 85 or 86 also apply; but the operation of that law must be compatible with the administration of the Community system.[6]

**143**    **British legislation.**   The principal British legislation relating to restrictive practices is contained in the Restrictive Trade Practices Acts 1956 to 1968, the Monopolies and Mergers Acts 1948 to 1965, and the Resale Prices Act 1964.   Under the Fair Trading Bill (the Bill) published on November 30, 1972, the existing monopolies and mergers legislation will be replaced by the wide provisions contained in that Bill, and the Restrictive Trade Practices Acts will be extended in certain respects, principally to cover the supply of services.   The Fair Trading Bill also contains provisions relating to consumer trade practices and to restrictive labour practices.

**144**    **The Restrictive Trade Practices Acts.**   Broadly speaking, the Restrictive Trade Practices Act 1956, Part I, (the Act of 1956) provides that certain agreements made between two or more persons carrying on business within the United Kingdom in the production or supply of goods, or in the application to goods of any process of manufacture, under which two or more parties accept restrictions as set out in section 6 of that Act, must be registered with the Registrar of Restrictive Trading Agreements (to be replaced under the Bill by a Director-General of Fair Trading).   Clause 98 of the Bill provides, broadly, that the provisions of Part I of the Act of 1956 will apply to services designated

[6] *Post,* §§ 148 *et seq.*

by the Secretary of State.    Failure to register a registrable agreement is a breach of section 7 of the Restrictive Trade Practices Act 1968 (the Act of 1968) and renders the agreement void in respect of the relevant restrictions.    Once registered the Registrar (or Director) has a duty to bring the agreement before the Restrictive Practices Court.[7]    Under section 20 of the Act of 1956 the court has jurisdiction to declare the restrictions contained in the registered agreement to be contrary to the public interest and to enjoin the parties from giving effect to those or any restrictions to the like effect.    Under section 21 of the Act of 1956, the restrictions contained in a registered agreement may be " justified " if the court is satisfied that the agreement has benefits which enable the restriction to satisfy one or more of the " gateways " set out in that section; and further that the restriction is not unreasonable having regard to the balance between the benefits the restriction may bring and any detriment the agreement is likely to cause to the public or persons not parties to the agreement.[8]

**145**    **Monopolies and mergers.**    The Monopolies and Mergers Acts 1948 to 1965 are expected in due course to be replaced by clauses 40 to 88 of the Fair Trading Bill.    Those clauses widen considerably the existing circumstances in which the Secretary of State for Trade and Industry may refer to the Monopolies Commission for investigation and report certain monopoly situations in relation to the supply of goods or services and certain mergers.    Under the Bill, the Director-General as well as the Secretary of State may refer certain monopoly situations to the Monopolies Commission, which will be known as " The Monopolies and Mergers Commission."    Under clauses 7 to 12 the proportion of the market by reference to which monopolies are defined is reduced from $33\frac{1}{3}$ per cent. under existing legislation to 25 per cent. Guide lines are provided for the Commission in considering whether any matters are or are not contrary to the public interest.[9]

**146**    **Resale Prices Act, 1964.**    Under section 1 of the Resale Prices Act 1964 any term or condition of a contract for the sale

---

[7] S. 1 (2) of the Act of 1956.
[8] See s. 21 (1) (*a*)–(*g*) of the Act of 1956
[9] Clause 79.

of goods between a supplier and a dealer, or any agreement between a supplier and a dealer in relation to such a sale shall be void in so far as it purports to establish or provide for the establishment of minimum prices to be charged on the resale of the goods in the United Kingdom. The effect of section 1 and the other provisions of the Act is broadly to make resale price maintenance unlawful within the United Kingdom, except where particular classes of goods have been exempted by order of the Restrictive Practices Court. Only two such orders have been made, in respect of books and medicaments.[10]

**147**    **The Common law.** In addition to legislation there is a substantial body of common law principles relating to restraint of trade.[11]  In so far as the Treaty provisions apply in any situation where those principles also apply, the application of the common law is broadly governed by the same principles as those now set out below in relation to the application of British domestic legislation.

#### (ii) British law and Community law
**148**    **In general.** Many of the agreements which fall within Part I of the Act of 1956 (as amended and extended by the Act of 1968 and by the Bill) are unlikely to involve questions of Community law. Article 85 (1) is concerned only with agreements that are liable to affect trade *between* Member States. Consequently, most agreements the scope and effect of which is limited to the United Kingdom fall outside the Treaty. Conversely, agreements relating to exports fall outside the Act of 1956.[12]

However, there are still agreements which after January 1, 1973, will fall under both the Act of 1956 and the prohibitions contained in the Treaties. In certain circumstances Article 85 of the EEC Treaty may apply to restrictive agreements made between parties carrying on business in the United Kingdom, if the agreement is capable of affecting trade between Member States.[13]  Also, Article 85 (1) and the Act of 1956 may both apply to restrictive agreements where two parties carry on business in the United

---

[10] See *Re Net Book Agreement 1957* (1964) L.R. 4 R.P. 484; [1962] 1 W.L.R. 1347. *Re Medicaments Reference (No. 2)* [1970] 1 W.L.R. 1339.
[11] See generally *Chitty on Contracts*, 23rd Ed. Vol. I, paras 861 *et seq.*
[12] See s. 8 (8); but see s. 31, also clause 94 of the Bill.
[13] See *post*, § 236.

Kingdom, and other parties are situated in other Member States. Similarly, questions relating to Community law may arise in the course of an investigation by the Monopolies and Mergers Commission, particularly in respect to export agreements which fall under clause 9 of the Bill. When these latter circumstances arise it is necessary to consider both the relevant provisions of national law and the relevant provisions of Community law.

**149**    **The European Communities Act 1972, section 10.**    Section 10 of the European Communities Act 1972 deals with the relationship between Part I of the Act of 1956 and Community law. It makes no provision in respect of the monopolies and mergers legislation or in respect of the Resale Prices Act 1964 or the common law. Where questions of conflict between the respective jurisdictions arise in relation to these latter matters, reference can only be made to the general principles of Community law set out below.[14] As far as Part I of the Restrictive Trade Practices Act 1956 is concerned, section 10 provides that the Act of 1956 still applies to an agreement irrespective of whether the agreement also falls under the relevant EEC legislation; but certain changes are made to ensure that the operation of the United Kingdom legislation is fully compatible with the administration of the Community systems.[15]

**150**    **Section 10.**    Section 10 (1) makes it clear that all requirements of the Act of 1956 continue to apply to an agreement, notwithstanding either that the agreement may be void under Article 85 (2) of the EEC Treaty or that the agreement may have been exempted under Article 85 (3). However, in order to avoid conflict with Community legislation, where agreements fall both under the Act of 1956 and under the Treaty provisions, the Restrictive Practices Court and the Registrar (Director) are given

---

[14] *Post,* § 153.
[15] S. 10 also makes provision in relation to the ECSC: s. 10 (1) and 10 (2). However, it is widely held that, under Community law, national authorities have no competence to regulate restrictive practices within the ECSC (or at least to regulate the agreements falling within Article 65 of the ECSC Treaty), this power being exclusively reserved to Community institutions under the Treaty (see *e.g.* the submissions of the Advocate-General in *Wilhelm* v. *Bundeskartellamt* (14/68) [1969] C.M.L.R. 100, 106, 113). Having regard to Community law, and to s. 2 (1) and 2 (4) of the European Communities Act 1972, the effect of s. 10 in relation to agreements falling within the ECSC Treaty remains to be determined.

a discretion in the discharge of their respective functions. The court is given a discretion not to exercise its powers under section 20, which gives it jurisdiction to declare the restrictions contained in a registered agreement to be contrary to the public interest and to enjoin the parties from giving effect to those or any restrictions to the like effect. In declining or postponing the exercise of this jurisdiction the court may have regard to the operation of Article 85 or to the purpose and effect of exemptions granted under Article 85 (3). Similarly the court may, in the light of those Community considerations, exercise its jurisdiction under section 22 of the Act of 1956 to discharge any previous declaration or order. This latter jurisdiction may be exercised notwithstanding section 22 (2), which provides that the provisions as to the public interest as defined by section 21 of the Act of 1956 apply to applications under section 22. Similarly, the Registrar (Director) who has a duty under section 1 (2) of the Act of 1956 to bring registered agreements before the court, is given a discretion not to take proceedings in respect of any agreements, so long as he thinks it appropriate to do so.[16]

**151**      **Section 10 (2).** S. 19 of the Act of 1956 authorises the Registrar to make regulations for the purposes of the registration of agreements falling under section 6 (1) of the Act of 1956. Section 11 (2) of the Act of 1956 provides that the particulars of registrable agreements duly furnished pursuant to those regulations shall be entered or filed in the Register maintained by the Registrar under section 11 of that Act. Section 10 (2) of the European Communities Act gives the Registrar power to make regulations requiring that he be kept informed of steps taken or decisions given in respect of the agreement under Community proceedings, and that such information shall be entered or filed in the Register.

**152**      **Section 10 (3).** Section 10 (3) of the European Communities Act is to be replaced by clause 116 of the Fair Trading Bill.[17] Clause 116 (1) restricts, subject to penalties, the disclosure of information with respect to any particular business obtained under

---

[16] Curiously, the Registrar's (Director's) discretion is expressed differently to that of the court: he must have regard to the operation of Article 85 (1) *and* to the purpose and effect of an exemption under Article 85 (3), whereas the court may have regard to those matters in the alternative.

[17] S. 10 (3) itself is repealed by Sched. 13 of the Bill.

the Acts of 1956 and 1968, or the Bill.   However, under clause 116 (2) (*b*) it is provided that clause 116 (1) does not apply to a disclosure made in pursuance of a Community obligation within the meaning of the European Communities Act 1972.[18]

**153**   **Principles of Community law.**   In the exercise of the discretions vested in the Registrar (Director) and the Restrictive Practices Court under section 10 (1) of the European Communities Act 1972, and in dealing with other situations not provided for under that Act where there may be a dual jurisdiction, regard must be had to the relevant principles of Community law. In the absence of any regulation or directive as to the relationship between Community and national law as provided for under Article 87 (*e*) of the Treaty, the relevant principles are those laid down by the European Court of Justice in *Wilhelm* v. *Bundeskartellamt*.[19]   That case was referred to the European Court in the course of parallel proceedings into the same set of circumstances that were being conducted by the Commission and the German Federal Cartel Office (the Bundeskartellamt) respectively. The European Court said [20]

> "The EEC Treaty instituted its own legal order, integrated into the legal systems of Member States, and which has priority before their courts.   It would be contrary to the nature of such a system to accept that the Member States may take or maintain in force measures liable to compromise the useful effect of the Treaty."

Consequently, the Court held, " [C]onflicts between the Community rule and the national rules on competition should be resolved by the application of the principle of the primacy of the Community rule.

"It follows from the foregoing that in the case where national decisions regarding an agreement would be incompatible with a decision adopted by the Commission at the end of the proceedings instituted by it, the national authorities are required to respect its effects.

"In the cases in which, during national proceedings, it appears possible that the decision whereby the Commission will put an

---

[18] See *post*, § 1216.
[19] (14/68) [1969] C.M.L.R. 100.
[20] [1969] C.M.L.R. 100, 119, 120.

end to proceedings in progress concerning the same agreement may conflict with the effects of the decision of the national authorities, it is for the latter to take appropriate measures."

The Court held that as long as no regulation under Article 87 (e) of the Treaty[21] has provided otherwise, national authorities may apply their internal laws to agreements, even where the agreement is being examined by the Commission, provided that the application of the national law does not prejudice the full and uniform application of Community law or the effect of acts in implementation of it. It appears to follow that national authorities may not take actions which would result in the condemnation of an agreement which has been exempted under Article 85 (3) either by way of an individual decision by the Commission or by way of a block exemption.

**[The next paragraph is 201]**

---

[21] *Ibid.*

# CHAPTER 2

## ARTICLE 85 (1): GENERAL PRINCIPLES

### 1. IN GENERAL

**201    Article 85 (1).**  Article 85 (1) provides that " the following shall be prohibited as incompatible with the common market: all agreements between undertakings, decisions by associations of undertakings and concerted practices which may affect trade between Member States and which have as their object or effect the prevention, restriction or distortion of competition within the common market, and in particular those which:

(*a*) directly or indirectly fix purchase or selling prices or any other trading conditions;

(*b*) limit or control production, markets, technical development or investment;

(*c*) share markets or sources of supply;

(*d*) apply dissimilar conditions to equivalent transactions with other trading parties, thereby placing them at a competitive disadvantage;

(*e*) make the conclusion of contracts subject to acceptance by the other parties of supplementary obligations which, by their nature or according to commercial usage, have no connection with the subject of such contracts."

**202**    In deciding whether any particular transaction falls within Article 85 (1) it is necessary to consider the matter from three aspects: (i) whether there exists an agreement, decision or concerted practice made between or observed by " undertakings " or, in the case of a decision, by " an association of undertakings "; (ii) whether trade between Member States may be affected thereby; and (iii) whether competition within the common market may thereby be prevented, restricted or distorted. Each of the above conditions must be fulfilled before the prohibition in Article 85 (1) is applicable.  In this chapter, a general examination is made of the principles which governs each of these requirements.

## 2. UNDERTAKINGS

**203** **Undertakings.** The word " undertaking " is a wide term that
has not been judicially defined for the purposes of the EEC
legislation.[1] Prima facie, there seems no reason why the term
should not include almost any legal or natural person having the
capacity to enter into legally binding agreements. Thus " undertakings " within the meaning of Article 85 (1) may cover many
different forms of legal enterprise ranging from a small shop to
a large industrial concern including, for example, public and
private companies, partnerships, unincorporated associations,
sole traders and state owned corporations.[2] Moreover, Article
85 (1) is not limited in its application to undertakings which
carry on any particular type of activity. Undertakings engaged
in the supply of services are " undertakings " within the meaning
of the Treaty, as well as undertakings engaged in the manufacture,
processing or distribution of goods. Thus in *Re Gema*[3] the
Commission held that a German authors rights society was
an undertaking within Article 86; there is no reason to suppose
that the decision would have been different under Article 85. But
it may be doubted whether bodies which are not engaged in any
commercial activity at all are undertakings within Article 85 (1),
*e.g.* trade unions.

**204** **Subordinate undertakings.** One question that arises is whether
an agreement between a parent company and a controlled
subsidiary or between two companies which are under the
common control of a third is an agreement between " undertakings." There is as yet no European Court decision which
directly decides whether bodies which are legally separate from
but economically dependent on other bodies remain separate
undertakings for the purposes of Article 85 (1).[4] It is not,

---

[1] References to " undertakings " are to be found in Arts. 52 and 58 of the EEC
Treaty. Both the ECSC Treaty (Art. 80) and the Euratom Treaty (Art. 196)
contain definitions of " an undertaking " for the purposes of those Treaties.
Cases under the ECSC Treaty concerning the meaning of " undertaking "
include Cases 32 and 33/58, 5 Rec. 275, 295; Cases 42/59 and 49/59, 7 Rec. 101;
Case 19/61 8 Rec. 675, 681, and Case 36/62, 9 Rec. 583, 601.
[2] As to State and public corporations see Art. 90. And see *ante,* § 119. For
associations of undertakings, see *post*, §§ 209, 210.
[3] J.O. 1971 L134/15, [1971] C.M.L.R. D35. See *post*, §§ 731 *et seq.*
[4] For decisions under the ECSC Treaty see Note 1, *supra.* See also the argument
of the Advocate-General in *Béguelin* (22/71) [1972] C.M.L.R. 81, 87–89.

however, necessary to resolve this question since both the Commission and the Court have held that, in practice, there can be no agreement falling under Article 85 (1) between bodies that are not economically autonomous of each other.[5] Consequently, agreements between such bodies are not apt to prevent, restrict or distort competition and they therefore fall outside Article 85 (1). The basis of these decisions is further discussed below.[6]

**205**    **Undertakings outside the common market.** An undertaking situated outside the common market is still an undertaking within the meaning of Article 85 (1) and an agreement made by such an undertaking may still fall within the prohibition provided the effects of the agreement are felt within the common market.[7] With regard to the question of jurisdiction, the Commission may assert jurisdiction over such undertakings where they engage in prohibited conduct within the EEC, either by themselves or through subsidiary undertakings.[8]

### 3. AGREEMENTS, DECISIONS AND CONCERTED PRACTICES

#### (a) *Agreements*

**206**    **Generally.** The word "agreements" (accords) in Article 85 (1) may mean agreements which are intended to be legally binding upon the parties.[9] An alternative and tenable view is that "agreements" may mean a "gentleman's agreement" or "arrangements" binding in honour only.[10] However, even if the word "agreement" in Article 85 (1) is limited to legally binding agreements, an agreement or arrangement which is not legally binding upon the parties will amount to a "concerted practice."[11] Ordinarily, if parties co-operate in such a way as to

---

[5] *ICI* v. *EC Commission* (48/69) [1972] C.M.L.R. 557, 629. See *Béguelin* (22/71) [1972] C.M.L.R. 81, 95; *Re Christiani & Nielsen*, J.O. 1969 L165/12, [1969] C.M.L.R. D36; *Re Kodak*, J.O. 1970 L147/24, [1970] C.M.L.R. D19.

[6] *Post*, §§ 250 *et seq.*

[7] *Béguelin* (22/71) [1972] C.M.L.R. 81, 95.

[8] *ICI* v. *EC Commission* (48/69) [1972] C.M.L.R. 557, 628–9. And see *post*, § 1209.

[9] See *e.g.* Oberdorfer, Gleiss, Hirsch, *Common Market Cartel Law*, p. 13. Mathijsen, *A Guide to European Community Law*, p. 82.

[10] See *e.g.* Deringer, *The Competition Law of the European Economic Community*, p. 11; Mégret, Wailbroeck & others, *Editions de l'Université de Bruxelles* (1972), p.6. See also the decision of the Commission in the *Quinine* case, J.O. 1969 L192/5; [1969] C.M.L.R. D41. *Cf.* the definition of agreement to include "an arrangement" in s. 6 (3) of the Restrictive Trade Practices Act 1956.

[11] *Post*, §§ 211 *et seq.;* and see the *Quinine* case [1969] C.M.L.R. D41, D58–D59.

infringe the Treaty, little will turn upon the precise form which that co-operation takes.[12]   The Treaty places no limit on the kinds of agreements which may fall within Article 85 (1).   Thus both " horizontal " agreements (*e.g.* agreements between a group of suppliers or a group of acquirers *inter se*) and " vertical " agreements (*i.e.* agreements between a supplier and one to whom he supplies) may fall within Article 85 (1).[13]

**207**    **Accession agreements.**   Agreements already in existence on January 1, 1973 which fall within Article 85 (1) solely as a result of accession are throughout this work referred to as Accession agreements.[14]   Accession agreements are those which, having been made before January 1, 1973, now " affect trade *between Member States* " and " prevent, restrict or distort competition *within* the common market " only as a result of the enlargement of the Community to include the United Kingdom, Ireland and Denmark.   Such agreements are those which previously fell outside the Treaty in that they only affected trade between an acceding member state and an original member state, or between two acceding member states, or restricted competition only outside the EEC.   Thus Accession agreements do not include agreements which affected trade between the then Member States and restricted competition within the then common market, prior to January 1, 1973, notwithstanding that such agreements were made by undertakings who were, at that time, situated outside the Community.[15]

**208**    **Validity of Accession agreements.**   Accession agreements will fall within Article 85 (1) if their effects continue to be felt within the enlarged common market after that date.[16]   Their validity in

---

[12] See the judgment of the European Court in the *Quinine* cases *ACF Chemiefarma* v. *EC Commission* (41/69), *Boehringer Mannheim* v. *EC Commission* (45/69), *Buchler* v. *EC Commission* (44/69) 8 C.M.L.Rev. 86 at p. 90, where the Court was content to describe the whole complex of formal and informal arrangements in these cases as " the performance of a forbidden cartel " without finding it necessary to distinguish the legal nature of the various forms of cooperation. But *cf.* the arguments of the Advocate-General in the *Quinine* cases, 8 C.M.L. Rev. 86, 90 and in *ICI* v. *EC Commission* (48/69) [1972] C.M.L.R. 557, 586–587.

[13] *Italy* v. *EEC Council & Commission* (32/65) [1969] C.M.L.R. 39; *La Technique Minière* v. *Maschinenbau Ulm* (56/65) [1966] C.M.L.R. 357.

[14] See the definition contained in Art. 25 of Reg. 17, App. 2, *post*.

[15] See *post*, §§ 240 *et seq.*

[16] *Sirena* v. *Eda* (40/70) [1971] C.M.L.R. 260, 274; *post*, §§ 910 *et seq.*

respect of any period prior to January 1, 1973 is not affected by accession.[17]   Certain transitional arrangements relating to accession agreements are discussed below.[18]

### (b)  *Decisions by Associations of Undertakings*

**209**   **Decisions.**   The expression " decision " in Article 85 (1) has not been the subject of judicial interpretation.   In cases where the Commission has found the existence of a " decision," the " decision " concerned has been that of a trade association made in accordance with the rules of the association and binding upon the members of the association in their capacity as such.[19]   The term " decision " is sufficiently wide to include the actual constitution of a trade association as well as the regulations made thereunder.[20]   Although it is doubtful whether a recommendation made by an association which is not legally binding is a decision, observance of such a recommendation by the members of the association may give rise to a " concerted practice." [21]

**210**   **Associations of undertakings.**   The " associations of under-takings " with whose decisions [22] the Commission has to date been concerned have been trade associations.   However, under the Treaty the word " associations " is not limited to any par-ticular type of association, either formal or informal whether with or without legal personality.   The Commission has held [23] that a *de facto* international association without legal personality, the members of which were twelve national associations of undertakings, was itself " an association of undertakings " within Article 85 (1).

---

[17] *Bosch* v. *de Geus* (13/62) [1962] C.M.L.R. 1; *post*, §§ 405, 415.
[18] For notification of Accession agreements see *post*, §§ 501–509, 517 *et seq.;* for the provisional validity of accession agreements duly notified or exempt from notification under Art. 4 (2) of Reg. 17 see §§ 410 *et seq.*
[19] See *e.g.* the decision of September 30, 1958 relating to aggregated rebates taken at the general meeting of the Association of German Ceramic Tiles Producers in *Re German Ceramic Tiles Agreement* J.O. 1971 L10/15, [1971] C.M.L.R. D6. See also the decision relating to exports in *Re VVVF,* J.O. 1969; L168/22 [1970] C.M.L.R. D1.
[20] See *e.g. Re ASPA*, J.O. 1970 L148/9, [1970] C.M.L.R. D25.
[21] *Post*, §§ 211.   But see now *VCH* v. *EC Commission* (8/72) [1973] C.M.L.R. 7.
[22] *Ante*, § 209.
[23] *Re Cecimo* J.O. 1969 L69/13, [1969] C.M.L.R. D1.

### (c) *Concerted Practices*

**211**    **In general.** The inclusion of "concerted practices" in Article 85 (1) (pratiques concertées) is intended to bring within the Treaty informal co-operation between undertakings that is not characterised by any formal agreement or decision. Such a provision is necessary to prevent the circumvention of Article 85 (1) by arrangements of an informal nature which may serve the parties' purposes just as well as more formal agreements.[24]

**212**    **The Dyestuffs case.** The leading case on what constitutes a concerted practice under Article 85 (1) is *ICI and others* v. *EC Commission*[25] (the *Dyestuffs* case). The facts of that case were as follows. In January 1964 nearly all the undertakings that produced aniline dyestuffs in Italy and Benelux simultaneously increased prices for certain categories of their products by a uniform 15 per cent. Between October and December 1964 certain of the undertakings concerned announced further uniform price increases which were to take effect on January 1, 1965. On that date the producers in Germany simultaneously introduced the 15 per cent. increase previously introduced in Italy and Benelux; while on the same day all producers in the five countries uniformly increased by 10 per cent. the price of those products not covered by the 15 per cent. increase. In 1967, at a meeting held on August 18, one of the producer undertakings announced its intention to raise its prices by a further 8 per cent. as from October 16, 1967, while two others said they were considering an increase. In mid-September 1967 all the parties concerned announced uniform price increases of 8 per cent., increased to 12 per cent. in France, to take effect from October 16, 1967 in all countries except in Italy. In its decision[26] the Commission had held that the parties were guilty of concerted practices in the fixing and introduction of price increases, and it imposed fines upon them.[27] As proof of the concerted practices, the Com-

---

[24] *Cf.* the definition of an agreement under s. 6 (3) of the Restrictive Trade Practices Act 1956 to include " any agreement or arrangement whether or not it is intended to be enforceable by legal proceedings." And see note 32, *infra*. See also U.S. cases as to the meaning of " conspiracy " under the Sherman Act, 1890; A. D. Neale, *The Anti Trust Laws of the U.S.A.* 2nd Ed., pp. 32–91.
[25] (48, 49/69, 51–57/69) [1972] C.M.L.R. 557. See Mann, 22 I.C.L.Q. 35. See also *Quinine* cases, note 12, *supra*; *Re Sugar Cartel*, Commission decision, January 2, 1973.
[26] J.O. 1969 L195/11; [1969] C.M.L.R. D23.
[27] See *post*, §§ 1201 *et seq.*

mission relied *inter alia* upon the identity of the rates of increase
and the products to which they applied in each country, the
similarity of the dates upon which the increases were announced
or applied, the simultaneous despatch of instructions to subsidiaries and representatives, the identity of form and content of
those instructions, and the fact of informal contact between the
undertakings. The parties themselves contended that the price
increases merely reflected parallel behaviour in an oligopolistic
market where each producer followed the price-leader which
initiated the increase (usually the one with the strongest market
position in each Member State). This behaviour, it was argued,
was quite natural in a closely knit industry where all producers
were equally affected by the continual erosion of their margins.

**213    The Court's decision.** The European Court, on appeal,[28]
held that the participating undertakings were guilty of concerted
practices. In summary, the Court said [29] that Article 85 (1)
distinguished the concept of " a concerted practice " from that of
"an agreement " or " a decision between undertakings " in order
to bring within the prohibition of that Article " a form of co-
ordination between undertakings which, without going so far as
to amount to an agreement properly so called, knowingly substitutes a practical co-operation between them for the risks of
competition." [30] The Court said that whilst parallel behaviour
by itself did not constitute a concerted practice, it may be a strong
indication of such a practice if it leads to market conditions that
are different from those which would prevail under free competition. In order to decide the question whether market
conditions diverge from the competitive it is necessary to examine
the market for the products in question. The Court found that
the market for dyestuffs was fragmented and divided along
national lines. The similarity of the rates of, and the timing of,
the price increases could not be explained away as the result of
parallel yet independent behaviour prompted by market forces.
The Court found that in fact the 1964, 1965 and 1967 price
increases revealed a progressive *co-operation* between the parties.
In particular, the prior announcements of the 1965 and 1967
price increases enabled the undertakings to eliminate in advance,

[28] Under Art. 173 of the Treaty; *post*, §§ 1229 *et seq.*
[29] See [1972] C.M.L.R. 557, 621–628.
[30] *Ibid.* at p. 622.

between themselves, uncertainty as to their mutual behaviour on
the various markets. The general and uniform increases were
explicable only by the convergent *intention* of the parties to
increase prices while at the same time avoiding any risk of a change
in the conditions of competition. The Court said [31]: "While it
is permissible for each manufacturer to change his prices freely
and to take into account for this purpose the behaviour, present
and foreseeable of his competitors, it is, on the other hand, contrary to the competition rules of the Treaty for a manufacturer
to co-operate with his competitors, in whatever manner, to
determine a co-ordinated course of action relating to an increase
in prices, and to ensure its success by the prior elimination of all
uncertainty as to mutual behaviour relating to the essential
elements of this action, such as rates, subject matter, date and
place of the increases."

**214**    **Conduct intended to co-ordinate commercial policies.** In the
light of the *Dyestuffs* case, it is submitted that a concerted practice
will be held to exist where: (*a*) the parties intend that the commercial conduct of the parties shall be maintained or altered in a
particular way; (*b*) they take positive steps with the common
object of realising that intention; and (*c*) the steps that they take
have the effect of maintaining or altering their commercial
conduct.

It must therefore be possible to point to positive steps taken
by the parties to achieve a common goal, steps that they would
not have taken but for their intention to co-ordinate their
commercial policies. It follows from the foregoing that concerted
practices include not only unenforceable agreements and
" arrangements " as defined for the purposes of the Restrictive
Trade Practices Act 1956[32]; conduct that falls short of an arrange-

---

[31] *Ibid.* at p. 627.
[32] The meaning of " arrangement " was considered in *Re British Basic Slag's
Application* [1962] 1 W.L.R. 986; affirmed [1963] 1 W.L.R. 729. Cross J., at
first instance, held that there was an arrangement where the parties had communicated to each other in some way and that, as a result of a communication,
each had intentionally aroused in the others an expectation that it would act in
a certain way. In the Court of Appeal, Willmer L.J. laid down a test similar to
that propounded by Cross J. Danckwerts L.J. said that no general principle
could be laid down; each case depended on its own circumstances. Diplock L.J.
agreed that an arrangement is something whereby the parties accept mutual
rights and obligations but he went on to say *obiter* that it is sufficient to constitute
an arrangement if: (i) one party makes a representation as to his future conduct
with the expectation and intention that such conduct on his part will operate as

ment because of the absence of a sense of mutual obligation may
nevertheless constitute a concerted practice given a common
*intention* on the part of the parties, their *positive steps* to realise
that intention and the *effect* of those steps in achieving a result
that would not otherwise have been achieved.[33] As a matter of
evidence, parallel behaviour may be a strong indication of a
concerted practice if it leads to conditions of competition which
do not correspond to the normal conditions of the market.[34]

4. THE RESTRICTION OF COMPETITION

(a) *Generally*

**215**   **In general.**  Article 85 (1) is not applicable to an agreement
unless that agreement first has as its object or effect the prevention,
restriction or distortion of competition within the common
market.  Whether any particular agreement has any such object
or effect is closely connected with the question whether that
agreement also " affects trade between Member States."  That
latter question is dealt with in the next section of this chapter.[35]
Both sections, however, are interrelated and should be read
together.

**216**   **Restraints on competition.**  There is no doubt that Article
85 (1) strikes at agreements which prevent, restrict or distort
competition as between the parties themselves.  Article 85 (1) is

an inducement to the other to act in a particular way; (ii) such representation is
communicated to the other who has knowledge that the first so expected and
intended; and (iii) such representation and the conduct of the first in fulfilling it
operates as an inducement to the other to act in that particular way.  As a result
of *Basic Slag* it is probable that wherever the facts give rise to a sense on the part
of one or more of the parties that if he or they act or do not act in a particular
way, the others will feel that he or they have acted in an untrustworthy or
unreliable fashion, then there is sufficient understanding between the parties to
amount to an agreement for the purposes of Part I of the Act.  But *cf.* the test
laid down in *Re Mileage Conference, etc. Agreement* [1966] 1 W.L.R. 1137, at
pp. 1156–1159.  This test may go beyond the test in *Basic Slag* but on the facts
of that case there would almost certainly be a concerted practice within Article
85 (1).
[33] Certain conduct falling short of a concerted practice may fall within Art. 86.
See *post,* §§ 712 *et seq.*  See also *Re Sugar Cartel,* Commision decision, January
2, 1973.
[34] [1972] C.M.L.R. 557, 622–3.  See also the decision of the Commission in the
*Quinine* case, J.O. 1969 L192/5, [1969] C.M.L.R. D41, where it was held that
where parties claim to have terminated an agreement, and their market behaviour
continues to be convergent, there is a heavy onus upon them to show that they
are not continuing to act in concert; and see the Commission's Press Release,
June 19, 1970 relating to concerted practices in the flat glass industry.
[35] *Post,* § 230.

also concerned with agreements which present competition between one of the parties to the agreement and third parties. This important principle was firmly established by the decision of the European Court in *Grundig-Consten*,[36] a case concerning an exclusive distributorship agreement. Since this case is the foundation of much of the Community law of competition,[37] it is convenient to set out shortly the facts.

**217    Grundig-Consten: the facts.** Under an exclusive distributorship agreement made between Grundig, a manufacturer, and Consten, a distributor, Consten was appointed exclusive distributor in France of Grundig radios, televisions and related equipment. Consten undertook, *inter alia*, not to sell competing products and not to deliver any Grundig products directly or indirectly outside France. Grundig, for its part, undertook not to deliver its products directly or indirectly to anyone in France except Consten. At the same time Grundig assigned to Consten the trademark " GINT " which was affixed to all Grundig products in addition to the " Grundig " mark. This assignment enabled Consten to sue any third party importing Grundig products into France for infringement of the trademark " GINT." Before entering into the contract with Consten, Grundig had imposed on all its other concessionaires outside France, and upon its German wholesalers, obligations not to deliver directly or indirectly outside their respective contract territories.

**218    Grundig-Consten: restrictions on competition.** The purpose of the Grundig system was to protect Consten, as far as possible, from competition from imports of Grundig products obtained from outside France (*i.e.* parallel imports). By imposing export bans on each concessionaire, and by assigning to Consten the trademark " GINT " Grundig sought to protect Consten absolutely from such imports (absolute territorial protection). The Commission, in a decision,[38] held that the agreement restricted competition within the meaning of Article 85 (1). Since

---

[36] *Consten & Grundig* v. *EEC Commission* (56/64, 58/64) [1966] C.M.L.R. 418.
[37] For aspects of this case dealing with " effect on trade between Member States," see §§ 232 *et seq., post*; for aspects concerned with industrial property rights, see § 909, *post*. For considerations relating to Art. 85 (3), see §§ 603–604; 612, *post;* for exclusive dealing aspects, see §§ 810 *et seq., post*.
[38] J.O. 1964 2545/64, [1964] C.M.L.R. 489.

Grundig and its concessionaires were prevented from delivering to other vendors within France, and since Consten could prevent indirect imports by an action for infringement of the " GINT " mark, Consten was free of competition from other distributors of Grundig products.[39]   On appeal to the European Court,[40] it was argued that in determining whether " competition " was restricted within the meaning of the Treaty the Commission should not have considered only competition as between distributors of Grundig products; rather, they should have considered the whole market for radio, televisions and related products, in which Grundig faced fierce competition from other brands.   The Court held[41] that it was sufficient, for the purposes of Article 85 (1), if the agreement had the object or effect of restricting competition between distributors of the same brand of products.   Where the agreement prevented other distributors on a national market from obtaining supplies of well known branded goods, Article 85 (1) was applicable.   The Court substantially upheld an order imposed by the Commission under Article 3 (1) of Regulation 17[42] the effect of which was to prevent Consten from relying either upon the agreement or upon the trademark " GINT " and French national law in order to prevent " parallel imports " of Grundig products.

**219**   **Favourable effects of agreement irrelevant.**  The result of *Grundig-Consten* is that where an agreement has the object or effect of preventing competition between the parties, or between one of the parties and third parties, that agreement falls within Article 85 (1), notwithstanding that the *overall* effect of the agreement may be to increase competition within the common market.[43] The operation of this general principle may be seen not only in relation to exclusive dealing agreements,[44] but also, for example, in the Commission's decisions relating to exclusive patent

---

[39] Consten could also seek to rely on the French law of unfair competition under which an exclusive distributor may sue a competitor who fails to respect his exclusive dealing rights.   For a general exposition of the laws of unfair competition in the EEC see Ulmer *La Répression de la concurrence déloyale dans les états membres de la CEE*, Tome I, Droit Comparé, especially at pp. 204–5.

[40] Under Art. 173 of the Treaty.

[41] [1966] C.M.L.R. 418, 472–4.

[42] In its decision J.O. 1964 2545/64, [1964] C.M.L.R. 489; for Art. 3 (1) of Reg. No. 17 see *post.*, §§ 1202 *et seq.*

[43] See [1966] C.M.L.R. 418, 472–4.

[44] *Post*, §§ 801 *et seq.*

licences.[45]   An exclusive patent licence may well have a favourable effect on competition in that the licensee obtains the opportunity to exploit a patented product which was previously the sole preserve of the licensor.   However, the Commission has held[46] such an agreement may fall within Article 85 (1) because, by granting an *exclusive* licence for a given territory, the licensee has deprived himself of the power to grant licences for that territory to any other undertaking. This in turn prevents competition in the patented products between the licensee and third parties.   The benefits which flow from such agreements fall to be considered under Article 85 (3); they do not prevent the application of Article 85 (1).

**220**  **Unilateral restrictions sufficient.**  It follows from the above that, in contrast to the Restrictive Trade Practices Act 1956,[47] an agreement may fall within Article 85 (1) even though only one party accepts restrictions thereunder.   Thus resale price maintenance agreements, which may prevent one party from competing on price with third parties, fall under Article 85 (1).[48]  Similarly, patent, know-how and trademark licences which only contain unilateral restrictions on the licensee may in certain circumstances fall within the prohibition.[49]   Indeed, it should be recognised that whenever one of the parties to an agreement accepts a restriction relating to his future commercial activities towards third parties, competition may well be prevented, restricted or distorted within the meaning of Article 85 (1).

### (b) *The Object or Effect of the Agreement*

**221**  **Object or effect: the test to be applied.**  The principles to be applied in establishing whether an agreement has as its object or effect the prevention, restriction or distortion of competition within the common market were first considered by the European Court in the *L.T.M.*[50] case.   In that case the Court was asked to consider the validity under Article 85 (1) of an agreement whereby

---

[45] See further *post*, §§ 944 *et seq.*
[46] *Re Davidson Rubber*, J.O. 1972 L143/31, [1972] C.M.L.R. D52; *post*, §§ 944 *et seq.*
[47] See s. 6 (1), to be amended by the provisions of the Fair Trading Bill, Part X.
[48] *Post*, §§ 318 *et seq.*
[49] *Post*, §§ 931 *et seq.*
[50] *La Technique Minière v. Maschinenbau Ulm* (56/65) [1966] C.M.L.R. 357.

a French company was granted the exclusive right to sell in France levelling machines manufactured by a German company. In dealing with the question as to whether the agreement had as its " object or effect " the restriction of competition, the Court said[51] "the fact that these are not cumulative but alternative conditions, indicated by the conjunction 'or,' suggests first the need to consider the very object of the agreement in the light of the economic context in which it is to be applied.  The alterations in the play of competition envisaged by Article 85 (1) should result from all or some of the clauses of the agreement itself.  Where, however, an analysis of the said clauses does not reveal a sufficient degree of harmfulness with regard to competition, examination should then be made of the effects of the agreement and, if it is to be subjected to the prohibition, the presence of those elements which establish that competition has in fact been prevented, restricted or distorted to a noticeable extent should be required. The competition in question should be understood within the actual context in which it would occur in the absence of the agreement."

**222     The object.**   Thus, the object of the agreement should be considered first in the light of its economic context, before considering the effects of the agreement.  This is the practice which is commonly but not invariably followed by the Commission in the reasoning which accompanies its decisions on negative clearance and applications for exemption under Article 85 (3).[52]  It is not however necessary to determine *the* object of the agreement.  Article 85 is concerned with agreements that have a restriction of competition among a number of objects.[53]

**223     Object alone insufficient.**   In *Grundig-Consten* the Court said[54] " For the purpose of applying Article 85 (1) it is superfluous to take into account the concrete effects of an agreement once it appears that it has the object of restricting, preventing or distorting competition."  This widely expressed statement has been

---

[51] *Ibid.* at p. 375.
[52] See *e.g. Re Rieckermann's Agreement*, J.O. 1968 L276/25, [1968] C.M.L.R. D78.
[53] The French text speaks of "tous accords . . . qui ont pour objet ou pour effet."
[54] [1966] C.M.L.R. 418, 475.

subject to criticism[55] and does not appear to be consistent with the Court's other decisions.[56] In practice, for the purpose of applying Article 85 (1), it will generally be insufficient to determine " the object " of the agreement without also taking into account its intended effects. First, it must be said that even if an agreement had as its object the prevention or distortion of competition without that effect being present, it would not fall within Article 85 (1) unless it was also capable of affecting trade between Member States. An agreement only " affects trade between Member States " within the meaning of the Treaty if the concrete effects of the agreement, actual or potential, are likely to endanger the creation of a single market between the States.[57] In practice, one can never say whether an agreement is apt to " affect trade between Member States " without examining its effects on competition; for unless there is an adverse effect on competition, the agreement cannot affect trade " in a manner likely to endanger the creation of a single market between the States." Indeed at this point the two concepts of Article 85 (1) clearly overlap.

Secondly, it will generally be insufficient merely to consider " the object " of the agreement because of the operation of the *de minimis* rule which is dealt with in more detail below.[58] Under that rule agreements which have as their object restrictions on competition none the less fall outside Article 85 (1) where they are unlikely to affect competition to any noticeable extent.[59]

**224**    **Noticeable effect on competition: the economic and legal context.** In *Volk* v. *Vervaecke*[60] the European Court established the rule that an agreement falls within Article 85 (1) only where it prevents, restricts or distorts competition and affects trade between Member States to a *noticeable* extent. In deciding whether an agreement has the effect of preventing, restricting or

---

[55] *e.g.* by Oberdorfer, Gleiss, Hirsch, *op. cit.*, p. 33, and by the Advocate-General in *Volk* v. *Vervaecke* (5/69) [1969] C.M.L.R. 273, 278–9. Both argue that this remark was *obiter*.

[56] *e.g.* those decisions where the Court emphasises that it is necessary to consider the whole economic circumstances of the agreement, particularly *LTM* (56/65) [1966] C.M.L.R. 357, 375; *Volk* v. *Vervaecke* (5/69) [1969] C.M.L.R. 273, 281; *Brasserie de Haecht* (23/67) [1968] C.M.L.R. 26, 40.

[57] See *post*, §§ 230 *et seq.*

[58] *Post*, §§ 245 *et seq.*

[59] See *e.g. Re Safco*, J.O. 1972 L13/44, [1972] C.M.L.R. D83; *Re Socemas*, J.O. 1968 L201/4, [1968] C.M.L.R. D28; *Re Limeburners*, J.O. 1969 L122/8, [1969] C.M.L.R. D15.

[60] (5/69) [1969] C.M.L.R. 273; *post*, § 245.

distorting competition within the common market to a noticeable extent, it is necessary to consider the whole economic context in which the agreement operates. This principle may be seen in the judgment of the European Court in the *Brasserie de Haecht* [61] case, where the Court said that the effects of agreements must be observed in the context in which they occur " *i.e.* in the economic and legal context in which such agreements, decisions and practices are to be found, or where they might, together with others, amount to a cumulative effect on competition. It would be futile to consider an agreement, a decision or a practice as regards its effects if the latter could be separated from the market in which they appear, and could only be examined detached from the bundle of effects, convergent or not, in the midst of which they are produced. Thus to judge whether it is hit by Article 85 (1) a contract cannot be isolated from its context *i.e.* from the factual or legal circumstances resulting in it having the effect of preventing, restricting or distorting competition."

225     **The relevant factors.**   Thus, in contrast to the approach of the Restrictive Trade Practices Act 1956,[62] the economic consequences of the agreement must always be considered for the purpose of deciding whether Article 85 (1) is contravened.[63]   Among the factors which are relevant when considering whether an agreement prevents, restricts or distorts competition to any noticeable extent are the following: the nature and quantity of the products which are the subject matter of the agreement; the positions of the parties in the market; the number of parties to the agreement or, where applicable, to other agreements forming part of a network; and the existence of relevant industrial property or analogous rights protected by national laws.[64]   The agreement must be judged having regard to the competition which would occur in the absence of the agreement.[65]   Regard must be had not only to

---

[61] (23/67) [1968] C.M.L.R. 26.  See also *LTM* (56/65) [1966] C.M.L.R. 357, 375–7.
[62] Where the economic consequences are considered only in the context of justification under s. 21, and not for the purposes of deciding whether the agreement is registrable under s. 6 (1).
[63] See also " effect on trade between Member States " *post*, §§ 230 *et seq.*
[64] See generally *LTM* (56/65) [1966] C.M.L.R. 357, 375–7; *Béguelin* (22/71) [1972] C.M.L.R. 81, 97; *Volk* (5/69) [1969] C.M.L.R. 273, 281.  As to industrial property rights, see *Sirena* (40/70) [1971] C.M.L.R. 260; *Consten & Grundig* v. *EEC Commission* (56/64, 58/64) [1966] C.M.L.R. 418; *post*, §§ 908 *et seq.*
[65] *LTM* (56/65) [1966] C.M.L.R. 357, 375.

actual, but also to potential, restrictions on competition. The operation of all these factors may be seen in the decisions of the Commission [66] and of the Court.[67] If, having regard to the relevant factors the agreement affects competition only insignificantly, it will fall outside Article 85 altogether.[68] The circumstances in which this principle of *de minimis* may apply are further considered below.[69]

**226    Article 85 (1) (a)–(e).**  Article 85 (1) sub-paragraphs (a) to (e) illustrate certain particular agreements which, bearing in mind the relevant factors set out above, commonly have as their object or effect a restriction of competition within the common market. The types of agreement there set out are considered in detail in the next following chapter. They are agreements, decisions or concerted practices which (*a*) directly or indirectly fix purchase or selling prices or any other trading conditions [70]; (*b*) limit or control production, markets, technical development or investment [71]; (*c*) share markets or sources of supply [71]; (*d*) apply dissimilar conditions to equivalent transactions with other trading parties, thereby placing them at a competitive disadvantage [72]; and (*e*) make the conclusion of contracts subject to acceptance by the other parties of supplementary obligations which, by their nature or according to commercial usage, have no connection with the subject of such contracts.[73] These illustrations, however, are not exhaustive. Agreements which do not fall within one of the examples set out in Article 85 (1) (a)–(e) may still fall within the general prohibition under that Article. In this respect the Treaty differs fundamentally from section 6 (1) of the Restrictive Trade Practices Act 1956, which closely defines the types of agreements falling within that legislation.

---

[66] Many examples may be given; but see particularly the decisions in *Re Sopelem-Langen*, 1972 J.O. L13/47; [1972] C.M.L.R. D77 and *Re Henkel-Colgate*, 1972 J.O. L14/14; *post*, §§ 1104 *et seq.* See also, generally *Specialisation Agreements*, *post*, §§ 1001 *et seq.* and *Re Transocean Marine Paint*, J.O. 1967 163/10; [1967] C.M.L.R. D9.
[67] *e.g. Sirena* (40/70) [1971] C.M.L.R. 260.
[68] *Volk* v. *Vervaecke* (5/69) [1969] C.M.L.R. 273.
[69] *Post*, §§ 245 *et seq.*
[70] *Post*, §§ 303 *et seq.*
[71] *Post*, §§ 325 *et seq.* and see §§ 331 *et seq.*
[72] *Post*, §§ 313, 323.
[73] *Post*, §§ 314, 324.

**227**     **Competition within the common market.** One important
consideration also to be borne in mind when considering the
relevant factors set out above is that competition must be
prevented, restricted or distorted within the *common market*.
Thus *e.g.* agreements relating exclusively to exports from the
common market to third countries do not restrict competition
*within* the common market.   On the other hand agreements
between undertakings situated outside the common market may
restrict competition within the common market.   The whole
topic of agreements which relate to trade between the EEC and
third countries is considered below.[74]

**228**     **Agreements between associated companies.** One particular
class of agreements which may not prevent, restrict or distort
competition to a noticeable extent are those made between
companies in the same group, or subject to common control, or
which are otherwise " interconnected." [75]   Broadly speaking, such
agreements fall outside the Treaty.   The basis for this conclusion,
however, has been variously expressed by the Commission and the
European Court, and for this reason such agreements are dealt
with separately below.[76]

**229**     **Co-operation agreements.** Finally, not every form of co-
operation between undertakings leads to a restriction on competition.   The principal type of agreement which falls outside the
Treaty is an agreement between undertakings which, although
carrying on business at the same level of trade, are not in actual
or potential competition with each other.[77]   Although each
agreement will depend upon its own circumstances, certain forms
of co-operation which do not restrict competition are set out in
the Commission's Notice of July 29, 1968.[78]   Although it
expressly applies to all undertakings regardless of size, this
Notice was particularly intended to offer guidance to small and
medium-sized undertakings.   When considering whether any

---

[74] *Post*, §§ 243 *et seq.*
[75] *Cf.* the definition of " inter-connected bodies corporate," under the **Restrictive
Trade Practices Act 1956, s. 36 (1).**
[76] *Post*, § 250.
[77] See *e.g. Re Wild & Leitz*, J.O. 1972 L61/27, [1972] C.M.L.R. D36; *Re Alliance
de Constructeurs Français de Machines-Outils*, J.O. 1968 L201/1, [1968] C.M.L.R.
D23.
[78] App. 12, *post*. Sometimes known as " the block negative clearance."

particular type of co-operation falls within the Treaty it should be borne in mind that a co-operation agreement between small undertakings is much less likely to offend against Article 85 (1) than an equivalent agreement between large undertakings. It must, however, be emphasised that the Notice is only a guide and is not intended to be a comprehensive and definitive statement of the circumstances in which an agreement will fall outside Article 85 (1).[79] The agreements to which it relates are discussed in the next following chapter and in other parts of this work. They comprise agreements which in each case have the following sole objects:

(1) An exchange of opinion or experience; joint market research; the joint carrying out of comparative studies of undertakings or industries; the joint preparation of statistics and calculation models.[80]

(2) Co-operation in accounting matters; joint furnishings of credit guarantees; joint business or tax consultant agencies.[81]

(3) The joint implementation of research and development projects; the joint placing of research and development contracts; the sharing out of research and development profits among participating undertakings.[82]

(4) The joint use of production facilities and storage and transport facilities.[83]

(5) The setting up of working partnerships for the common execution of orders, where the participating undertakings do not compete with each other in the work to be done or where each of them by itself is unable to execute the orders.[84]

(6) Joint selling arrangements or joint after-sales and repair services, where the undertakings do not compete in the products covered by the agreement.[85]

(7) Joint advertising.[86]

---

[79] See *e.g. Re Henkel-Colgate*, J.O. 1972 L14/14; *post*, §§ 1107 *et seq.*
[80] *Post*, §§ 315–316.
[81] *Post*, § 317.
[82] *Post*, §§ 1101 *et seq.*
[83] *Post*, App. 12.
[84] *Post*, App. 12.
[85] *Post*, §§ 337 *et seq.*
[86] *Post*, §§ 351 *et seq.*

(8) The use of a common label to designate a certain quality, where the label is available to competitors on the same conditions.[87]

### 5. EFFECTS ON TRADE BETWEEN MEMBER STATES

**230**     **National law and Community law.** An agreement, decision or concerted practice does not fall within Article 85 (1) unless it may affect trade between Member States. Broadly speaking, it is the capacity of the agreement to affect trade between Member States which serves to distinguish agreements which are prohibited by Community law from those which are prohibited, if at all, only under national restrictive practices legislation.[88] Whether any agreement affects trade between Member States is closely connected with the question of whether it also prevents, restricts or distorts competition. This section should therefore be read together with the last preceding section.[89]

**231**     **General principles.** The European Court of Justice has now laid down the broad principles to be applied when deciding whether an agreement may affect trade between Member States.[90] In summary, those principles are

(1) An agreement " may affect trade between Member States " within the meaning of the Treaty if it appears, after consideration of its objective legal or factual elements, that the agreement may reasonably be expected to exercise a direct or indirect, actual or potential effect upon the flow of trade between Member States which may hinder the creation of a common market among those states and obstruct the economic interpretation aimed at by the Treaty.

(2) In considering whether a particular agreement falls within the above definition, it is necessary to assess the agreement within the whole surrounding economic and legal context.

**232**     **Harm to the objectives of the EEC.** Fundamentally, the agreements which fall under Article 85 (1) are those which affect

[87] *Post*, § 353.
[88] *Consten & Grundig* v. *EEC Commission* (56/64, 58/64) [1966] C.M.L.R. 418, 472, see *ante*, §§ 139 *et seq.*
[89] *Ante*, §§ 215 *et seq.*
[90] See *Consten & Grundig* v. *EEC Commission* (56/64, 58/64) [1966] C.M.L.R. 418, 470; *LTM* (56/65) [1966] C.M.L.R. 357, 375; *Brasserie de Haecht* (23/67) [1968] C.M.L.R. 26, 40; *Volk* v. *Vervaecke* (5/69) [1969] C.M.L.R. 273, 281; *Cadillon* v. *Firma Höss Maschinenbau* (1/71) [1971] C.M.L.R. 420, 428. See also *VCH* v. *EEC Commission* (8/72) [1973] C.M.L.R. 7.

trade between Member States in such a way as to hinder the economic integration of the Community and create obstacles to the creation of a single common market. In the *L.T.M.* case the Court said [91] that Article 85 (1) could apply only if: " Considered on the basis of a series of objective legal or factual elements, the agreement is such as to lead to a reasonable expectation that it may be able to exercise an influence, whether direct or indirect, actual or potential on trade between Member States capable of hindering the realisation of a single market among the said States. In this respect, examination should particularly be made whether the agreement is capable of partitioning the market in certain products between Member States." Dealing with the agreement in question the Court said [92]: "In particular it is necessary to know whether the agreement is in a position to partition one market for given products between Member States and thus render more difficult the economic interpenetration desired by the Treaty." In *Grundig-Consten* the Court said [93] that an agreement falls within Article 85 (1) " if it is capable of endangering, either directly or indirectly, in fact or potentially, freedom of trade between Member States in a direction which could harm the attainment of the objects of a single market between states."

**233**    **The relevant factors.** In determining whether an agreement may, actually or potentially, affect trade between Member States within the meaning of the Treaty it is necessary to assess the agreement within the whole surrounding economic and legal context.[94] Thus it is impossible to know whether an agreement is prohibited under Article 85 (1) without considering the actual or potential operation of the agreement in the market. For this purpose it is necessary to take into account the same factors which, as already indicated, must be considered when deciding whether an agreement has as its effect the prevention, restriction or distortion of competition.[95] Reference should be made to each of those factors previously discussed. In particular it is necessary to consider the existence of similar contracts of the same type.[96]

[91] (56/65) [1966] C.M.L.R. 357, 375; and see *ante*, § 221.
[92] *Ibid.*
[93] [1966] C.M.L.R. 418, 472.
[94] *LTM* (56/65) [1966] C.M.L.R. 357, 375; *Brasserie de Haecht* (23/67) [1968] C.M.L.R. 26, 40.
[95] *Ante*, § 225.
[96] *Brasserie de Haecht*, note 94, *supra.*

It is also important to consider whether trade between Member
States may be affected by the agreement when combined with
industrial property and analogous rights conferred by the national
laws of Member States.[97]  All these matters should be borne in
mind, remembering that the test is whether the agreement may
contribute to the perpetuation of national markets and hinder
the creation of a *common* market.  Thus, even if the agreement
leads to an increase in the *volume* of inter-State trade, that agreement falls within Article 85 (1) if the agreement by the use of
*national* boundaries and *national* laws tends to fragment what
ought to be a common market.[98]  It must be emphasised that
" trade " between Member States relates to the provision of
services as well as to the supply of goods.

**234     Perpetuation of national markets: import and export pro-
hibitions.**  Those agreements which contribute most to the perpetuation of national markets are those which directly or
indirectly prevent the free import and export of goods and services
between Member States.  Thus, in *Grundig-Consten*,[99] the isolation
of the French market was achieved by (i) Grundig's undertaking
not to export to anyone in France except Consten; (ii) the
obligation imposed on other Grundig concessionaires and
wholesalers not to export into France, and (iii) the assignment of
the " GINT " mark which enabled Consten to use French
national industrial property law to defeat would-be importers
endeavouring to breach the Grundig system.  The decisions of
the Commission and of the European Court in *Grundig-Consten*
show that the Treaty strikes particularly at bars to exports and
imports to and from other Member States.[1]  At the same time,
these decisions show that national laws which operate to preserve
national markets may not be used to prevent imports and exports
and defeat the objectives of the Treaty.  The decisions of the
Commission and the European Court in effect prevented Consten

[97] See *Consten & Grundig* v. *EEC Commission* (56/64, 58/64) [1966] C.M.L.R. 418,
475; *Sirena* (40/70) [1971] C.M.L.R. 260, 272 *et seq.; Béguelin* (22/71) [1972]
C.M.L.R. 81, 96.
[98] *Consten & Grundig* v. *EEC Commission* (56/64, 58/64) [1966] C.M.L.R. 418,
471–2, see also *Re German Ceramic Tiles*, J.O. 1971 L10/15, [1971] C.M.L.R.
D6, D16.
[99] J.O. 1964 2545/64, [1964] C.M.L.R. 489; (56/64, 58/64) [1966] C.M.L.R. 418.
[1] See also *Re Pittsburg Corning Europe*, J.O. 1972 L272/35, [1973] C.M.L.R. D2;
*Re WEA-Filipacchi*, J.O. 1972 L303/52.

from using the rights conferred under French national law to preserve its exclusive position on the French market.[2]

**235    Wide circumstances in which trade may be affected.** It should not be thought, however, that trade between Member States is affected only where agreements contain direct or indirect prohibitions against imports or exports. In accordance with the principles of general application laid down by the European Court, the whole operation of the agreement in the market must be considered.[3] Where the effect of an agreement is to contribute to the preservation of individual national markets, to the detriment of the effective freedom of movement of the products concerned, Article 85 (1) will be applicable.[4] The decisions of the Commission, moreover, show that where the undertakings concerned are situated in different Member States, and there is a noticeable restriction of competition within the common market, it may almost invariably be said that trade between Member States is affected within the meaning of the Treaty.[5] Indeed, once it is shown that competition is noticeably prevented, restricted or distorted within the common market, it may not be difficult to identify some respect in which trade between Member States is affected. Thus, in *Davidson Rubber*[6] the holder of a patent granted exclusive patent licences to licensees in different Member States. The Commission held that competition was restricted in that the licensor had deprived himself of the opportunity to grant a licence in respect of the patented products to any other licensee in a particular Member State. Although each licensee was free to export to other Member States, it was held that such an agreement affects trade between Member States; since the licensor could not grant a licence to any third party situated in the territory of a licensee, third parties were deprived of the possibility of being granted a right to exploit the patent and, consequently, the potential opportunity of exporting to other parts of the common market.

---

[2] Including the French Law of unfair competition, *ante*, note 39. For the effect of the Treaty generally on the internal laws of Member States, see § 139, *ante*.
[3] See *ante*, § 233.
[4] *ICI* v. *EEC Commission* (48/69) [1972] C.M.L.R. 557, 628.
[5] See *e.g.* decisions relating to specialisation agreements, §§ 1001 *et seq.*, *post*.
[6] J.O. 1972 L143/31, [1972] C.M.L.R. D52, *post*, §§ 944 *et seq.*

**236     Agreements between undertakings in the one Member State.**
There is no reason in principle why an agreement between
undertakings in one Member State should not fall within Article
85 (1). Clearly this is the case if the agreement relates directly to
imports or exports between Member States, as in the case of an
agreement containing terms affecting export to or re-import from
other EEC countries. However, the prohibition may also apply
if the domestic agreement indirectly affects trade between Member
States by making import or export between them more difficult.
Whether any particular agreement has this effect to a noticeable
degree is a question of fact. For example, an agreement to limit
production may deprive a party to the contract of the ability to
export or restrict customers in other Member States as to their
choice of supplier.[7] An exclusive purchase obligation may involve
a restriction on capacity to import; and if it is part of a network
of like agreements, may prevent the penetration of a national
market by foreign suppliers.[8]

**237     National cartel agreements.** In practice, those domestic
agreements which are most likely to affect trade between Member
States are collective cartel arrangements. The prohibition of
Article 85 (1) does not extend merely to import and export
cartels. Collective exclusive dealing agreements between domestic
manufacturers on the one hand and domestic traders on the other
may fall within Article 85 (1),[9] as may the collective enforcement
by manufacturers upon traders of " approved " channels of
distribution.[10] National agreements which operate fixed or
minimum price schemes,[11] or recommended price schemes [11] or
through which resale price maintenance [12] is observed may also
fall under the Treaty, at least where the provisions of the agreement extend to imported products. Although not all national
cartels will be caught by Article 85 (1),[13] their effect on inter-State

---

[7] *Re Lightweight Paper,* J.O. 1972 L182/24, [1972] C.M.L.R. D94, para. 10.
[8] *Brasserie de Haecht* (23/67) [1968] C.M.L.R. 26, 40.
[9] *La Convention Faience, Bulletin,* No. 5, 1964, Annex II; *post,* §§ 331 *et seq.*
[10] *Re ASPA,* J.O. 1970 L148/9, [1970] C.M.L.R. D25; *post,* § 333.
[11] *Re VCH,* J.O. 1972 L13/34, [1973] C.M.L.R. D16; *VCH* v. *EEC Commission*
(8/72) [1973] C.M.L.R. 7. The Court said: "a restrictive agreement extending
to the whole territory of a Member State by its very nature consolidates the
national boundaries, thus hindering the economic interpenetration desired
by the Treaty and so protecting national production."
[12] *Re ASPA, supra.*
[13] See " joint selling agreements " *post,* § 337. But *Cf. Re VCH* (8/72), *supra.*

trade requires careful consideration in each case. This is particularly so when collective arrangements in one Member State may discriminate directly or indirectly against nationals of another Member State. For example, in *Re German Ceramic Tiles Discount Agreement*,[14] where the members of the German association of ceramic tile manufacturers gave German purchasers aggregated rebates which increased according to the total volume of supplies purchased from all the members of the association, it was held that the scheme affected inter-State trade by discouraging German purchasers from obtaining supplies from outside Germany.

**238    De minimis rule.** As with restrictions upon competition, it must be remembered that under the *de minimis* rule, an agreement will not fall under Article 85 (1) unless it affects trade between Member States to a *noticeable extent*.[15] The operation of this rule is considered below.[16]

**239    Trade with third countries.** The question of how far agreements may " affect trade between Member States " when one or more of the participating undertakings is outside the Community, or when the agreement relates to exports outside the EEC is considered in the next section.[17]

### 6.    THE EXTRA-TERRITORIAL EFFECT OF ARTICLE 85 (1) [18]

#### (a) *Trade Within the EEC*

**240    Agreements where one undertaking is situated outside the EEC.** The criteria for the application of Article 85 (1) are that trade *between* Member States must be affected and that competition *within* the common market should be prevented, restricted or distorted. Provided those criteria are satisfied, it is immaterial whether one or some of the parties to the agreement are situated outside the EEC. The location of the parties is irrelevant,

---

[14] J.O. 1971, L10/15 [1971] C.M.L.R. D6.  See also " loyalty rebates " scheme in *Cobelaz No.* 1, J.O. 1968 L276/29, [1968] C.M.L.R. D45.
[15] *Volk* v. *Vervaecke* (5/69) [1969] C.M.L.R. 273.
[16] *Post,* §§ 245 *et seq.*                                              [17] *Post,* §§ 240 *et seq.*
[18] For the associated territories, etc. to which Art. 85 (1) applies see Art. 227 of the Treaty, as amended by Art. 26 of the Accession Treaty.  For the extra territorial application of restrictive trade practices legislation see: International Law Association: Report of 51st Conference (1964) pp. 304–592.  Report of 52nd Conference (1966), pp. 26–142 and 866–868; Report of 53rd Conference (1968), pp. 53–404; Report of 54th Conference (1970), pp. 151–246.

provided the agreement has its effects within the EEC.[19]   Thus
an agreement which concerns imports into one Member State from
a non-EEC country, which obstructs the re-export of the goods
into any Member State, may well be prohibited under Article
85 (1).   In the *Béguelin* [20] case, the agreement between a Japanese
firm and its French exclusive distributor which prevented the
French firm from re-exporting the imported products into another
Member State was held to fall within the Treaty.   Again, in
*Henkel-Colgate*,[21] the Commission held that an agreement between
an American corporation trading within the common market and
a German firm to set up a joint research subsidiary in Switzerland
fell within the Treaty where the agreement would result in a
restriction on competition in research between two companies
competing within the common market.   The Commission has
reached similar conclusions in respect of patent licence and
know-how agreements between American companies and licensees
within the EEC.[22]

**241**   **Agreements where both undertakings are outside the EEC.**
It follows from the foregoing that, in principle, there is nothing
to prevent the Treaty applying to an agreement between two
undertakings where both are situated outside the EEC, provided
only that the agreement produces the prohibited effects within the
common market.   If this is right, then one result of Accession will
be to bring within the jurisdiction of the Commission for the
first time parties who have hitherto been operating agreements
(pre-Accession agreements) to which Article 85 (1) has been
applicable, perhaps for some years past.[23]

**242**   **Agreements restricting exports into the common market.**   In
certain circumstances, an agreement may fall within Article 85 (1)

[19] *Béguelin* (22/71) [1972] C.M.L.R. 81; *Sirena* (40/70) [1971] C.M.L.R. 260;
*cf. ICI* v. *EEC Commission* (48/69) [1972] C.M.L.R. 557, 628. See also Commission's view on agreements relating to limitations on Community imports
from Japan, J.O. 1972 C111.
[20] Note 19, *supra.*
[21] J.O. 1972 L14/14.
[22] *Re Davidson Rubber*, J.O. 1972 L143/31, [1972] C.M.L.R. D52; *The Burroughs
decisions*, J.O. 1972 L13/50, 53, [1972] C.M.L.R. D67, D72. See also *Re
Raymonds*, J.O. 1972 L143/39, [1972] C.M.L.R. D45.
[23] As to the possibility of the imposition of fines in respect of such agreements, see
*post*, § 1209.

if an undertaking in a third country is prevented by the agreement from exporting into the EEC. Such a restriction occurred in *Re Raymond*[22] which concerned a patent licence agreement between the French licensor and a Japanese licensee who was prevented from exporting the patented products into the common market as a whole. The Commission found, on the special facts of the case, that competition *within* the common market was not likely to be restricted since the Japanese undertaking was unlikely, for technical reasons, to export to or manufacture in the common market. On the other hand, there is no reason in principle why such a provision should not restrict competition within the common market; and if it could be shown that there was a realistic possibility that the goods, once imported into the EEC, would subsequently cross the frontier of another Member State, then the agreement would also affect trade between Member States. Consequently Article 85 (1) would be applicable.[24]

### (b) *Agreements Relating Solely to Trade Outside the EEC*

**243**    **Exports to third countries.** Broadly speaking, agreements which relate solely to trade outside the EEC have no noticeable effect on trade between Member States or competition within the common market. Thus in *Re Omega*,[25] where the Swiss watch firm imposed on its exclusive distributors an export ban in respect of countries outside the EEC, it was held that this did not fall within the Treaty. Similarly, exclusive dealing agreements which relate only to exports to third countries,[26] joint selling agreements,[27] joint tendering agreements,[28] or the joint fixing of export prices,[29] in respect of markets outside the EEC, and patent licences granted to undertakings outside the EEC,[30] have all been held not to contravene Article 85 (1).

**244**    **Examination of individual circumstances required.** However, although there has been no reported decision by the Commission holding that an agreement relating to exports outside the EEC

---

[24] See also *Re Grosfillex*, J.O. 1964 915/64, [1964] C.M.L.R. 237.
[25] J.O. 1970 L242/22, [1970] C.M.L.R. D49; *post*, §§ 840 *et seq.*
[26] *Re Grosfillex*, J.O. 1964 915/64, [1964] C.M.L.R. 237; *Re Rieckermann*, J.O. 1968 L276/25, [1968] C.M.L.R. D78; *post*, §§ 833 *et seq.*
[27] See *post*, §§ 337, 345.
[28] *Re DECA*, J.O. 1964 2761/64, [1965] C.M.L.R. 50.
[29] *Re VVVF*, J.O. 1969 L168/22, [1970] C.M.L.R. D1; see *post*, § 306.
[30] *Re Raymond*, note 22, *supra*.

falls within Article 85 (1), it is none the less the Commission's practice carefully to examine the likely effect of each such agreement before reaching that conclusion. Thus in *Re Rieckermann* [31] which concerned an exclusive dealing agreement whereby a German undertaking appointed a German export agency as its sole agent for sales to Japan, the agreement involved a prohibition against the export agency making any sales within the common market. On the special facts, the Commission held that competition would not be restricted within the common market, but it so held only after duly considering the effects of the agreement. Export agreements to non-Member countries should always be considered carefully to see whether, in fact, they may have effects within the Community.

## 7. THE DE MINIMIS RULE

**245     Agreements of minor importance.** An agreement which would otherwise fall within Article 85 (1) none the less falls outside the prohibition where it is unlikely either to affect trade between Member States or to restrict competition to any noticeable extent. This principle was established by the decision of the European Court in *Volk* v. *Vervaecke*.[32] There a German manufacturer of washing machines, Volk, granted the Belgian firm Vervaecke the exclusive right to distribute the machines in Belgium and Luxembourg. Volk undertook to ensure that Vervaecke would be absolutely protected against parallel imports and Vervaecke undertook not to sell competing machines. A dispute arose. Vervaecke alleged the agreement was void under Article 85 (1). It transpired that Volk's production of washing machines was very small, 2,361 units in 1963 and 861 in 1966— about 0·2 per cent. and 0·05 per cent. respectively of production in Germany. The European Court said [33] that the requirements of Article 85 (1) must be considered in the actual context in which the agreement exists. Consequently, it held, " an agreement escapes the prohibition of Article 85 where it affects the market

---

[31] Note 26, *supra;* for examples of the Commission's reasoning see also: *Re VVVF*, note 29, *supra; Re Raymond*, note 22, *supra; Re Kodak*, J.O. 1970 L147/24, [1970] C.M.L.R. D19.
[32] (5/69) [1969] C.M.L.R. 273.  See also *Cadillon* v. *Firma Höss Maschinenbau* (1/71) [1971] C.M.L.R. 420.
[33] [1969] C.M.L.R. 273, 283.

insignificantly, account being taken of the weak position of the
parties in the market in the products in question." [34]

Clearly the question whether the agreement has only " such
a significant effect " must be considered as much in relation to
its capacity to restrict, prevent or distort competition as in relation
to its ability to affect trade between Member States. In the
*Béguelin* [35] case the European Court stated the matter succinctly:
" To bring into play the prohibition set out in Article 85, the
agreement must *noticeably* affect trade between Member States
and competition". [36]

**246**   **Meaning of " noticeably."** Whether or not trade between
Member States is actually or potentially affected " to a noticeable
degree," or competition " noticeably " restricted within the
common market is a question of fact in each case. Some guidance
may be obtained from two sources. First, following the *Volk* [37]
decision, the Commission on May 27, 1970 issued a Notice
Concerning Agreements of Minor Importance [38] in which it
attempted a definition of the phrase " noticeable effect."
Secondly, in several decisions granting negative clearance [39] the
Commission has in practice applied the principle of the *Volk* case.

**247**   **Notice of May 27, 1970.** The Notice of May 27, 1970 states
that in the Commission's view, agreements between undertakings
engaged in the production or distribution of goods do not fall
within Article 85 (1) where (i) the products covered by the
agreement do not represent, in the part of the common market in
which the agreement produces its effect, more than 5 per cent. of
the amount of business done in identical products or in products
considered by the consumer to be similar by reason of their
properties their price or their use, and (ii) the total annual

---

[34] *Ibid.* For the effect of *Volk* on exclusive dealing agreements where " absolute
territorial protection " exists, see *post*, § 816.
[35] (22/71) [1972] C.M.L.R. 81.
[36] [1972] C.M.L.R. 81, 96. The French text, (*ibid.* pp. 103 *et seq.*) uses the word
" sensible " which has usually been translated as " noticeably." Although not
an exact translation, it is probably more accurate than " perceptibly " or
" significantly."
[37] Note 32, *supra.*
[38] J.O. 1970 L64/1; App 13, *post.*
[39] *Re SAFCO*, J.O. 1972 L13/44, [1972] C.M.L.R. D83; *Re SOCEMAS*, J.O.
1968 L201/7, [1968] C.M.L.R. D28; *Re Limeburners*, J.O. 1969 L122/8, [1969]
C.M.L.R. D15; *post*, § 249. See also the *Burroughs decisions*, J.O. 1972
L13/50, 53, [1972] C.M.L.R. D67, D73; *post*, §§ 944 *et seq.*

turnover of the undertakings taking part in the agreement does not exceed 15 million units of account or, in the case of commercial undertakings, 20 million units of account.[40] Further, the Commission does not regard Article 85 (1) as applying if the above limits as to market share and turnover in all products are exceeded by less than 10 per cent. in any two consecutive financial years. In calculating turnover, regard must be had not only to the turnover of the parties, but also to that of certain associated undertakings, including those in which the parties hold more than 25 per cent. of the capital or working capital.[40a]

**248**     **Comment on Notice of May 27, 1970.** The Notice of May 27, 1970 raises certain difficulties. In practice, it may not be easy to identify the part of the common market in which the agreement has its effects; nor may it be easy to ascertain whether the products concerned represent less than 5 per cent. of the " relevant market " according to the stated definitions. The distinction drawn between " undertakings " and " commercial undertakings " in relation to the calculation of turnover is obscure .[41] Also it appears to follow that an agreement which initially falls under the terms of the Notice may subsequently become unlawful if the parties prosper and exceed the prescribed limits as to market share and turnover. More important than these matters, however, is the fact that the Notice is for general guidance only. It is without prejudice to the ruling of the European Court of Justice,[42] and is not binding upon national courts. Thus, there may be circumstances in which the Notice has no application (*e.g.* certain restricted or very special markets), even if the criteria set out in the Notice are complied with.[43] Conversely, as the Notice itself states,[44] the defined limits will affect trade between Member States and competition to more than an insignificant degree. In all the circumstances, therefore, the Notice must be treated with caution. Only in those cases where it is clear beyond

---

[40] See para. 6 of the Notice. The unit of account is fixed in terms of gold. Prior to the devaluation of the U.S. dollar in 1972, one unit of account was equal to one U.S. dollar.

[40a] See para. 8 of the Notice.

[41] Commercial undertakings are thought to be " dealers " as distinct from " manufacturers ".

[42] Para. 5, *ibid.*

[43] See the arguments of the Advocate-General in *Cadillon* (1/71) [1971] C.M.L.R. 420, 427 and the arguments of both the Commission and the Advocate-General in *Béguelin* (22/71) [1972] C.M.L.R. 81, 90.

[44] At para. 4 of the Notice.

argument that the agreement concerned satisfies both the letter
and the spirit of the Commission's Notice may the parties safely
rely upon it.

**249    Decisions relating to negative clearance.**    Perhaps more helpful
indications as to the operation of the *de minimis* rule may be
obtained from certain decisions of the Commission relating to
negative clearance.   Thus, in *SAFCO* [45] there was an agreement
between French producers of preserved vegetables who conferred
upon their agency SAFCO the exclusive right to export their
products to Germany.   Membership of the association was
limited to undertakings of less than 500 employees and a capital
of not more than 5 million French francs.   Before the agreement,
the undertakings either did not export their products at all, or did
so only on a very small scale.   At the time of the decision the
combined exports of tinned vegetables by the members of the
association to their main foreign market West Germany did not
exceed 1 to 2 per cent. of German consumption of tinned vegetables
as a whole or 7 to 8 per cent. of German consumption for certain
particular types of tinned vegetables.   The Commission granted
negative clearance on the ground that competition was not
" noticeably " restricted.   Similarly, in SOCEMAS [46] an association of 69 small and medium sized French firms set up a joint
import purchasing agency.   Arguably, such an arrangement would
fall within Article 85 (1) if it noticeably restricted the freedom of
supplies to supply the members of SOCEMAS individually.
However, the members of SOCEMAS were still free to purchase
individually from abroad and imports from EEC countries carried
out through SOCEMAS amounted to only 0·1 per cent. of the
turnover of the members.   The imports of any given product
through SOCEMAS did not exceed 1 per cent. of the annual
production of any Member State.   The purchases abroad made by
SOCEMAS represented only a very minor part of the different
markets in the products in question and this position was unlikely
to change in future.   On these facts, the Commission granted
negative clearance, holding that the activities of SOCEMAS had
no significant effect on the position of suppliers.

[45] J.O. 1972 L13/44, [1972] C.M.L.R. D83.  See also *Re Limeburners*, J.O. 1969
L122/8, [1969] C.M.L.R. D15, and the *Burrough's decisions* J.O. 1972 L13/50,
53, [1972] C.M.L.R. D67, 72; *post*, § 944.
[46] J.O. 1968 L201/7, [1968] C.M.L.R. D28.

## 8.  AGREEMENTS WITH SUBSIDIARY UNDERTAKINGS

**250     In general.**  Broadly speaking, agreements between parent and subsidiary or between subsidiary companies in the same Group, or subject to a common control, fall outside Article 85 (1).  In each case the test to be applied is whether the subsidiary, although having a distinct legal personality, does not determine its behaviour on the market in an autonomous manner, but essentially carries out the instructions given to it by the parent company.[47]  If the subsidiary does not enjoy any real autonomy in the determination of its course of action, then Article 85 (1) does not apply to agreements between it and its parent, who together form one economic unit.  The criteria to be applied are essentially *economic* rather than legal.

**251     Basis of the rule.**  The basis of the rule set out above has been variously expressed.  It has been said that " agreements " between bodies that are not economically autonomous of each other are not " agreements between undertakings."[48]  It has also been said that " agreements " between parent and subsidiary are not really " agreements " at all, but simply a parent company imposing its will on subsidiaries. [49]  A view that has found some favour is that in the case of a parent and a subsidiary there can be no competition between the parties, and hence any apparently restrictive agreement between them cannot restrict competition within the meaning of Article 85 (1).  This reasoning was the basis for the Commission's decision in *Christiani and Nielsen,*[50] which concerned an agreement between a parent and a wholly owned subsidiary.  There the Commission said that before Article 85 (1) could apply, there must be competition between the two undertakings which was capable of being restricted by the agreement.  It was necessary to examine all the circumstances to see whether, in fact " autonomous activity of the subsidiary with regard to the parent company is possible on the economic

---

[47] *ICI* v. *EEC Commission* (48/69) [1972] C.M.L.R. 557, 629. See also *Béguelin* (22/71) [1972] C.M.L.R. 81, 95.  This principle would appear to overrule the Commission's recommendation in *Remington Rand*, EC Press Release, June 11, 1969.  For the application of Art. 86 to a parent and a subsidiary see *Re CSC-ZOJA*, J.O. 1972 L299/51.
[48] *e.g.* by the Advocate-General in *Béguelin* (22/71) [1972] C.M.L.R. 81, 88.
[49] By the Commission in *Re Kodak* J.O. 1970 L147/24, [1970] C.M.L.R. D19.
[50] J.O. 1969 L165/12, [1969] C.M.L.R. D36.

plane." [51]  In that case, the subsidiary was subject to the directions
of the parent with whom it would not be expected to compete,
and the Commission described the agreement as " merely distribution of tasks within a single economic entity." [51]  In the
*Béguelin* [52] case the European Court came close to endorsing the
Commission's reasoning in *Christiani and Nielsen*, [50] but in the
*ICI* case the Court contented itself with the general statement [53]:
" When the subsidiary does not enjoy any real autonomy in the
determination of its course of action on the market, the prohibitions imposed by Article 85 (1) may be considered inapplicable
in the relations between the subsidiary and the parent company
with which it then forms one economic unit."

**252**    **Application of the rule.**  Whatever the basis of the rule, it
may now be considered established that if, as a matter of fact,
one undertaking is not economically autonomous of another, an
agreement between them will fall outside Article 85 (1).  Hence
agreements between parents and *wholly* owned subsidiaries will
generally fall outside Article 85. However, the rule may not be
so easy to apply in the case of *partly* owned subsidiaries where
there are substantial minority shareholders.  Difficulties may also
arise where, perhaps for tax reasons, a subsidiary in a Member
State is accorded considerable local independence of action.
Ultimately, the question must be one of fact.  Perhaps the most
appropriate question to pose is: Could the " subsidiary," if it so
wished, go against the wishes of the " parent "?  Where the
answer is no, Article 85 (1) will not apply. [54]

**253**    **Principal and agents.**  It is probably because an agent enjoys
no economic autonomy of his principal that, in the Commission's
view, agreements between principal and agent in which the latter
merely makes contracts for and on behalf of the former, fall
outside the Treaty. [55]

**[The next paragraph is 301.]**

[51] [1969] C.M.L.R. D36 and D39.
[52] Note 47, *supra.*
[53] [1972] C.M.L.R. D557, 629.
[54] For Art. 86 see *Re CSC-ZOJA*, J.O. 1972 L299/51.
[55] See Notice on Exclusive Representation by Commercial Agents, December 24,
1962; App. 10, *post.*  See also *post*, §§ 805 *et seq.*

CHAPTER 3

# ARTICLE 85 (1): COMMON TYPES OF AGREEMENT

## 1. IN GENERAL

**301** **Purpose of this chapter.** The purpose of this chapter is to illustrate, by way of example, the general principles governing the application of Article 85 (1) that have been discussed in the previous chapter. Article 85 (1) may be applicable in many different circumstances, including those set out in Articles 85 (1) (*a*)–(*e*). Accordingly, the agreements here dealt with display a wide variety. Broadly speaking, the principle adopted is to discuss in this chapter those agreements which, typically, fall within Article 85 (1) and those agreements which, typically, fall outside Article 85 (1) altogether. Many of the types of agreements discussed in this chapter to which Article 85 (1) applies are those which have not hitherto benefited from an exemption under Article 85 (3). The main classes of agreements to which Article 85 (1) applies, but in respect of which exceptions under Article 85 (3) have been granted, are dealt with in separate chapters later in this book. Such agreements include exclusive dealing,[1] specialisation[2] and research and development[3] agreements. The problems raised by industrial property rights under the Community law of competition are also discussed separately in a later chapter.[4]

**302** **Plan of this chapter.** In this chapter the first class of agreements dealt with are those relating to agreements between undertakings as to prices and conditions of sale. Those agreements concerned with limitations as to markets and as to production are discussed next. Thirdly, collective exclusive dealing agreements are considered, followed by joint purchasing agreements, joint selling agreements and other agreements relating to joint sales promotion.

---

[1] §§ 801 *et seq., post.*
[2] §§ 1001 *et seq., post.*
[3] §§ 1101 *et seq., post.*
[4] §§ 901 *et seq., post.*

## 2. AGREEMENTS RELATING TO PRICES AND CONDITIONS OF SALE

### (a) *Generally*

**303** **In general.** Article 85 (1) (*a*) provides that agreements, decisions and concerted practices prohibited under Article 85 (1), in that they prevent, restrict or distort competition within the common market and affect trade between Member States, include, in particular, those which " directly or indirectly fix purchase or selling prices or any other trading conditions." This wide provision applies to horizontal and vertical agreements. It covers both agreements, decisions and concerted practices that directly fix prices, and those that indirectly do so. Whether any particular arrangement or practice has the object or effect of " directly or indirectly " fixing prices must be a question of fact in each case. The simplest example of a vertical agreement which directly fixes prices is a resale price maintenance agreement. Where horizontal agreements are concerned a typical example is an express agreement between suppliers to observe uniform prices. On the other hand the parties may in fact observe uniform prices as a result of some very informal co-operation between them. In such cases there may be " a concerted practice " to fix prices.[5] Moreover the indirect effect of each agreement must be considered. Thus agreements as to discounts, rebates and uniform terms of sale may indirectly fix prices. Again a cartel agreement could fix a price to which members were not obliged to adhere; but if they undersold they might be required to pay into a pool a percentage of the difference between their actual price and the cartel price. Such an agreement could be regarded as an agreement which indirectly fixed prices, or if it resulted in price fixing, the parties could be said to be operating a " concerted practice to fix prices." Such a case may also arise where the parties agree list prices but remain free to give whatever discounts they please off the list prices. From one point of view such an agreement " directly fixes prices," irrespective of the actual identity or similarity of the net prices. Alternatively such an agreement could be said " indirectly to fix prices "; or if the agreement operated in such a way as to fix prices, it could be said that the parties were engaging in " concerted practices " which directly

---

[5] See *e.g. ICI* v. *EEC Commission* (48/69) [1972] C.M.L.R. 557.

or indirectly fixed prices. Whether such agreements fall under the Treaty must be judged according to the particular circumstances of each case.

(b) *Agreements Between Suppliers and Acquirers* inter se

**304** **Horizontal agreements as to prices and conditions.** Agreements, decisions or concerted practices made between or observed directly or indirectly by two or more suppliers or acquirers *inter se*, as to the prices to be charged, quoted or paid for goods or services of any description within the common market, generally restrict competition. Given a noticeable restriction on competition an agreement will ordinarily affect trade between Member States sufficiently to bring the agreement within Article 85 (1) where the undertakings concerned are situated in different Member States. Horizontal price fixing agreements made between undertakings situated in the same Member State [6] will contravene the Treaty where they relate to the prices and conditions upon which exports may be made to other Member States [7] or the prices at which or conditions upon which goods imported from another Member State may be resold. [8] Agreements between suppliers in the same Member State which fix the selling prices of non-imported goods in the home market may in certain circumstances affect trade between Member States. [9] The application of these principles may be illustrated by the decisions of the Commission discussed in the following paragraphs.

**305** **International price fixing cartels.** Price fixing cartel arrangements made between undertakings situated in different Member States often include restrictions other than those relating to price, which fall within Article 85 (1). In the *Quinine* case,[10] for example, the restrictions accepted by the parties related to prices,

---

[6] Where the agreement in question is made between two or more persons carrying on business within the U.K. in the production or supply of goods or in the application to goods of any process of manufacture (or in the supply of services), the application of the Restrictive Trade Practices Acts (and the Fair Trading Bill) fall to be considered in addition to the Treaty provisions.

[7] § 306, *post.*

[8] § 307, *post.*

[9] § 308, *post.*

[10] See J.O. 1969 L192/5, [1969] C.M.L.R. D41. On appeal, see *ACF-Chemiefarma* v. *EEC Commission* (41/69); *Boehringer Mannheim* v. *EEC Commission* (45/69); *Buchler* v. *EEC Commission* (44/69), all noted at 8 C.M.L.Rev. 86.

market divisions, sales quotas and limitations on production. The undertakings concerned were situated in Holland, Germany and France.  By a series of agreements and concerted practices, the parties jointly fixed the prices and discounts at which, and other conditions of sale upon which, they would sell quinine and quinidine-based products in the various national markets of the EEC.  They also agreed the amount and timing of price increases. This uniform pricing policy was, the Commission found, the basis of the whole cartel.  In addition the parties agreed, in effect, to keep out of each other's national markets; to observe a quota system in respect of exports, including exports to Member States, whereby each party agreed to sell a certain annual quota and, if such quota were exceeded, to buy an equivalent amount of quinine from a party who had not reached his quota; finally, certain undertakings agreed not to manufacture quinidine.  The Commission held [11] that the agreement restricted competition within the common market, and that freedom of inter-State trade was adversely affected where the agreements on prices relating to exports between Member States, and the other restrictions accepted by the parties, contributed to the protection of national markets and prevented purchasers from benefiting from the competitive behaviour that would have occurred between the parties in the absence of the cartel.  An international cartel which " concerted " prices and price increases (although imposing no other restrictions) was held to fall under Article 85 (1) in the *Dyestuffs* case,[12] where the uniform pricing behaviour of the undertakings concerned restricted competition between them and contributed to the perpetuation of fragmented national markets within the EEC.

**306**    **National export cartels.**  Agreements between undertakings situated in the same Member State fall under Article 85 (1) where the parties fix the prices or conditions of sale in respect of exports to be made to other Member States.  This may be seen in *Re VVVF*,[13] where the members of a Dutch association of paint manufacturers agreed, *inter alia*, to observe fixed minimum prices and uniform sales conditions in respect of export sales

[11] [1969] C.M.L.R. D41, D57.
[12] J.O. 1969 L195/11, [1969] C.M.L.R. D23; *ICI* v. *EEC Commission* (48/69) [1972] C.M.L.R. 557; and see *ante*, §§ 211 *et seq.*  See also *Re Sugar Cartel*, Commission decision, January 2, 1973.
[13] J.O. 1969 L168/22, [1970] C.M.L.R. D1.

from Holland, including sales to other Member States.   They also
agreed to ensure that wholesalers did not resell below the minimum export prices, [14] and to inform the Group secretariat of their
current products, prices and monthly sales.[15]   Before granting
a negative clearance, the Commission required that the parties
cease to give effect to such restrictions in so far as they related
to exports to other Member States.   In so far as the restrictions
related to markets outside the EEC, the Commission held, on
the facts, that Article 85 (1) was not infringed.[16]   Similar principles
to those applied by the Commission in *VVVF* can be seen in
certain aspects of the Commission's decisions relating to national
joint selling agreements.[17]

**307**    **Price fixing in relation to imported goods.**   The *VCH* [18]
decision illustrates that agreements between suppliers in the
same Member States that fix the prices at which, and conditions
upon which, they will resell products imported from other
Member States may fall under Article 85 (1).   Under the agreement in question, members of an association of Dutch cement
merchants were, *inter alia*, required to resell in accordance with
the standard conditions of sale laid down by the association.
Moreover, in respect of deliveries of 100 tons or less they agreed
to observe common fixed prices.   For deliveries of over 100 tons,
the association recommended prices and fixed obligatory minimum prices.   The parties to the agreement controlled about
two-thirds of the Dutch market.   About one-third of their total
sales related to products imported from Belgium and West
Germany.   The Commission held that the agreement restricted
competition and affected trade between Member States, particularly to the detriment of Belgian and German producers who
would have been able, in the absence of the agreement, to increase
their share of the Dutch market.

**308**    **Other " national " price fixing agreements.**   Whether other
price fixing agreements  made between undertakings situated

[14] For resale price maintenance in respect of exports see § 310 and also § 320, *post*.
[15] For price information agreements see § 315.
[16] See *ante*, §§ 243 *et seq*.
[17] *Post*, §§ 337 *et seq*.
[18] J.O. 1972 L13/34, [1973] C.M.L.R. D16.   See also *VCH* v. *EEC Commission*
(8/72) [1973] C.M.L.R. 7, and see §§ 311 and 620, *post*.   For agreements relating
to resale price maintenance in the U.K. see § 320, *post*.

in the same Member State fall within the Treaty will be a question of fact in each case. Almost certainly an agreement between two small manufacturing firms in Birmingham as to the prices at which they will supply their customers in the Midlands would not " affect trade between Member States " although it would fall under section 6 (1) (*a*) of the Restrictive Trade Practices Act 1956.[19]  On the other hand, a national price fixing agreement will fall under the Treaty, even if it relates only to products of domestic manufacture, if it noticeably affects trade between Member States.  This is particularly the case where the effect of the agreement is to discriminate against nationals of other Member States,[20] or to lead to the continued isolation of a national market.  Thus, in *Re German Ceramic Tiles Agreement*,[21] an association of manufacturers collectively agreed to give uniform discounts in respect of purchases made from them. This prevented producers individually negotiating discounts with their customers, and suppressed competition in relation to discount rates.  Moreover, the uniform discounts were calculated according to the quantity of the purchases which a particular customer had made from all the producers of ceramic tiles in Germany over a given period.  Thus, if a particular customer went outside Germany for an order, his total purchases from German producers would be lower, and hence the discount to which he would be entitled on purchases made within Germany would be lower also.  The effect of the agreement, therefore, was to concentrate orders upon the German producers, even in cases where non-German producers offered more favourable terms. The scheme accordingly operated to the detriment of producers outside Germany, who had to overcome the artificial barrier erected by the discriminatory discount structure which rendered access to the German market more difficult.  The Commission held that in the circumstances competition was restricted and trade between Member States adversely affected within the meaning of the Treaty.

**09**        **Fixing of purchase prices.**  It should be remembered that competition may be restricted within the meaning of Article

[19] And see clause 90 of the Fair Trading Bill.
[20] See Art. 7 of the Treaty. See also *VCH* v. *EEC Commission* (8/72) [1973] C.M.L.R. 7; *Re Cimbel*, J.O. 1972 L303/24; *Re GISA*, J.O. 1972 L303/45.
[21] J.O. 1971 L10/15, [1971] C.M.L.R. D6, and see *post*, §§ 313, 334 and 618.

85 (1) where two or more undertakings combine to fix, directly or indirectly, the prices at which they will purchase goods or services.[22]  If, for example, a group of purchasers agree upon the prices at which they will acquire supplies of a given product, they restrict their ability to purchase individually at different prices.  This situation has not arisen very frequently in the Commissions decisions.  But in the *Quinine* case [23] the parties did at one time operate a system (determined before the entry into force of Regulation 17) whereby they 'jointly agreed their individual purchase prices for raw materials.

**310**   **Collective enforcement of resale price maintenance.**  In *Re ASPA* [24] a national scheme for the collective enforcement of resale price maintenance, which applied both in relation to products of domestic manufacture and in relation to imported goods, was held to fall within Article 85 (1).  Other features of the scheme included collective exclusive dealing provisions and collective boycotts.[25]  In *Re VVVF* [26] a collective agreement to observe r.p.m. in respect of exports was held to fall within Article 85 (1).

**311**   **Collective recommendation of resale prices.**  In the *VCH* [27] case the parties following the Commission's adverse decision under Article 85 (1), abandoned their collective agreement to observe certain fixed or minimum prices, and agreed that their association should confine itself to a system of " target " (*i.e.* recommended) prices, and uniform conditions of sale.  On appeal to the European Court against the Commission's decision, the association contended that Article 85 (1) did not apply to their agreement as amended.  On the question of recommended prices, the Court held that " target " prices affected the free play of competition, as did fixed prices, because they enabled all operators to make reasonably accurate forecasts as to the price policy of their competitors.  Where " price rules " extended over the whole territory of one Member State, the Court held that such agreements were in themselves conducive to national market seg-

[22] See also joint purchasing agreements, *post*, § 335.
[23] J.O. 1969 L192/5, [1969] C.M.L.R. D41 at D50–51, D68–D69.
[24] J.O. 1970 L148/9, [1970] C.M.L.R. D25.
[25] See also Restrictive Trade Practices Act 1956, s. 24.
[26] Note 13, *supra*.
[27] J.O. 1972 L13/34, [1973] C.M.L.R. D16; see also *VCH* v. *EEC Commission* (8/72) [1973] C.M.L.R. 7. See § 307, *ante*; *post*, § 620.

regation, impeding the process of economic interpenetration under the Treaty while protecting domestic production. It is probable that in certain cases, agreements between two or more suppliers to " recommend resale prices " are capable of falling under the Treaty.

**312    Collective use of standard conditions.** As has been seen,[28] agreements whereby the parties sell on standard terms as to prices, rebates, discounts, etc. may well contravene Article 85 (1). The Commission has, however, stated [29] that " no objection can be raised against the use of standardised printed forms; their use must, however, not be combined with an understanding or tacit agreement on uniform prices, rebates or conditions of sale." It is thought therefore that where an association merely prepares and makes generally available a standard form of contract, neither that fact nor the use of the standard form by members in the exercise of their individual discretion will fall within Article 85. However, a recommendation by a trade association as to the use of standard conditions of sale may give rise to a " concerted practice " falling within Article 85 (1).

**313    Collective discrimination.** Article 85 (1) (*d*) indicates that among the agreements prohibited under Article 85 (1) are those which " apply dissimilar conditions to equivalent transactions with other trading parties thereby placing them at a competitive disadvantage." This provision strikes at agreements whereby parties co-operate to discriminate against certain customers, for instance by giving them less favourable terms, as to prices, credit, discount, or delivery, etc. Such measures may be adopted collectively, for example, to force customers to observe a resale price maintenance scheme,[30] or to encourage customers to buy only from a national cartel *e.g.* by granting rebates only to those customers who have in fact refrained from purchasing outside the cartel territory.[31] The provision also covers vertical agreements, *e.g.* requiring a distributor to discriminate between his

[28] §§ 303–311, *ante.*
[29] Notice on Co-operation Agreements, App. 12, *post.*
[30] As in *Re ASPA,* note 25, *supra*; § 310, *ante.*
[31] As in *Re German Ceramic Tiles Agreement,* J.O. 1971 L10/15, [1971] C.M.L.R. D6; *ante,* § 308; and see § 618, *post.* See Collective exclusive dealing, *post,* § 331; *Re Pittsburgh Corning Europe,* J.O. 1972 L272/35, [1973] C.M.L.R. D2.

customers; and where in a sole contract the supplier is obliged to treat other customers less favourably in equivalent transactions. Agreements between parties which discriminate against third party nationals of other Member States purely on the grounds of their nationality are particularly liable to fall within Article 85 (1). How far one undertaking may independently discriminate against other parties with whom he deals is considered below.[32]

**314**    **Collective " tying."** Article 85 (1) (*e*) establishes that " making the conclusions of contracts subject to acceptance by the other parties of supplementary obligations, which, by their nature or according to commercial usage, have no connection with the subject of such contracts " is prohibited under Article 85 (1). This provision aims at " tie-in " transactions. Such transactions typically occur where one party agrees to supply the other only on condition that the purchaser accepts not only the goods he requires but also other goods and services offered by the supplier. An extreme form of tie-in transaction known as " full line forcing " occurs where the purchaser is obliged to take the whole range of the supplier's goods. Article 85 (1) (*d*) clearly shows that agreements between parties to impose tie-in obligations on third parties are covered by the Treaty.

**315**    **Price information agreements.** Agreements whereby parties exchange information as to prices and conditions of sale, orders, turnover, investments, etc., may lead to restrictions on competition.[33] The exchange of such information may facilitate the avoidance of price competition as between the parties, even where the parties have not reached any overt agreement as to their pricing policies. Such agreements may indirectly fix prices or give rise to concerted pricing practices. If in any particular sector the prices of the undertakings concerned are characterised by a uniformity that one would not expect to find in conditions of free competition, and if at the same time the parties are exchanging information as to their prices, etc., the exchange of information will afford some evidence that the parties are guilty

---

[32] *Post*, § 323.
[33] See *Re VVVF*, J.O. 1969 L168/22, [1970] C M.L.R. D1; *ante*, § 306. See also Notice in Co-operation Agreements, App. 12, *post*. And see *Re CRN-1971*, J.O. 1972 L303/7; *Re Cimbel*, J.O. 1972 L303/24.

of a concerted practice in relation to their pricing policies.  Price
information agreements of the kind here discussed are capable of
falling under Article 85 (1).[34]

**316    Other information agreements.**  On the other hand, it is
desirable that commercial enterprises should be able to inform
themselves about current conditions in the market.  In the Commission's view,[35] agreements which have as their sole object joint
procurement of information which is necessary to enable the
participating enterprises to determine their future market behaviour freely and independently do not have the purpose or
effect of restricting competition.  However, the Commission's
opinion is subject to qualifications, and the effects of an information agreement must be carefully considered in every case.
The danger is that an exchange of information may lead to
collision between the parties and give rise to concerted practices.
In order to fall outside Article 85 (1) the agreement should not in
fact limit firms' freedom to determine their prices independently,
nor should it result in the co-ordination of market behaviour.
In particular, express or tacit recommendations may fall under
Article 85 (1) where they subsequently induce the parties to behave
in a parallel manner in the market.  Broadly speaking, however,
agreements limited to an exchange of opinions or experience, or
joint market research, or joint studies of undertakings or
industries, or joint preparation of statistics and calculation models
will fall outside Article 85 (1).[36]

**317    Joint financial services.**  The Commission's view is that
co-operation over financial matters, which generally do not concern the economic decisions made by undertakings, falls outside
Article 85 (1).[37]  Thus co-operation in accounting matters (*e.g.*
to standardise accounting methods) will normally fall outside
the Treaty.  This applies also to the joint provision of credit
guarantees, and to joint debt-collecting associations, provided

---

[34] Following intervention by the Commission, insurance companies in four EEC
countries abandoned an information agreement whereby information " normally
treated as secret and not exchanged among competitors " relating to rates of
premium, etc. was exchanged.  See European Community Information Service,
Community News, April 1, 1969.
[35] See Notice in Co-operation Agreements, App. 12, *post.*
[36] *Ibid.*
[37] *Ibid.*

that they do not influence price formation. The joint use of
" business or tax consultant " agencies is similarly not regarded as
being restrictive of competition.

### (c) Vertical Agreements Between Individual Suppliers and Acquirers

**318**   **Vertical agreements as to prices and conditions.** In this section
of this chapter are considered those agreements entered into
between a supplier and a person to whom he supplies goods. The
principal matters which arise for consideration are how far the
supplier may impose upon the acquirer terms as to the resale
price of the goods, and other conditions upon which the goods
may be supplied. In so far as such problems arise where the
supplier is acting collectively with other suppliers, reference
should be made to the last preceding section.[38]

**319**   **Resale price maintenance: the Commission's view.** In its
First Report on Competition Policy, the Commission states [39]
that purely national systems of resale price maintenance do not,
in general, fall under the Treaty.[40] To the extent that such
systems are limited to imposing upon retailers established in one
Member State an obligation to observe resale prices in respect of
the resale within the national territory of products delivered by a
manufacturer established in that State, or by his distributor,
trade between Member States is not generally affected within the
meaning of Article 85 (1). In the Commission's view,[41] the
question of resale price maintenance is essentially a question for
national, rather than Community, competition policy. However,

---

[38] *Ante*, §§ 310–314; and see also collective exclusive dealing, *post*, § 331.

[39] First Report on Competition Policy (1972), para. 55.

[40] For a short account of resale price maintenance systems in the Member States
see *Resale Price Maintenance*, studies edited by *B. S. Yamey* (1966); Denmark
at pp. 166 *et seq.*; " The Six " at pp. 181 *et seq.*; Ireland at pp. 219 *et seq.* and
the U.K. at pp. 251 *et seq.* Briefly, resale price maintenance is prohibited, subject
to exceptions in favour of limited classes of particular products, in Denmark,
France, Italy and Luxembourg. In Holland, r.p.m. survives subject to controls.
In Ireland, r.p.m. is controlled through " fair trading rules " laid down by the Fair
Trade Commission. In Germany, r.p.m. agreements must be notified to the
Bundeskartellamt and may be permitted, under certain conditions. In Belgium,
r.p.m. is permitted. For an up to date account of the position in the United
Kingdom, see Chitty, *Contracts*, 23rd ed., Vol. II, paras. 1350 *et seq.* R.p.m.
is now only permitted in respect of books and medicaments: see *Re Net Book
Agreement*, [1962] 1 W.L.R. 1347, (1964) L.R. 4 R.P. 484, *Re Medicaments
Reference*, [1970] 1 W.L.R. 1339. See also *Joliet* (1971) 16 *Anti-Trust Bulletin* 589.

[41] See note 39, *ante*. This view may change following *VCH* v. *EEC Commission*
(8/72) [1973] C.M.L.R.7.

the Commission wishes to ensure that middlemen and consumers at all times have the chance of obtaining supplies on the most favourable conditions at the place of their choice within the common market.

**320**    **Article 85 (1): resale price maintenance in the United Kingdom.** It follows from the foregoing that purely " domestic " resale price maintenance agreements fall outside Article 85 (1). Agreements relating to resale price maintenance within the United Kingdom (now only in relation to books and medicaments) [42] will be caught by Article 85 (1) in so far as they purport to determine the prices at which goods imported from another Member State may be resold within the United Kingdom,[43] or in so far as they purport to determine the prices at which goods exported from the United Kingdom may be resold within the Community.[44] However, it must be remembered that resale price maintenance agreements made between only two parties and under which only one party accepts restrictions, even if they fall within Article 85 (1), are not required to be notified to the Commission.[45] How far such agreements continue to be valid and enforceable, whether or not they are notified to the Commission, is further considered below.[46]

**321**    **Provisions designed to preserve national systems of resale price maintenance.** In Germany, resale price maintenance systems that have been notified to the Bundeskartellamt may be operated provided they are " watertight " *i.e.* enforced in such a manner that *all* undercutting is prevented.[47] This requirement means that the price fixing undertaking must bind all its customers to observe the stipulated prices, and must also take action against price-cutters. Moreover, the system in effect requires the price fixing undertaking to impose upon its customers export and reimport bans in order to prevent the products being exported outside Germany and then reimported into Germany by a third

---

[42] See note 40, *ante*; as to notification of agreements where the undertakings concerned are situated in the same Member State, see § 529, *post*.

[43] *Ante*, § 307. See also *post*, §§ 321–323.

[44] *Ante*, § 306. See also *post*, §§ 321–323.

[45] See *post*, § 532.

[46] See *post*, §§ 413–414.

[47] See generally, OECD, *Guide to Legislation on Restrictive Business Practices* (1972), Vol. II, Germany, Pt. 20, p. 8.

party and sold at a lower price. If this latter operation can be done without any breach of a reimport prohibition, the system is " incomplete " and thus unenforceable. It can be seen that such a system tends to isolate the German national market. In *Agfa-Gevaert* [48] the Commission held that the resale price mainten- ance system imposed by the parties in Germany, including as it did bans on exports and reimports, fell under Article 85 (1) notwithstanding that it was authorised under German law. The effect of the agreement was to protect artificially the German market and the Commission did not consider that the application of Article 85 (3) was appropriate. Accordingly, the parties abandoned their system of resale price maintenance within Germany as did, at the same time, two other camera manufac- turers, Kodak and Zeiss-Ikon-Voigtlander.[49] The effect of the Commission's decision has been seriously to weaken the system of r.p.m. prevailing in Germany. It also illustrates the principle that import and export laws may not be imposed to preserve resale price maintenance permitted under national laws.

**322** **Individual conditions of sale.** One important matter to be considered is how far and in what circumstances the other conditions upon which a single undertaking independently decides to sell to its customers may fall under Article 85 (1). In *Re Kodak* [50] the Commission held that a company's standard conditions of sale constituted " agreements between under- takings " because they necessarily formed part of the contracts made between the Kodak companies and each of their purchasers. It follows that standard conditions of sale independently adopted by single undertakings may fall within Article 85 (1). In that case the Commission insisted upon the removal of terms in the company's standard conditions of sale which purported to impose upon purchasers an obligation not to resell the goods by way of import or export to another Member State. The Com- mission reached a similar decision in *Re Omega*.[51] It follows from these decisions that an undertaking cannot generally include

[48] *Bulletin of the European Communities*, No. 2—1970, Pt. 2, chap. 1, no. 5.
[49] See First Report on Competition Policy (1972), p. 62n. See also press release in " Europe," No. 1173 (new series), December 1, 1972: announcement of the revision of the " Du Pont de Nemours " standard conditions of sale.
[50] J.O. 1970 L147/24, [1970] C.M.L.R. D19.
[51] J.O. 1970 L242/22, [1970] C.M.L.R. D49; and see *post*, § 840. See also note 49, *supra*.

in its conditions of sale restrictions upon import and export within the common market. In both *Re Kodak* and *Re Omega* restrictions relating to the resale of the products in question only to middlemen who were technically qualified, fell outside Article 85.

**323** **Discrimination.** The *Kodak* decision also raises the question as to how far a single undertaking may, as an act of independent commercial policy, discriminate between customers as to terms of sale, without contravening Article 85 (1).[52] As has been seen, Article 85 (1) (*d*) prohibits " agreements between undertakings " which apply dissimilar conditions to equivalent transactions with other trading parties thereby placing them at a commercial disadvantage. How far does this provision compel an undertaking without a dominant position within the meaning of Article 86 to sell on equivalent terms to all comers? Despite the weight of academic opinion to the contrary,[53] the *Kodak* case has been considered by some to suggest that agreements between one seller and various buyers whereby equivalent transactions are treated differently, to the competitive disadvantage of some buyers, may fall under Article 85 (1), at least where the discrimination is on the grounds of nationality.[54] In *Re Kodak*, the Company's conditions of sale as notified contained a provision that payment for all transactions with Kodak in a given national territory should be made to the Kodak subsidiary situated in that territory. The Commission held [55] that such a provision could be interpreted to mean that " should the Kodak companies in the common market sell in another Member State to purchasers other than the Kodak company installed in that State, such purchasers should pay for the supplies to the latter company and at the prices charged by it,

---

[52] For agreements between two parties relating to discrimination against third parties, see § 313, *ante*; and see *Re Pittsburgh Corning Europe*, J.O. 1972 L272/35, [1973] C.M.L.R. D2; for the position under Art. 86, see §§ 723 *et seq.*, *post.*

[53] See Canenbley, *Das Diskriminierungsverbot in den Wettbewerbsregeln des Vertrages zur Grundung der Europäischen Wirtschaftsgemeinschaft Artikel 85 Absatz 1, Buchstabe(d), Artikel 86 Buchstabe(c) EWG Vertrag*, Marburg (1970).

[54] *Cf.* the U.S. Robinson-Patman Act. See Scheuermann, *Journal of World Trade Law*, Vol. 5, pp. 533 *et seq.* and authorities cited, *ibid.* at p. 538. See also Mégret, Waelbroeck & others, *op. cit.* at p. 45. See also the Commission's Press Release of May 22, 1967; and written answer No. 117/60 to parliamentary question (M. Vredeling) J.O. 1971 C74 (July 24, 1971).

[55] [1970] C.M.L.R. D19, D22.

thus losing all interest in making any direct imports, whatever the respective price levels ". For example, suppose that prices of Kodak products were low in Belgium and high in France. If the Belgian Kodak Company sold to an importer in France, the French importer would have to pay for those imports at the price ruling in France and not at the cheaper price ruling in Belgium.[56] The Commission held that such conditions of sale " had the effect of isolating the markets of each Member State and of excluding from competition in one or more Member States the prices charged in each of these markets ". Kodak agreed to delete the offending provisions, and replaced them with conditions which made it impossible for Kodak to maintain prices at appreciably different levels in different common market countries. Under the new conditions of sale, no Kodak subsidiary could export at a price above that charged in its domestic market. Although it should be emphasised that Kodak voluntarily abandoned the right to charge customers in different Member States different prices in respect of broadly equivalent transactions, the case may suggest that one undertaking may not discriminate as to prices to be charged to a purchaser merely on the grounds of his nationality or country of establishment.[54]

**324**  **Tying-transactions.** As has been seen Article 85 (1) shows that among the prohibited " agreements between undertakings " are those which " make the conclusion of contracts subject to acceptance by the other parties of supplementary obligations, which by their nature or according to commercial usage, have no connection with the subject of such contracts." The view has been expressed [57] that this sub-paragraph applies only to agreements between two parties to impose tie-in obligations on third parties. This, it is submitted is too narrow an interpretation. A " tying " transaction will usually involve the imposition of an exclusive purchase obligation which will deprive the acquirer of the opportunity to obtain the goods elsewhere and deprive

---

[56] In October 1969 the European Community Statistical Office found that top prices for four types and makes of Kodak camera commonly on sale in five of the member countries—data for France was not available—ranged from 8 to 30 per cent. above the lowest price for each type. For all photographic apparatus and supplies the Statistical Office in 1969 found a range of up to 12 per cent. (in Luxembourg) above the cheapest country for these products (Belgium)— European Communities Information Service: Press Release, July 3, 1970.

[57] See Oberdorfer, Gleiss, Hirsch, *Common Market Cartel Law*, para. 71.

suppliers of an outlet.[58]  If the necessary requirement of effect
on trade between Member States is also present a " tying "
contract made between a single supplier and a single purchaser
under which the latter accepts such " supplementary obligations,"
may fall under the Treaty.

### 3.  AGREEMENTS LIMITING MARKETS OR PRODUCTION

**325**   **In general.**   Article 85 (1) (*b*) illustrates that among typical
agreements that infringe the Treaty are those which " limit or
control production, markets, technical development or investment."   Article 85 (1) (*c*) similarly refers to agreements to
" share markets or sources of supply."   Agreements to divide
markets within the common market, especially along national
boundaries, have been consistently condemned by the Commission.[59]   Agreements to limit or control production, etc. often
occur as part of an express or implied agreement to divide the
market, or to limit or control the ability of the parties to encroach
upon each others market share.   This may be achieved directly
or indirectly.   For example, a cartel agreement may allocate
quotas to its members; if a member sells more than his quota he
may have to pay so much per sale into a pool which is then divided
between the members *e.g.* pro rata to their shortfall below their
quotas.[60]   When considering arrangements between parties
which relate, directly or indirectly, to a limitation on markets or on
production, the question in every case is whether there exists an
agreement, decision or concerted practice the object or effect of
which is to prevent, restrict or distort competition within the
common market and which affects trade between Member
States to a noticeable extent.

**326**    **Market sharing.**    A classic case in which Article 85 (1) is
infringed is where the parties agree to keep out of each others
market in different Member States.   Such was the case in *Re*

[58] For requirements contracts, see *post*, § 836.  See also Reg. 67/67, Art. 2 (2)
which permits an exclusive dealing agreement to impose an obligation to
purchase complete lines of products without losing the benefit of the block
exemption under Art. 85 (3).
[59] See §§ 326, 327, *post*.  See also collective exclusive dealing agreements, *post*,
§§ 331 *et. seq.* See *Re Sugar Cartel*, Commission decision, January 2, 1973. For a
restriction on sale of machinery to competing manufacturers see *Bulletin*, No. 10,
1972, p. 57.
[60] See *e.g.* the *Quinine* cartel, J.O. 1969 L192/5, [1969] C.M.L.R. D41, § 305, *ante*.

*Van Katwijk* [61] where a Belgian and a Dutch manufacturer of certain tubes agreed not to compete with each other in the other's national market. The Dutch manufacturer agreed to keep wholly out of the Belgian market and the Belgian manufacturer agreed to sell no more than a fixed quota of products on the Dutch market. The Commission held Article 85 (1) to be applicable and refused an exemption under Article 85 (3). [62]

**327**   **Division of markets and quotas.** As has been seen, agreements relating to division of markets are often accompanied by arrangements relating to quotas. Thus in the *Quinine* case, [63] the parties agreed to observe delivery quotas, and parties exceeding their quotas in relation to particular markets had to purchase, from producers who had not reached their quotas, an equivalent amount of quinine. In addition, in that case the French members of the cartel agreed not to manufacture synthetic quinidine, a restriction which protected the monopoly position of the German and Dutch members of the cartel. Similarly in *Re Lightweight Paper*, [64] an agreement was held to fall within Article 85 (1) where the parties observed a system of production quotas, combined with a compensation system to ensure observance of those quotas. The quotas were observed in relation to certain types of products and merely had the effect of crystallising the mutual trading position of the parties.

**328**   **Standardisation agreements.** One particular type of agreement which may limit or control production or markets is where the parties undertake not to manufacture or sell products which do not conform to certain common standards, dimensions or types. By such an agreement the parties may restrict their ability to compete by offering differentiated products. The exact application of Article 85 (1) to such agreements remains uncertain. There has been no relevant decision of the Commission relating solely to standardisation agreements, [65] primarily because such

---

[61] J.O. 1970 L242/18, [1970] C.M.L.R. D43.
[62] See *post*, § 621.
[63] Note 60, *supra*; § 305, *ante*. See also *Re CRN-1971*, J.O. 1972 L303/7; *Re Cimbel*, J.O. 1972 L303/24.
[64] J.O. 1972 L182/24, [1972] C.M.L.R. D94; *post*, §§ 1001 *et seq.* See also *Re Transocean Marine Paint Association*, J.O. 1967 163/67, [1967] C.M.L.R. D9. *Cf. Re Limeburners*, J.O. 1969 L122/8, [1969] C.M.L.R. D15, where there was no noticeable restriction on competition.
[65] But see *Transocean Marine Paint Association*, note 64, *supra*.

agreements, in themselves are not subject to notification.[66] Under Regulation 2821/71 the Commission has power to issue a block exemption [67] in respect of standardisation agreements but it has not yet done so.

**329**   **Sale of goodwill.** Another particular aspect of agreements which limit markets are those types of agreement commonly entered into between the vendor of an undertaking and its purchaser, whereby the vendor agrees, for a limited period, not to compete within the market of the undertaking purchased. The purchaser may similarly agree not to compete within the market remaining to the vendor. The application of Article 85 (1) to such agreements is unclear. In one decision of the Commission, *Re Nicholas Frères*,[68] a negative clearance was granted in a case which involved an agreement between one undertaking within and one outside the common market. The decision has several unsatisfactory features.[69]

**330**   **Exemption under Article 85 (3).** Agreements limiting or dividing markets, as such, have never benefited from exemption under Article 85 (3). Agreements relating to limitation of production, and, in so far as they contained reciprocal exclusive dealing provisions, to division of markets, have been exempted where the Commission considered that the specialisation achieved under the agreement brought resultant benefits.[70]

### 4. COLLECTIVE EXCLUSIVE DEALING

**331**   **In general.**   "Collective" [71] exclusive dealing agreements most frequently occur where national groups of suppliers covenant among themselves to supply exclusively only through certain channels or where reciprocal exclusive supply and purchase arrangements are entered into between national groups of suppliers on the one hand and groups of acquirers on the other

---

[66] Under Art. 4 (2) (iii) (*a*) of Reg. 17; *post*, §§ 528 *et seq.* See First Report on Competition Policy (1972), para. 38.

[67] See *post*, § 609.

[68] J.O. 1964 2287/64, [1964] C.M.L.R. 505.

[69] Deringer, *The Competition Law of the European Economic Community*, p. 37, note 5 comments " the decision is not perfectly clear because it obviously represents a compromise within the EEC Commission. Therefore, it is impossible to draw any conclusions from it." The reasoning of the decision is somewhat difficult to follow.

[70] See *post*, §§ 1001 *et seq.*

[71] For bilateral exclusive dealing agreements see §§ 801 *et seq.*, *post.*

hand.  Such agreements often contain additional provisions relating to quotas, minimum prices and import and export bans Collective exclusive dealing agreements fall under Article 85 (1) because they contribute to the continued division of the national market.  Where there is a national exclusive dealing agreement producers in other Member States find that outlets are closed to them, while acquirers within the national territory are deprived of the opportunity to seek supplies from elsewhere in the common market as well as from suppliers in their own national territory.[72] The Commission has held Article 85 (1) to be applicable in a large number of such cases,[73] and hitherto none of the arrangements concerned has benefited from an exemption under Article 85 (3).

**332**     **Agreements between groups of suppliers and groups of acquirers.** The application of Article 85 (1) to collective exclusive dealing between national groups of suppliers on the one hand and groups of acquirers on the other may be illustrated by the very first intervention by the Commission, in 1963, in a recommendation [74] addressed to an association of Belgian tile manufacturers and traders.  There the manufacturers of tiles had agreed to supply only those traders who were members of the association and the traders had agreed to obtain supplies solely from those manu-facturers who were also members.  The Commission took the view that such an arrangement restricted competition and affected trade between Member States in that the manufacturers limited their outlets (including export outlets) and the traders were prevented from obtaining the best offer of supplies from anywhere within the common market.  This was particularly important in a situation where the parties to the agreement com-prised most of the national manufacturers of the products con-cerned and a large proportion of the national distributors.  On the Commission's view becoming known, the members abandoned the agreement.  Many equivalent collective exclusive dealing agreements within Member States have similarly been ter-minated.[72]

**333**     **Agreements between suppliers.**  Agreements whereby national groups of suppliers covenant among themselves to supply only

[72] See First Report on Competition Policy, paras. 19–24.
[73] See the cases set out *ibid.*  And see *Re CRN-1971*, J.O. 1972 L303/7; *Re Belgian Central Heating Agreement*, J.O. 1972 L264/22, [1972] C.M.L.R. D130.
[74] *Bulletin of the European Communities*, No. 5—1964, annex II.

through certain channels may also fall within Article 85 (1). Thus in *Re ASPA* [75] a group of Belgian manufacturers and importers of toiletries covenanted to observe a regulation whereby their products could be obtained by wholesalers or retailers only from the members of the association or from their " approved " wholesalers. In addition the members agreed collectively to impose resale price maintenance conditions in respect both of imports and products of local manufacture. Any retailer or middleman who obtained products otherwise than through the exclusive official channel of distribution, or who failed to observe resale prices was liable to have supplies cut off altogether. The Commission held that the restrictions limited competition in branded goods imported into Belgium. The fact that the trader's freedom to obtain supplies through by-passing the ASPA network was curtailed was liable to hinder imports from other Member States.

334    **Aggregated rebates cartels.** A national cartel agreement whereby the members agree to give discounts according to the total purchases made by customers from a group of producers as a whole is in many ways equivalent to a collective exclusive dealing agreement and may accordingly fall under Article 85 (1). [76]

## 5. JOINT PURCHASING

335    **Joint purchasing.** Joint purchasing arrangements between competitors within the common market may fall within Article 85 (1). The " bark pool " and the joint purchases from American strategic reserves which were features of the *Quinine* case afford an illustration of such arrangements. [77] Article 85 (1) may also be infringed even if the agreements are made between undertakings which are not themselves competing. In such cases the agreements may lead to a restriction on competition through restricting demand—*i.e.* suppliers may find it more difficult to make individual sales to members of a joint purchasing agreement. That these latter agreements are contrary to the Treaty is also the view of the Commission. [78] A joint purchasing agreement which

[75] J.O. 1970 L148/9, [1970] C.M.L.R. D25.
[76] See *Re German Ceramic Tiles*, J.O. 1971 L10/15, [1971] C.M.L.R. D6, *ante*, § 308.
[77] See *ante*, § 309, note 23.
[78] First Report on Competition Policy, paras. 40–41.

involves imports from other Member States will not, however, fall under Article 85 (1) unless it restricts competition to a noticeable extent. [79]

**336**   **Joint purchasing: Article 85 (3).** The Commission has not yet had cause to issue an exemption under Article 85 (3) in respect of a joint purchasing agreement but it regards those matters as important—on the one hand, the desirability of retailers being able to obtain supplies throughout the common market on terms and conditions that compare fairly with those obtainable by large concerns, and on the other hand, the desirability of avoiding the creation of powerful groups of purchasers who might be able to put supplies under undue pressure.[80] No doubt the Commission have both these matters in mind when granting an exemption. Another circumstance that might be relevant is whether it is in fact necessary for the parties to combine to combat the power of an existing powerful supplier;[81] equally the Commission may be expected to have regard to its policy of encouraging co-operation between medium and small-sized undertakings. At the present time, however, it is not possible to predict whether any given agreement would benefit from exemption under Article 85 (3).

## 6. JOINT SELLING

**337**   **In general.** As has been seen, Article 85 (1) may be infringed where the parties deprive themselves of their freedom to fix prices independently or to sell as they choose throughout the common market.[82] One particular situation where Article 85 (1) may be applicable is where the parties create a similar result by entering into a " joint selling agreement." Joint selling agreements take a number of forms. The type which has attracted most attention under Community law has been the joint sales agency: the parties to a joint sales agency agreement jointly confer, usually upon a trade association,[83] the exclusive right to sell their products upon particular markets. The trade association fixes common

---

[79] *Re Socemas*, J.O. 1968 L201/4, [1968] C.M.L.R. D28; *ante*, § 249.
[80] See note 78, *supra*.
[81] *Cf:* Restrictive Trade Practices Act 1956, s. 21 (3); *Re National Sulphuric Acid Association's Agreement*, [1963] 1 W.L.R. 848, and also (*No. 2*), L.R. 6 R.P. 210.
[82] *Ante*, § 303–334.
[83] The legal form the joint sales agency takes is not material.

prices and conditions of sale, and the total receipts are divided among the members in proportion to the quantities they have supplied, every undertaking receiving the same price for its products. A variation of the joint sales agency is the "joint tendering cartel" the members of which do not tender for contracts in competition with each other, but agree which undertakings should tender for what work, and how the latter should be divided amongst themselves. Bilateral joint selling agreements also occur, and sometimes a similar result is achieved by reciprocal exclusive dealing agreements [84] and joint marketing subsidiaries. Although similar principles apply to such agreements, this part of this chapter is primarily concerned with the decisions relating to collective joint selling.

**338**    **Joint selling to other Member States.** Joint selling agreements concerning exports to other Member States may contravene Article 85 (1). This principle was established by the Commission in a number of decisions relating to Belgian, French and Italian agencies for the joint selling of fertilizers, of which the decision in *Le Comptoir français de l'Azote* (CFA) [85] is typical. In that case the agreement which was submitted for negative clearance was made between all the French producers of nitrogen and related in particular to nitrogen fertilizers. The parties set up CFA to sell nitrogen products on their behalf both in France and in export markets, including those within the EEC. Every three years the parties would inform CFA of the quantities which they would deliver to it over the next three years, and CFA would decide which quantities should be sold in France and which should be exported, particularly within the common market, and at what price. In addition CFA operated a price equalisation scheme whereby each member received the same price for products sold in France and products exported. As long as the French internal price was higher than that freely obtainable on export markets the members of CFA had no incentive to export individually. In fact, the members did not actually make any

[84] See *e.g. Re Wild & Leitz*, J.O. 1972 L61/27, [1972] C.M.L.R. D36, and the decisions relating to specialisation agreements; *post*, §§ 1001 *et seq.*
[85] J.O. 1968 L276/29, [1968] C.M.L.R. D57. See also *Re Cobelaz (No. 1)*, J.O. 1968 L276/13, [1968] C.M.L.R. D45; *Re Cobelaz (No. 2)*, J.O. 1968 L276/19, [1968] C.M.L.R. D68; *Re Supexie*, J.O. 1971 L10/12, [1971] C.M.L.R. D1; *Re Seifa*, J.O. 1969 L173/8.

exports otherwise than through the CFA. The Commission held that the agreement as it stood fell within Article 85 (1) but granted negative clearance when the parties amended the agreement to limit joint sales by CFA solely to the French market and countries outside the EEC.

**339**    **Exclusivity.** The CFA agreement did not itself confer upon CFA exclusive selling rights, but the members did not export individually and there was a strong disincentive to do so. The Commission held Article 85 (1) to be applicable.[86] Similarly, a joint sales agency will contravene Article 85 (1) even if the parties are free to export to other EEC countries, and to decide their own prices, if the agency operates a price equalisation scheme whereby the total export revenues of the members are divided equally among them.[87] In such a case there is no incentive for the members to compete *inter se*. Where the parties have conferred upon the agency the *exclusive* right to export to other Member States, Article 85 (1) clearly applies.[88]

**340**    **The de minimis rule.** Agreements for joint selling to other Member States will, in accordance with general principles,[89] fall outside Article 85 (1) where they do not noticeably restrict competition or affect trade between Member States. This will typically be the case in respect of agreements made between undertakings who are not competing in the products covered by the agreement[90] or which are made between medium and small-sized undertakings.[91]

**341**    **Joint selling to other Member States: Article 85 (3).** There is no reported instance where exemption under Article 85 (3) has been granted in respect of a joint selling agreement to other Member States, although the case for such an exemption was strongly argued in the *NCH* decision.[92]

---

[86] *Cf. Re Seifa* and *Re Supexie*, note 85, *supra*.
[87] *Belgaphos*, EC Press Release, June 1970.
[88] As in *Cobelaz Nos. (1) and (2)*, note 85, *supra*.
[89] *Ante*, § 245.
[90] *Re Alliance de Constructeurs Français de Machine-Outils*, J.O. 1968 L201/1, [1968] C.M.L.R. D23.
[91] *Re SAFCO*, J.O. 1972 L13/44, [1972] C.M.L.R. D83, *ante*, § 249.
[92] J.O. 1972 L22/16; *post*, § 619. *Cf.* the position under the ECSC Treaty, Art. 65 (2), and decisions thereunder, *e.g.* at [1972] C.M.L.R. D105–D111.

**342**    **Joint selling on the national market.**    Hitherto, the relevant
decisions of the Commission have been to the effect that a joint
selling agreement between competing manufacturers, limited in
its operation to the national market, falls outside Article 85 (1).[93]
Thus, in *Cobelaz (No. 1)* [94] the Belgian producers of nitrogen
fertilizers agreed to confer upon Cobelaz, a joint selling agency,
the exclusive right to sell their products only in Belgium or to
countries outside the EEC.    In Belgium the members delivered
all their products to Cobelaz, in accordance with a maximum
quota fixed annually.    A price equalisation scheme assured that
they each received the same price.    Cobelaz was responsible for
fixing a uniform sales price to wholesalers and also for enforcing
uniform conditions of sale.    Cobelaz sold only to " approved
wholesalers."    Although this agreement restricted competition
within the common market, the Commission held that trade
between Member States was not affected for three main reasons.
First, the individual freedom of the parties to import products
from other Member States was unaffected by the agreement.
Secondly, the agreement (as amended)[95] did not directly affect
the parties' freedom to export to other Member States, nor did it
indirectly do so since the parties were free to determine the
quantities they would export themselves and those they would
make available to Cobelaz.    There were no other provisions of
the scheme which might influence the parties' actions.    The
price equalisation scheme would not in fact, discourage intra-
EEC exports.[96]    Thirdly, purchasers from Cobelaz were free to
import and export products from other Member States.    Accordingly, the Commission held that Article 85 (1) did not apply and
it therefore granted negative clearance.

**343**    **Elimination of " extra territorial " effects.**    Before granting
the negative clearance sought in *Cobelaz (No. 1)* the Commission
insisted on the elimination of many aspects of the agreement
which might affect trade between Member States.    These included
not only the concerted practice which extended Cobelaz's
exclusive right to Luxembourg, but also the price equalisation

[93] Although s. 6 (1) of the Restrictive Trade Practices Act 1956 would apply.
[94] J.O. 1968 L276/13, [1968] C.M.L.R. D45.
[95] See *post*, § 343.
[96] *Cf.* the treatment of the price equalisation scheme in *Re Cobelaz (No. 2)*, J.O.
1968 L276/19, [1968] C.M.L.R. D68, D75.

scheme in so far as it applied to exports, the obligation to market one product (coking sulphate of ammonia) in priority to others, a prohibition against export imposed on purchasers from Cobelaz by the uniform conditions of sale, and the practice of granting " loyalty " and " stock adjustment " rebates to Belgian purchasers who refrained from obtaining supplies from abroad.

**344** **Present status doubtful.** The Commission's decisions in *Cobelaz (No. 1)* and similar cases have been criticised, principally on the grounds that they failed to take into account the disadvantageous position of potential exporters to Belgium faced with a powerful selling agency on the national market.[97] However, it appears that the Commission may be ready to reconsider the position. It has announced [98] that it is examining the position *de novo*.

**345** **Joint selling to third countries.** Joint selling arrangements limited solely to countries outside the EEC are not generally apt to affect trade between Member States or to restrict competition within the common market. This was established by the decision of the Commission in *DECA*.[99] The rules of the Dutch Engineers and Contractors Association required the members to inform its central office of possible contracts open for tender in countries not within the EEC. If a member proposed to tender for certain contracts he was again required to inform the other members, who would consider collectively who would tender and how the available work would be divided between them. The Commission held that neither these rules nor the collaboration of the participants had any direct or indirect effect on competition within the common market. In the fertilizer cases [1] the Commission also granted negative clearance to export sales agencies, although in both the *Cobelaz* cases [2] and the *CFA* [3] the export selling agency to third countries comprised an international cartel operated through Nitrex S.A. in Zurich, which itself fixed export prices and conditions of sale. The Commission insisted upon certain

[97] See written question No. 29/72 (M. Vredeling), J.O. 1968 L276/13.
[98] See First Report on Competition Policy, para. 13 and written answer to Question No. 163/72 (M. Dewulf): Press Release 25/26, September 1972.
[99] J.O. 1964 2761/64, [1965] C.M.L.R. 50.
[1] Note 85, *supra*.
[2] § 342, *supra*; note 85, *supra*.
[3] § 338, *supra*; note 85, *supra*.

amendments to the price equalisation schemes in so far as they related to exports.

**346    Joint after sales service.**  The Commission has said[4] that there is no restraint of competition where several manufacturers, without acting in concert with each other, arrange for an after sales and repair service of their products to be provided by an independent undertaking.  In this situation, Article 85 (1) does not apply even if the manufacturers are competing *inter se.*

### 7.    AGREEMENTS RELATING TO SALES PROMOTION

**347    In general.**  Related to, but quite distinct from, joint selling agreements are agreements made as to the manner and methods by which the parties may seek to promote their products.  The Commission has now provided guidance upon the application of Article 85 (1) to agreements restricting participation in trade fairs, and to agreements concerning joint advertising and the use of a common label to designate a certain quality.

**348    Trade fairs.**  In certain circumstances agreements which relate to the holding of trade fairs and exhibitions may fall within Article 85 (1).  The Commission hitherto has dealt with two cases[5] in both of which an international association of national trade associations imposed a prohibition against exhibiting at trade fairs other than that organised by the association itself.  In *Re Cematex*,[5] for example, the international trade association for the textile machinery industry organised an international exhibition " ITMA " every few years.  " ITMA " was the only large international event in Europe devoted to textile machinery, and the members of Cematex, who included most of the major European manufacturers, accepted an obligation not to exhibit at any other textile machinery exhibition in Europe in any year that " ITMA " was held, or in the year before or the year after.  Manufacturers who did so either by themselves or their agents could be excluded from participation in " ITMA ".  *Re Cecimo*[5] concerned a similar agreement relating to the exhibition of machine tools at the trade fair " EMMO."

[4] Notice on Co-operation Agreements, App. 12, *post.*
[5] *Re Cecimo*, J.O. 1969 L69/13, [1969] C.M.L.R. D1; *Re Cematex*, J.O. 1971 L227/26.

**349**    In both *Re Cematex* and *Re Cecimo* the Commission held that Article 85 (1) was infringed.   In *Re Cematex* there was a competitive restriction upon the freedom of organisers of exhibitions other than " ITMA," in that only in one year out of four were the products of the Cematex manufacturers available to them; there was a competitive restriction upon the manufacturers themselves since they were deprived of their commercial freedom to promote their products at other fairs; and there was a competitive restriction on the freedom of wholesalers, agents and distributors who were similarly deprived of the opportunity to exhibit the manufacturers' products elsewhere.   Trade between Member States was affected because the restrictions related to the freedom of the organisers to organise, and of the manufacturers and distributors to sell at, fairs and exhibitions held in other Member States.   The Commission made similar findings in *Re Cecimo*.

**350**    **Trade fairs: exemption under Article 85 (3).**[6]   However, in both *Re Cematex*[5] and *Re Cecimo*,[5] the Commission granted, subject to conditions,[7] exemptions under Article 85 (3).   The Commission required the agreements to be amended in certain respects, but held that the remaining restrictions were counterbalanced by the advantages of rationalising and concentrating such exhibitions.

**351**    **Joint advertising: where unobjectionable.**   Joint advertising does not constitute a restraint upon competition, at least so long as it is limited to drawing the buyer's attention to the products of an industry or to a common brand, and the parties to the agreement are not wholly or partly prevented from carrying out their own publicity.[8]   This principle, which was announced by the Commission in its Notice on Co-operation Agreements,[9] was established by the negative clearance granted in *Re Association pour la Promotion du Tube d'Acier soudé électriquement*.[10]   This association was formed by Belgian and Luxembourg producers for the purpose of promoting electrically welded steel tubes.   One of its activities was to place, on behalf of its members, joint

---

[6] See generally, §§ 601 *et seq.*
[7] See §§ 633 *et seq.*
[8] Notice concerning Co-operation Agreements, App. 12, *post.*   First Report on Competition Policy, para. 36.
[9] App. 12, *post.*
[10] J.O. 1970 L153/14, [1970] C.M.L.R. D31.

publicity in favour of electrically welded steel tubes; but no member was prohibited from advertising individually. The Commission held [11] that the placing of joint publicity, which is limited to calling the attention of consumers to the characteristics and qualities of a product manufactured by several undertakings, does not restrict competition, at least where the undertakings concerned remain free to place their own individual publicity for their own products. Similarly, no exemption is necessary where the joint advertising only covers products in respect of which the parties are not competing, for then there is no restriction on competition.[12]

**352    Joint advertising: where objectionable.** Article 85 (1) may apply where undertakings accept restrictions on their freedom to promote their products individually, for that would be an important restriction on their competitive freedom.[13] Even if the parties remain legally free to advertise individually, it is doubtful whether Article 85 (1) would be avoided if joint advertising between competing undertakings went beyond promoting the generic products of a particular industry or a common brand or quality label.[14] The Commission has further said that joint advertising may be objectionable where the structure of the market is oligopolistic and advertising plays an important role in competition between undertakings.[15] If the agreement contravenes Article 85 (1), an exemption under Article 85 (3) is required. Such exemptions have been granted where restrictions on individual promotion were ancillary to agreements leading to the rationalisation of resources [16] or specialisation.[17]

**353    Common quality labels.** Joint advertising is often closely related to the common adoption by an association of undertakings of a label or trademark which is used to designate a certain quality. In general terms, the use of such a common

---

[11] [1970] C.M.L.R. D31, D35.

[12] *Re Wild & Leitz,* J.O. 1972 L61/27, [1972] C.M.L.R. D36; *sed quaere* how far the Commission considered future competition in this case.

[13] *Cf.* the restrictions on exhibiting at trade fairs in *Re Cecimo* and *Re Cematex* discussed *ante,* §§ 348–350.

[14] See Notice on Co-operation Agreements, App. 12, *post.*

[15] First Report on Competition Policy (1972), para. 36. *Cf. Henkel-Colgate,* J.O. 1972 L14/14, *post,* §§ 1107 *et seq.*

[16] *Re Cecimo; Re Cematex,* note 5, *supra;* §§ 348–350, *ante.*

[17] *e.g. FN-CF,* J.O. 1971 L134/6. See §§ 1004 *et seq.*

quality label does not restrict competition where the label is freely available to competitors whose products meet the stipulated quality conditions.[18] This principle is again seen in *Re Association pour la Promotion du Tube d'Acier soudé électriquement*.[19] There, in addition to its joint promotional activities, the association owned a trademark which took the form of a label stuck to the tubes made by the members. Use of the trademark was restricted to those producers who manufactured tubes to the standards laid down by the International Standards Organisation. The agreement did not prevent the members from manufacturing products with different characteristics not covered by the joint mark. Membership of the association and use of the mark was freely available to any producer of electrically welded steel tubes who manufactured his products to the required standards. Negative clearance was granted. In the Commission's view, there would have been no restriction on competition even if the members of the association had additionally undertaken to accept a quality control, to issue uniform instructions for use of the products in question, or to use the label for all those products meeting the required specification.[20] However, the use of a common label may fall within Article 85 (1) where it is linked to other restrictions, such as manufacturing or selling products *only* of the guaranteed quality, observing minimum prices, or delivering only to a limited class of customers.[21]

**[The next paragraph is 401.]**

---

[18] Notice on Co-operation Agreements, App. 12, *post*.
[19] J.O. 1970 L153/14, [1970] C.M.L.R. D31; *ante*, § 351.
[20] Notice on Co-operation Agreements, App. 12, *post*.
[21] *Re VVVF*, J.O. 1969 L168/22, [1970] C.M.L.R. D1; *ante*, § 306. *Cf. Re Transocean Marine Paint Association*, J.O. 1967 163/67, [1967] C.M.L.R. D9.

# CHAPTER 4

## ARTICLE 85 (2)

### 1. NULLITY

**401** **General consequences of infringement.** Broadly speaking, if an agreement, decision, or concerted practice falls within Article 85 (1),[1] two quite separate consequences follow. First, the validity of the agreement or decision may be affected under civil law. Article 85 (2) of the Treaty provides that any agreements or decisions prohibited pursuant to Article 85 (1) are " automatically void." As will be seen below,[2] there are important exceptions to this provision; but the purpose of Article 85 (2) is to render agreements and decisions falling within Article 85 (1) unenforceable in the civil courts of the Member States. Secondly, the parties may be exposed to the risk of the Commission taking proceedings under Regulation 17 to enforce the prohibition contained in Article 85 (1). Under Article 15 (2) of that Regulation the Commission may impose fines upon undertakings if they intentionally or negligently infringe the Treaty. Under Article 3 (1) thereof the Commission may also require undertakings to bring to an end infringements of the Treaty. Under Article 16 (1) (*a*) thereof such a requirement may be enforced by the imposition of penalty payments in respect of each day that the infringement continues. The Commission's powers of enforcement are discussed in more detail in Chapter 12.[3] In this chapter the consequences under civil law of an agreement falling within Article 85 (1) are discussed.

**402** **Civil consequences: in general.** If Article 85 (2) applies to an agreement without qualification,[4] the consequences which result from the agreement being " void " under that Article depend

---

[1] The full text of Art. 85 is set out at App. 1, *post*.
[2] *Post*, §§ 410 *et seq.*
[3] *Post*, §§ 1201 *et seq.*
[4] For a full discussion of the concept of " provisional validity " see *post*, §§ 410 *et seq.*

upon the relevant principles of general application laid down by the European Court of Justice.[5] It is, however, national courts which have the task of applying Article 85 (2). In exercising this jurisdiction the questions which arise are:

(1) How far, if at all, are agreements falling within Article 85 (1) enforceable in a national court?

(2) How far may provisions of an agreement falling within Article 85 (1) be severable?

(3) What legal remedies, if any, are available to a third party who has been or may be damnified by the operation of an Article 85 (1) agreement?

Some tentative comments relating to these problems are set out below.

**403**    **Provisional validity.** The doctrine of " provisional validity " forms an important exception to the general application of Article 85 (2).[6] " Provisional validity," which is discussed more fully in the next section,[7] applies only to agreements in existence at the date of entry into force of Regulation 17 on March 13, 1962 (old agreements)[8] which were notified to the Commission in due time for the purpose of obtaining exemption under Article 85 (3), or in respect of which the notification requirements have been relaxed under the provisions of Article 4 (2) of Regulation 17.[9] In essence, the European Court has held [10] that these agreements must be regarded as enforceable pending a decision by the Commission granting or refusing an exemption under Article 85 (3).[11] But such agreements are only " provisionally " valid in that if the Commission reaches an adverse decision the " validity " comes to an end; and it is most probable that the old agreement

---

[5] *LTM* (56/65) [1966] C.M.L.R. 357. For the role of the European Court of Justice see *post*, § 409.

[6] See *Bosch* v. *Geus* (13/61) [1962] C.M.L.R. 1; *Portelange* v. *Smith Corona* (10/69) 7 C.M.L.Rev. 1970, 234; *Bilger* v. *Jehle* (43/69) 8 C.M.L.Rev. 1971, 241; *Brasserie de Haecht* (*No. 2*) (48/72), February 6, 1973.

[7] *Post*, §§ 410 *et seq.*

[8] See § 411, *post*; and for " Accession agreements " and provisional validity, see § 418, *post*.

[9] For notification see §§ 411–413, 504 *et. seq., post*. For Article 4 (2) agreements see §§ 413–414, 422, 528 *et. seq., post*.

[10] See the decisions cited at note 6, *supra*.

[11] Under Arts. 6, 8, 9 of Reg. 17, or exercising its powers under Art. 7 of Reg. 17, *post*, §§ 415, 523–524; or under Art. 15 (6) of Reg. 17, *post*, § 513. The Commission's decision under Arts. 6 and 7 of Reg. 17 may be of retroactive effect.

thereupon becomes void with effect retroactively to the date of entry into force of Regulation 17.[12]

Agreements coming into existence after the date of entry into force of Regulation 17 (new agreements) do not benefit from " provisional validity."[13] However, where such new agreements have been notified, or fall within Article 4 (2) of Regulation 17, a national court may have a discretion to stay proceedings in which the civil validity of such an agreement is in issue. This power is also discussed more fully in the next section.[14] In this section the effects of Article 85 (2) are considered in general terms in respect of all agreements which have not been notified to the Commission and which do not fall within Article 4 (2) of Regulation 17.

**404    Effect of Article 85 in English law.** It is clear that following the United Kingdom's accession to the Treaty of Rome [15] the provisions of Article 85 of the Treaty and the Regulations made thereunder will be directly applicable in English law as from the date of accession.[16] Accordingly it will be the duty of English courts to give effect to those provisions as from that date. The question now considered is what is the effect in English law of Article 85 (2) in respect of an agreement falling within Article 85 (1) which has not been notified to the Commission in due time under Articles 4, 5 or 25 of Regulation 17 and is not exempt from notification under Articles 4 (2) and 5 (2) thereof? This question is discussed in broad terms; more detailed guidance on the general topic of " illegality " in the law of contract should be sought from standard textbooks.[17]

**405    Article 85 (2): as between the parties.** Under Article 1 of

---

[12] *Brasserie de Haecht (No. 2)* (48/72), February 6, 1973; *post,* § 417. But *cf. Bilger* (43/69) 8 C.M.L.Rev 1971, 241.
[13] *Brasserie de Haecht (No. 2)* (48/72), February 6, 1973; *post,* § 419.
[14] §§ 419, 421–422, *post.*
[15] In accordance with the Treaty of Accession and the Decision of the Council of the European Communities of January 22, 1972. Cmnd. 4862, I and II.
[16] Art. 1 of Reg. 17. *Bosch* v. *de Geus* (13/61) [1962] C.M.L.R. 1. European Communities Act 1972, s. 2 (1).
[17] For " illegality " generally, and a more detailed treatment of contracts rendered void or prohibited by statutory provisions in English law, see Chitty, *Contracts,* 23rd ed., Vol. 1, Chap. 16; Cheshire and Fifoot, *Law of Contract,* 7th ed., Part IV, Chaps. III–VI.

Regulation 17, agreements, decisions and concerted practices
falling within Article 85 (1) are prohibited, no prior decision to
that effect being required.[18]   Accordingly the nullity imposed by
Article 85 (2) affects an agreement falling within Article 85 (1) as
from the date of entry into force of Regulation 17,[19] unless the
agreement benefits from provisional validity.[20]   In the case of
accession agreements *i.e.* those already in existence as at
January 1, 1973, and falling within Article 85 (1) solely as a result
of accession, nullity takes full effect from January 1, 1973 unless
the agreement is notified before July 1, 1973.[21]   Subject to the
question of severance discussed below, the civil consequences of
such nullity must be considered from two aspects.   First, it is clear
that neither party to the agreement will be permitted to enforce it
—to allow such a contract to be enforced would be to give effect
to a void agreement.[22]   The second aspect relates to monies paid
under the agreement.   Does the fact that the agreement is void
mean that the parties to the agreement are able to recover anything paid thereunder (as *e.g.* in English law where the agreement
is void for mistake)?   At the present time this question has
not yet been resolved.   Is the problem to be determined according
to the national law applicable to the agreement, or according to
Community law?   In the *LTM* case the European Court held
that Article 85 (2) was a provision which aimed at ensuring
respect for the Treaty and should " only be interpreted in the
light of its purpose within the Community and should be limited
to that context."[23]   This suggests that the consequences of
Article 85 (2) are a matter for Community law.   Accordingly,
the problem of the recovery of monies paid under the agreement
should be determined by the European Court, which has not yet
pronounced on this point.   On the other hand, it has not been
authoritatively decided whether national courts may resolve the
problem by applying their own national laws.   It is therefore
relevant to consider what the position would be if the consequences of Article 85 (2) fell to be decided under English law.

[18] Subject to Arts. 6, 7 and 23 of Reg. 17.
[19] March 13, 1962.
[20] *Bosch* v. *de Geus* (13/61) [1962] C.M.L.R. 1. *Post*, §§ 410 *et seq.*
[21] *Post*, § 418; see also § 519.
[22] *Béguelin* (22/71) [1972] C.M.L.R. 81, 87.
[23] (56/65) [1966] C.M.L.R. 357, 376.   In the C.M.L.R. translation " finalité "
is incorrectly translated as " finality."

In this context it is considered that agreements falling within
Article 85 (1) are not merely void, but are also " illegal " in that
they are directly prohibited by Article 85 (1) and Article 1 of
Regulation 17.   Infringement of this prohibition is subject to
administrative sanctions.[24]   Consequently it is submitted that
in actions for recovery of monies paid under a contract void by
virtue of Article 85 (2), it would be proper to apply the maxim *in
pari delicto potior est conditio defendentis*.[25]   The effect of this
maxim is that one party cannot recover what he has given to the
other under a prohibited contract if he has to rely on the illegality
in order to do so.   It is considered that to permit a party to recover
monies paid on the grounds that the agreement was " void "
under Article 85 (2) would be to allow a cause of action " founded
upon a transgression of a positive law of this country." [26]   But
there may be circumstances where the doctrine of *in pari delicto*
would not apply, *e.g.* if the contract were still executory.[27]

**406**    **Severance.**   In the *LTM* case the European Court held [28] that
Article 85 (2) applies only to those individual elements of the
agreement which fall within the prohibition of Article 85 (1),
provided that those elements are severable from the agreement
as a whole.  If the offending provisions are not severable, then the
whole agreement is void.  In order to decide which provisions are
severable, it is necessary to apply the relevant national law.[29]
It follows, therefore, that an English court would have to consider
whether those parts of the agreement which were prohibited by
Article 85 (1) were severable from the remainder.  If so, the
unobjectionable parts of the agreement would be enforceable.
In considering contracts governed by English law, the principles
to be applied are those of the common law.

Any detailed account of severance in English law is outside

---

[24] Under Art. 15 of Reg. 17; but under Art. 15 (4) decisions by the Commission
imposing fines should not be regarded as imposing criminal penalties.  See
*post*, §§ 1205 *et seq.*
[25] Chitty, *op. cit.*, para. 939 *et seq.*; Cheshire and Fifoot, *op. cit.*, pp. 325 *et seq.*
[26] *Holman* v. *Johnson* (1775) 1 Cowp. 341, 343.
[27] *Kearley* v. *Thomson* (1890) 24 Q.B.D. 742.   *Taylor* v. *Bowers* (1876) 1 Q.B.D.
291; and see generally Chitty, *op. cit.*, para. 939 *et seq.*, Cheshire and Fifoot,
*op. cit.*, pp. 325 *et seq.*
[28] (56/65) [1966] C.M.L.R. 357, 376; see also *Grundig & Consten* v. *EEC Commission*
(56/64, 58/64) [1966] C.M.L.R. 418, 474 and 475.
[29] *LTM* (56/65) [1966] C.M.L.R. 357, 376; for practice in German courts see *Re
Yoga Fruit Juices* [1969] C.M.L.R. 123, *Re Vat 69* [1969] C.M.L.R. 266.

the scope of this work, but certain general considerations should be borne in mind.[30]   First, the courts will not sever contractual provisions where this involves making a new contract for the parties.   Thus, where contracts have contained provisions in restraint of trade, the courts have been prepared to sever the unreasonable parts only where this can be done merely by striking out the offending clauses.[31]   But even where such clauses may be " blue-pencilled " the court will not sever clauses in restraint of trade where to do so would " alter entirely the scope and intention of the agreement." [32]   Whether any particular clause or clauses may be severed from an agreement in such case must be a question of the proper construction of that agreement.

**407**       **Claims by third parties.**  It is at present an open question as to whether parties who suffer injury as a result of an agreement falling within Article 85 (1), which is void under Article 85 (2), may recover damages from or take proceedings for an injunction against the parties to the agreement.[33]   At the present time there is no reported decision dealing directly with this matter in any national or European court.[34]   It could be argued that third parties could bring an action in appropriate circumstances for breach of a " statutory duty " imposed by the combined effects of section 2 of the European Communities Act 1972, and Article 85 of the Treaty.[35]   Alternatively, it could be argued that the giving effect to Article 85 (1) restrictions which have not been duly notified constituted the use of unlawful means and that a third party whose legitimate business interests were thereby injured

---

[30] For more detailed accounts of the doctrine of severance, see Chitty, *op. cit.*, paras. 949 *et seq.;* Cheshire and Fifoot, *op. cit.*, pp. 358–363.

[31] See *e.g. Goldsoll* v. *Goldman* [1914] 2 Ch. 603; [1915] 1 Ch. 292.   *Ronbar Enterprises Ltd.* v. *Green* [1954] 1 W.L.R. 815.

[32] *e.g. Attwood* v. *Lamont* [1920] 3 K.B. 571.

[33] See generally " Actions for Damages by Third Parties under English Law for Breach of Article 85 of the EEC Treaty " by P. Rew, 8 C.M.L.Rev. 1971, 462; " La Réparation des conséquences dommageables d'une violation des Articles 85 and 86 " Etudes de la CEE (Série Concurrence No. 1), Bruxelles, 1966.

[34] See the decision of the Bundesgerichtshof under Arts. 4 (6) and 60 of the ECSC Treaty: April 14, 1959, BGHZ, 30, 74.

[35] An action in conspiracy would be unlikely to succeed, unless it could be shown that the defendants had acted for an improper motive and not merely to advance their own trade interests: *Mogul SS. Co. Ltd.* v. *McGregor, Gow & Co.* [1892] A.C. 25; see *Crofter Hand Woven Harris Tweed Co. Ltd.* v. *Veitch* [1942] A.C. 435.

could sue in tort at common law.[36]   In essence, whether Article
85 confers such rights depends upon the proper construction of
the Treaty.   Ultimately therefore the question must be resolved
by the European Court.   At the present time, however, it cannot
be safely assumed that breaches of Article 85 (1) are not action-
able by third parties.

**408     Claims against third parties.**   In *Béguelin* the European
Court held that agreements falling within Article 85 (1) could not
be relied upon in proceedings against third parties.[37]   This ruling
was given with reference to the French law of unfair competition,
which gives exclusive concessionaires certain rights against third
parties who attempt to sell the contract products in their territory.
It is thought that no action for inducing breach of contract would
lie against a third party where the contract itself was void under
Article 85 (2).[38]   Moreover, infringement proceedings to enforce
industrial property rights against third parties may fail where such
proceedings are " the object, means or consequence " of an
agreement falling under Article 85 (1).[39]

**409     Jurisdiction of the English courts.**   Certain limitations on the
jurisdiction of English courts to pronounce on agreements
falling under Article 85 of the Treaty should be noted.   First,
the courts have no jurisdiction to decide on the application of
Article 85 (3) to an agreement; this is reserved to the Commission.[40]   Hence, in the case of agreements not benefiting from
provisional validity, the court is solely concerned with the effect,
in English law, of the nullity of the agreement.[41]   Secondly, it

---

[36] See *Daily Mirror Newspapers Ltd.* v. *Gardner* [1968] 2 Q.B. 762; *Brekkes* v.
*Cattel* [1972] 1 Ch. 105.   And see *post*, § 420.
[37] (22/71) [1972] C.M.L.R. 81, 98.
[38] See *Joe Lee Ltd.* v. *Dalmeny* [1927] 1 Ch. 300, and generally Clerk and Lindsell,
*Torts*, 13th ed., para. 794.
[39] See *Grundig & Consten* v. *EEC Commission* (56/64, 58/64) [1966] C.M.L.R. 418;
*Sirena* v. *Eda* (40/70) [1971] C.M.L.R. 260; *Parke Davis & Co.* v. *Probel* (24/67)
[1968] C.M.L.R. 47.   For the application of Art. 86 see *post* § 726 and for the
application of Arts. 30–36 to industrial property rights see § 912, *post*.
[40] Art. 9 (1) of Reg. 17.
[41] But see §§ 410 *et seq.*, especially § 419.   Decisions of national courts since 1967
regarding unnotified agreements include, Belgium: *Van Heuven Meiren* v. *Buitoni*
[1967] C.M.L.R. 241, 243 (dismissing an action for damages for breach of an
agreement on the ground that the agreement was void under Art. 85 (1) ); *Schott*
v. *Remacle* [1967] C.M.L.R. 55 (deciding that Art. 85 (1) was not applicable to
a sole agency agreement); *Onckelincx* v. *Ets. Beaumaine* [1970] C.M.L.R. 122
(holding that a price fixing scheme among wholesalers did not fall within Art.

appears that if the Commission has "initiated a procedure" under Articles 2, 3 or 6 of Regulation 17, the court has no jurisdiction to apply Article 85 (1) to the agreement in question.[42] Thirdly, under Article 177 of the Treaty, if any question concerning the interpretation of the Treaty, or the validity and interpretation of the acts of the institutions of the Community, should arise in the courts of a Member State, a national court may, and a national court of final resort must, refer the matter to the European Court of Justice for a preliminary ruling. Questions relating to whether parties to an Article 85 (1) agreement may recover monies paid thereunder, or to whether third parties can recover damages under Article 85 (1) may be suitable questions for such a reference. The extent and operation of Article 177 is, however, outside the scope of this work.[43]

## 2. PROVISIONAL VALIDITY

**410** **Provisional validity and notification.** Under the doctrine of "provisional validity" agreements already in existence at the date of entry into force of Regulation 17, which would otherwise become void under Article 85 (2), are to be regarded as enforceable while the possibility remains of the Commission granting exemption under Article 85 (3). This possibility exists only if the agreement is notified to the Commission, or if the agreement is of a kind exempted from notification, under the provisions of Regulation 17. In order to understand the decisions of the European Court relating to provisional validity, it is first necessary to explain the notification requirements of Regulation 17. In this section the rules as to notification are outlined first. Then the doctrine of provisional validity is considered in relation

85 (1)); *N.V. Canoy Herfkens* v. *Maison Kessels* [1969] C.M.L.R. 148 (considering the application of Art. 85 (1) to a sole distributorship agreement). France: *Lavecire France S.a.r.l.* v. *Ets. Isobel* [1969] C.M.L.R. 249 (sole agency agreement outside Art. 85 (1)). Germany: for decisions relating to application of Article 85 (1) to sole distributorship agreements see *Re " Asbach Uralt " Brandy* [1969] C.M.L.R. 172; *Re Vat 69* [1969] C.M.L.R. 266; *Re Yoga Fruit Juices* [1969] C.M.L.R. 123.

[42] Under Art. 2, in relation to an application for negative clearance; under Art. 3 in relation to a complaint by third parties or an investigation initiated by the Commission itself; under Art. 6 in relation to an application for exemption under Art 85 (3). For the meaning of " initiates a procedure " see § 421, *post.*

[43] For a short account see Mathijsen, *A Guide to European Community Law* (Sweet and Maxwell/Matthew Bender) (1972) paras. 3–59 *et. seq.;* and see Lagrange, " The European Court of Justice and National Courts," 8 C.M.L.Rev. 1971, 313.

to the several categories of agreements which receive different treatment under those rules. Basically, Regulation 17 contains two sets of rules relating to notification, transitional rules and general rules.[44]

**411** **Notification: transitional rules.** The first set of rules may be described as the transitional rules. Those rules originally applied to agreements which were already in existence on March 13, 1962, the date on which Regulation 17 came into force (old agreements) and now also apply to those agreements existing on January 1 1973 which fall within Article 85 (1) solely as a result of Accession (Accession agreements). The transitional rules applicable to old agreements—*i.e.* those in existence on March 13, 1962— are set out in Articles 5, 6 (2) and 7 of Regulation 17.[45]

Article 5 (1) of Regulation 17 provides that the date for notifying old agreements was November 1, 1962, or if the agreement was bilateral, February 1, 1963. Article 6 (2) of Regulation 17 provides that if old agreements were duly notified within the appropriate time limits, and are subsequently granted exemption under Article 85 (3) of the Treaty, the Commission's decision may be made to take effect retroactively, to a date earlier than the date of notification. Article 7 of Regulation 17 provides that if old agreements were notified within the time limits, and the parties cease to give effect to them or modify them in such a way that they no longer fall within Article 85 (1) of the Treaty or that they satisfy Article 85 (3), the Commission may declare Article 85 (1) inapplicable to the agreement for any period prior to the modification or abandonment of that agreement. Broadly speaking, the transitional rules set out above apply to accession agreements *i.e.* agreements existing on January 1, 1973 which fall within Article 85 (1) solely as a result of Accession. To benefit from the advantages of notification such agreements should be notified before July 1, 1973.[46]

**412** **Notification: general rules.** Agreements falling within Article 85 (1) other than old agreements and Accession agreements do not benefit from the transitional arrangements; such agree-

---

[44] For a full discussion of notification see §§ 501 *et seq., post.*
[45] See further *post,* §§ 517 *et seq.*
[46] Under Art. 25 of Reg. 17; *post,* §§ 517 *et seq.*

ments (new agreements) were or are subject to Article 85 (1) at the time of their formation. New agreements comprise agreements that were or are made after March 13, 1962, restricting competition within the common market and affecting trade between the Six; or agreements made after January 1, 1973, restricting competition within the enlarged common market and affecting trade between the nine Member States. Under Article 4 (1) of Regulation 17 new agreements can only obtain exemption under Article 85 (3) if notified to the Commission for that purpose. If such an exemption is subsequently granted, it cannot take effect from a date earlier than notification.[47]

**413**     **Agreements exempt from notification: Article 4 (2) of Regulation 17.** Under Article 4 (2) and Article 5 (2) of Regulation 17 the requirements of notification have been relaxed in respect of certain agreements. Such agreements, whether old, Accession or new agreements, need not be notified for the purpose of obtaining exemption. Broadly, these agreements comprise any agreement:

(1) to which the parties are undertakings in one Member State and the agreement does not relate either to imports or to exports between Member States; or

(2) to which not more than two undertakings are party and the agreement *only* (a) restricts the freedom of one party as to the prices at which and conditions of business upon which goods obtained from the other may be resold, or (b) imposes restrictions upon the assignee or user of industrial property rights or know-how; or

(3) that has as its *sole* object (a) the development or uniform application of standards or types, (b) joint research and development, and (c) specialisation in manufacturing, where the market share and turnover of undertakings concerned do not exceed certain limits.[48]

**414**     **Validity of agreements within Article 4 (2) of Regulation 17.** When considering the validity of agreements falling within

---

[47] See generally *post*, §§ 501 *et seq.* Art. 6 (2) and Art. 7 of Reg. 17 do not apply to new agreements.

[48] For a detailed treatment of Art. 4 (2) and Art. 5 (2) agreements see § 528, *post*; see also §§ 957, 1043, 1113, *post*. Exemption may be granted retroactively to the date of the agreement. Art 6 (2) of Reg. 17.

Article 4 (2) of Regulation 17 which have not been notified,[49] it is first necessary to distinguish between " old Article 4 (2) agreements " and " new Article 4 (2) agreements." It is also necessary to consider the cases of *Bilger* and *Brasserie de Haecht* (*No. 2*).[50] In *Bilger* the European Court held that an agreement falling under Article 4 (2) of Regulation 17 and not notified remained valid until its invalidity had been established. The nullity of the agreement could take effect only prospectively—*i.e.* from the date on which the nullity was established.[51] This rule, the Court held, applied to both " new " and " old " Article 4 (2) agreements. However, in *Brasserie de Haecht* (*No. 2*) the Court clearly held that " new Article 4 (2) agreements " were void *ab initio* under Article 85 (2). Such agreements do not enjoy any " provisional validity " and are to be treated no better than other notified new agreements.[52] To this extent *Brasserie de Haecht* clearly overrules dicta to the contrary in *Bilger*. However, the question that also arises is how far the *Bilger* decision has been implicitly overruled by *Brasserie de Haecht* (*No. 2*) in respect of " old Article 4 (2) agreements." It is thought, in the light of both decisions, that such agreements continue to enjoy " provisional validity " until a decision by the competent authorities to the contrary. However, it appears to follow from *Brasserie de Haecht* (*No. 2*) that, upon an adverse decision by the competent authorities, the agreement becomes void with retroactive effect to the date of entry into force of Regulation 17. On this latter point it is submitted that *Bilger* can no longer be safely relied on.

**415     Validity of old agreements falling under transitional rules: Bosch.** The validity of old agreements existing at the time of the entry into force of Regulation 17 (other than Article 4 (2) agreements) was established by the European Court in *Bosch* [53]

---

[49] As far as provisional validity is concerned, it is submitted that Art. 4 (2) agreements which have been notified are governed by the same rules as other agreements which have been notified; see *post*, §§ 415–420.

[50] *Bilger* (43/69) 8 C.M.L.Rev. 1971, 241; *Brasserie de Haecht* (48/72), February 6, 1973; *post*, § 419. See also *Bosch* v. *de Geus* (13/61) [1962] C.M.L.R. 1, 29; *Béguelin* (22/71) [1972] C.M.L.R. 81, 97.

[51] The Court held in *Bilger* that this nullity could be established by national authorities, including national courts. See *post*, § 422. It is submitted that the reasoning in *Bilger* applies equally where nullity has been established by the Commission.

[52] See *post*, § 419.

[53] (13/61) [1962] C.M.L.R. 1, 27–31.

and its decision in *Portelange*.[54]  In *Bosch* the Court held that
if the agreement had been duly notified within the time limits
set out under Article 5 (1) of Regulation 17 it could not be
considered void as long as the possibility remained of the Commission granting an exemption under Article 85 (3) or exercising
its powers under Article 7 (1) of Regulation 17.[55]  Accordingly,
the Court said that agreements notified in due time must be considered as " temporarily valid " until the Commission had
declared that neither the provisions of Article 85 (3) nor the
provisions of Article 7 (1) of Regulation 17 might be applied to
the agreement.  The Court said it would be contrary to the principle of legal security to render agreements void before it was
possible to tell which ones were caught by Article 85 as a whole
*i.e.* agreements falling within Article 85 (1) could not be treated
as void under Article 85 (2) unless it was shown that they could
not qualify for exemption under Article 85 (3).  The Court held
also that all old agreements were to be considered fully valid up
until March 13, 1962 unless they had been held contrary to
Article 85 by express decisions of authorities acting prior to that
date under the limited transitional powers contained in Articles
88 or 89 (2) of the Treaty.[56]

**416**     **The Portelange decision.**  In *Portelange*[57] the Court gave
more guidance on the provisional validity of an old agreement
in existence on March 13, 1962 and duly notified to the Commission.[58]  In that case, one of the parties to an exclusive dealing
agreement claimed damages in a Belgian court in respect of its
premature determination.  The Belgian court asked the European
Court to rule upon the consequences of the " provisional validity "
accorded to duly notified agreements as a result of the *Bosch* case.
The European Court held that until the Commission had taken
a decision under Article 85 (3), every agreement which had been
duly notified must be considered as valid and fully binding upon
the parties.  However, the Court said that if the Commission

[54] (10/69) 7 C.M.L.Rev. 1970, 234.  And see Arts. 88 and 89 (2).
[55] For Art. 7 (1) of Reg. 17 see *ante*, § 411; and also *post*, §§ 523–524.
[56] The transitional powers of the Commission and the authorities of Member
States between March 25, 1957 and March 17, 1962 are of little practical significance.  See *ante*, §§ 117–118.
[57] (10/69) 7 C.M.L.Rev. 1971, 234.
[58] But *cf. Brasserie de Haecht (No. 2)* (48/72), February 6, 1973; *post*, §§ 417–419.

informs the parties under Article 15 (6) [59] of Regulation 17 that the agreement is unlikely to be exempted, from the date of that communication onwards the parties give effect to the agreement " at their peril."

**417    Effect of Portelange and Bosch.**   The effect of the *Portelange* decision is that old agreements duly notified within the time limits are enforceable unless and until the Commission issues a decision under Article 85 (3) of the Treaty or under Article 15 (6) of Regulation 17. If the Commission issues an adverse decision under Article 85 (3) of the Treaty, it is clear that the agreement is void from that moment on. It is not entirely clear whether the agreement is then also void in respect of the period before the Commission's decision. The question must now be seen in the light of *Brasserie de Haecht (No. 2)*.[58] One view is that as a result of *Portelange* duly notified agreements are enforceable until the Commission issues an adverse decision, whereupon such agreements become void with prospective effect. The following considerations may be advanced in support of this view.

(i) Although in *Portelange* the Court did not deal specifically with the question of retroactive effect, it did hold that old agreements duly notified must be taken as fully valid (" recoivent leur plein effet " [60]) pending a decision by the Commission. If, during the period prior to the Commission's decision, such agreements are always subject to the risk of subsequently becoming void with retrospective effect, it is difficult to see how they can meaningfully be regarded as " fully valid."

(ii) In principle, if old agreements duly notified may subsequently become void retrospectively to the date of entry into force of Regulation 17, that causes uncertainty pending the grant or refusal of exemption, and jeopardises the very legal security with which the Court was concerned in *Portelange* and *Bosch*.

(iii) It was held in *Bilger* [61] that old Article 4 (2) agreements may be declared void only with prospective effect;[62] there is no reason why old agreements duly notified under Article 5 (1) should be treated differently.[63]

---

[59] See *post*, § 513.          [60] 15 Rec. 309.
[61] (43/69) 8 C.M.L.Rev. 1971, 241.          [62] See §§ 413–414, *ante*.
[63] But *cf. Bosch* [1962] C.M.L.R. 1, 29 where the Court apparently drew a distinction between agreements falling within Art. 5 (1) and agreements falling within Art. 5 (2), regarding the former as " temporarily valid " and the latter as " valid."

The view that *Portelange* decides that upon the refusal of an
exemption an old agreement is void *only with effect thereafter*
received some support.[64]  On the other hand, the cogency of this
view had been seriously weakened by *Brasserie de Haecht*
(*No. 2*)[65] which (overruling *Bilger* in part) decides that agreements falling within Article 85 (2) may be void with retroactive
effect.  While it is true that that decision was dealing primarily
with new agreements, it is submitted that the tenor of the *Brasserie
de Haecht* (*No. 2*) decision supports the better view that duly
notified old agreements become void with retroactive effect
following an adverse decision by the Commission.  In addition,
it may be said (a) that if duly notified agreements are not retrospectively void when a decision under Article 85 (3) is refused,
then little meaning can be attached to the Commission's powers
under Article 7 (1) of Regulation 17 or under Article 6 (2) to
grant exemption retrospectively of its decision; (b) that the Court
in *Portelange* did not say that the nullity of the agreement takes
effect only as from the date of the Commission's decision[66];
and (c) that in *Bosch*[67] the Court said " The refusal of the Commission, moreover, to issue a declaration under Article 85 (3) in
respect of agreements falling within Article 85, necessitates their
nullity from the date of entry into force of Regulation 17."  The
practical effects of provisional validity are further discussed
below.[68]

**418**      **Validity of Accession agreements.**  It is submitted that the
rules developed by the European Court in respect of agreements
in existence on March 13, 1962 should also apply to Accession
agreements.  Upon that assumption the rules of provisional
validity discussed above[69] may therefore be summarised in
relation to Accession agreements, as follows.  First, all such
agreements are fully valid until January 1, 1973.  Next, unnotified

[64] See *e.g.* annotations by Maas and Van der Wielen at 8 C.M.L.Rev. 1971, 246–7;
Ulmer, Aussenwirtschaftsdienst des Betriebs-Beraters (AWB), 1970, p. 193;
Mégret, Waelbroeck and others, at p. 169, by whom the decisions were
criticised.
[65] (48/72), February 6, 1973.
[66] This is the Commission's view; Answer to written question No. 4/71, J.O. 1971
C57/6.  The view that agreements denied exemption do become void retrospectively is supported by Oberdorfer, Gleiss and Hirsch, *Common Market
Cartel Law*, para. 307; Mathijsen *op. cit.*, para. 2–14.
[67] [1962] C.M.L.R. 1, 29.
[68] *Post*, §§ 421–422.          [69] *Ante*, §§ 414–417.

Accession agreements falling within Article 4 (2) of Regulation 17 are enforceable until declared void by the competent authorities; thereupon they most probably become void with retroactive effect.[70] As to agreements not falling within Article 4 (2) of Regulation 17 the position is:

(i) If duly notified within six months of accession, such agreements remain enforceable until the Commission has issued a decision under Article 85 (3) of the Treaty or Article 15 (6) of Regulation 17.[17]

(ii) It follows that if duly notified within six months of accession, such agreements are enforceable during the period between January 1, 1973 and the date of notification.

(iii) Upon an adverse decision by the Commission such agreements probably become void with retroactive effect.[71]

(iv) If Accession agreements are not duly notified within six months of accession, they become void with effect from January 1, 1973. If they are later notified, they are probably to be treated as notified new agreements thereafter,[72] remaining void in respect of the period between January 1, 1973, and the date of notification. The practical effect of these rules is considered below.[73]

**419    Validity of new agreements.** The validity of new agreements made after March 13, 1962 or January 1, 1973, as the case may be, is now governed by the decision of the European Court in *Brasserie de Haecht* (*No. 2*)[74] It is clear that the principles there laid down apply equally to all new agreements, whether or not they fall within Article 4 (2) of Regulation 17. In essence, the European Court has held that new agreements do not enjoy " provisional validity." A notified new agreement, or an unnotified new agreement falling within Article 4 (2), must be regarded as void, even during the period prior to any decision by the Commission under Article 85 (3). The Court said that in the period prior to the Commission's decision the parties carried out the agreement at their own risk. Notifications in accordance with Article 4 (1) of Regulation 17 did not affect the nullity of the agreement under Article 85 (2) and the same applied to new agreements falling within Article 4 (2) of Regulation 17. The Court, however, also held that in a proper case the national judge

[70] *Ante,* § 414.  [71] *Ante,* §§ 416–417.
[72] *Post,* § 419.  [73] *Post,* §§ 421–422.  [74] (48/72) February 6, 1973.

could stay the proceedings in order to ascertain the Commission's position, except where it is clear beyond doubt that the agreement is contrary to Article 85.[75]

**420**     **Agreements not likely to be exempted under Article 85 (3).** One other problem is whether old notified agreements which are so clearly contrary to the provisions of the Treaty that they are most unlikely to benefit from an exemption under Article 85 (3) also benefit from provisional validity. In the *Parfums Marcel Rochas* [76] decision the Commission argued that export prohibitions in a notified agreement which gave " absolute territorial protection " to exclusive concessionaires should not benefit from the doctrine of provisional validity. The European Court said that, subject to the Commission invoking its powers under Article 85 of the Treaty and Regulation 17, the clauses at issue in that case did not alter the full effects of the provisional validity of notified agreements.[77] This decision may suggest that Accession agreements which have little chance of obtaining exemption under Article 85 (3) may benefit from provisional validity.

**421**     **Duly notified agreements before English courts.** What courses of action are open to an English court if the effect under Article 85 (1) of a duly notified agreement falling within that Article is raised as an issue in the course of domestic litigation? First it appears that if the Commission has " initiated a procedure " under Articles 2, 3 or 6 of Regulation 17, national courts are not competent to apply Article 85 (1) to the agreement in question at all. This would seem to follow from the decision of the European Court in *Bilger* [78] where the words " national authorities " in Article 9 (3) of Regulation 17 were interpreted to include national courts. The meaning of the important phrase " initiated a procedure " is not yet clear, but it may scarcely be doubted that the Commission does not " initiate a procedure " within the meaning of Article 9 (3) merely on receipt of a

---

[75] See also §§ 420–422, *post.*
[76] *Parfums Marcel Rochas Vertrieb G.m.b.H.* v. *Bitsch* (1/70) [1971] C.M.L.R. 104. Cf. *Daily Mirror Newspapers Ltd.* v. *Gardner* [1968] 2 Q.B. 762; *Brekkes* v. *Cattel* [1972] 1 Ch. 105; *ante,* § 408; but see now *Brasserie de Haecht (No. 2)* (48/72), February 6, 1973.
[77] (1/70) [1971] C.M.L.R. 104, 117.
[78] (43/69) 8 C.M.L.Rev. 1971, 241, 243–5, criticised by Mégret, Waelbroeck, and others, *op. cit.*, p. 159.

notification.[79] Thus it is necessary to consider the position that arises where an agreement has been notified but the Commission has not yet initiated a procedure. In the case of notified agreements the Commission has exclusive jurisdiction to decide whether the agreement may benefit from Article 85 (3), and hence, has exclusive jurisdiction to put an end to any provisional validity the agreement may have.[80] Accession agreements, it is submitted, must be treated as enforceable, under the doctrine of provisional validity, until the Commission has pronounced. Subject to the general principles applying to injunctive relief, it would be proper to enforce by injunction, pending the Commission's decision, an Accession agreement which had been duly notified. Whether an English court should proceed to hear actions for damages for breach of such an agreement pending such a decision, is more doubtful. One appropriate course would be to stay the proceedings, since if the Commission's final decision is adverse, the agreement most probably becomes void with retroactive effect.[81]

[79] Relevant decisions of national courts on this point include: *Brinkhof N.V.* v. *N.V. Nederlandse Spoorwegen and Deutsche Bundesbahn* [1970] C.M.L.R. 264 (Holland; a decision under Reg. 1017/68). France: *Laffort* v. *Laboratoires Sarbach* [1968] C.M.L.R. 257. See now *Brasserie de Haecht No. 2* (48/72), February 6, 1973.

[80] But see *ante*, § 420 and *post*, § 422.

[81] *Brasserie de Haecht (No. 2)* (48/72), February 6, 1973; *ante*, § 417; Oberdorfer, Gleiss and Hirsch, *Common Market Cartel Law*, 2nd ed., at para. 307 consider that damages can be recovered prior to the Commission's decision but may require to be repaid. French and Belgian courts have preferred to stay proceedings upon the grant of appropriate interim relief. See Mégret, Waelbroeck and others, p. 163. Some decisions of national courts relating to the enforcement of provisionally valid agreements include *Ass. Gén. des Fabricants Belges de Ciment Portland Artificiel* v. *S.A. Carrière Dufour* [1965] C.M.L.R. 193; [1967] C.M.L.R. 250 (Belgium: provisionally valid agreement—stay of proceedings pending Commission's decision. The agreement in question was later found by the Commission to fall outside Art. 85 (1): see *Re Limeburners Agreement*, J.O. 1969 L122/8 [1969] C.M.L.R. D15; *ante*, §§ 245 *et seq.*). Contrast the decision of the Gerichtshof, Amsterdam of June 28, 1961, enforcing a provisionally valid agreement against an unwilling party by interim injunction. Exemption under Art. 85 (3) was finally refused on October 20, 1970, the parties being required by the Commission to put an end to the agreement which the order of the Dutch Court had enforced for nine years. See *Re Van Katwijk's Agreement*, J.O. 1970 L242/18, [1970] C.M.L.R. D43; *post*, § 621. See also *Sieverding* v. *Hemes* [1967] C.M.L.R. 66 (Belgium: for purposes of civil action, notification subsequent to issue of writ disregarded); *Societé B.A.P.* v. *Madimpex* [1967] C.M.L.R. 148 (France: stay of proceedings pending Commission's decision under Art. 85 (3); grant of interim injunction); *Hofma* v. *Grundig* [1967] C.M.L.R. 1; *General Electrics Imports Co.* v. *Sieverding* [1967] C.M.L.R. 13 (Holland and Belgium respectively; injunctions to enforce duly notified agreements); *Advance Transformer Co.* v. *Bara* [1972] C.M.L.R. 497 (Belgium: validity of agreement falling within Art. 85 (1) terminated prior to March 13, 1962; *Bosch* v. *de Geus* (13/61) [1962] C.M.L.R. 1 followed); *Re Retail Price*

It is submitted that damages should not be recoverable in respect
of breaches committed in the period prior to the Commission's
decision, where the agreement is subsequently refused an exemption under Article 85 (3) or the Commission refuses to apply
Article 7 (1) of Regulation 17.[82]   In the case of new agreements,
it is now clear that such agreements do not benefit from provisional
validity, even though notified, during the period prior to the
Commission's decision.[83]   It is submitted that such new agreements should ordinarily not be enforceable during this period,
but in a proper case the Court might stay the proceedings upon
terms, pending the position of the Commission becoming
known.[84]

**422**     **Article 4 (2) agreements before English courts.**   It is submitted
that unnotified Accession agreement falling within Article 4 (2) of
Regulation 17 must be accorded provisional validity in the same
way as Accession agreements duly notified.[85]   It appears from the
decision of the European Court in *Bilger* [86] that English courts
do have jurisdiction to bring to an end the provisional validity of
Accession agreements falling within Article 4 (2) of Regulation 17.
It is, however, not yet certain how this jurisdiction should be
exercised.   Very difficult questions may arise if, for example, the
validity of a tied house agreement is in issue.[87]   It is not clear how
far the court may continue to exercise jurisdiction if the parties
proceed to notify the agreement in question to the Commission;
or how far the court may take into account the provisions of
Article 85 (3).   Where the validity of an unnotified new agreement
falling within Article 4 (2) of Regulation 17 is in issue, the
principles set out in *Brasserie de Haecht* (*No. 2*) apply.[88]

[The next paragraph is 501.]

*Maintenance for Film* [1972] C.M.L.R. 62 (Germany: enforcement of provisionally valid agreement by injunction).
[82] See *ante*, § 415 and *post*, §§ 523–524.
[83] *Brasserie de Haecht* (*No. 2*) (48/72), February 6, 1973.
[84] *Ibid.*                [85] See *ante*, §§ 414, 418.
[86] (43/69) C.M.L.Rev. 1971, 241.   *Bilger* held that a national court may bring
such provisional validity to an end only with *prospective* effect, but see now
*Brasserie de Haecht* (*No. 2*) (48/72), February 6, 1973.
[87] See *Brasserie de Haecht* v. *Wilkin* (23/67) [1968] C.M.L.R. 26; *post*, §§ 836 *et seq.*
The Bundesgerichtshof has distinguished the *Bilger* decision and held that
German courts do not have jurisdiction to treat as void agreements falling
under Art. 4 (2) of Reg. 17: Decision of April 9, 1970. See 9 C.M.L.Rev. 1972,
242.
[88] (48/72), February 6, 1973.   See *ante*, § 419.

CHAPTER 5

## NOTIFICATION

### 1. Application for Negative Clearance and Notification

**501**   **In general.**   Application for negative clearance is the procedure under which undertakings or associations of undertakings may obtain a declaration from the Commission that the agreement in question falls outside Articles 85 and 86 altogether.[1] Notification is the procedure necessary in order to obtain an exemption under Article 85 (3) of the Treaty.   Only the Commission is empowered to grant such exemption.[2]   Pending the grant or refusal of exemption by the Commission, the effect of notification and the rules relating thereto [3] is substantially to mitigate the normal consequences which flow from a contravention of Article 85 (1).

**502**   **Object of negative clearance.**   Under Article 2 of Regulation 17 the Commission may certify, upon application of the parties, that on the basis of the facts known to it there are no grounds for action on its part under Article 85 (1) or Article 86 of the Treaty in respect of an agreement, decision or practice.   The object of applying for negative clearance is to establish whether any particular agreement falls within Article 85 (1) or not.   If the application is successful, the Commission will issue a declaration that " there is no reason for the Commission in the light of the information available to it to intervene under the Treaty."   Such a declaration must be distinguished from the declaration made by the Commission, when granting an exemption under Article 85 (3), that " the provisions of Article 85 (1) are declared inapplicable to the agreement."   Confusingly, under the Treaty " a declaration of inapplicability " is given when the Commission exempts under Article 85 (3) an agreement to which Article 85 (1) applied; an

---

[1] Art. 2 of Reg. 17.
[2] Art. 9 (1) of Reg. 17.
[3] Arts. 4–7 of Reg. 17.

agreement to which Article 85 (1) does not apply at all receives
" negative clearance." [4]

**503**    **Effect of negative clearance.**  Technically, a negative clearance
has no binding effect on the courts of the Member States.  In
the Commission's view, a decision on negative clearance may be
revised upon the discovery of further information or fresh facts
unknown to the Commission at the time of its decision,[5] or even
in the event of a change in judicial interpretation of the law.[6]
Unlike the notification of an agreement for the purpose of
obtaining exemption under Article 85 (3), an application for
negative clearance cannot give the agreement provisional validity [7]
nor are the parties protected from fines,[8] during the period prior
to the Commission's decision.  However, applications for negative clearance and notifications for the purpose of obtaining
exemption under Article 85 (3) must both be made on the same
form, Form A/B.[9]  For the purposes of obtaining the temporary
advantages which flow from notification,[10] and which do not
flow from applications for negative clearance, it is always
desirable to make a combined application, both for negative
clearance and, alternatively, for exemption under Article 85 (3).
The procedure for making such applications is described below.[11]

**504**    **Object of notification.**  As has been seen, two consequences
normally follow if an agreement, decision or concerted practice
falls within Article 85 (1).  First, the Commission may impose
fines upon each of the participating undertakings if they either
intentionally or negligently infringe the Treaty.[12]  Secondly, by
virtue of Article 85 (2), any agreements or decisions prohibited
pursuant to Article 85 (1) are automatically void.[13]  However,
once the Commission grants an exemption pursuant to Article

---

[4] Compare the declarations made by the Commission in *Davidson Rubber Co.*
where certain agreements received negative clearance and others exemptions:
J.O. 1972 L143/31, [1972] C.M.L.R. D52; *post*, §§ 946 *et seq.*
[5] *Guide Pratique*, Part II (II).
[6] Answer to Deringer, Parliamentary Question J.O. 1962 76/2136.
[7] *Ante*, §§ 403, 410 *et seq.*
[8] §§ 513, 1205 *et seq.*  Although fines may be imposed only for intentional or
negligent infringements, if parties had filed an application for negative clearance,
imposition of a fine would be unlikely.
[9] *Post*, §§ 535, 536.  Forms A, B and B1 are no longer in use.
[10] *Post*, §§ 512–514, 520–525.
[11] *Post*, §§ 534 *et seq.*  For procedure following the application, see *post* § 1221.
[12] Art. 15 (2) of Reg. 17.  *Post*, §§ 1205 *et seq.*          [13] *Ante*, §§ 401 *et seq.*

85 (3) [14] and so long as that exemption remains in force,[15] the parties do not infringe Article 85 (1) by giving effect to the agreement. Consequently, they are not liable to be fined and the agreement is fully valid and enforceable. The object of notification, therefore, is to obtain the ultimate benefits of an exemption under Article 85 (3). In addition to the final benefit of an exemption, notification itself results in certain temporary advantages to the parties. These advantages vary according to which of the categories of agreements set out in Articles 4, 5 and 25 of Regulation 17 the particular agreement belongs. In general terms they may be summarised as follows:

(i) Until the grant or refusal of an exemption, the parties obtain protection from the imposition of fines.[16]

(ii) Upon the grant of an exemption, the parties to a duly notified agreement may benefit from the power of the Commission to declare the exemption applicable with retroactive effect.[17]

(iii) Until the grant or refusal of an exemption, the parties may be able to enforce certain agreements subject to transitional provisions under the doctrine of provisional validity.[18]

(iv) In the case of certain agreements subject to transitional provisions [19] the parties may benefit from the power of the Commission to declare, in cases where these agreements have been modified or abandoned, that Article 85 (1) was inapplicable to the agreement during any period prior to the modification or abandonment.[20]

Since the time taken by the Commission to reach a decision upon the grant or refusal or any exemption is usually about two years, and often longer,[21] the protection from fines and the other matters mentioned above represent not inconsiderable advantages.

[14] Under Arts. 8 and 9 of Reg. 17.
[15] Art. 8 (1) of Reg. 17. See *post*, §§ 633 *et seq.*
[16] Art. 15 (5) and (6) of Reg. 17. See *post*, §§ 513, 520. For fines, see *post*, § 1205.
[17] Art. 6 of Reg. 17; *post*, §§ 514, 522.
[18] See *ante*, §§ 403, 410 *et seq.*, *post*, §§ 515, 525.
[19] *Post*, §§ 508, 517 *et seq.*
[20] Art. 7 of Reg. 17; *post*, §§ 523–524.
[21] The shortest time in which the Commission has reached a decision was seven months in *Re Henkel-Colgate*, J.O. 1972 L14/14. There the parties made exemption a condition precedent to the agreement. In *Re Lightweight Paper*, J.O. 1972 L182/24, [1972] C.M.L.R. D94, the Commission's decision of July 26, 1972 was given in respect of an agreement notified on October 31, 1962.

**505**    **Consequences of failure to notify.**  Although it is sometimes
said that there is no duty to notify, in that the failure to notify
does not in itself attract any penalties, the omission of notification
has certain consequences which are the converse of the advantages described above.  Most important, as long as the agreement
is unnotified, the parties deprive themselves of the opportunity to
obtain the benefit of an exemption under Article 85 (3).  In
addition, again in general terms, there are the following further
disadvantages:

(1) Parties who give effect to an unnotified agreement falling
within Article 85 (1) are liable to be fined for acts committed
while the agreement was unnotified.[22]

(2) In the case of agreements subject to transitional provisions,
the parties may lose the benefit of provisional validity.[23]

**506**    **Article 4 (2) agreements.**  To the above general principles, there
are two important exceptions.  First, agreements falling within
Article 4 (2) of Regulation 17 do not require to be notified
in order to obtain an exemption under Article 85 (3).  However,
such agreements may be notified and there may be advantages in
notifying them, depending upon whether the agreement falls within Article 4 (2) or Article 5 (2) of Regulation 17.[24]  Article 4 (2)
relates to agreements coming into force after March 13, 1962, or
January 1, 1973 (new agreements); Article 5 (2) applies transitional
provisions in respect of agreements already in existence on those
dates (either "old" or "Accession" agreements).[25]  Such
agreements are more fully discussed below.[26]

**507**    **Block exemptions.**  The second exception to the above general
principles is that certain other classes of agreements benefit from
block exemptions under Article 85 (3).[27]  Agreements falling
within the terms of such block exemptions, which at present relate
to exclusive dealing agreements [28] and specialisation agreements,[29]
do not require notification.

**508**    **General rules and transitional rules.**  In respect of those

[22] Art. 15 of Reg. 17; *post*, §§ 1205, 1208–1209.    [23] *Ante*, §§ 403, 410 *et seq.*
[24] *Post*, § 528.
[25] For the meaning of "new," "old" and "Accession" agreements, see further
§ 508, *post*.
[26] *Post*, §§ 528 *et seq.*    [27] *Post*, §§ 609 *et seq.*
[28] Under Reg. 67/67.  See *post*, § 818.    [29] *Post*, § 1023.

agreements which require notification in order to obtain exemption under Article 85 (3) (*i.e.* agreements neither falling within Article 4 (2) of Regulation 17 nor benefiting from block exemption) it is important to remember that there are two sets of rules, transitional rules and general rules. This complexity derives from the need to make transitional arrangements, originally for agreements which were already in existence on March 13, 1962, the date on which Regulation 17 came into force (old agreements), and now for those agreements existing on January 1, 1973 which fall within Article 85 (1) solely as a result of accession (Accession agreements). The transitional rules applicable to old agreements are contained in Articles 5, 6 (2) and 7 of Regulation 17. Under Article 25 of Regulation 17 these transitional rules are broadly applied to Accession agreements, *i.e.* agreements already in existence on January 1, 1973 that fall within Article 85 (1) solely as a result of accession. But agreements falling within Article 85 (1) other than old agreements and Accession agreements do not benefit from these transitional arrangements; such agreements (new agreements) were and are subject to Article 85 (1) at the time of their formation; they fall within a different set of rules which are contained in Article 4 and Article 6 (1) of Regulation 17.

**509** **Plan of this chapter.** In this chapter, the general rules of notification relating to new agreements (apart from Art. 4 (2) agreements) are described first. These rules concern all those agreements coming into force after March 13, 1962, apart from Accession agreements already in existence on January 1, 1973 and falling within the Treaty solely as a result of accession. Next, the transitional rules are dealt with, first with regard to the position of Accession agreements and then, briefly, with regard to agreements in existence on March 13, 1962, but in both cases excluding Article 4 (2) agreements. The position of Article 4 (2) agreements is then considered in relation to new agreements, old agreements and Accession agreements. Finally, the procedure for notification is dealt with. Although in this chapter reference will be made only to agreements, it must be remembered that decisions and concerted practices are subject to, and may benefit from, notification.[30]

[30] Arts. 4 to 7 of Reg. 17.

## 2. NOTIFICATION: GENERAL RULES

**510**     **Generally.** The general rules discussed are those relating to
the notification of " new " agreements, *i.e.* (i) those which came
into effect between March 13, 1962 and January 1, 1973 and which
affected trade between the original Member States and restricted
competition within the then common market, and (ii) agreements
that came into effect after January 1, 1973 that affect trade
between the nine Member States and restrict competition within
the enlarged common market. The phrase " new agreement,"
although relative in concept, thus covers all agreements not
subject to transitional arrangements.

**511**     **Article 4 of Regulation 17.** Article 4 (1) of Regulation 17
provides that all new agreements which came into force after
March 13, 1962, or after the date of accession, as the case may
be, in respect of which the parties seek exemption under Article
85 (3), must be notified to the Commission. No exemption can
be granted unless notification is made. However, Article 4 (2)
provides that certain agreements need not be notified to the
Commission. Those agreements are discussed separately below.[31]
In this section the new agreements which do not fall within Article
4 (2) are considered.

**512**     **Effect of notification.** As long as a new agreement falling
within Article 85 (1) of the Treaty and outside Article 4 (2) of
Regulation 17 remains unnotified, the agreement is void [32] and
the Commission may impose fines in respect of infringements.[33]

**513**     **(a) Fines.** Fines may not be imposed after notification and
prior to the Commission taking a decision under Article 85 (3),
provided the parties do not go beyond the agreement that has
been notified.[34] Under Article 15 (6) of Regulation 17 the
Commission may inform the parties that after a preliminary
examination it feels that the application of Article 85 (3) is not
justified. If the parties continue to give effect to the agreement
after receiving such a communication, they may then be fined.

[31] *Post,* §§ 528 *et seq.*
[32] Art. 85 (2) of the Treaty. For consequences of nullity see *ante,* §§ 401 *et seq.*
[33] Art. 15 (2) of Reg. 17. *Post,* §§ 1205 *et seq.*
[34] Art. 15 (5) of Reg. 17. See *Pittsburgh Corning Europe,* J.O. 1972 L272/35,
[1973] C.M.L.R. D2.

In *Re Noordwijks Cement Accoord* [35] the European Court held that a communication from the Commission under Article 15 (6) must fully set out the reasons why Article 85 (3) cannot be applied. Since this decision, the Commission has made almost no use of the provisions of Article 15 (6) of Regulation 17, presumably because it is just as easy to issue a final decision under Article 85 (3).

**514**     **(b) Retroactivity.** If the Commission decides to grant an exemption under Article 85 (3) then under Article 6 (1) of Regulation 17 it is empowered to grant the exemption with retroactive effect to the date of notification.[36] Such a retroactive exemption will render the agreement fully valid and enforceable for the period fixed by the Commission. Such a retroactive exemption cannot take effect from a date earlier than notification. Hence, until the agreement is notified, the parties deprive themselves of the opportunity of obtaining retroactive exemption under Article 6 (1) even if Article 85 (3) is in fact satisfied during this period.[37]

**515**     **(c) Provisional validity.** In *Brasserie de Haecht (No. 2)* [38] the European Court held, in relation to new agreements falling under Article 4 (1), that such agreements do not obtain the advantages of provisional validity even though notified to the Commission.[39] In such cases the parties make the agreement at their own risk and notification is without suspensory effect. However, in a proper case a national court has a discretion to stay the proceedings, pending a decision by the Commission if any question arises as to the civil validity of a duly notified agreement. This jurisdiction should not be exercised where it is clear beyond doubt that the agreement infringes Article 85.[40]

---

[35] (8–11/66) [1967] C.M.L.R. 77 (*the Cimenteries case*).
[36] For the circumstances in which it will exercise this power, see *ante*, §§ 631 *et seq.* However, once an agreement has been notified the power to give retroactive exemption under Art. 6 (1) may not be of significance since duly notified agreements enjoy provisional validity pending the Commission's decision; see *post*, § 515, but see also *ante*, § 419.
[37] See *e.g. Re Sopelem and Langen & Co.*, J.O. 1972 L13/47, [1972] C.M.L.R. D77 at p. D82.
[38] (48/72), February 6, 1973.
[39] See *ante*, §§ 410–422.
[40] *Brasserie de Haecht (No. 2)*, note 38, *supra*.

**516**     **Late notification and omission to notify.** Agreements can
always be notified late (*i.e.* after the agreement has come into
effect), but they do not obtain any of the benefits of notification
during any period in which the agreement was unnotified.
Omission to notify results in the loss of an opportunity to obtain
exemption, including potentially retroactive exemption, and
possibly, a fine for practising the prohibited agreement prior to
the notification. It has been suggested that, since an agreement
falling within Article 85 (1) is void under Article 85 (2), notification requires the consent of all the parties to the agreement
before such notification can affect the legal position of the parties
*inter se*.[41]

### 3.  NOTIFICATION: TRANSITIONAL RULES

#### (a)  *Accession Agreements*

**517**     **Article 25.** Articles 5, 6 (2) and 7 of Regulation 17 contain
transitional provisions in favour of agreements that were already
in existence on March 13, 1962. Under the " Act concerning the
Conditions of Accession and the Adjustments to the Treaties "
(the Act) annexed to the Decision of the Council of the EEC of
January 22, 1972, amendments and adaptations are made to the
existing Regulations, Decisions and Directions of the Community
to take account of the accession of the new Member States.[42]
The Act amends Regulation 17 by adding thereto a new Article
25.[43] This Article makes transitional arrangements for all
agreements in existence on January 1, 1973 and falling within the
Treaty solely as a result of accession. This part of this chapter is
concerned with those Accession agreements which fall outside
Article 4 (2) of Regulation 17.[44]

**518**     **Provisions of Article 25.** Agreements originally in force on
March 13, 1962 obtained the benefit of the transitional provisions
of Articles 5, 6 (2) and 7 if they were notified within a certain
period from the " date of entry into force " of Regulation 17.
The main effect of Article 25 is to provide that as far as Accession
agreements are concerned, the date of accession shall be sub-

---

[41] Mégret, Waelbroeck and others, p. 125; but Reg. 27, Art. 1 (1), *post*. §§ 534 *et
seq.* suggests that any party may notify unilaterally.
[42] J.O. 1972 L73/12, 14, Cmnd. 4862, I and II.
[43] J.O. 1972 L73, 92, Cmnd. 4862, II, p. 74.
[44] For Art. 4 (2) agreements see *post*, § 528.

stituted in every place where the phrase " date of entry into force " appears in Regulation 17. In addition Article 25 (2) and (3) provide:

> " (2) Accession agreements must be notified pursuant to Article 5 (1) and Article 7 (1) and (2) of Regulation 17 within six months of accession;
>
> (3) no fines may be imposed for any act done prior to notification of an Accession agreement, provided that the agreement is notified within six months."

The combined effect of Article 25 and Articles 5, 6 (2) and 7 of Regulation 17 in respect of agreements not falling within Article 4 (2) of Regulation 17 is discussed in the next following paragraphs.

**519**    **Date for notification.** Accession agreements not falling within Article 4 (2) of Regulation 17 must be notified " within six months of Accession." The Accession of the United Kingdom occurred at midnight on January 1, 1973. Accordingly, it is considered that Accession Agreements must be notified by June 30, 1973. Under Article 3 of Regulation 27,[45] the effective date of a notification is the date upon which it is received by the Commission, unless the notification is sent by registered post, in which case it is deemed to have been received on the date shown on the postmark of the place of posting. Accordingly, in order to be valid, notification must either be in the Commission's hands by June 30, 1973, or be sent by registered mail bearing a postmark not later than June 30, 1973.

**520**    **Effect of timely notification.** If Accession agreements are notified by June 30, 1973, then

(i) no fines can be imposed for acts committed prior to notification [46];

(ii) the benefit of an exemption can be made effective from a date earlier than that of notification and back to January 1, 1973 [47];

(iii) the parties can obtain the advantages of Article 7 (1) [48];

(iv) the agreement probably has provisional validity.[49]

---

[45] *Post*, § 538.
[46] Art. 25 (3) of Reg. 17.
[47] Art. 25 and Art. 6 (2) of Reg. 17.
[48] *Post*, §§ 523, 524.
[49] *Ante*, §§ 403, 410 *et seq.*

**521**　　**Fines.** The protection against fines extends to acts committed prior to notification and continues until the Commission declares that application of Article 85 (3) cannot be justified or issues a communication under Article 15 (6) of Regulation 17.[50]

**522**　　**Retroactive exemptions.** Although in the case of new agreements exemption cannot be made effective earlier than the date of notification, in the case of Accession agreements exemption can be granted with effect from the date when Article 85 (1) became applicable (*i.e.* January 1, 1973), provided that such agreements are notified in due time.[51] But this advantage may be of limited significance since, under the doctrine of provisional validity, duly notified agreements are probably enforceable in respect of the period between January 1, 1973 and the Commission's decision.[52]

**523**　　**Article 7 (1).** Article 7 (1) of Regulation 17, as amended by Article 25, provides that if Accession agreements are notified to the Commission by June 30, 1973, and the parties cease to give effect to them or modify them in such a way that they no longer fall under Article 85 (1), or that they satisfy Article 85 (3), the Commission can declare that the prohibition of Article 85 (1) " shall apply only for the period fixed by the Commission." Hitherto, the Commission has always declared, pursuant to Article 7 (1), that the prohibition of Article 85 (1) was inapplicable as from the date of entry into force of Regulation 17, in all cases where the parties have so modified their agreements as to entitle them either to negative clearance or to exemption under Article 85 (3).[53] There is no reason to suppose that the Commission will not adopt a similar practice in respect of Accession agreements. However, duly notified Accession agreements are probably provisionally valid until a decision of the Commission refusing

[50] Art. 25 (3) of Reg. 17; also see *ante*, § 513.
[51] Art. 6 (2) of Reg. 17.
[52] See *ante*, §§ 415–418.
[53] For an example in the case of exemption under Art. 85 (3) see *Re Lightweight Paper*, J.O. 1972 L182/24, [1972] C.M.L.R. D94, D101. For an example in the case of a negative clearance see *Re Supexie*, J.O. 1972 L10/12, [1971] C.M.L.R. D1, D5; for a refusal to apply Art. 7 (1) see *Re German Ceramic Tiles*, J.O. 1971 L10/15, [1971] C.M.L.R. D6, D20.

exemption under Article 85 (3),[54] or refusing to apply the provisions of Article 7 (1).

524    **Dissenting parties.** The second sentence of Article 7 (1) provides that any decision under the Article " cannot apply as against undertakings and associations of undertakings who have not expressly consented to the notification." The purpose of this limited provision is to ensure that the exercise by the Commission of its powers under Article 7 (1) should not affect the legal position of those parties who did not consent to the notification of the agreement.

525    **Provisional validity.** Accession agreements will probably benefit from the doctrine of provisional validity, the effects of which have been discussed in Chapter 4.[55]

526    **Late notification or omission to notify.** It follows from Article 25 that until June 30, 1973 parties to Accession agreements benefit from provisional validity[56] and relief from the liability to be fined.[57] These advantages continue after June 30, 1973 only if Accession agreements are notified by that date. Similarly only notification by that date enables the parties to take advantage of Article 7 (1). Late notification, after June 30, 1973, can always be made, possibly only with the consent of the parties,[58] but the agreement will be void from January 1, 1973 onwards. Furthermore, the parties may be liable to be fined for acts committed before notification. The advantages of Article 7 (1) will not be available if the agreement is notified and subsequently obtains exemption under Article 85 (3); the exemption cannot take effect from a date earlier than notification.[59]

### (b) *Agreements in Existence on March 13, 1962*

527    **Transitional rules.** The rules relating to the notification of agreements in existence on March 13, 1962 may be summarised as follows. Under Article 5 (1) of Regulation 17, existing agree-

---

[54] *Ante*, §§ 415–418.
[55] See *ante*, §§ 415–418.
[56] *Ante*, § 419.          [57] Art. 25 (3).          [58] See *ante*, § 516.
[59] Art. 6 of Reg. 17, *e.g.* see *Re Davidson Rubber*, J.O. 1972 L143/31, [1972] C.M.L.R. D52, D62. Compare the fate of the Davidson-Maglum contract in that case.

ments not falling within Article 4 (2) had to be notified before November 1, 1962, or in the case of bilateral contracts, before February 1, 1963. If they were so notified, they could obtain the benefits of retroactive exemption under Article 6 (2) with effect from a date earlier than that of notification. They could also obtain the benefit of Article 7 (1) and, under Article 15 (5), relief from liability to be fined.

### 4. Agreements Falling Within Article 4 (2) of Regulation 17

**528**     **Notification of Article 4 (2) agreements.** The requirements of notification have been relaxed in favour of agreements falling within Article 4 (2) of Regulation 17. Such agreements are not required to be notified to the Commission for the purpose of obtaining exemption under Article 85 (3). In considering the position of Article 4 (2) agreements, it is again necessary to distinguish between old agreements, Accession agreements and new agreements.[60] One rule, however, is common to all such agreements: If the Commission grants an exemption in respect of an agreement falling within Article 4 (2) such exemption may take effect retroactively to the date of the agreement and not merely to the date of the notification.[61] Bearing in mind that common factor, the additional rules applying only to Accession agreements falling within Article 4 (2) may be summarised as follows:

    (i) even if unnotified, such agreements probably remain provisionally valid until such time as their nullity is established by a decision of the competent authorities. It is probable that such agreements then become void retroactively in the event of such adverse decision [62];

    (ii) parties to unnotified Article 4 (2) Accession agreements are technically subject to the possibility of a fine,[63] but in practice the imposition of such a fine seems unlikely;

    (iii) Accession agreements falling within Article 4 (2) and notified before July 1, 1973 may benefit from Article 7 (1) and (2) of Regulation 17.[64]

---

[60] For " old," " new," and " Accession " agreements, see *ante*, § 508.
[61] Art. 6 (2) of Reg. 17.
[62] See *ante*, §§ 413–414.
[63] Arts. 15 (2) and 15 (5) of Reg. 17.
[64] Art. 25 (2) of Reg. 17.

Thus, notification before July 1, 1973 (i) protects the parties from fines from January 1, 1973 until a Commission decision and (ii) enables the parties to benefit from Article 7 (1) of Regulation 17. Notification after July 1, 1973 protects the parties as from the date of notification, but they would not benefit from Article 7 (1). On the other hand, notification at any time does not materially increase the provisional validity already enjoyed by the agreement: and the Commission seems unlikely to impose fines in respect of unnotified Article 4 (2) agreements. New Article 4 (2) agreements do not enjoy provisional validity,[65] whether notified or not, nor do they benefit from Article 7 (1) and (2) of Regulation 17. Parties are protected from fines as from the date of notification.

**529**    **Scope of Article 4 (2): domestic agreements.**    Article 4 (2) (i) relaxes the notification requirements in respect of agreements between undertakings situated in the same Member State which " involve neither imports nor exports between Member States." Article 4 (2) (i) is thus concerned with those agreements which fall under Article 85 (1) in that they affect trade between Member States, but at the same time do not " involve imports or exports " between those States. This problem was considered by the European Court in the *Bilger* [66] case. That decision concerned a " requirements " contract between a brewery and the owner of an inn, both situated in Germany. The Court held that a contract between a producer and an independent dealer both situated in the same Member State, in which the latter agreed to buy exclusively from the former, did not " involve imports or exports " where the execution of the agreement did not involve the goods in question crossing any national frontiers. Hence, an exclusive supply contract of the type discussed in *Bilger* is not subject to notification, even though the effect of that agreement may be to prevent the dealer from importing products from another Member State: such an agreement does not *directly* involve imports or exports. Thus, it is fairly clear that *e.g.* tied house contracts and " solus " petrol agreements, even if they fall under Article 85 (1),[67] need not be notified where the parties are from

---

[65] *Brasserie de Haecht (No. 2)* (48/72), February 6, 1973; *ante,* § 419.
[66] (43/69) 8 C.M.L.Rev. 1971, 241.   See also *ante,* § 414 and see *Re Patent Licence Rights* [1971] C.M.L.R. 564 (a German decision).
[67] *Post,* § 836.

the same Member State. It is not, however, clear how far the *Bilger* decision affects national exclusive dealing agreements where a manufacturer in one Member State seeks to prevent his distributors in that State from *exporting* to other Member States. If, for example, a manufacturer in the United Kingdom agrees to supply his sole distributor with products for resale only within a defined part of the United Kingdom, *e.g.* Kent, it may be argued that such an agreement does not involve imports or exports, and is not subject to notification.[68] If this is right, it may also be that the agreement continues to fall within Article 4 (2) even if the manufacturer undertakes to supply goods " for resale only within any part of the United Kingdom." Such a restriction has exactly the same effect as the restriction against selling outside Kent—it prevents exports from the United Kingdom. It remains to be seen whether an agreement, which has the effect of preventing exports in circumstances where the area to which the distributor is confined is co-terminous with that of a Member State, falls outside Article 4 (2). If, of course, the agreement contains an express ban on exports it is more difficult to argue that the agreement does " not involve imports or exports." The result of the *Bilger* decision may be that a national exclusive dealing agreement may fall within Article 4 (2) if it only indirectly achieves a ban on exports without containing any express prohibition. Where the agreement contains no direct or indirect ban on exports, then the problem of " involving imports and exports " does not arise, and the agreement is not subject to notification.

**530**    **The Commission's view.** In the *Guide Pratique* [69] the Commission states that purely regional arrangements for specialisation or exclusive rights, which only indirectly affect imports and exports, are not subject to notification by virtue of Article 4 (2) (i); nor are price arrangements or arrangements limiting production between undertakings in a single Member State, provided that imports and exports are not concerned; thus a national arrangement permitting exports but prohibiting re-imports, or a national arrangement for joint buying in another Member State will be subject to notification. Further the Commission regards Article

[68] See submissions of Adv.-Gen. Gand in *Bilger* (43/69) 16 Rec. 127; CMR § 8112.
[69] Part II (III), (3).

4 (2) (i) as having no application where the agreement in question discriminates in its treatment of domestic products and imported products, or where the provisions of the agreement itself are applied to imported goods, *e.g.* in fixing the resale price. Thus a cartel agreement between Dutch liquorice producers which, *inter alia,* fixed uniform prices for imported products and sought to prevent wholesalers from taking imported supplies, was, in the Commission's view, notifiable.[70] If parties are in doubt as to whether their agreement " involves imports or exports " between Member States, the prudent course is to notify.

**531**    **Resale price maintenance and conditions of sale.**  Article 4 (2) (ii) (a) relaxes the notification requirements in respect of agreements between only two undertakings where the sole effect is to restrict the freedom of one party to determine the prices at which or conditions of business on which goods obtained from the other may be resold.  This provision applies whether or not the parties are situated in the same Member State and whether or not the goods concerned are exported to some other Member State.  But it applies only where the *sole* restriction accepted is a unilateral restriction on one party as to prices and terms of resale.[71]  An agreement may be " between only two undertakings " even if it is one of a series of identical agreements.[72]

**532**    **Other provisions of Article 4 (2).**  Article 4 (2) (ii) (b) exempts from notification agreements imposing unilateral restrictions upon the assignee or user of industrial property rights, or upon a person entitled under a contract to make use of know-how relating to manufacture or to the application of industrial processes.[73]  Article 4 (2) (iii)[74] exempts from notification agreements having as their *sole* object (a) the development or uniform application of certain standards or types[75]; (b) joint research and development[76]; (c) specialisation in manufacture,

[70] Reply to Written Question 440/70 (Vredeling), J.O. 1971 C29/9.
[71] For the position of resale price maintenance in the common market see *ante,* §§ 318 *et seq.*
[72] *Parfums Marcel Rochas* (1/70) [1971] C.M.L.R. 104.
[73] See *post,* § 957.
[74] As amended by Reg. 2822/71.
[75] *Ante,* § 328.
[76] *Post,* §§ 1101 *et seq.*

including agreements necessary for its achievement, where the products concerned do not hold more than 15 per cent. of the relevant market and the total turnover of the participating undertakings does not exceed 200 million units of account.[77]

**533     Agreements within more than one category.** The several categories of Articles 4 (2) (i), (ii) and (iii) are not expressed in the alternative. Thus, if an agreement falls within more than one category (*e.g.* a domestic agreement under Art. 4 (2) (i) which also imposes restrictions on the assignee of industrial property rights under Art. 4 (2) (ii) (b) ) it does not thereby lose the benefit of Article 4 (2). One particular problem arises under Article 4 (2) (iii). If an agreement has as its object not only standardisation (Art. 4 (2) (iii) (a) ) but also joint research and development (Art. 4 (2) (iii) (b) ) and specialisation (Art. 4 (2) (iii) (c) ), is the agreement subject to notification where its *cumulative* objects do not extend beyond those permitted under Article 4 (2) (iii)? While in many cases there may be no good reason to deprive an agreement of the benefit of Article 4 (2) in these circumstances, it may also be true that the competitive effects of, for example, a specialisation agreement differ according to whether it also contains additional provisions relating to research and development or standardisation. It must therefore be doubtful whether an agreement falls within Article 4 (2) when it contains provisions the objects of which relate to more than one of the permitted objects set out in Article 4 (2) (iii).[78]

## 5. NOTIFICATION PROCEDURE

**534     Regulation 27.** The procedure by which notification under Articles 4 and 5 of Regulation 17 should be made is set out in Regulation 27 as amended.[79] This Regulation also deals with the procedure for making applications for negative clearance under Article 2 of Regulation 17. The rules for notification described here also apply, *mutatis mutandis*, to applications for negative clearance.

[77] *Post*, §§ 1001 *et seq.* esp. §§ 1043 *et seq.*
[78] *Cf. Registrar of Restrictive Trading Agreements* v. *Schweppes* (*No. 2*) [1971] 2 All. E.R. 1473.
[79] By Reg. 1133/68.

**535** **Procedure.** Any contracting party may notify the agreement, but notice must be given to all parties who do not join in the notification.[80] If notifications are made jointly a joint representative must be appointed.[81] All persons signing notifications on behalf of undertakings must produce proof that they are authorised to act.[82] Seven copies of the notification must be filed [83] on Form A/B [84] set out in the Annex to the Regulation, together with seven copies of supporting documents which may be duly certified copies.[85] Notifications must be completed in one of the Community languages,[86] translations of any original documents being supplied.[87] Agreements may be notified late.[88] Fines may be imposed for false information supplied on form A/B.[89]

**536** **Form A/B.** The contents of this form appear from the specimen set out in Appendix 2. Copies of it may be obtained from the Information Service of the European Communities, 23 Chesham Street, London S.W.1, and other Information Offices of the EEC in Member States. Copies are also obtainable from the Commission, 200 Rue de la Loi, Brussels, from the Department of Trade and Industry, Victoria Street, London S.W.1 and from Chambers of Commerce in the Member States. It should be noted that Form A/B may be used both as an application for negative clearance and as a notification for the purpose of obtaining an exemption. Application for negative clearance should not be made without completing the part relating to notification, but it may be left to the Commission to decide which is appropriate.[90] The form provides that the parties are free to produce further arguments in support of their contentions.[91] For

[80] Art. 1 (1) of Reg. 27.
[81] Art. 1 (3).
[82] Art. 1 (2).
[83] Art. 2 (1).
[84] The Separate Forms A, B and B1 provided by Art. 4 of Reg. 27 are no longer in use; see Reg. 1133/68.
[85] Art. 2 (2).
[86] But not in Erse. See Reg. No. 1, Art. 1, as amended by Art. 29 of the Act concerning the Conditions of Accession and Adjustments to the Treaties, Annex 1, XIV (1), J.O. 1972 L/73, Cmnd. 4864, II, 134.
[87] Reg. 27, Art. 2 (3).
[88] But see *ante*, §§ 516, 526.
[89] Art. 15 (1) of Reg. 17.
[90] See *ante*, § 503.
[91] See Form A/B, Part VI.

the purposes of notification it is not necessary to complete in detail Parts IV and V of the Form (which require reasons in support of an application for negative clearance or for an exemption). These may be supplemented later. The parties are entitled to expect the Commission to assist in establishing the relevant facts and circumstances by its own investigation.[92]

**537    Standard form contracts.** In the case of a contract which the notifying party concludes regularly with specified persons or groups of persons, it is sufficient to annex to Form A/B the text of the standard form. Agreements which are a copy of this standard form benefit from the notification of the standard contract as from the date when that notification takes effect.[93]

**538    Date when notification takes effect.** Notification takes effect on the date when it was received by the Commission, or in the case of a notification made by registered post, from the date shown on the postmark in the country of posting.[94]

**539    Secrecy.** Under Article 20 (2) of Regulation 17 the Commission, authorities of Member States, their servants and officials are under an obligation not to disclose any information received by them as a result of the application of Regulation 17, provided that such information is " of the kind covered by professional secrecy " *e.g.* information transmitted to the Commission in confidence. Further, the information obtained by the Commission may be used only for the purpose for which it was supplied.[95] There is no public register of agreements which have been notified.[96] Under Article 19 (3) of Regulation 17, prior to reaching a favourable decision the Commission must publish the gist of the notification and invite interested third parties to submit their comments. In such publication the Commission must have regard to the legitimate interests of undertakings in the protection of their business interests.

---

[92] *Grundig and Consten* v. *EEC Commission* (56/64, 58/64) [1966] C.M.L.R. 418.
[93] *Parfums Marcel Rochas Vetriebs G.m.b.H.* v. *Bitsch* (1/70) [1971] C.M.L.R. 104, 116, 117. And see *Brasserie de Haecht* (*No. 2*) (48/72), February 6, 1973.
[94] Art. 3 of Reg. 27.
[95] Art. 20 (1) of Reg. 17.
[96] See also Written Answer to Question No. 45/70 J.O. 1970 C86.

**540** **Post notification procedure.** The procedure following receipt
of the notification is fully described in Chapter 12. The Commission has never made a formal decision under seven months
(in *Re Henkel-Colgate*,[37] an exceptional case where the agreement
was expressed to be subject to the Commission's approval). The
average time taken is about two years, often longer. Within
a very much shorter time, however, the Commission may inform
the parties informally that, in their view, an exemption is unlikely
to be granted or that the agreement falls outside Article 85 (1)
altogether. In some circumstances the parties may be prepared
to accept the Commission's views without the necessity of the
Commission taking any formal decision.

[The next paragraph is 601.]

[37] J.O. 1972 L14/14. Compare a period of nearly 10 years in *Re Lightweight Paper*, J.O. 1972 L182/24, [1972] C.M.L.R. D94.

CHAPTER 6

## ARTICLE 85 (3)

### 1. INTRODUCTION

**601**     **Agreements in respect of which exemption may be granted.**
Article 85 (3) of the Treaty provides [1] that the provisions of
Article 85 (1) may be declared inapplicable in the case of " any
agreement or category of agreements between undertakings, any
decision or category of decisions of associations of undertakings
and any concerted practice or category of concerted practices "
which fulfils all of the following four conditions:

   (a) contributes to improving the production or distribution
       of goods or to promoting technical or economic progress,
       and
   (b) allows consumers a fair share of the resulting benefit, and
   (c) imposes on the parties only restrictions which are in-
       dispensable to the attainment of these objectives, and
   (d) does not afford such undertakings the possibility of
       eliminating competition in respect of a substantial part
       of the products in question.

Article 85 (3) in effect provides one "gateway" through which
an agreement may pass if each one of the four conditions is
satisfied.

**602**     **Powers of the Commission.**     The Commission is the only
body which has power to grant or refuse an exemption pursuant
to Article 85 (3).[2]  However, its jurisdiction to grant exemption
for individual agreements can be exercised only in respect of
agreements which have been notified.[3]  As far as the future is
concerned, the Commission has power to declare the exemption
only in respect of a specified period.  In addition, it has powers to
attach conditions and obligations to the exemption, or to revoke

---

[1] The full text of Art. 85 is set out in App. 1, *post*.
[2] Art. 9 (1) of Reg. 17.
[3] Arts. 4 (1), 5 (1) and 25 of Reg. 17; but see also Art. 4 (2) of Reg. 17.  For
notification generally see §§ 501 *et seq*.  For notification procedure see §§ 534
*et seq*.

it.[4] As far as the past is concerned, the Commission has power in appropriate circumstances to declare the prohibition of Article 85 (1) inapplicable with retroactive effect.[5] The procedure which the Commission must observe following notification but before the grant or refusal of an exemption is set out in Chapter 12.[6]

**603**  **The Burden of proof.** The burden of showing that Article 85 (3) is satisfied lies primarily upon the undertakings concerned, but the Commission is under an obligation to co-operate in the establishment of the relevant facts and circumstances. The parties are entitled to receive a fair and adequate examination of their contentions.[7] In reaching its decisions the Commission is prepared to act on the basis of probabilities.[8]

**604**  **Discretionary power of the Commission.** Article 85 (3) provides that the Commission *may* grant an exemption if the four conditions of that Article are satisfied. Although it is doubtful whether the Commission could lawfully deny an exemption if all the requirements for a favourable decision were in fact fulfilled, in practice the Commission retains a considerable discretion in the application of Article 85 (3). This derives from the limited nature of the review of the Commission's decisions, against which an appeal lies to the European Court under Article 173 of the Treaty.[9] The European Court has held that the exercise of the Commission's powers under Article 85 (3) necessarily implies complex economic judgments, and the European Court must respect the character of those judgments. Provided that the Commission has (i) followed the correct procedure, (ii) taken into account all the material facts, (iii) applied a proper interpretation of the principles of the Treaty, and (iv) set out the reasoning upon which it bases its conclusions, the Court will not interfere with the Commission's economic assessments.[10] Hence, within the limits of procedural and interpretative control by the Court, the

[4] Art. 8 of Reg. 17; see *post*, §§ 633 *et seq.*
[5] Arts. 6 and 7 of Reg. 17; see *post*, §§ 631, 632.
[6] *Post*, §§ 1221 *et seq.*
[7] *Consten and Grundig* v. *EEC Commission* (56/64, 58/64) [1966] C.M.L.R. 418, 477.
[8] *Re ACEC-Berliet*, J.O. 1968 L201/7, [1968] C.M.L.R. D35, 40.
[9] *Post*, §§ 1227 *et seq.*
[10] *Consten and Grundig* v. *EEC Commission* (56/64, 58/64) [1966] C.M.L.R. 418, 477.

Commission is free to use Article 85 (3) to develop a competition policy for the European Community.

605    **Policy of the Commission.** Broadly speaking, the policy of the Commission under Article 85 (3) has been to encourage co-operation between undertakings where that co-operation is likely to produce favourable economic results and lead to increasingly effective competition within the common market.[11] Thus, hitherto, the main types of agreement in respect of which the Commission has granted individual exemptions are exclusive dealing,[12] specialisation,[13] research and development,[14] patent licence and know-how agreements.[15] Bilateral exclusive dealing agreements, once they have been freed from export and reimport prohibitions which might perpetuate divisions between national markets, have been considered to contribute to improving the distribution of goods. Specialisation agreements have been approved where the Commission has considered that they would encourage co-operation between firms so that they could better compete with large undertakings and make better, more rational, use of resources. Joint research and development agreements and patent and know-how licences lead to technical progress, promoting scientific innovation and development. The Commission's policy of promoting co-operation in these cases is now reflected in the Regulations relating to block exemptions for certain categories of agreements.[16]

06    Within the Commission's general policy of promoting co-operation where the results are likely to be beneficial, even at the expense of permitting restrictions on competition as between the parties, one particular factor has been important. In order to promote more effective competition with large undertakings, the Commission has sought to encourage co-operation between medium and small-sized firms. Thus in *Re Transocean Marine Paint Association*,[17] a group of small marine paint manufacturers situated all over the world (including five common market

[11] See generally First Report on Competition (1972) paras. 1–58.
[12] See also *post*, §§ 801 *et seq.*
[13] See also *post*, §§ 1011 *et seq.*
[14] See also *post*, §§ 1101 *et seq.*
[15] See also *post*, §§ 901 *et seq.*
[16] *Post*, § 609.
[17] J.O. 1967 163/10, [1967] C.M.L.R. D9.

countries) were endeavouring to establish, against fierce competition, a common brand of " Transocean " paint. The Commission held that the restrictions accepted by the parties would enable the group to ensure that Transocean paint was widely distributed and readily available at many points round the world; this in turn would enable the members to compete more successfully with strong international groups.

**607** However, each case ultimately depends very much on its own facts and the particular circumstances of the parties. In *Re Lightweight Paper* [18] the undertakings concerned were situated in the same Member State and held 80 per cent. of the national market. The Commission approved a specialisation agreement under which the principal French manufacturers of cigarette and other lightweight papers each agreed to limit their production only to certain types and qualities of paper. Again in *Re Henkel-Colgate* [19] the Commission granted, albeit subject to a number of conditions, exemption in respect of a research and development agreement between two of the four largest suppliers of detergents in the common market, who together had a very substantial market share, despite the fact that the effect of the agreement was to eliminate competition as between the parties in one vital area, that of research.

**608** As those, and other,[20] decisions demonstrate, there are dangers in attempting to lay down principles which apply generally to decisions under Article 85 (3). However, certain types of agreement have been consistently refused exemption.[21] These are, in particular, market sharing agreements [22] and agreements relating to price fixing [23] and quotas.[24] More particularly Article 85 (3) has never been applied in respect of agreements tending to lead to the protection of a particular national market, such as collective exclusive dealing agreements,[25] national

[18] J.O. 1972 L182/24, [1972] C.M.L.R. D94; *post*, § 630 and see § 1009.
[19] J.O. 1971 L14/14, *post*, § 630; and see § 1107.
[20] See *e.g. FN-CF*, J.O. 1971 L134/6; *MAN-SAVIEM*, J.O. 1972 L31/29.
[21] See First Report on Competition (1972) para. 1.
[22] *Re Van Katwijk's Agreement*, J.O. 1970 L242/18, [1970] C.M.L.R. D43; *post*, § 621.
[23] *Re* VCH, J.O. 1972 L13/34, [1973] C.M.L.R. D16 and (8/72) [1973] C.M.L.R. 7. See *post*, § 620.
[24] *Re Lightweight Paper*, J.O. 1972 L182/24, [1972] C.M.L.R. D94.
[25] See *ante*, §§ 311 *et seq.*

aggregated rebate schemes [26] or collective national price fixing agreements which regulate the prices of imported or exported goods,[27] or joint selling agreements relating to export markets within the EEC.[28] The possibility of an exemption being granted in respect of agreements to discriminate between customers or suppliers according to their Member State may be regarded as extremely remote.[29]

**609** **Block exemptions.** In addition to carrying out its policy by means of individual exemptions, the Commission has been given power to make regulations exempting certain categories of agreements *en bloc*. Regulations 19/65 empowers the Commission to exempt certain types of exclusive dealing agreements and certain types of licensing agreements, while Regulation 2821/71 gives a similar power in respect of certain standardisation, research and development and specialisation agreements. The Commission has exercised its powers to grant block exemptions in respect of exclusive dealing agreements under Regulation 67/67, [30] and has also published Regulation 2779/72 which now exempts certain specialisation agreements. [31] Agreements which fall within the conditions set out in these Regulations of the Commission providing for " block exemption " automatically benefit from the declaration of the inapplicability of Article 85 (1) contained therein and do not require to be notified.[32]

2. THE BENEFITS OF THE AGREEMENT

**610** **In general.** In order to obtain individual exemption under Article 85 (3) the parties must first show that the agreement is likely to have a beneficial effect in any one of four respects, namely, that it may contribute (i) to an improvement in the production of goods or (ii) to an improvement in the distribution of

---

[26] *Re German Ceramic Tile Agreement*, J.O. 1971 L10/15, [1971] C.M.L.R. D6; *post*, § 618.
[27] *Re VCH*, J.O. 1972 L13/34, [1973] C.M.L.R. D16 and (8/72) [1973] C.M.L.R. 7. See *post*, § 620.
[28] *Re Nederlandse Cement Handelsmaatschappij*, J.O. 1972 L22/16; *post*, § 619.
[29] See *Pittsburgh Corning Europe*, J.O. 1972 L272/35, [1973] C.M.L.R. D2.
[30] *Post*, §§ 818 *et seq.*
[31] *Post*, §§ 1023 *et seq.*
[32] Notification requirements are also relaxed in favour of agreements within Art. 4 (2) of Reg. 17; see *ante*, § 528.

goods or (iii) to technical progress or (iv) to economic progress.[33] It is sufficient if there is a reasonable probability that the benefits relied upon will materialise in the future.[34]

**611**   **Objective benefit necessary.** Whether any of the four benefits set out above are present must be judged not merely subjectively from the point of view of parties to the agreement but from the point of view of persons other than the parties.[35]   In continental jurisprudence this requirement is expressed by saying that the benefits must be " objective " benefits and that their effects must be judged " objectively." It is not sufficient, however, merely to consider the position of consumers, whose interests are protected under the second limb of Article 85 (3). The position of the parties' competitors must be considered and the advantages of the agreement judged from the point of view of the economy of the common market as a whole.[36]

**612**   **Benefit must be sufficient to balance reduction in competition.** In *Grundig-Consten*, the European Court held that the objective advantages to be obtained from the agreement must be sufficient to compensate for the consequent reduction in competition.[37]   In practice, the Commission has tended to balance on the one hand the advantages to be obtained from the agreement, and on the other hand the disadvantages resulting from the elimination of competition, judging the matter in relation to the situation which would prevail if the agreement did not exist.[38]   In several decisions the Commission has refused an exemption where the advantages claimed for the agreement did not outweigh the disadvantages resulting from restrictions on competition.[39]   In particular, an exemption will be refused where it cannot be shown

---

[33] Useful comparisons may be made between the decisions of the Commission under Article 85 (3) and the judgments of the Restrictive Practices Court in relation to the justification of registrable agreements under section 21 of the Restrictive Trade Practices Act 1956. See Chitty, *Contracts*, 23rd ed., Vol. II, paras. 1231 *et seq.*

[34] *Re ACEC-Berliet*, J.O. 1968 L201/7, [1968] C.M.L.R. D35, 40.

[35] *Consten and Grundig* v. *EEC Commission* (56/64, 58/64), [1966] C.M.L.R. 418, 478–9.

[36] *Re German Ceramic Tile Agreement*, J.O. 1971 L10/15, [1971] C.M.L.R. D6, D19.

[37] [1966] C.M.L.R. 418, 478.

[38] *e.g. Re German Ceramic Tile Agreement*, J.O. 1971 L10/15, [1971] C.M.L.R. D6, D19.

[39] See *post*, §§ 617–621. See also *Re CRN-1971*, J.O. 1972 L303/7; *Re Cimbel*, J.O. 1972 L303/24.

that the restrictions on competition contained in the agreement
are more likely than competition itself to produce the economic
benefits relied upon.[40]

**613      Improvements in production: examples.** Broadly speaking,
those agreements which have been exempted on the grounds that
they improve production have been specialisation [41] and research
and development [42] agreements. Improvements in production
have been held to result where the agreement has led to reduced
production costs, or increased productivity, for example because
the parties are enabled to concentrate their manufacture, or to
manufacture in long runs, to eliminate unprofitable production
or to draw up manufacturing programmes more easily.[43]
Improvements in production have also been found where the
agreement allows the parties to increase automation, to improve
quality control or to achieve standardisation of types.[44] The
Commission has also held that the elimination of duplication in
research,[45] or in surveys and investment,[46] contributes to an
improvement in production.

**614      Improvements in distribution: examples.** Improvements in
distribution have resulted in exemptions being granted in respect
of exclusive dealing agreements [47] and specialisation agreements,[48]
agreements rationalising trade fairs,[49] and in one case to enable
an association of small- and medium-sized paint manufacturers
to compete more effectively with larger organisations.[50] As far
as exclusive dealing agreements are concerned, the improvements

[40] *Re Vereeniging van Cementhaddelaren*, J.O. 1972 L13/34; *post*, § 620; *Re
Belgian Central Heating Agreement*, J.O. 1972 L264/22, [1972] C.M.L.R. D130,
D142.
[41] *Post*, §§ 1001 *et seq.*
[42] *Post*, §§ 1101 *et seq.*
[43] See *e.g. Re ACEC-Berliet*, J.O. 1968 L201/7, [1968] C.M.L.R. D35, D40; *Re
Clima Chappée*, J.O. 1969 L195/1, [1970] C.M.L.R. D7; *Re Jaz-Peter*, J.O.
1969 L195/5, [1970] C.M.L.R. 129; *Re FN-CF*, J.O. 1971 L134/6; *Re Sopelem-
Langen*, J.O. 1972 L13/47; *Re MAN-SAVIEM*, J.O. 1972 L31/29; *Re Lightweight
Paper*, J.O. 1972 L182/24, [1972] C.M.L.R. D94. *Post*, §§ 1001 *et seq.* and
1101 *et seq.*
[44] *Re FN-CF*, note 43, *supra.*
[45] *e.g. Re ACEC-Berliet*, note 43, *supra*; *Re FN-CF*, note 43, *supra.*
[46] *Re Clima Chappée*, J.O. 1969 L195/1, [1970] C.M.L.R. D7.
[47] See *post*, §§ 801 *et seq.* esp. §§ 818 *et seq.*
[48] And see *post*, §§ 1001 *et seq.*
[49] *Re Cecimo*, J.O. 1969 L69/13, [1969] C.M.L.R. D1. *Re Cematex*, J.O. 1971
227/26.
[50] *Re Transocean Marine Paint Association*, J.O. 1967 163/10, [1967] C.M.L.R. D9;
*ante*, § 606.

in distribution, which led first to exemption of individual agreements and then to block exemption under Regulation 67/67,
were the more effective organisation of sales activities, continuity
of supply, easier access to the market and proper provision of
after-sales and guarantee services.[51]  In *Re Omega* [52] a selective
distribution arrangement not falling under Regulation 67/67
was exempted under Article 85 (3) where only by limiting the
number of approved retailers selling certain expensive products
could the manufacturers ensure that the retailers received sufficient
turnover to enable them to offer proper sales and promotional
services to their customers.   In considering specialisation agreements, the Commission has been satisfied of improvements in
distribution where the parties have been able to offer a more
complete range of products, reduce distribution costs, facilitate
their access to new markets or increase supplies available on the
market.[53]   Rationalisation of trade fairs has been held to improve
distribution where concentration saves heavy promotional
expenditure, avoids " shopping around " and enables demand to
be met more easily.[54]   Restrictions on production and on marketing have also been exempted in the interests of promoting the wide
distribution of a paint sold in common by small manufacturers
under a uniform trademark.[55]

**615**     **Technical progress.**  The promotion of technical progress has
only recently emerged as a distinct benefit qualifying an agreement
for exemption under Article 85 (3).   Indeed, in many of the
decisions of the Commission, it is generally discussed in the same
context as improvements to production, to which it is clearly
closely related.   Up to the present time, the relevant decisions
have been concerned with research and development, specialisation, and patent licences and know-how agreements.   Technical

---

[51] *Post*, §§ 818 *et seq*; for individual exemptions prior to Reg. 67/67 see *post*, § 815.
[52] J.O. 1970 L242/22, [1970] C.M.L.R. D49; *post*, §§ 625 and 801 *et seq*.  *Cf.*
as to restrictions relating to deliveries to qualified traders, *Re VCH*, J.O. 1972
L13/34, [1973] C.M.L.R. D16, and (8/72) [1973] C.M.L.R. 7.
[53] See the decisions cited at note 43, *supra;* and see §§ 1001 *et seq.*, *post*.
[54] *Re Cecimo*, J.O. 1969 L69/13, [1969] C.M.L.R. D1; *Re Cematex*, J.O. 1971
L227/26.
[55] *Re Transocean Marine Paint Association*, J.O. 1967 163/10, [1967] C.M.L.R.
D9; *ante*, § 606.  In that case the principal restriction accepted by the parties
was an obligation not to supply outside a designated territory except on payment
of a small commission to another party from whose designated territory the
order had come.

progress has been held to result from the concentration of technical research, or from the fruits of joint research,[56] exchange of technical information, specialised co-operation in manufacture and the offer of improved products.[57] In *Re Henkel-Colgate*,[58] the Commission relied solely on " technical progress " in order to exempt a joint research agreement which would inevitably lead to a reduction in competition in research in an oligopolistic market. In *Re Davidson Rubber Co.*,[59] the Commission held that exclusive patent and know-how licences contributed to technical progress where the agreement enabled European manufacturers of car accessories to exploit a new process for moulding elbow rests and cushions for motor cars and to adapt it to European tastes and requirements.

**616**    **Economic progress.** The decisions of the Commission up to the present time do not give any precise indication as to the meaning of the phrase " economic progress " in Article 85 (3). It has been held that the rationalisation of trade fairs may promote " economic progress "[60] and it has also been said that rationalisation achieved by a specialisation agreement will generate " increased competitiveness, technical improvements and economic progress."[61] In *Re Davidson Rubber Co.* [62] it was held that the exclusive patent and know-how licences relating to the new process also contributed to economic, as well as technical, progress. " Economic progress " however is a category that has not yet been fully exploited by those seeking exemptions under Article 85 (3). It may be that it is most appropriate to agreements relating to services where clearly improvements in the production or distribution of goods are inappropriate.

**617**    **Objective requirements not satisfied.** As already indicated,[63] the first limb of Article 85 (3) will not be satisfied unless judged objectively, from the point of view of the common market as a whole, the benefits of the agreement outweigh the disadvantages

---

[56] See *e.g. Re ACEC-Berliet, Re MAN-SAVIEM, Re FN-CF* (all cited at note 43, *supra*). *Re Henkel-Colgate*, J.O. 1971 L14/14.
[57] *e.g. Re Jaz-Peter*, J.O. 1969 L195/5, [1970] C.M.L.R. 129, 136, 137.
[58] J.O. 1971 L14/14.
[59] J.O. 1972 L143/31, [1972] C.M.L.R. D52.
[60] *Re Cecimo*, J.O. 1969 L69/13, [1969] C.M.L.R. D1.
[61] *Re Clima Chappée*, J.O. 1969 L195/1, [1970] C.M.L.R. D7, D12.
[62] Note 59, *supra*.                     [63] See §§ 611–612, *ante*.

resulting from the restrictions on competition. In each of the cases where an individual exemption has been granted these requirements have been satisfied. It is convenient now to illustrate certain cases where those requirements have not been satisfied. The following decisions also indicate the Commission's policy towards agreements which tend to fix prices, or to isolate national markets, or to divide markets between the participants.[64]

**618** **Re German Ceramic Tiles Agreement.** In *Re German Ceramic Tiles Agreement* [65] it was argued that an aggregated rebates cartel among German manufacturers, whereby rebates were paid to traders calculated on their total purchases from all German manufacturers, improved production and distribution. The scheme was alleged to improve distribution by encouraging market transparency, allowing a wider degree of choice and permitting the continuation of specialist advisory services. It was also said that the scheme enabled the smaller German manufacturers to specialise their production. The Commission held that specialisation would occur anyway among small undertakings in conditions of free competition. It also held that the effect of the scheme was to isolate the German market from the competition of non-German producers. Any benefits which resulted from the agreement did so only at the expense of producers in other Member States, who found themselves at a serious competitive disadvantage on the German market as a result of the cartel. This in turn led to a deterioration in the distribution of foreign products on the market. The Commission held that the alleged improvements merely benefited the parties and the objective improvements required under Article 85 (3) were not present.

**619** **The NCH case.** The *Nederlandse Cement Handelsmaatschappij (NCH)* [66] decision concerned a joint selling agency of German producers selling cement into the Dutch market. In this case, it was said that a centralised sales service kept costs down, as did more rational use of transport, a limitation on transhipment centres at Dutch ports, and economies of adver-

---

[64] See *ante*, § 608. See also *Re CRN-1971*, J.O. 1972 L303/7; *Re Cimbel*, J.O. 1972 L303/24; *Re Belgian Central Heating Agreement*, J.O. 1972 L264/22, [1972] C.M.L.R. D130, D142.
[65] J.O. 1971 L10/15, [1971] C.M.L.R. D6.
[66] J.O. 1972 L22/16.

tising. It was argued that if the members had to deliver individually, costs would rise. It was also said that the scheme enabled prompt deliveries to be made, and knowledge of the market reduced risks. The Commission however held that the scheme involved a serious reduction in competition. In all the circumstances the advantages of the agreement did not outweigh the disadvantage resulting from that reduction.

**620** **The VCH case.** The same point is illustrated from another aspect by the *VCH* [67] case, which concerned the resale price fixing scheme of an association of Dutch cement merchants. The association fixed prices to be charged by members for deliveries of less than 100 tonnes, and recommended prices for deliveries above that amount. Sales to non members were restricted. It was alleged that the scheme enabled cement of uniform quality to be sold under economical conditions by trained dealers. The Commission held that the scheme could not improve the quality of the cement and that it was not shown that other advantages alleged from the agreement could not exist if there was free competition, including competition from wholesalers who had hitherto been excluded from the market. In other words, when judged in the light of the situation which would exist in the absence of the agreement, that of free competition, it was impossible to say that the agreement would result in any benefits which would not flow from the increased efficiency ordinarily to be expected in a competitive market. Consequently, an exemption under 85 (3) was refused.

**621** **The Van Katwijk case.** In *Re Van Katwijk's Agreement* [68] there was a market sharing agreement between one Belgian and one Dutch manufacturer of certain tubes whereby the Dutch manufacturer agreed to keep wholly out of the Belgian market and the Belgian manufacturer agreed to sell no more than a fixed quota of products on the Dutch market. Without detailing the arguments adduced in favour of an exemption, the Commission held [69] that such an agreement could not improve production and

---

[67] J.O. 1972 L13/34, [1973] C.M.L.R. D16. And see (8/72) [1973] C.M.L.R. 7.
[68] J.O. 1970 L242/18, [1970] C.M.L.R. D43.
[69] [1970] C.M.L.R. D43, D47.

distribution, and that " the elimination pure and simple " of a competitor, either wholly or partially, did not promote technical or economic progress.

### 3. THE BENEFITS FOR CONSUMERS

**622    Consumers.** In order to satisfy the second limb of Article 85 (3) the agreement should allow consumers a fair share of the resulting benefit. This requirement therefore contains three elements (i) " consumers " (ii) " a fair share " and (iii) " a resulting benefit." The first question is whether the expression " consumers " is limited to end users (or even consumers in the popular sense of such users who acquire the goods otherwise than for the purposes of a trade or business) or whether the expression includes trade purchasers whether they acquire the goods for use in the manufacture of other goods or even simply for resale. There is no authority that assists one to answer this question, but the use of the word " utilisateurs " in the French text of the Treaty [70] suggests that at least trade users are included in the expression " consumers." [71] It is however clear that the test of objectivity of benefit [72] excludes the parties themselves from the class of consumers, even though, in their capacity as consumers, they benefit from the agreement, *e.g.* a buyers' cartel.

**623    A fair share.** There is no authoritative definition of the words " a fair share." In practice the Commission has merely been concerned to ensure that the advantages of the agreement will enure to consumers and not merely to the parties themselves, without troubling with the precise meaning of the phrase " a fair share." From the practical point of view, the parties must show a reasonable probability that the benefits to be expected from the agreement will be passed on in reasonable measure to the consumer. [73] This requirement is generally satisfied by showing that the benefits which come from the agreement will perforce be passed on because of the pressure from competitors. [74] If the

[70] German " verbraucher "; Italian " utilizzatori "; Dutch " gebruikers."
[71] See also *Re Davidson Rubber*, J.O. 1972 L143/31, [1972] C.M.L.R. D52.
[72] *Ante*, §§ 611, 617–621.
[73] See *e.g. Re ACEC-Berliet*, J.O. 1968 201/7, [1968] C.M.L.R. D35, D40; *Re Clima Chappée*, J.O. 1969 L195/1, [1970] C.M.L.R. D7, D12.
[74] See *e.g. Re Transocean Marine Paint Association*, J.O. 1967, 163/10, [1967] C.M.L.R. D9, D18; *Re Cecimo*, J.O. 1969 L69/13, [1969] C.M.L.R. D1, D11; *Re Sopelem-Langen*, J.O. 1972 L13/47, [1972] C.M.L.R. D77, D81.

agreement has been made for the purpose of obtaining competitive advantages, that fact in itself ensures that consumers are likely to obtain " a fair share " of the resultant benefit.[75]  If the agreement is related to the launching of a new product, the difficulties of penetrating the market may themselves ensure that exploitation of consumers is impossible.[76]  Sometimes parties will be able positively to demonstrate that benefits from the agreement are already being passed on in reasonable measure by referring to developments that have occurred since the coming into operation of the agreement—for example product improvements or cost reductions.[77]

**624**  **Resulting benefits.**  The Commission does not always draw a very clear distinction between the improvements in production and distribution which the agreement will bring, and the benefits resulting therefrom.  However, the benefits which have been held to satisfy this part of the Article 85 (3) include improved supply,[78] production of a new [79] or improved [80] product or a greater range of products.[81]  One resulting benefit to which the Commission attaches particular importance is that the agreement will lead to lower costs or lower prices to consumers,[82] particularly as a result of rationalisation measures taken under a specialisation agreement,[83] or the sharing of the high costs of research.[84]

### 4.  INDISPENSABLE RESTRICTIONS

**625**  **Elimination of unnecessary restrictions.**  In order to satisfy the third limb of Article 85 (3), the restrictions in the agreement must not go beyond what is necessary for realising its benefits.[85]  In practice, the Commission insists upon the abandonment of restrictions which are not essential to achieving the advantages

[75] *Re Henkel-Colgate*, J.O. 1972 L14/14.
[76] *Re ACEC-Berliet*, J.O. 1968 L201/7, [1968] C.M.L.R. D35, D40.
[77] *e.g. Re FN-CF*, J.O. 1971 L134/6; *Re Lightweight Papers*, J.O. 1972 L182/24, [1972] C.M.L.R. D14.
[78] See *e.g.* Reg. 67/67, preamble; App. 6, *post; Re Transocean Marine Paint Association*, J.O. 1967 163/10, [1967] C.M.L.R. D9, D17.
[79] *Re ACEC-Berliet*, J.O. 1968 L201/7, [1968] C.M.L.R. D35, D40.
[80] *e.g.* see *Jaz-Peter*, J.O. 1969 L195/5, [1970] C.M.L.R. 129.
[81] *e.g. Re Clima Chappée*, J.O. 1969 L195/1, [1970] C.M.L.R. D7.
[82] *e.g. Jaz-Peter*, [1970] C.M.L.R. 129, 138; *Re Clima Chappée* [1970] C.M.L.R. D7, D12; *Re Cecimo*, J.O. 1969 L69/13, [1969] C.M.L.R. D1 at D11.
[83] *e.g. Re FN-CF*, J.O. 1971 L134/6.
[84] *Re Henkel-Colgate*, J.O. 1972 L14/14.
[85] *Re Cecimo*, J.O. 1969 L69/13, [1969] C.M.L.R. D1.

which may be derived from the agreement. Thus, before obtaining approval of the selective distribution agreement in *Re Omega*,[86] the parties had to abandon restrictions which prevented the Omega general agents and concessionaires from obtaining supplies from or exporting to other Member States.

**626    Restrictions that are unnecessary.** The Commission has consistently held that the " absolute territorial protection " of a sole distributor (*i.e.* the protection of the distributor against imports of similar goods) is not indispensable to improvements in distribution which may result from exclusive dealing agreements.[87] Similarly, in specialisation agreements which often involve reciprocal exclusive dealing, the Commission has been careful to see that the parties do not impose any resale restraints upon their customers, nor any restraints upon their own freedom to sell to third parties in countries that are not covered by the agreement.[88] In *Re Lightweight Paper*,[89] where the parties had a strong market position, the Commission considered that a restriction on producing certain types of product was the only restriction necessary for achieving the specialisation aimed at by the agreement.

**627    Restrictions that are indispensable.** Under Regulation 67/67 [90] the Commission has accepted certain restrictions as indispensable to exclusive dealing agreements. In an individual decision, *Re Omega*,[91] certain restrictions relating to selective distribution and falling outside Regulation 67/67 were held on the special facts of that case to be indispensable for ensuring retailers sufficient turnover to enable them adequately to promote the contract products. As far as specialisation agreements are concerned, certain restrictions which the Commission accepts as indispensable are now the basis of the new Regulation relating to the block exemption of specialisation agreements.[92] But again, in individual

[86] J.O. 1970 L242/22, [1970] C.M.L.R. D49, and see *ante*, § 614; *post*, § 840.
[87] *Re Grundigs Agreement*, J.O. 1964 2545/64, [1964] C.M.L.R. 489. *Re Consten-Grundig* v. *EEC Commission* (56/64, 58/64) [1966] C.M.L.R. 418; *cf.* Reg. 67/67; see *post*, §§ 811 *et seq.* See also First Report on Competition Policy, para. 49.
[88] *e.g. Re Clima Chappée*, J.O. 1969 L195/1, [1970] C.M.L.R. D7; *post*, § 1005.
[89] J.O. 1972 L182/24, [1972] C.M.L.R. D94; *post*, § 1019.
[90] *Post*, §§ 818 *et seq.*
[91] Note 86, *supra.* And see *post*, §§ 840 *et seq.*
[92] *Post*, §§ 1023 *et seq.*

decisions,[93] the Commission has permitted, on the particular facts, restrictions which are wider than those found in that block exemption *e.g.* reciprocal exclusive supply provisions.[94]    In the case of trade fairs, it has been held that restrictions on exhibiting at other fairs are a *sine qua non* of achieving a rationalisation of such exhibitions.[95]    Restrictions on divulging the results of joint research or technical collaboration are necessary to protect the parties to the agreement.[96]    The exclusivity granted in patent and know-how licences may be indispensable to attaining economic and technical progress, at least where it is necessary to protect licensees who may have to risk substantial investment in developing and adapting a new process[97].

## 5.  COMPETITION

**628**    **Elimination of competition.**  The " tail piece " of Article 85 (3) is that the agreement must not afford the parties the possibility of eliminating competition in respect of a substantial part of the products in question.  This requirement is closely related to the other limbs of Article 85 (3) in that, unless there is sufficient competition from competing products, the agreement will rarely satisfy the conditions that the advantages to be gained outweigh the disadvantages of the restrictions on competition [98] and that consumers will receive a fair share of the resulting benefit.[99]    In practice, no exemption under the EEC Treaty has been refused only for the reason that the agreement eliminated competition.

**629**    **Conditions to be satisfied.**  There is no authoritative definition of the words " elimination of competition in respect of a substantial part of the products in question."  However, in one

---

[93] See the cases cited at note 43, *supra*; and see *post*, §§ 1005–1022.
[94] See *post*, §§ 1023 *et seq*  In certain respects this regulation permits restrictions which appear to be wider than those permitted in individual decisions.  See *post*, § 1036.
[95] *Re Cecimo*, J.O. 1969 L69/13, [1969] C.M.L.R. D1.  *Re Cematex*, J.O. 1971 L227/26.  But similar restraints may not be permissible in relation to exhibitions of consumer goods rather than exhibitions of capital goods.  First Report on Competition (1972), para. 43.
[96] *Re Henkel-Colgate*, J.O. 1972 L14/14.  *Re Transocean Marine Paint Association*, J.O. 1967 163/10, [1967] C.M.L.R. D9.
[97] *Re Davidson Rubber*, J.O. 1972 L143/31, [1972] C.M.L.R. D52.
[98] *Ante*, §§ 611, 612, 617–621.
[99] *Ante*, §§ 622–624.

decision in a different context under Article 65 (2) of the ECSC Treaty [1] the European Court held that certain coal producers controlled " a substantial part of the products in question " where they sold and distributed coal, compressed fuel and coke in proportions varying between 26·1 per cent. and 43·7 per cent. of total sales within that common market. In practice, under the EEC Treaty, the Commission has usually contented itself with a finding that there is no possibility of competition being eliminated since the parties to the agreement are exposed to a lively competition from other manufacturers.[2] In this respect it is necessary to take into account competition both from producers in the same and other Member States, and from products imported from outside the EEC.[3] In several decisions there are detailed descriptions of the markets for the products in question.[4] It is also necessary to consider whether the parties may, as a result of this agreement, have the opportunity of substantially eliminating competition at any time in the future. If this is the case, the Commission may grant exemptions subject to conditions.[5]

**630      Henkel-Colgate and Lightweight Paper.** Despite the requirement that competition must not be eliminated in respect of a substantial part of the products in question, the Commission may be prepared to grant an exemption even though the collaborating parties have a significant share of the markets in question. Thus in *Henkel-Colgate* [6] the parties to the agreement were the third and fourth largest world producers of soaps and detergents after Procter and Gamble and Unilever. These four firms between them controlled 80 per cent. of the EEC market. Barriers to entry were high. Henkel and Colgate agreed to set up a joint research subsidiary. This would effectively prevent them from competing *inter se* in research, which in turn would mean they were not competing in the drive to find new, marketable products. Although the parties had a large market share, the Commission held that they could not themselves eliminate competition in respect of " a substantial part of the products in

---

[1] *Verkaufsgesellschaft Geitling Ruhrkohlen* v. *The High Authority* (13/60) [1962] C.M.L.R. 113. For the ECSC Treaty see *ante*, § 106.
[2] *e.g. Re Sopelem-Langen*, J.O. 1972 L13/47, [1972] C.M.L.R. D77.
[3] *e.g. Lightweight Paper*, J.O. 1972 L182/24, [1972] C.M.L.R. D94.
[4] *e.g. FN-CF*, J.O. 1971 134/6; *MAN-SAVIEM*, J.O. 1972 L31/29.
[5] *Post*, § 636.
[6] J.O. 1972 L14/14; *post*, § 1107.

question." They were still free, apart from the research agreement, to trade independently. The Commission found that they had not jointly a dominant position for the products concerned in any single market of the EEC, and that the research agreement would in fact promote competition with the other two large undertakings. The Commission granted an exemption whilst imposing stringent conditions.[7] In *Re Lightweight Paper* [8] the parties held 80 per cent. of the French market and 70 per cent. of the Benelux market in cigarette papers, and 15 per cent. of the common market production of other thin papers. Under a specialisation agreement each party agreed to restrict his production to certain types of paper only. The Commission held that there was no substantial elimination of competition in respect of the market for cigarette papers in the EEC. There was strong competitive pressure from German, Italian, Austrian and American undertakings, the parties to the agreement were faced by powerful buyers, and there was no reason why a world market for the products should not develop.

### 6.  POWERS RELATING TO GRANT OF AN EXEMPTION

#### (a) *Retroactivity*

**631**     **Retroactive effect.**   Under Articles 6 and 7 of Regulation 17 the Commission has power, in certain circumstances, to declare that the exemption it has granted in respect of an agreement under Article 85 (3) shall have effect retroactively.[9]  In the case of agreements coming into force after March 13, 1962 [10] (apart from Accession agreements) [11] the exemption cannot have retroactive effect to a date earlier than the date of notification, except in the case of agreements falling within Article 4 (2) of Regulation 17. If an exemption is sought in respect of an agreement falling within Article 4 (2), any exemption subsequently granted can be backdated to the date of the agreement.[12]  In the case of agreements

---

[7] See §§ 633 *et seq., post.*
[8] J.O. 1972 L182/24; *post*, § 1019.
[9] See *ante*, §§ 514 and 522–523.
[10] The implementing date of Reg. 17.
[11] See *ante*, §§ 517 *et seq.*
[12] Art. 6 (1) of Reg. 17.  For Art. 4 (2) agreements see *ante*, §§ 528 *et seq.*  Hitherto the circumstances in which an exemption may be granted to an Art. 4 (2) agreement have not arisen.

which were already in force on March 13, 1962 and which were duly notified within the appropriate time limits,[13] and in the case of Accession agreements which have been notified before July 1, 1973, the exemption can also be back-dated to March 13, 1962 or January 1, 1973 as appropriate.[14]  Also, if such agreements do not qualify for exemption under Article 85 (3) when notified, but are subsequently modified in order to do so, the Commission has a discretionary power to fix retroactively a period in respect of which the prohibition of Article 85 (1) shall not apply.[15]

**632      Commission's exercise of its powers.**   Where agreements in existence on March 13, 1962 have been duly notified in good time and subsequently modified so as to enable an exemption to be granted under Article 85 (3), the Commission's uniform practice has been to declare Article 85 (1) inapplicable in respect of the period between March 13, 1962 and the date of the grant of the exemption.   It may be expected that the Commission will follow the same practice in respect of Accession agreements. Agreements which have come into force after March 13, 1962, and which have obtained exemption, have invariably been exempted retroactively to the date of notification, provided that they fulfilled the requirements of Article 85 (3) at that date. [16]

### (b) *Conditions Attached to Exemption*

**633      Powers of the Commission.**   Under Article 8 (1) of Regulation 17 the Commission has power to grant exemption only for a specified period and to attach conditions and obligations.   Under Article 8 (2), the exemption may be renewed if the conditions of the Treaty continue to be fulfilled.   Under Article 8 (3) the Commission has power to revoke an exemption if there has been a change in any of the facts which were fundamental in the making of the decision, or if a stipulation attached to the exemption has been infringed, or where the exemption has been gained by the giving of false information, or where those concerned have abused the exemption that has been granted to them.   In the latter three cases, the decision may be revoked with retroactive effect.

[13] *Ante*, § 527.
[14] Art. 6 (2) and Art. 25 of Reg. 17; *ante*, §§ 517 *et seq.* esp. 522.
[15] Art. 7 of Reg. 17; *ante*, § 523.
[16] *e.g. Re Sopelem-Langen*, J.O. 1972 L13/47, [1972] C.M.L.R. D77.

**634      Exercise of powers: specified period.** The Commission has generally been prepared to grant exemption for the period necessary to ensure that the benefits of the agreement are realised. In practice the period of exemption has been either five [17] or ten years,[18] usually as from the date of notification. Exceptionally, a period of twelve years has been granted, but only where the agreement concerned trade fairs which themselves took place only every four years.[19]

**635      Renewal and revocation.** The Commission has not hitherto had occasion to exercise its powers to renew or revoke any exemption it has granted.[20]

**636      Conditions and stipulations.** The Commission has frequently exercised its powers to attach conditions and stipulations to exempted agreements. In order to supervise the operation of the agreement and maintain effective competition in the market the Commission has in a number of cases required the parties to submit periodic and detailed reports relating to the operation of the agreement.[21] The Commission has also imposed obligations which ensure that the agreement will not be operated in a discriminatory fashion. This in *Re Cecimo* [22] a trade association was obliged to report any occasions upon which members were expelled, or new members refused admission. Similarly *Omega* [23] is obliged to report any withdrawals of the status of " Omega concessionaires " from retailers.

Finally, the Commission has been concerned to see that the parties do not abuse their position by dividing up the market or using the agreement for anti-competitive purposes. Thus in *Re Henkel-Colgate* [24] the parties are required to inform the Commission of all licences granted by their joint research subsidiary—a provision designed to prevent market sharing by

[17] *e.g. Re Lightweight Paper,* J.O. 1972 L182/24, [1972] C.M.L.R. D94; *Re Henkel-Colgate,* J.O. 1972 L14/14.
[18] *Re FN-CF,* note 43, *supra.*
[19] *Re Cematex,* J.O. 1971 L227/26.
[20] But the exemption in *Transocean Marine Paint Association,* note 96, *supra,* was due to expire on December 31, 1972.
[21] *e.g. Re MAN-SAVIEM,* J.O. 1972 L31/29. *Re Lightweight Paper,* J.O. 1972 L182/24, [1972] C.M.L.R. 94.
[22] J.O. 1969 L69/13, [1969] C.M.L.R. D1; see also *Re Cematex,* J.O. 1971 227/26.
[23] J.O. 1970 L242/22, [1970] C.M.L.R. D49, D63.
[24] J.O. 1972 L14/14.

means of patent licence agreements. They are also required to report all acquisitions of interests as between the parties and all exchanges of executive staff between the two groups. This requirement is specifically designed to ensure that the joint research collaboration in that case will not lead to integration of the two concerns or a substantial diminution of trading competition between them. Similar conditions were imposed in *Re Lightweight Paper*.[25]

**[The next paragraph is 701.]**

[25] J.O. 1972 L182/24, [1972] C.M.L.R. D94.

CHAPTER 7

## ARTICLE 86

### 1. IN GENERAL

**701**    Article 86 of the Treaty provides as follows [1]: " Any abuse by one or more undertakings of a dominant position within the common market or a substantial part of it shall be prohibited as incompatible with the common market in so far as it may affect trade between Member States.    Such abuse may, in particular, consist in:

> (*a*) directly or indirectly imposing unfair purchase or selling prices or other unfair trading conditions [2];
>
> (*b*) limiting production, markets or technical development to the prejudice of consumers [3];
>
> (*c*) applying dissimilar conditions to equivalent transactions with other trading parties, thereby placing them at a competitive disadvantage [4];
>
> (*d*) making the conclusion of contracts subject to acceptance

As at November 30, 1972 the Commission had instituted proceedings under Art. 86 and published decisions in only two cases; for a summary of those decisions see §§ 731–742, *post;* those cases have only an indirect bearing on many of the important problems which are likely to arise under Art. 86, and since it is likely that there will be an increase in the volume of proceedings taken by the Commission in this area of Community law, it has been considered necessary to make a number of general propositions in the text about the most likely meaning of the very general expressions used in this Article.    See now also *Re Sugar Cartel*, Commission decision, January 2, 1973; *Re CSC-ZOJA*, J.O. 1972 L299/51; see also Joliet, *Monopolization and Abuse of Dominant Position* (1970); the Commission's Memorandum on Concentration (1966); and First Report on Competition Policy (April 1972) at pages 74 to 82.    The Commission has power to carry out a general investigation into an economic sector where there is a suggestion that competition may be restricted; in carrying out any such investigation the Commission has the right to require undertakings which appear to be in a dominant position to supply relevant particulars of their size and practices so that the Commission may appraise the situation in the light of Art. 86: see Art 12 of Reg. 17 § 1215, *post*.    As to the provisions in the laws of Member States regulating an abuse of a dominant position, see OECD Guide to Legislation on Restrictive Business Practices.    See also OECD, *Market Power* (1970).

[2] Compare Art. 85 (1) (*a*) and see §§ 303 *et seq., ante.*
[3] Compare Art. 85 (1) (*b*) and see § 325, *ante.*
[4] Compare Art. 85 (1) (*d*) and see §§ 313, 323, *ante.*

[ 148 ]

by the other parties of supplementary obligations which, by their nature or according to commercial usage, have no connection with the subject of such contracts.[5] "

702     Conduct of the kind prohibited by Article 86 requires the presence of three factors: the existence of a dominant position, the abuse of that position and the possibility that trade between Member States may be affected by it.

## 2. DOMINANT POSITION [6]

703     **General.** In their decision in *Re Continental Can Co. Inc.*[7] the Commission defined dominant position as follows: " Undertakings are in a dominant position when they have the power to behave independently, which puts them in a position to act without taking into account their competitors, purchasers or suppliers. That is the position when, because of their share of the market, or of their share of the market combined with the availability of technical knowledge, raw materials or capital, they have the power to determine prices or to control production or distribution for a significant part of the products in question. This power does not necessarily have to derive from an absolute domination permitting the undertakings which hold it to eliminate all will on the part of their economic partners, but it is enough that they be strong enough as a whole to ensure to those undertakings an overall independence of behaviour, even if there are differences in intensity in their influence on the different partial [8] markets."

[5] Compare Art. 85 (1) (c) and see §§ 314, 324, *ante.*
[6] For the determination of a dominant position in relation to industrial property rights see *Parke, Davis & Co.* v. *Probel* (24/67) [1968] C.M.L.R. 47, 59 (patents); *Sirena s.r.l.* v. *Eda s.r.l.* (40/70) [1971] C.M.L.R. 260, 275 (trade marks); *Deutsche Grammophon G.m.b.H.* v. *Metro-SB-Grossmärkte G.m.b.H. & Co. K.G.* (78/70) [1971] C.M.L.R. 631, 658 (record manufacturer's right of protection similar to copyright). For a general discussion of these cases in relation to industrial property rights in the EEC, see §§ 901 *et seq.* See also the Commission's Memorandum on Concentration (1966), Part III in which the Commission indicated that, in its view, it would appear that as a rule an enterprise which acted as the " price leader " in an oligopolistic situation occupied a market dominating position.
[7] J.O. 1972 L7/25, [1972] C.M.L.R. D11, D27; see §§ 739–742, *post*; see also *Europemballage Corporation and Continental Can Co. Inc.* v. *EEC Commission* (6/72), *The Times*, February 26, 1973.
[8] As in *Re Continental Can Co. Inc.* where the Commission held that a dominant position was exercised in relation to the supply of light metal containers for preserved meat and shellfish and in the supply of metal tops for glass jars; and see §§ 739–742, *post*. *Cf.* the decision of the European Court, *post*, § 742.

**704**    The Treaty nowhere defines " dominant position " and in any
attempt to expand or give meaning to the expression, there is
a risk that it is only replaced by criteria equally or more inexact.
In the first two cases in which the Commission has issued a
decision under Article 86 the position was clear: Gema,[9] a
German authors' rights society, although not possessing a legal
monopoly under German law, was the only society established
in Germany for the protection of authors' rights in musical works;
Continental Can Co. Inc.,[10] by virtue of its financial, technical
and commercial strength in world markets and in the German
market for the supply of light metal containers, had substantial
market strength in Germany [11] in respect of the supply of light
metal containers for certain major applications.

**705**    The Commission has emphasised " overall independence of
behaviour " [12] as the principal test of a dominant position, which
can only be satisfied by examining the relative strengths of
undertakings which compete in the supply or acquisition of goods
or services within a particular market.  In applying this test it is
submitted that a distinction is to be drawn between an undertaking in a leading position and an undertaking in a dominant
position.  The presence in the market of an undertaking which
enjoys a leading position is not incompatible with the existence
in that market of effective competition; however the presence in
the market of an undertaking in a dominant position assumes
that the competitiveness in the market which could ordinarily be
relied upon to have a material influence upon the activities of such
an undertaking, and in particular to prevent or restrict any
significant unfair or anti-competitive behaviour, is not present;
in those circumstances an external discipline is required to regulate
the economic power and activities of such an undertaking in so
far as they conflict with Article 86 and the general aims of the
Treaty.[13]

[9] J.O. 1971 L134/15, [1971] C.M.L.R. D35; see also [1972] C.M.L.R. D115.
[10] J.O. 1972 L7/25, [1972] C.M.L.R. D11.  See now also *Re Sugar Cartel* (Commission decision), January 2, 1973; *Re CSC-ZOJA*, J.O. 1972 L299/51.
[11] *Ibid.*, where the Commission held that Germany was a substantial part of the
common market; and see as to the definition of substantial part of the common
market, § 710, *post.*
[12] See § 703, *ante.*
[13] See in particular, Art. 3 (*c*) (" the abolition, as between Member States, of
obstacles to freedom of movement for persons, services and capital "), Art. 3 (*f*)
(" the institution of a system ensuring that competition in the common market

**706**    It is submitted that such a test, which may embrace all the circumstances which have led to and support the existence of a dominant position, is the most appropriate test to apply to the regulation of economic power. The determination of the existence of a dominant position solely by reference to quantitative figures of market share is unhelpful as it gives little guide as to the competitiveness of an industry, except in the extreme cases where a market share of 90 per cent. or over may be a sufficient indication by itself of the existence of a dominant position.

**707**    **The market.** The first priority is to define the market in respect of which an undertaking enjoys a dominant position and to examine the conduct of the undertaking and its competitors over a sufficient period of time to enable accurate conclusions to be drawn about the structure and likely future structure of that market. Many factors may be relevant; analyses over time of market shares, divided as between various sub-markets or sub-groups of products, within a more general description of goods; the overall financial and commercial strength of an undertaking which might enable it to withstand cyclical changes in the market more readily than competitors; the extent of any arrangements made either with competitors, suppliers or purchasers which may reduce even further the competitiveness of the market; the ability of an undertaking to incur substantially higher overhead costs in the form of research and development expenditure and expensive management and labour training schemes while at the same time selling at market prices and earning better profits than competitors; the volume of business in the relevant descriptions of goods or services in relation to that of competitors, individually rather than collectively; the ability of an undertaking to control over a period of time its prices and trading conditions without apparent regard for those of competitors.

The distinction between an undertaking in a leading position and one in a dominant position may be illustrated by the following example of a typical market situation: a leading company may have a market share of 65 to 70 per cent. but the remainder of the market may be supplied by two companies, both financially

is not distorted ") and Art. 7 (" within the scope of application of this Treaty, and without prejudice to any special provisions contained therein, any discrimination on grounds of nationality shall be prohibited ").

strong, divisions of powerful organisations determined to increase market share and develop new products.  Such companies could have a material influence upon the firm enjoying the large market share which could ignore them only at its peril.  That situation may be contrasted with that of an undertaking which has a market share of about 70 per cent. but where the remainder of the market is supplied by a large number of small firms each selling a small product range in regional markets.  None of those small firms would be likely to have a material influence on the activities of the larger firm which might appropriately be described as enjoying a dominant position.

**708**    **Description of goods or services.**  A dominant position can be exercised only in relation to the supply or acquisition of goods or services of a certain description and within a particular market.  As the Commission showed in its decision in *Re Continental Can Co. Inc.*[14] it is prepared to seek to regulate an abuse of economic power in relation to the supply of goods to be used in specific applications.  In that case the Commission drew a distinction between a powerful position in the supply of a generic description of goods (light metal containers) and a dominant position in the supply of those goods for preserved meat and shellfish and the supply of metal caps for glass jars.[15] There are inevitably problems in the determination of the most appropriate description of goods by which to test the existence and abuse of a dominant position.

Goods which have the same generic description, *e.g.* motor vehicles, may be manufactured in different ways, have different technical characteristics and functions and sell into different markets.  If the demand for motor vehicles for commercial use is supplied by a single undertaking it might be unrealistic to allege that the relevant market is that for the supply of all motor vehicles for all applications.  In each case questions will turn on the degree to which goods supplied by one undertaking can be substituted for goods supplied by other undertakings, and the extent to which, in spite of the possibility of substitution, goods of a certain physical description represent and are recognised as a homogeneous and commercially distinct class.

[14] J.O. 1972 L7/25, [1972] C.M.L.R. D11.
[15] *Ibid.* at D27, D28; but see now *Europemballage Corporation and Continental Can Co. Inc.* v. *EEC Commission*, (6/72) *The Times*, February 26, 1973.

**709**    The importance of defining the appropriate market is most acute where the very existence of a dominant or monopoly position itself is prohibited; Article 86 prohibits only an abuse of a dominant position. In practice however, the market is to be determined by investigating all relevant facts to discover first whether an undertaking enjoys that " overall independence of behaviour " in relation to the goods or services which it supplies that would enable it to abuse that position, and secondly whether it has in fact abused that position. Clearly the narrower the market is defined the more likely it is that other goods or services will be competitive and the less likely it will be that an undertaking will enjoy overall independence of behaviour even though no other undertaking supplies precisely the same goods or services for the same applications.

**710**    **The common market or a substantial part of it.**  For Article 86 to apply, one or more undertakings must have a dominant position within the common market or a substantial part of it. In its decisions in *Re Gema*[16] and in *Re Continental Can Co. Inc.*[17] the Commission held that Germany was a substantial part of the common market; in *Re Continental Can Co. Inc.* the Commission also held that North Germany and Benelux was a substantial part of the common market. Therefore if a substantial part is to be defined by reference to territory alone it follows that the United Kingdom, France and Italy are all likely to be held to be substantial parts of the common market. The position is unclear as to the smaller Member States and in such cases the question is likely to be resolved by reference to the commercial importance of the supply of certain goods or services within a national market or part of one in relation to the total supply of such goods or services within the common market and the extent to which that national market is isolated from competitive pressures which characterise the rest of the common market.

**711**    Article 86 is concerned with the supply of goods or services *within* the common market; therefore in considering whether an undertaking has a dominant position the extent of competition

---

[16] J.O. 1971 L134/15, [1971] C.M.L.R. D35; see also *Re Gema (No. 2)*, J.O. 1972 L166/22, [1972] C.M.L.R. D115
[17] J.O. 1972 L7/25, [1972] C.M.L.R. D11.

from imported products into Member States is relevant, just as the nationality of the undertaking alleged to be in a dominant position is irrelevant; such an undertaking may supply goods within the common market through an agent or independent distributor or sell to a subsidiary or associate company responsible for reselling within the common market; whatever the mechanism by which goods or services are supplied the Commission will institute proceedings against the undertaking which is responsible for controlling the activities of its subsidiaries, associates or agents whether or not the undertaking itself is established for fiscal or other purposes within a Member State.[18]

**712**     **One or more undertakings.**[19]     Article 86 is probably not confined to the activities of a single monopolist. Article 86 provides that abuse by one or more undertakings of a dominant position shall be prohibited and the expression " one or more undertakings " is not, it is thought, limited to an undertaking and its subsidiary companies or to an undertaking and those of its associated companies whose policy it is effectively able to control or materially to influence.

**713**     **Oligopoly.**     It has yet to be determined whether Article 86 will apply to a situation of shared monopoly where two or more undertakings, none of which is in a dominant position in the market, collectively act in a manner similar to that in which an undertaking in a dominant position would or might act. In such a situation the Commission might consider that there was no effective competition in the market, even though there had been no agreement or concerted practice between the undertakings.

**714**     **Restriction of competition.**     There is no authority as to whether Article 86 applies to a situation where two or more undertakings, in the absence of agreement or concerted practice,[20] restrict competition in the supply of goods or services by pursuing a

---

[18] In *Re Continental Can Co. Inc.* J.O. 1972 L7/25, [1972] C.M.L.R. D11; (see §§ 739–742, *post*) the Commission instituted proceedings against Continental Can Co. Inc. of New York (U.S.A.) and its subsidiary Europemballage Corporation of Wilmington, Delaware (U.S.A.) and Brussels (Belgium), and held that they were companies acting directly within the common market and undertakings within the meaning of Art. 86 of the Treaty affirmed on appeal, Case (6/72); for the application of Art. 85 to companies established outside the common market, see §§ 240 *et seq., ante,* and § 1209, *post.*

[19] For the meaning of the expression " undertaking " see § 213, *ante*; see also Art. 90 (2) of the Treaty.

[20] For the meaning of the expression " concerted practice " see §§ 211 *et seq., ante.*

course of common conduct. If for example a small number of major suppliers of a particular description of goods have entered into long term exclusive supply agreements and effectively foreclosed substantially all the important points of distribution, the Commission might institute proceedings on the ground that new entry to the market is virtually impossible and that competition between undertakings in the market has been unreasonably and excessively restricted. However there seems no reason in principle why Article 86 should not apply to certain situations of shared monopoly or to situations where a few undertakings pursue a common course of conduct which restricts competition to such a degree that the maintenance of effective competition in the market is substantially impaired.

715    **The relationship between Article 85 and Article 86.** Two or more undertakings may collectively enjoy a dominant position within the common market and it is submitted that it is irrelevant how that dominant position has been achieved; it may have been achieved by an agreement or a concerted practice of the kind falling within Article 85 (1) or by a process of concentration, which has resulted, for example, in a duopoly, or by the pursuit of a common course of conduct. There may therefore be situations where the Commission has power to institute proceedings both under Article 85 and Article 86. Since the two Articles are not mutually exclusive, the Commission probably has the power of requiring parties to an agreement to put an end both to the agreement in pursuance of which they have acted so as to restrict competition and to the specific acts themselves, in so far as they are abuses by one or more undertakings of the dominant position which they hold by virtue of the agreement.

### 3. ABUSE OF A DOMINANT POSITION

716    **General.** Article 86 aims at the regulation of abuse of economic power in market conditions where a dominant position exists; there is no provision in Article 86 or anywhere in the Treaty that the dominant position itself may operate against the interests of the Community and no provision for the prior notification and regulation of mergers.[21] This reflects the attitude of the

---

[21] As to whether Art. 86 applies to mergers, see §§ 739–742, *post*; *cf* Art. 66 of ECSC Treaty. A Regulation relating to prior notification of mergers is contemplated.

signatories to the Treaty that industries within Member States were characterised by too many small undertakings and that larger units were required to be competitive with the strong United States companies. Attitudes within the Community may now be changing, as the Commission indicated in 1965 in a memorandum on the concentration of enterprises within the common market,[22] but the very general provisions of Article 86 are not to be interpreted so as to cover all activities by undertakings in a dominant position which might be considered to restrict competition.

**717**    Abuse, it is submitted, is the use of a dominant position to act in an unreasonable way which, in conditions of effective competition, would be unlikely to be permitted by suppliers or customers or would not be practicable in view of likely action by competitors. It is action which is taken as a result of and by the use of the economic power of the undertaking. This definition, it is submitted, gives due weight to the word " abuse " and to the idea of " exploitation,"[23] that is conduct which is practicable only by virtue of the existence of the dominant position and which is unreasonable or unfair when viewed in the light of the illustrations in Article 86 (a) to (d) [24] and the general aims of the Treaty.[25]

**718**    **Abuse by reason of adverse economic effect.**  It is a matter to be determined whether the expression abuse also covers unreasonable conduct of the kind illustrated in the sub-paragraphs of Article 86, and of a similar kind, if pursued by an undertaking in a dominant position though not as a result of, and by the use of, its economic power as such.  In such a case abuse of a dominant position lies in the fact that its adverse effects on suppliers, customers or competitors may be expected to be substantially greater and of more permanence than if that conduct were pursued by a less important undertaking.  In substance the question is whether community law will include in its concept of " abuse "

---

[22] See the Commission's Memorandum on concentration within the common market: Competition Series No. 3, 1966, Part III.
[23] See the French text of Art. 86 which includes the words " exploiter de façon abusive."
[24] See §§ 719–724, post.
[25] See note 13, ante.  See also now *Europemballage Corporation and Continental Can Co. Inc.* v. *EEC Commission* (6/72) *The Times*, February 26, 1973.

such unreasonable practices carried on by an undertaking in a dominant position which are aimed at preserving that dominant position. It is submitted that that approach would be consistent with both the wording of Article 86 and the general aims of the Treaty; abuse of a dominant position is determined not by the motive with which action is taken, for malice and ill-will are irrelevant, but by its economic effect on trade between Member States. An undertaking may have pursued a particular trading policy for twenty years or more; as a result of mergers and acquisitions it may have established for itself a dominant position. The continuation of such a policy, whether it is based on tying agreements or a network of exclusive dealing agreements, may clearly have substantially greater consequences because the economic effect of the restrictions is commensurably greater than when the undertaking first sought to establish a foothold in the market. It is not action which is taken by the use of a dominant position; it is action which, because of the existence of a dominant position, the ordinary forces of competition could not be expected to erode or influence, so as to promote equality of opportunity for other individuals and undertakings throughout the common market. In practice however such action when taken by an undertaking in a dominant position is likely to be at least facilitated by that position[25a].

**719**    **Particular abuse.** Sub-paragraphs (*a*) to (*d*) of Article 86 illustrate the kind of abuse which is prohibited. Article 86 provides that " Such abuse may, in particular, consist in:

> (*a*) directly or indirectly imposing unfair purchase or selling prices or other unfair trading conditions;
>
> (*b*) limiting production, markets or technical development to the prejudice of consumers;
>
> (*c*) applying dissimilar conditions to equivalent transactions with other trading parties, thereby placing them at a competitive disadvantage;
>
> (*d*) making the conclusion of contracts subject to acceptance by the other parties of supplementary obligations which, by their nature or according to commercial usage, have no connection with the subject of such contracts."

[25a] And see *Europemballage Corporation and Continental Can Co. Inc.* (6/72) *The Times*, February 26, 1973.

**720**     The illustrations are not exhaustive.  However they indicate the general area of prohibited conduct and the Commission may be expected to have particular regard to them in identifying conduct of the kind falling within the prohibitions in Article 86. It may therefore be of assistance to indicate the broad types of abuse with which the sub-paragraphs deal, each of which represents a classic situation of abuse of economic power.

**721**     **(a) Directly or indirectly imposing unfair purchase or selling prices or other unfair trading conditions.**  Selling prices may be unfairly low or unfairly high; unfairly low selling prices may be charged in regional markets or over a limited period of time to discourage potential competitors from entering or seeking to expand their share of a market, or to drive existing competitors out of the market or so cripple their activities as to offer them the choice of bankruptcy or acquisition by the undertaking in the dominant position.  Unfairly high selling prices may make it more difficult for customers to resell at economic prices or may add unduly to their costs if they are using the products as raw materials; that might have an effect on the ability of those users to compete in trade between Member States.

Trading conditions may be unfair if they unreasonably restrict the freedom of a customer or supplier in its relations with third persons.  Thus different considerations may apply to exclusive dealing agreements when one party is an undertaking in a dominant position; so far from promoting the most economic and efficient distribution of goods they may serve to entrench the dominant position by foreclosing major outlets of distribution to actual and potential competitors.

In each case it will be necessary to examine the nature and effect of any restrictions, the conduct which might be expected if the restrictions were qualified or brought to an end, and the extent to which the advantages which in many cases accrue to customers and suppliers from the existence of an undertaking in a dominant position might be threatened by the abandonment of some of its more important trading policies.

**722**     **(b) Limiting production, markets or technical development to the prejudice of consumers.**  The important words in (b) are " to the prejudice of consumers."  As the pattern of demand in an industry changes, an undertaking in a dominant position will, like other producers, tend to rationalise production, divert activities into different markets and change the emphasis of its research and development activities. Since the Treaty permits the existence and continued operation of undertakings in a dominant position, their activities, to fall within sub-paragraph (b) must be to the prejudice of consumers and, it is submitted, such prejudice must outweigh the advantages which the same or other purchasers derive from the conduct which is alleged to be an abuse; such conduct could include a failure to increase production capacity to meet increase in demand, with the result that consumers suffer from higher prices and longer delays; failure to supply goods for which there is a significant demand, although there is often a conflict between continuing a policy of increased specialisation and making available a wide range of goods some of which may be obsolescent; delay in introduction of new products and processes until established products have made a satisfactory profit contribution.

The Commission endeavoured to justify its decision in *Re Continental Can Co. Inc.*[26] by reference to sub-paragraph (b); the argument was that sub-paragraph (b) was concerned with the internal activities of an undertaking as distinct from conduct towards customers, suppliers and competitors and would cover the acquisition of a competing enterprise by an undertaking in a dominant position, provided that that acquisition eliminated competition which might otherwise have been expected; examining the conduct from the viewpoint of economic effect it was similar to action which unreasonably prevented another undertaking from offering potential competition.

**723**    **(c) Applying dissimilar conditions to equivalent transactions with other trading parties, thereby placing them at a competitive disadvantage.**[27] Again the important words in sub-paragraph (c) are " thereby placing them at a competitive disadvantage." Differences in terms and conditions of supply or acquisition as between different customers or suppliers are not abuses unless the

[26] Argument of the Commission at the hearing before the European Court of the Appeal of Continental Can Co. Inc. against the decision of the Commission; see also the Commission's Memorandum on concentration within the common market: Competition Series No. 3, 1966, Part III, para. 65.
[27] *Cf.* a similar provision under Art. 85 (1); §§ 313, 323, *ante.*

economic effect is to place those who obtain the worst or less good terms at a competitive disadvantage.

The absence of uniformity in prices or conditions in selling to customers who carry on business in different Member States might in certain circumstances be an abuse within (c). An undertaking in a dominant position might be required by the Commission to sell at the same ex-works prices to such customers so as not to restrict the competitiveness of the industry at the next stage of supply. The Commission's decision in *Re Gema* [28] indicates the importance which the Commission attaches to promoting equality of opportunity for undertakings and individuals in Member States and any discrimination on the ground of nationality is likely to be held to be an abuse.

Attention should be paid to the requirement in Article 86 (c) that the transactions should be equivalent; in *Re Gema* [29] the Commission decided that the imposition of a higher fee on importers of records than on German manufacturers was unreasonable in that it tended to restrict competition between importers and manufacturers by placing the importers at a competitive disadvantage. It is also a question to be determined to what extent conditions may differ in transactions which are not equivalent and whether Article 86 (c) or (a) would apply in such a case.

**724**      **(d) Making the conclusion of contracts subject to acceptance by the other parties of supplementary obligations which, by their nature or according to commercial usage, have no connection with the subject of such contracts.**[30] The typical case prohibited under (d) will be that of an undertaking which refuses to supply goods in respect of which it enjoys a dominant position unless the purchaser also acquires other goods from that undertaking, either of a particular description or of a full range (full line forcing). By the imposition of such an obligation an undertaking in a dominant position can extend that position to cover other goods in respect of which there may be effective competition or at least obtain a competitive advantage by the use of the dominant position. Since sub-paragraph (d) is only an illustration of the

[28] J.O. 1971 L134/15, [1971] C.M.L.R. D35; see also *Re Gema (No. 2)*, J.O. 1972 L166/22, [1972] C.M.L.R. D115.
[29] *Ibid.*
[30] *Cf.* a similar provision under Art. 85 (1); §§ 314, 324, *ante.*

kind of abuse at which Article 86 aims, it is to be determined
whether it is necessary to impose an obligation in order for the
conduct to be prohibited; or whether it is sufficient if the pricing
and discount structures are calculated to have the same economic
effect.

725      **Trade between Member States.**   Article 86 prohibits an abuse
of a dominant position within the common market or a substantial
part of it in so far as it may affect trade between Member States.
There is no distinction drawn in the Treaty, and none seems
necessary, between the meaning of this expression in Article 85
and its meaning in Article 86.[31]   The existence of a dominant
position involves the lack of effective competition, whether from
within or outside a Member State and it is likely that most abuses
of a dominant position, in so far as they tend unfairly to protect
that position will be held to affect trade between Member States.
In *Re Gema* [32] the Commission held it to be an abuse to discriminate between individuals on the ground of nationality; in that
case individuals could not effectively seek representation of their
rights through any society other than one established in their
country even though international rights were concerned.
However a material effect on trade between Member States
must be established; otherwise Article 86 will not apply and the
abuse must be remedied, if at all, by national authorities within
Member States.

726      **Industrial property rights.**   Any undertaking to which a
national authority has granted an industrial property right has,
subject to the national law governing the exercise of that right,
an exclusive right in the nature of a monopoly.   The mere fact of
being a patentee, however, or the owner of a trade mark or
other similar right does not put an undertaking into a dominant
position within Article 86.   Thus in *Parke Davis* [33] where the
holder of a patent exercised his rights to prevent the importation
of products covered by the patent from a Member State which

---

[31] For the meaning of the expression " trade between Member States " see § 230,
*ante*.
[32] J.O. 1971 L134/15, [1971] C.M.L.R. D35; see also *Re Gema (No. 2)*, J.O. 1972
L166/22, [1972] C.M.L.R. D115; and see §§ 731–737, *post*.
[33] *Parke, Davis & Co.* v. *Probel* (24/67) [1968] C.M.L.R. 47.   See also *post*, §§ 901
*et seq*.

did not afford similar protection, the European Court held that [34] " for an act to be prohibited (under Article 86) it is . . . necessary to find the existence of three elements: the existence of a dominant position, an improper exploitation of it, and the possibility that trade between Member States may be affected by it. Although a patent confers on its holder a special protection within the framework of a State, it does not follow that the exercise of the rights so conferred implies the existence of the three elements mentioned. It could only do so if the utilisation of the patent could degenerate into an improper exploitation of the protection."

In that case the fact that the price of the patented product was higher than that of the imported product was held not sufficient to establish an " abuse." Again, in *Sirena*,[35] where the issue under Article 86 was the use of a trade mark right to prevent the importation of products covered by the trade mark which were lawfully marketed in another Member State, the Court held that [36] " The owner of a trade mark does not enjoy a ' dominant position ' within . . . Article 86 merely because he can prohibit third parties from marketing products bearing the same mark in the territory of a Member State. Since this Article provides that the dominant position must extend to at least a ' substantial part ' of the common market, it is necessary in addition that the trade mark owner should have the power to prevent the main- tenance of effective competition in a considerable part of the market in question, taking into account, in particular, the possible existence and the position of producers or distributors who market similar or substitute products. With regard to the improper exploitation of a dominant position, the higher price of the product, although it does not *per se* constitute sufficient proof, may nevertheless become so, in view of its size, if it does not seem objectively justified."

727    An undertaking in a dominant position may not use industrial property rights in such a way as to abuse its dominant position.

[34] [1968] C.M.L.R. 47, 59.
[35] *Sirena s.r.l.* v. *Eda s.r.l.* (40/70) [1971] C.M.L.R. 260. See also *post*, §§ 901 *et seq.* esp. 908 *et seq.*
[36] [1971] C.M.L.R. 260, 275 and see also *Deutsche Grammophon G.m.b.H.* v. *Metro-SB-Grossmärkte G.m.b.H. & Co. K.G* (78/70) [1971] C.M.L.R. 631, 658 in which a similar judgment was reached to that in the *Parke, Davis* and *Sirena* cases, *supra*, in relation to a record manufacturer's right of protection within a Member State and the relationship between prices charged for protected products and prices for reimported products. §§ 912 *et seq.*

In some cases the ownership of a patent may have enabled an undertaking to achieve a dominant position in respect of the supply of goods of a certain description; where there are no effective substitutes and no effective competition Article 86 is likely to prohibit any abuse by that undertaking of the dominant position which patent protection enables it to enjoy. However it has to be borne in mind that the monopoly granted in respect of industrial property rights may be for a limited period of time, thus limiting the possibility of significant abuse, and that it is in the nature of those rights, especially patent rights, that the holder is entitled to a reward for his inventiveness which he is under no obligation to share with competitors. It remains to be seen whether in any circumstances it can ever be an abuse to refuse to offer licences to competitors upon payment of reasonable royalties, or to discriminate between competitors in granting licences, or to impose onerous terms relating to the distribution of goods manufactured in accordance with the patent licence which might discourage competitors from applying for licences or from competing within the same territory[36a].

**728** Article 86 may also apply to a situation where a patentee charges excessively high prices [37] in commercial or geographical areas, where there are no substitute products and extremely low prices in commercial or geographical areas, and where competition from non-patented products would be substantial were it not for the uneconomic market price set by the undertaking in the dominant position.

**29** Whereas authorities in Member States may see disadvantages to the public interest in an undertaking earning, as a result of patent or similar protection, excessively high profits within that Member State and take remedial action to reduce the level of profits, it has yet to be determined how far the Commission will go in connecting excessively high profits earned by a firm in a dominant position with an adverse effect on inter-State trade, a factor which must be positively established if Article 86 is to apply.

[36a] See also *CSC-ZOJA*, J.O. 1972 L299/51.
[37] See § 726, *ante*.

#### 4. ACTIVITY OF THE COMMISSION UNDER ARTICLE 86

**730**    **General.** Between 1962 and 1972 there were only two decisions of the Commission under Article 86. However, the lack of decisions is no indication as to the changes in pricing policy and in the terms and conditions of supply which undertakings, believing themselves to be in a dominant position, have voluntarily made. Decisions of the Commission and of the European Court under Article 85 have established the rules of competition for restrictive trading agreements; the sub-paragraphs of Article 86 illustrate the kind of abuse at which Article 86 strikes and the fact that an abuse of a dominant position is prohibited *ab initio* is likely to have had a further important influence in encouraging firms to cease certain practices which would be most likely to be condemned.

**731**    **Re Gema.**[38] In December 1970 the Commission instituted proceedings[39] against Gema, a German authors' rights society, of Berlin. Its decision was published in June 1971.

Gema was the only society in Germany managing the rights of authors of musical works. It was of great commercial value to authors who would otherwise find it impracticable to manage their rights effectively and, through certain exclusivity agreements, it had acquired the power to exercise in Germany the rights enjoyed by other authors' rights societies established in other Member States. It had therefore a powerful position within Germany and one which was unlikely successfully to be challenged. The Commission investigated the constitution of the society, its practices and the fees which it had imposed on users of authors' rights in order to determine whether any part of its constitution or any of its practices was an abuse of its dominant position.

---

[38] J.O. 1971 L134/15, [1971] C.M.L.R. D35; see also *Re Gema (No. 2)*, J.O. 1972 L166/22, [1972] C.M.L.R. D115. See also the Commission's First Report on Competition Policy (1972), paras. 82–88, in which the Commission also indicates the measures which it has taken in respect of the practices of societies for the protection of authors' rights in other Member States. See now also *Re Sugar Cartel*, Commission decision, January 2, 1973; *Re CSC-ZOJA*, J.O. 1972 L299/51.

[39] The Commission instituted proceedings *ex officio* under Art. 3 of Reg. 17 (Ending of Infringements); for the powers of enforcement of the Commission see generally Chap. 12, *post*.

The Commission found that Gema had abused its dominant position principally in the ways discussed in the following paragraphs.

**732    Discrimination.**  Gema had discriminated against nationals of other Member States.[40]   Under its constitution, composers and authors who were nationals of other Member States but who did not have a fiscal residence in Germany were denied full benefits of ordinary membership: they could have no influence on the management of Gema and they were not entitled to certain supplementary benefits operated through a scheme which afforded benefits to full members.  There was also discrimination against German publishing houses with economic and personal links in other countries.

**733    Unnecessary obligations.**  Gema had bound its members by obligations which were not necessary.[41]   The Commission held that it was not necessary for Gema to require the assignment of authors' rights for all categories and for the whole world.  Only for the territory in which it carried on direct activity, in the categories entrusted to it, could Gema reasonably require the exclusive assignment of all the works of an author, including his future works.  It was also wrong to exclude all claims of right and recourse to the courts in the event of dispute as to the funds to be distributed, to pay supplementary fees only to certain of its members although the sums were derived from contributions of all members and others, and to refuse full benefits of membership to those of its members who were economically dependent upon users of authors' rights; in the event of any conflict of interest Gema should adopt the least restrictive means of safeguarding authors' rights.  It was also an abuse unfairly to complicate the movement of its members to another authors' rights society: the length of the assignment agreement (six years), the obligation to assign all future works in all categories over that period even after resignation and the long waiting period before becoming eligible for certain pecuniary benefits all tended unfairly to prevent movement to another society.

[40] [1971] C.M.L.R. D35, D47.
[41] *Ibid.* at p. D48.

**734**   **A single market.**  Gema had prevented, through its system, the establishment of a single market in the supply of services of music publisher.[42]  The Commission found that the discrimination against music publishers of other Member States and against German music publishers with ties in other Member States prevented authors and composers choosing a foreign publishing house because it would not gain the full benefits of membership of Gema.

**735**   **Wrongful use of copyright.**  Gema had extended copyright, through contractual means, to non-copyright works.[43]  It was Gema's practice to charge record manufacturers the same fee whether the record (or a side of the record) was protected by copyright in full or only as to part.  The Commission held that such a contractual term between the owner and user of copyright work would not be accepted if Gema did not enjoy a dominant position and was an abuse of that position.

**736**   **Lack of uniformity in charges.**  Gema had discriminated against independent importers of gramophone records as compared with manufacturers of records.[44]  Gema levied the whole licence fee on records imported from other Member States although a licence fee had already been paid for the records, either to Gema or to another authors' rights society.  This had the effect of discriminating between manufacturers of records, who paid a single fee, and importers who effectively had to pay a double fee and who were put at a competitive disadvantage.  Gema had also discriminated against importers of tape recorders and optical sound recorders as compared with the German manufacturers of such recorders by pursuing against importers the consistent practice of levying a higher fee on imports of tape recorders and optical sound recorders than on the products when manufactured in Germany.[45]  It was important to provide the same initial conditions to the undertakings which offered these instruments for sale, irrespective of the question whether they were manufacturers or importers.

[42] *Ibid.* at p. D53.
[43] *Ibid.* at p. D53.
[44] *Ibid.* at p. D54.
[45] *Ibid.* at p. D55.

**737**    The Commission also held that the improper exploitation of its dominant position by Gema was capable of affecting trade between Member States and that Gema was not a public under-taking,[46] within Article 90 of the Treaty, nor were special or exclusive rights granted to it.

**738**    Although *Re Gema* might fairly be considered as of limited general application, it indicates the very broad approach which the Commission is prepared to take in identifying and remedying any action which appears to it to be an unreasonable exercise of economic power aimed at entrenching a dominant position or which has that economic effect.    The decision also highlights the fact that the definition of an undertaking for the purposes of Article 86 is wide: the Commission held that Gema was an undertaking since " in granting and managing for profit authors' rights in music it carried on contracting activity consisting in the supply of services with regard to both composers, authors and publishers and users of music." [47]   Such an undertaking must ensure that its rules and activities do not unreasonably prevent or restrict the freedom of choice of individuals to seek alternative and effective representation throughout the common market.

**739**    **Re Continental Can Co. Inc.**   Until the European Court gave its judgment in *Re Continental Can Co. Inc.* it remained uncertain whether Article 86 applies to the control of mergers and acquisitions.[48]   Article 86, unlike Article 66 of the ECSC Treaty,[49] contains no specific provisions dealing with the prior notification and regulation of mergers.   Nevertheless the Com-mission had formed the view [50] that Article 86 would apply in circumstances where an undertaking in a dominant position acquired a competitor and substantially eliminated actual or

---

[46] See § 203, *ante*, for the meaning of undertaking, and for the provisions of Art. 90 see § 119, *ante*.

[47] [1971] C.M.L.R. D35, D46.

[48] See now *Europemballage Corporation and Continental Can Co. Inc.* v. *EEC Commission* (6/72) *The Times*, February 26, 1973.   The general view at present is that Art. 85 (1) does not apply to mergers agreements.   See the Commission's memorandum on Concentration of Enterprises in the Common Market (1966), Part III; Oberdorfer, Gleiss and Hirsch, *Common Market Cartel Law* (1971), para. 20; Deringer, The Competition Law of the European Economic Community (1968), para. 169.

[49] For the detailed provisions in Art. 66 of the ECSC Treaty dealing with prior notification of mergers see *Sweet & Maxwell's European Community Treaties* (1972), pp. 24–26.

[50] See the Commission's Memorandum on Concentration (1966), Part III.

potential competition in any market. In 1970, when Continental Can Co. Inc. acquired control of a leading Dutch supplier of metal containers the Commission put that view to the test. The facts which gave rise to the institution of proceedings by the Commission and upon which the decision was based are set out below.[51]

**740   Continental Can: the facts.**   Continental Can Co. Inc. (Continental Can) of New York was the world's largest producer of metal containers and an important producer of paper and plastic containers and of machines to manufacture and use them. In 1969 it had acquired control of Schmalbach-Lubeca-Werke (Schmalbach) of Germany, the largest producer of light metal containers in continental Europe and, in 1970, through a wholly owned company Europemballage Corporation, it acquired control of Thomassen and Drijver-Verblifa of Holland (Thomassen) the largest producer of metal containers in Benelux.

Both Schmalbach and Thomassen had been licensees of Continental Can before the acquisitions and both had been formed by mergers within the German and Benelux industries respectively. In terms of size (calculated generally by reference to sales) Schmalbach was about 15 per cent. that of Continental Can and Thomassen about 50 per cent. that of Schmalbach. The main production of Schmalbach and Thomassen was of light metal containers, accounting for approximately 80 per cent. of Schmalbach's turnover and 88 per cent. of that of Thomassen; with regard to the market for cans for preserving sterilised food products, Schmalbach had a market share in Germany of 70 to 80 per cent. in cans used for meat products, and 80 to 90 per cent. in cans used for fish and shellfish. Thomassen had a 100 per cent. market share in Holland in respect of those types of cans and a 100 per cent. share in Belgium in respect of " open top " cans for meat products. In metal stoppers (other than crown corks) Schmalbach had a market share of 50 to 55 per cent. in Germany and Thomassen had a market share of 45 to 50 per cent. in Holland and 15 per cent. in Belgium. In addition to an examination of the respective market shares of the merged companies the Commission investigated products capable of being substituted for metal containers in various applications, the

[51] J.O. 1972 L7/25, [1972] C.M.L.R. D11; on appeal, the Court was not satisfied that all the facts had been proved (Case 6/72).

strength of actual and potential competition, the requirements of the customers and other general matters which might affect competition in the supply of metal containers of certain types.

**741    Continental Can: the Commission's decision.** The Commission's findings may be summarised as follows. As the sole shareholder of Europemballage which held 85 per cent. of the share capital of Schmalbach, Continental Can controlled those two undertakings; it was subject to the jurisdiction of the Commission because of the effects of its actions within the common market.

Continental Can had a dominant position in Germany (a substantial part of the common market) in the supply of light metal containers for preserved meats and fish and in the supply of metal caps for glass jars. That dominant position derived from Schmalbach's market share of the different sub-markets for light containers and from the economic, financial and technical importance of the group. The Commission was not satisfied that there was significant competition from other manufacturers or from substitute products.

Other factors which the Commission regarded as relevant were Schmalbach's strong position in the supply of metal and other containers for other applications (*e.g.* for drinks); Schmalbach's overall importance in relation to other suppliers; Continental Can's manufacture of machines necessary for the production and use of metal containers and Continental Can's ownership of important patents and technical know-how. All those advantages were accentuated by the economic importance of the group, which enabled it to raise finance with less difficulty than competitors and maintain a technical lead.

The Commission held that Continental Can's acquisition of Thomassen was an abuse of its dominant position. " For an undertaking in a dominant position to reinforce that position by means of a merger with another undertaking with the consequence that the competition which would have existed actually or potentially in spite of the existence of the initial dominant position is in practice eliminated for the products in question in a substantial part of the common market constitutes behaviour which is incompatible with Article 86 of the Treaty."[52]

[52] *Ibid*, at p. D31.

**742**    **Continental Can: the Court's decision.** On appeal, the
European Court held [53] that Article 86 may be infringed where
an undertaking already in a dominant position seeks to reinforce
that position, for example, to a point at which potential competitors no longer exist because all companies in a certain market
have become dependent on the dominant company. Thus, it
appears, there is no need to establish that the dominant company
is specifically using its dominant position for the purpose of
abuse; in certain circumstances the mere strengthening of a
dominant position may, in itself, be prohibited under the Treaty
where it substantially results in the elimination of competition.
On the facts, however, the Court held that the Commission's
*reasoning* was defective, particularly in specifying the precise
markets in which the appellants were dominant, and in failing to
state the degree of competition found in each market. Accordingly, the Court allowed the appeal. Exactly how the Commission will apply the principles now stated by the Court remains
to be seen.

## 5.  PROHIBITION OF ABUSE [54]

**743**    **General.** Article 86 provides that any abuse shall be prohibited. Under Article 1 of Regulation 17 no prior decision to
that effect is necessary. Therefore the activity which is prohibited
and in respect of which sanctions can be applied is the abuse and
not merely future activity in breach of any order or finding by
the Commission.

**744**    **Effect of Article 86 in English law.** Since Article 86 and the
regulations made under Article 87 of the Treaty will be directly
applicable in English law as from the date of accession, it will be
the duty of English courts to give effect to those provisions as from
that date, just as in the case of Article 85.[55] Therefore, for
example, an English court will recognise and apply the decisions

---

[53] *Europemballage Corporation and Continental Can Co. Inc.* v. *EEC Commission*
(6/72) *The Times*, February 26, 1973.
[54] For the Commission's powers of enforcement of Arts. 85 and 86 see Chap. 12,
*post*; provision is made in Art. 2 of Reg. 17 for a request for negative clearance
under Art. 86 as well as Art. 85; as for requests for negative clearance, see §§ 501–
504, *ante*.
[55] See §§ 401 *et seq., ante*.

of the European Court of Justice in relation to the application of
Article 86.[56]

It has yet to be determined whether a civil action for damages
or an injunction lies for breach of the obligation which is imposed
by Article 86. It could perhaps be argued that third parties could
bring an action in appropriate circumstances for breach of a
" statutory duty " imposed by the combined effect of Article 86
and the European Communities Act 1972.[57] Alternatively, it
could be argued that an infringement of Article 86 constituted the
use of " unlawful means " and that a third party whose legitimate
business interests were injured thereby could sue in tort at common law.[58] However, it is submitted that whether Article 86 is
capable of conferring such rights is a question which must
ultimately be resolved by the European Court as a matter of
interpretation of the Treaty. If such an action does lie further
questions will arise as to measure of damages, remoteness of
damages and available defences which would be appropriate in
such an action, and whether such matters are exclusively within
the jurisdiction of the national court.

Under the Monopolies and Mergers Acts 1948 and 1965 [59]
provision is made for the Secretary of State to regulate the
activities of a monopolist where such activities have been found
by the Monopolies Commission, to operate against the public
interest; any prohibition of future activities of a certain kind is
enforceable by the Secretary of State and there is no provision in
English law for third party actions if the monopolist acts in
breach of such a prohibition. Therefore if a remedy exists under
Article 86 it would represent a considerable change in the law
and in the rights of third parties.

**[The next paragraph is 801.]**

[56] See s. 3 (1) of the European Communities Act 1972.
[57] See § 407, *ante.*
[58] See *ibid.*
[59] To be replaced by the Fair Trading Bill.

# CHAPTER 8

# EXCLUSIVE DEALING AGREEMENTS

## 1. IN GENERAL

**801    Generally.** The agreements with which this chapter is concerned are agreements between suppliers and distributors of goods or services under which restrictions are accepted by the supplier or by the distributor or by them both. The restrictions on the supplier affect the distribution of such goods or services in the distributor's area otherwise than through the distributor. The restrictions on the distributor affect the distribution or acquisition for distribution of such goods or services other than goods or services acquired from the supplier. The details of such restrictions may vary in important respects and will be affected by the question whether the distributor is an agent of the supplier or a principal who acquires the goods for resale on his own account. In some cases the supplier may be restricted only as to the appointment of other agents or the sale to other distributors in the area; in other cases the supplier may also be restricted as to the supply of such goods direct to consumers or users. Again in some cases the distributor or agent may be restricted as to the other suppliers whose goods he may handle, or as to the goods (whether acquired from another supplier or manufactured by the distributor himself) that he will sell in the area. In some cases the restriction applies according to the area in which the distributor is situated, irrespective of the situation of the customer; in other cases the restriction applies according to the situation of the customer, irrespective of the area in which the distributor is situated.

Such agreements may then be very broadly classified as follows:
(i) Sole agency [1] supply or sole supply: the supplier is restricted as to the other agents or distributors through or to whom he will supply.

---

[1] The expression " sole agent " in the context of exclusive dealing agreements is sometimes loosely used to describe a sole distributor. In this chapter " agent " refers only to an agent strictly so called *i.e.* one who merely passes orders to his principal or makes contracts on his behalf.

(ii) Exclusive agency supply or exclusive supply: the supplier is restricted not only as in (i) but also in respect of direct supply to consumers or users; in this kind of case, as also in case (i), the supplier is sometimes said to confer upon the agent or distributor a " franchise."

(iii) Exclusive agency distribution or exclusive distribution: the agent or distributor is restricted as to the suppliers from whom he acquires goods, or as to the goods, whether acquired from someone else or manufactured by the agent or distributor, that he distributes; this type of agreement is often known as a " requirements contract " [2] and includes "solus" selling agreements for petrol and " tied-house " agreements for beer.

The third type of agreement may be combined with the first or second type of agreement, so that both supplier or distributor are in some degree tied to each other.

**802**    Exclusive dealing agreements may also be collective. Under " collective " exclusive dealing agreements groups of manufacturers covenant among themselves to supply only through certain channels. Such agreements are often found where reciprocal exclusive supply and purchase arrangements are entered into between groups of manufacturers on the one hand and groups of traders on the other. Collective exclusive dealing agreements are discussed elsewhere in this work.[3]

**803**    **Exclusive dealing agreements and Article 85.**  Although when considering the effect of the Treaty it is necessary to distinguish between the different types of exclusive dealing agreements, those agreements all have certain features which may bring them within Article 85 (1). The common factor among exclusive dealing agreements is that they either prevent traders from making use of alternative sources of supply, or they prevent suppliers from making use of alternative distributive arrangements. In this way, the restrictions contained in such agreements limit the competitive activities of third parties. For example, a sole dis-

[2] In this work the word " tying " will not be used in connection with " solus " or " requirements " contracts in order to avoid confusion with those agreements referred to in Art. 85 (1) (e). *Ante*, §§ 314, 324.

[3] *Ante*, §§ 331 *et seq.* Many national collective exclusive dealing agreements in the United Kingdom have been struck down under the Restrictive Trade Practices Act 1956.

tributorship agreement has the effect of preventing any other
distributor within the contract area from obtaining supplies
of the contract products directly from the manufacturer. A
" requirements " contract denies to other suppliers an outlet for
their products. These restrictions may become particularly acute
if the contract in question is part of a network of similar contracts. This may have the effect of closing wide areas to the
trading activities of third parties. For these reasons, exclusive
dealing agreements are capable of being caught by Article 85 (1),
which applies not only to agreements which restrict competition
between the parties themselves but also to agreements which
limit competition between one of the contracting parties and third
parties.[4]   On the other hand, many exclusive dealing agreements
may qualify for exemption under Article 85 (3). Certain types of
them benefit from the block exemption which is provided under
Regulation 67/67.[5]   A non-exclusive distribution agreement
which contains no territorial restrictions, and no other competitive restrictions on the distributor, falls outside Article 85 (1)
altogether.[6]

**804**    **Plan of this chapter.** The types of agreement referred to
above are the subject of this chapter. After a short discussion of
" sole agency " agreements, the main section of the chapter deals
with sole distributorship agreements. Then " requirements "
contracts are discussed. A separate section is devoted to the
important topic of selective distribution.

## 2.  AGENCY

**805**    **True agency agreements fall outside Article 85 (1).** In the
Commission's view [7] Article 85 (1) of the Treaty does not apply
to contracts concluded with sole or exclusive agents [8] in which
the latter agree, for a specified part of the common market, to
procure business on behalf of another undertaking or to close
transactions for the account of that undertaking. It is immaterial
whether or not the transaction is actually made in the agent's

---

[4] *Ante*, §§ 215–220.                                  [5] *Post*, § 818.
[6] *Re Mertens and Straet*, J.O. 1964 1426/64, [1964] C.M.L.R. 416.
[7] Announcement on Exclusive Agency Contracts made with Commercial Agents
    December 24, 1962, App. 10, *post*. And see now *Re Pittsburgh Corning Europe*,
    J.O. 1972 L272/35, [1973] C.M.L.R. D2.
[8] The notice appears to apply whether the agency is sole or exclusive. See § 801,
    *ante*.

name. The Commission argues that such agreements do not prevent, restrict or distort competition, since the agent has only an auxiliary function in the market, that of seeking buyers or sellers on behalf of his principal, in whose interests he is acting. The undertaking which employs such an agent remains entirely free to decide with whom it wishes to do business, in what products and for which territory. The agent always remains subject to his principal's directions. While it is true that the agent's obligation to serve only one principal in a particular market for a given length of time may result in restrictions on supply (the agent's freedom to place orders elsewhere) and demand (the principal's freedom to do business through other agents), the Commission feels that these restraints result from the special relationship between principal and agent whereby each party owes a special duty to protect the other's commercial interests. The Commission's view may derive some support from certain dicta of the European Court of Justice.[9]

**806    Incidence of risk decisive.** However, such contracts will fall outside the Treaty only if they are made with agents who act on behalf of their principals rather than as independent traders on their own account. The Commission considers [7] that the decisive criteria for distinguishing a sole agent from an independent trader is whether the agent in fact assumes any risk in connection with the transaction (apart from the common *del credere* guarantee). If he does so, the agent will normally be an independent trader, regardless of the appellation chosen by the parties to the contract. In particular the Commission considers that a party described as an agent is in reality an independent trader where he is required to or does in fact either hold considerable stocks as his own property, or maintain an after-sales service to customers at his own expense; or where he is able to determine prices and terms of business.

**807    Joint agents.** Different considerations arise where two or more parties in competition with each other (usually manufacturers) agree to appoint the same agent to transact business on their behalf. In such cases there may be a joint selling agreement falling within Article 85 (1).[10]

[9] *Italy* v. *EEC Council and Commission* (32/65) [1969] C.M.L.R. 39, 63.
[10] See *ante*, §§ 337 *et seq.*

### 3.  SOLE DISTRIBUTORSHIP AGREEMENTS [11]

#### (a) *General*

**808**     **Form and function.**[12]   A sole distributorship agreement is an agreement by which one party (the supplier) agrees to deliver certain products only to the other (the distributor) for resale, usually within a certain area.   The grant of such an exclusive right is intended to give the distributor an interest in the promotion of sales of the supplier's goods in the territory concerned.   In many cases, this may be the supplier's only means of penetrating the market.   Such agreements often include either a prohibition imposed on the distributor against dealing in products competing with those of the supplier or an obligation to obtain all his goods for resale only from the supplier.   This gives the sole distributor an added incentive to promote sales of the contract products.

**809**     **Additional protection of sole distributor.**   The exclusivity granted to the sole distributor may be enhanced by various means intended to ensure that he shall be the only distributor to market the contract products in the territories assigned to him.   These means principally consist of export bans imposed on other distributors of the same supplier. This may make it impracticable for third parties to obtain supplies.   Another means of achieving the same end is the assignment to the sole distributor of industrial property rights, especially trade mark rights.[13]   This is designed to enable the sole distributor to sue other importers for infringements of his rights.   In addition, the exclusivity may be protected by the " laws of unfair competition " in certain countries, particularly in France, under which a sole distributor may obtain an injunction against a competitor who fails to respect his exclusive rights by importing the contract products from elsewhere.[14]

**810**     **Plan of this section.**   The first topic discussed, is the impact of Article 85 upon sole distributorship agreements which relate directly to inter-State trade.   The circumstances in which par-

---

[11] The principles discussed in this chapter apply equally to " exclusive distributorship agreements."
[12] See also §§ 801 and 802, *ante.*
[13] See also §§ 905 *et seq., post.*
[14] See *ante*, § 218, note 39.

ticular agreements or clauses in agreements may fall under
Article 85 (1) are considered together with circumstances in which
sole distributorship agreements (including Accession agreements)[15] may benefit from exemptions. It is necessary to deal
separately with agreements relating solely to inter-State trade
and with agreements relating to trade with third countries outside
the EEC.

## (b) *Inter-State Agreements*

### (i) **Grundig-Consten and other decisions**

**811**      **In general.** Fundamentally, the Commission is favourably
disposed towards sole distributorship agreements provided they
are not too restrictive. As expressed in the Preamble of Regulation 67/67, which will be dealt with in this section, sole
distributorship agreements bring a number of benefits. By
appointing a sole distributor the supplier avoids numerous
dealings with a large number of traders; he is able to intensify
his sales effort and to rationalise his distribution, particularly
when international trade is concerned. But the Commission's
policy, the foundations of which were laid down in the leading
case of *Grundig-Consten*,[16] is to strike down the *additional*
protection of the sole distributor referred to above.[17] At the
same time, the Commission has, by means of Regulation 67/67,
granted block exemption under Article 85 (3) to many sole
distributorship agreements where this additional protection is
absent. But before discussing this Regulation it is necessary to
consider the principles of *Grundig-Consten* and other decisions.

**812**        **Grundig-Consten: the Commission's decision.** The Commission's decision in *Re Grundig-Consten* [18] is the foundation of
Community law relating to sole distributorship agreements. The
full facts of this case have already been set out in Chapter 2, to
which reference should be made.[19] Briefly, Grundig appointed
Consten as its sole distributor in France in respect of Grundig

---

[15] *Ante,* § 207.
[16] *Re Grundig-Consten,* J.O. 1964 2545/64, [1964] C.M.L.R. 489; *Consten and
Grundig* v. *EEC Commission* (56/64, 58/64) [1966] C.M.L.R. 418.
[17] § 809, *ante.*
[18] *Re Grundig-Consten,* J.O. 1964 2545/64, [1964] C.M.L.R. 489.
[19] *Ante,* §§ 217–219.

EXCLUSIVE DEALING AGREEMENTS

products. Consten agreed not to deliver any Grundig products directly or indirectly outside the contract territory of France. Grundig itself undertook not to deliver to anyone in France except Consten, and at the same time imposed restrictions upon its distributors in each of the other Member States, and upon its German wholesalers, which prevented them from exporting into France either. In addition, by a collateral agreement Consten was authorised to register in France the Grundig mark " GINT " which appeared on all Grundig products in addition to the " GRUNDIG " mark. In 1961, another French firm, UNEF managed to obtain Grundig products, imported them into France, and sold them at a lower price than Consten. When Consten sued UNEF in the French courts under the French law of unfair competition [20] and for infringement of the trademark " GINT," the French court stayed proceedings pending the Commission's decision upon the applicability of Article 85 (1).[21] The Commission found that both the sole distribution agreement between Consten and Grundig and the collateral agreement relating to the " GINT " trademark fell within Article 85 (1). The Commission gave three main reasons for its decision [22]: (i) the contractual arrangements reserved the trade between France and Germany in Grundig products entirely to Consten. No competing French undertaking could import these products without risk. Thus " parallel imports "—i.e. imports of the contract product by dealers other than Consten—were prevented and the French national market for those products was isolated in the hands of one enterprise; (ii) the prohibition on export imposed upon Consten under the agreement prevented exports from one Member State to another and consequently hindered the integration of national markets in the common market; (iii) the use of the " GINT " trademark to preserve Consten's exclusive French rights contributed to preserving the isolation of the French market in Grundig products. Consequently the agreements affected trade between Member States and restricted competition within the meaning of Article 85 (1). Moreover, the Commission refused an exemption under Article 85 (3) because of the " absolute territorial protection " accorded

[20] See ante, § 218, note 39.
[21] [1963] C.M.L.R. 176.
[22] [1964] C.M.L.R. 489, 494–497.

to Consten.[23] " Absolute territorial protection," a concept invented by the Commission, occurs where the distributor is wholly protected from competition from parallel imports. In this case, the contractual arrangements gave Consten a monopoly position in France. Prices of Grundig products in France were much higher than in Germany. The restriction on parallel imports prevented any equalisation of those prices taking place and hindered the creation of a true common market. The Commission said that absolute territorial protection was not indispensable to the attainment of improvements in distribution which the sole distributorship agreement might otherwise have offered. It therefore held [24] that the whole agreement fell within Article 85 (1) and granted an order under Article 3 (1) of Regulation 17 [25] enjoining the parties from taking " any and all measures " to prevent third parties from obtaining Grundig products for resale in the contract territory from any wholesaler or retailer of their choice. This order was intended not only to prevent Consten from invoking the clauses of the agreement, but also to prevent the use of either national trademark rights or the national laws of unfair competition to obstruct parallel imports.[26]

**813**      **The Court's decision.** Grundig and Consten appealed to the European Court of Justice against the Commission's decision.[27] In most, but not all, respects the Court confirmed the Commission's decision,[28] holding that competition was restricted within the meaning of Article 85 (1) where the agreement had the object or effect of restricting competition between distributors of the same branded products.[29] The distribution agreement isolated the French market for products of a well known brand and hence affected trade between Member States.[30] The Court also held that the exercise of the " GINT " trademark rights for the purpose of obstructing imports brought the agreement relating to the assignment of the trademark within Article 85 (1).[31] Further the Court refused to interfere with the Commission's

---

[23] *Ibid.*, pp. 497 *et seq.*                    [24] *Ibid.*, pp. 503, 504
[25] See *post*, §§ 1202 *et seq.*
[26] See also § 141 as to conflict between Community laws and national laws.
[27] Under Art. 173 of the Treaty, *post*, § 12.
[28] *Consten and Grundig* v. *EEC Commission* (56/64, 58/64) [1966] C.M.L.R. 418.
[29] *Ibid.* at pp. 472–474. See *ante*, §§ 218, 219.
[30] *Ibid.* at pp. 471 and 472. *Ante*, §§ 218, 219.
[31] See *post*, §§ 909 *et seq.*

refusal to grant exemption under Article 85 (3), holding that the Commission's reasoning was sufficient on this point.[32] Finally the Court substantially confirmed the order imposed on the parties.

**814    Result of Grundig-Consten: absolute territorial protection.** As a result of the decisions of the Commission and the Court in *Grundig-Consten*, a sole distributorship agreement falls within Article 85 (1) in so far as it confers on the sole distributor absolute territorial protection.[33] In practice this means that an undertaking by the supplier to procure that no other distributor exports into the contract area will be void; similarly a ban on export imposed on the sole distributor will also be avoided. To this general rule there are only minor exceptions.[34] Further, agreements which contain such provisions will almost invariably not qualify for exemption under Article 85 (3), although the Commission does not entirely exclude the possibility of a temporary exemption in rare circumstances.[35]

**815    Agreements not conferring absolute territorial protection.** However, the Court did not confirm the Commission's decision in *Grundig-Consten* in its entirety. It held [36] that the Commission had given no reasons for striking down the whole of the distribution agreement, as distinct from those clauses of the agreement which conferred upon Consten absolute territorial protection. In particular it held that the Commission had not sufficiently explained the reasons why the exclusivity clause (*i.e.* Grundig's commitment to supply no other distributor in France with the contract products) fell within Article 85 (1).[36] In the absence of such reasons, the Court annulled that part of the Commission's decision which condemned clauses other than

[32] [1966] C.M.L.R. 418, 477–480. See *ante*, §§ 603, 604, 612.
[33] Various car manufacturer's dealing agreements have been the subject of investigation. Formal complaints have been issued to Citroën: " Europe " No. 1128 (new series) 25/26, September 1972. Fines of 100,000 units of account (u.a.) have been imposed on Pittsburgh Corning Europe S.A. for isolating the German market, J.O. 1972 L272/35, [1973] C.M.L.R. D2; see also *WEA-Fillipachi*, J.O. 1972 L303/52.
[34] *Post*, § 817; and see *ante*, §§ 245 *et seq.*
[35] First Report on Competition Policy, para. 49.
[36] [1966] C.M.L.R. 418, 474, 475.

those which tended to obstruct parallel imports into France.[37] The question therefore arises, in what circumstances does an exclusive dealing agreement which does not confer absolute territorial protection fall within Article 85 (1)? This question was considered by the Court in the *LTM* case[38] in a judgment rendered very shortly before that of *Grundig-Consten*. In *LTM* the agreement conferred no absolute territorial protection and contained no ban on re-export. The Court held[39] that agreements merely granting sole distributorship rights do not *necessarily* fall within the Treaty. In every case it is necessary to take a large number of considerations into account, including "the nature and limited or unlimited quantity of the products covered by the agreement, the position and importance of the grantor, the position and importance of the concessionaire on the market in the products in question, the isolated nature of the agreement in question or its place among a network of agreements, the severity of the clauses intended to protect the exclusive right or the possibilities left open to other commercial dealings in the same products through export or parallel imports."[40] The Court's decision in *LTM* apparently overrules a number of previous decisions of the Commission in which it was held that the mere commitment by a supplier to deliver his goods to only one distributor within a specified part of the common market brings the agreement within Article 85 (1), at least where branded goods giving rise to consumer preferences are concerned.[41] As a result of the Court's decision it may not be easy in any given case to say whether or not a sole distributorship agreement without an absolute territorial protection clause or a ban on re-export falls within Article 85 (1).[42] But since a great number of agreements of this type fall within the block exemption provided by Regulation 67/67,[43] the problem may not often arise.

---

[37] *Ibid.* at p. 481. Under Art. 173 of the Treaty the Court may allow an appeal against the Commission's decision, *inter alia*, on the grounds of infringement of the Treaty or of any rule of law relating to its application. Art. 190 of the Treaty provides that the Commission shall state its reason for its decision. It was the lack of *reasoning* that resulted in the partial annulment of the decision.
[38] (56/65) [1966] C.M.L.R. 357.                           [39] *Ibid.* at pp. 376, 377.
[40] *Ibid.* at pp. 375, 376. See also *Béguelin* (22/71) [1972] C.M.L.R. 81, 94–96.
[41] See *Re DRU–Blondel*, J.O. 1965 2194/65, [1965] C.M.L.R. 180; *Re Hummel-Isbecque*, J.O. 1965 2531/65, [1965] C.M.L.R. 242; *Re Jallatte-Voss and Jallatte-Vandeputte*, J.O. 1966 37/66, [1966] C.M.L.R. D1.
[42] For some decisions of national courts in this field, see *ante*, § 409, note 41 and § 421, note 80.                                    [43] *Post*, § 817.

**816**    **The " de minimis " rule.**    A sole distributorship agreement
will fall outside Article 85 (1) altogether if it has no noticeable
effect on trade between Member States or competition.[44]    This
principle, which has been fully discussed in Chapter 2 above,[45]
was confirmed by the decision of the European Court in *Volk*
where the Court held [46] that such an agreement may not be caught
by the prohibition contained in the Treaty where the parties have
a weak position on the market in question, even if the agreement
grants absolute territorial protection.

**817**    **Parent and subsidiary companies.**    Agreements whereby a
parent company appoints as its sole distributor a subsidiary
which is not economically autonomous of the parent fall outside
Article 85 (1).[47]

**(ii) Regulation 67/67** [48]

**818**    **In general.**    Under Regulation 67/67, made by the Commission under the powers contained in Regulation 19/65,[49] many
sole distributorship agreements are exempted *en bloc* from the
prohibition contained in Article 85 (1).    This Regulation came
into force on May 1, 1967 and has now been extended until
December 31, 1982.[50]    Agreements made after May 1, 1967
which fall within Regulation 67/67 do not require to be notified.[51]
Transitional provisions have been made for Accession agreements
to be modified so as to fall within the block exemption.[52]    The
provisions of the Regulation do not apply to agreements in which
only undertakings from one Member State are party and which
concern the resale of goods within that Member State.[53]

**819**    **Agreements to which Regulation 67/67 applies.**    Article 1 of
Regulation 67/67 declares the prohibition of Article 85 (1)
inapplicable to " agreements to which only two undertakings are

[44] *Volk* v. *Vervaecke* (5/69) [1969] C.M.L.R. 273.
[45] *Ante,* § 241.
[46] (5/69) [1969] C.M.L.R. 273, 281–283.  See also *Cadillon* (1/71) [1971] C.M.L.R.
    420, 429.  But *cf. Béguelin* (22/71) [1972] C.M.L.R. 81, dispositif, at pp. 98, 99.
[47] *Béguelin* (22/71) [1972] C.M.L.R. 81, 95.  See also *ante,* §§ 250 *et seq.*
[48] App. 6, *post.*
[49] App. 5, *post.*
[50] Under Reg. 2591/72, amending Reg. 67/67.
[51] *Cadillon* (1/71) [1972] C.M.L.R. 420, 430.
[52] *Post,* § 824.
[53] Art. 1 (2) of Reg. 67/67.  For " national " sole distributorship agreements see
    *post,* § 830.

parties and by which: (a) one undertakes, with regard to the other, to supply certain products to the other alone with a view to their resale within a specified part of the common market territory, or (b) one undertakes, with regard to the other, to purchase from the other alone certain products with a view to their resale,[54] or (c) sole supply and purchase commitments, with a view to resale, of the type envisaged in the two preceding subparagraphs, have been entered into by the two undertakings." It does not matter whether the parties are established inside or outside the EEC.[55] But it should be noted that the Regulation only applies (i) where the contract is bilateral [56] and (ii) the products are delivered for resale and not *e.g.* for further processing or use. The Regulation also covers concerted practices falling within the above definition.[57]

**820**     **Permitted restrictions on sole distributor.** If the agreement falls within Article 1 of Regulation 67/67 it must then satisfy Article 2. Article 2 (1) sets out the only restrictions on competition which may be imposed on the distributor in addition to the exclusive obligations set out in Article 1 (1). These are obligations: (i) not to manufacture or distribute competing products for up to one year after the expiry of the contract, and (ii) not to advertise, or to establish a branch or warehouse outside the contract territory. If any restrictions on competition are imposed beyond the two permitted above, the agreement will not benefit from the exemption. Thus, although the manufacturer may legitimately restrain the distributor from *promoting* the products outside his area, the distributor must remain free to sell beyond his territory if he so wishes. In this sense the contract territory can be no more than an area of primary responsibility. It should also be noted that the distributor must be free to determine prices and terms of resale. A resale price maintenance obligation may take the agreement outside the block exemption-Article 2 (2) provides that Article 1 (1) may still apply not.

---

[54] As to " requirements " contracts see *post*, §§ 836 *et seq.*

[55] For agreements relating to trade with non-Member States see *post*, §§ 832 *et seq.*

[56] A network of distribution agreements may properly be treated as a series of bilateral contracts between the supplier on the one hand and each distributor on the other: *Parfums Marcel Rochas* (1/70) [1971] C.M.L.R. 104, 117.

[57] Reg. 67/67, Art. 8.

withstanding that the distributor is obliged to purchase complete lines or minimum quantities, to sell under the manufacturers' trademark or packaging, or to undertake sales promotion measures such as advertising, stock holding, providing after sales and guarantee services and employing qualified staff.

**821    Competing manufacturers.**   Article (3) (*a*) of Regulation 67/67 provides that the block exemption is excluded where competing manufacturers grant each other exclusive selling rights in their respective products.   Such an arrangement may result in market sharing.[58]

**822    Absolute territorial protection.**   Article 3 (*b*) provides that the exempting Regulation shall not apply where " the contracting parties make it difficult for middlemen and consumers to obtain the contract products from other dealers within the common market " particularly when the parties (i) exercise industrial property rights with a view to interfering with the supplying to resellers or users in other parts of the common market of products covered by the contract, properly marketed and put into circulation, or with the sale of the said products by those resellers or users in the territories covered by the contract; (ii) exercise other rights or adopt measures with a view to interfering with the supplying to resellers or users of products covered by the contract elsewhere in the common market, or with the sale of the said products by those resellers or users in the territory covered by the contract.   These provisions are intended to deal with the situations such as that which arose in *Grundig-Consten*.[59]   Article 3 (*b*) (i) and (ii) in effect provide that the exercise of industrial property or other rights for the purposes set out (*i.e.* in order to divide up the market and hinder the economic integration of the EEC) will render the exemption inapplicable.   Thus the bringing of an infringement action in respect of an alleged violation of a patent or trademark for the *improper purpose* of ensuring absolute territorial protection for the goods would remove the benefit of the exemption.   In the *Béguelin* case [60] the

[58] *Cf. Re Wild & Leitz*, J.O. 1972 L61/27, [1972] C.M.L.R. D36.  See also reciprocal exclusive dealing in specialisation agreements, § 1005 *et seq.*
[59] J.O. 1964 2545/64; (56/64, 58/64) [1966] C.M.L.R. 418.  See *ante*, §§ 812, 813.  See further *post*, §§ 909 *et seq.*  See also *ante*, §§ 217–219.
[60] (22/71) [1972] C.M.L.R. 81, 96, 97.

Court appears to have regarded the invocation of the French law of unfair competition as " an exercise of other rights or a taking of measures " which rendered Regulation 67/67 inapplicable. The treatment of industrial property and analogous rights in Article 3 (*b*) coincides with the principles developed by the Court in this respect.[61]

**823**   **Revocation.**  Under Article 7 of Regulation 19/65 the Commission has power to withdraw the benefit of the block exemption, where it finds, upon its own initiative or upon a request from Member States or interested third parties, that the operation of a particular agreement is incompatible with Article 85 (3) of the Treaty.  When withdrawing the benefit of the block exemption the Commission may then take a decision granting an exemption under Article 85 (3), but subject to conditions, notwithstanding that the agreement has not been notified.  It is not clear whether the Commission's decision to withdraw the benefit of the block exemption under Article 7 of Regulation 19/65 may have retroactive effect.[62]  Under Article 6 of Regulation 67/67 the Commission is under a duty to examine whether Article 7 of Regulation 19/65 is applicable in any given case, particularly if the contract products are not exposed to competition from similar products,[63] or if other manufacturers of similar products have difficulty in selling within the contract territory,[64] or if the distributor is abusing the exemption by denying supplies to certain buyers [65] or charging unreasonably high prices.[66]

**824**   **Transitional provisions: Accession agreements.**  Transitional arrangements have been made for sole distributorship agreements which were already in existence on January 1, 1973 and which fall within the Treaty solely as a result of accession (Accession agreements).[67]  Clearly the transitional arrangements will benefit not only agreements between parties in the " new " Member States, but also those agreements in the " old " Member States

---

[61] See *post*, §§ 901 *et seq.*  See in particular *Sirena* (40/70) [1971] C.M.L.R. 260, 272–275.
[62] See Art. 7 of Reg. 19/65 and Art. 8 (3) (*b*) (*c*) and (*d*) of Reg. 17.
[63] Art. 6 (*a*) of Reg. 67/67.
[64] Art. 6 (*b*) of Reg. 67/67.
[65] Art. 6 (*c*) (i) of Reg. 67/67.
[66] Art. 6 (*c*) (ii) of Reg. 67/67.
[67] *Ante*, § 207.

which formerly involved exports outside the common market *e.g.* to England or Ireland. The position of such agreements, may be summarised as follows:

(i) Those agreements which on January 1, 1973 already satisfy the requirements of Regulation 67/67 do not require to be notified and benefit from the block exemption as from that date.

(ii) Those agreements which do not on January 1, 1973 fulfil the conditions of Regulation 67/67 benefit from an amendment to Article 5 of that Regulation, made consequent upon accession,[68] which provides that the prohibition in Article 85 (1) of the Treaty shall not apply where they are modified within six months from the date of accession so as to fulfil the conditions contained in that Regulation. The result of this provision is that sole distributorship agreements not falling within Regulation 67/67 at the date of accession will, if modified before July 1, 1973 so as to fall within Regulation 67/67, be fully valid as from January 1, 1973, and will not require notification.

(iii) Sole distributorship agreements which are not modified before July 1, 1973, so as to fall within Regulation 67/67, will become void in the relevant respects as from January 1, 1973. If they have been notified before July 1, 1973 for the purpose of obtaining an individual exemption, they enjoy " provisional validity. "[69]

(iv) Agreements in existence on January 1, 1973 which do not fall within Regulation 67/67 and which are not notified by July 1, 1973, but which are subsequently modified after that date so as to fulfil Regulation 67/67, become fully valid at least from the date of the modification, even in the absence of notification.

**825    The original transitional provisions.**  When Regulation 67/67 first came into force on May 1, 1967, certain transitional arrangements were made in respect of agreements in existence at that time. Agreements in existence on March 13, 1962, the date when Regulation 17 came into force, and notified before February 1, 1963 benefit from the block exemption retroactively to the date when the requirements of Regulation 67/67 were fulfilled.[70] Agreements notified before February 1, 1963 which

[68] Cmnd. 4862, II, p. 75. See App. 6, *post.* Presumably the third and fourth sentences of Art. 5 may now be disregarded although they are not specifically amended by the Act of Accession.
[69] See generally §§401 *et seq.*, especially §§403, 410 *et seq.*
[70] Art. 4 (1) of Reg. 67/67.

were modified before August 2, 1967 to fulfil the conditions of Regulation 67/67 are also exempt from the provisions of Article 85 (1) for the period preceding the modification provided that the Commission has been notified of the modification before October 3, 1967.[71] All other agreements which were notified before May 1, 1967 benefit from the block exemption retroactively to the date when the conditions of Regulation 67/67 were fulfilled, but not for any period earlier than the date of notification.[72] It is undecided how far agreements made before May 1, 1967 which fulfil the conditions of Regulation 67/67 but have never been notified benefit from the exemption. Whatever their legal status prior to that date, it is the Commission's view, expressed in the *Cadillon* case,[73] that they qualify for exemption, from May 1, 1967. But in *Cadillon* the Court of Justice left this point open.

826 **(iii) Other agreements falling outside Regulation 67/67**
**In general.** If any particular agreement falls outside the provisions of Regulation 67/67 it is still open to the parties to notify the agreement to the Commission for the purposes of obtaining an individual exemption under Article 85 (3). One such exemption in *Re Omega*[74] is discussed later in this chapter.[75] In this part of this section some miscellaneous cases probably falling within Article 85 (1) but outside Regulation 67/67 are mentioned.

827

**Obligation on distributor not to resell before importation and payment of duty.** The Commission has published [76] the outline of an agreement between a Scotch whisky manufacturer and a French distributor whereby the distributor accepts a number of restrictions falling within Regulation 67/67, but in addition agrees not to resell the contract products " prior to their importation into the territory covered by the concession and before customs duties have been paid." It appears that such restrictions may impede sales to other Member States and therefore fall within Article 85 (1). The Commission has announced [76]

[71] Art. 5 of Reg. 67/67.
[72] Art. 4 (2) of Reg. 67/67.
[73] (1/71) [1971] C.M.L.R. 420, 428.
[74] J.O. 1970 L242/22, [1970] C.M.L.R. D49.
[75] *Post,* § 840 *et seq.*
[76] J.O. 1971 C9/1. Announcement under Art. 19 (3) of Reg. 17.

that it proposes to take a favourable decision in respect of this agreement, but this may no longer be so.

**828** **Restrictions on purpose for which goods may be resold.** The Commission has published [77] the terms of a standard form of agreement between a Scotch whisky manufacturer and a number of victuallers, ships' chandlers and the like, under which the acquirers agree not to resell the contract products except for duty free consumption (*e.g.* on ships), and to obtain an undertaking from subsequent purchasers that they will only resell the goods for that purpose. The Commission has also announced that it proposes to give a favourable decision in respect of this agreement. [77]

**829** **Exclusive distributorship for the whole common market.** In the Commission's view, [78] the question of whether a distribution agreement appointing one distributor for the whole common market area falls under Article 85 (1) is not yet decided. It may appear, on an analogy with the *Davidson Rubber* [79] decision that such an agreement does fall within Article 85 (1). If so, can Regulation 67/67 apply? Article 1 (1) (*a*) of that Regulation relates to agreements where one party agrees to deliver the contract products only to the other party for *resale within a specified area of the common market*. This wording suggests that an agreement in respect of the whole of the common market falls outside Regulation 67/67 and thus requires an individual exemption. [80]

(c) *Domestic Agreements*

**830** **In general.** Sole distributorship agreements made between two parties situated in the same Member State which concern the resale of products within that State fall outside Regulation 67/67. [81] The Commission's view is that such bilateral exclusive dealing agreements are only exceptionally capable of affecting trade between Member States and, consequently, it is only in exceptional circumstances that Article 85 (1) will apply. [82]

[77] J.O. *Ibid.*
[78] First Report on Competition Policy, para. 52.
[79] J.O. 1972 L143/31, [1972] C.M.L.R. D52.  See *post*, § § 944 *et seq.*
[80] See also Oberdorfer, Gleiss and Hirsch, *Common Market Cartel Law*, para. 713.
[81] Art. 1 (2) of Reg. 67/67.
[82] First Report on Competition Policy, para 52.

**831**    **Export restrictions.** However, many United Kingdom sole
distributorship agreements contain two principal territorial
restrictions. First, the sole distributor is restricted, as to sales on
the home market, to a particular area within the United Kingdom,
*e.g.* Kent. Secondly, the distributor is often expressly prohibited
from exporting the contract products outside the United
Kingdom. A direct export prohibition of the latter kind may
fall within Article 85 (1) in accordance with the principles
of the *Grundig-Consten* decision.[83] The question then arises as to
how a restriction of the first kind falls within the Treaty— for an
obligation to resell all the contract products only within Kent
may be equivalent to a direct ban on exports. At this point there
is first the question of fact—is the restriction capable of preventing
competition and affecting trade between Member States? In
answering this question the general principles and the relevant
factors discussed in Chapter 2 must be applied.[84] In very many
cases the mere fact that a distributor is limited to sales within a
particular part of a national territory will not make Article 85 (1)
applicable. Secondly, there is the further question of whether
the agreement may be of the type described under Article 4 (2) (i)
of Regulation 17.[85] That provision relaxes the notification requirements in respect of agreements between undertakings situated in
the same Member State which " involve neither imports nor
exports. " The circumstances in which a national sole distributorship agreement may be said not " to involve imports or exports "
have been considered in Chapter 5, to which reference should be
made.[86] Where such an agreement falls within Article 4 (2) (i)
of Regulation 17 then, in certain circumstances, the agreement
may benefit from " provisional validity."[87]


(d) *Trade with Third Countries*

**832 (i) Imports into the EEC**
   **Sole distributorship for imports.** A sole distributorship
agreement by which an undertaking situated in a country outside
the EEC appoints a sole distributor for a specified area within the

[83] (56/64, 58/64) [1966] C.M.L.R. 418. *Ante,* §§ 811–814.
[84] *Ante,* §§ 221–226.
[85] See generally §§ 528 *et seq., ante.*
[86] *Ante,* § 529.
[87] *Ante,* §§ 403, 410 *et seq.*

EEC is governed by the same rules as those already discussed in the context of inter-State agreements.[88] This is illustrated by *Béguelin*.[89] In that case a Japanese undertaking producing WIN lighters appointed sole distributors in France and Germany respectively. The agreements purported to confer absolute territorial protection on each distributor. The French sole distributor attempted to sue a " parallel importer," who had obtained the contract products from the German sole distributor, under the French law of unfair competition.[90] On a reference from the French court, the European Court held [91] that the fact that one party to the contract was the Japanese supplier situated outside the common market did not prevent the normal application of the Treaty principles, provided the agreement produced its effects within the common market. It follows that there is nothing in principle to prevent a sole distributorship agreement in relation to imports into the EEC from benefiting from Regulation 67/67.

**(ii) Exports from the EEC**

833      **Sole distributorship for exports.** Agreements under which one party appoints the other as his sole distributor in respect of a county outside the EEC generally fall outside Article 85 (1), since they do not usually have the object or effect of restricting competition *within* the common market. This general rule was established in two decisions of the Commission, *Re Grosfillex* [92] and *Re Rieckermann*.[93] The Commission has announced [94] that these decisions may be regarded as establishing the principles to be applied, first to export agreements concluded with a sole distributor in a third country, and secondly to such agreements concluded with an exporter within the EEC who is not organised for distribution within the common market.

834      **The Grosfillex case.** In *Re Grosfillex*,[92] a French firm appointed a Swiss undertaking, Fillistorf, as its exclusive distributor for its plastic household products in Switzerland. Grosfillex agreed to deliver only to Fillistorf in Switzerland,

---

[88] *Ante*, §§ 811–829.
[90] See *ante*, § 218, note 39.
[92] J.O. 1964 915/64, [1964] C.M.L.R. 237.
[93] J.O. 1968 L276/25, [1968] C.M.L.R. D78.
[94] First Report on Competition Policy, para. 51.

[89] (22/71) [1972] C.M.L.R. 81.
[91] [1972] C.M.L.R. 81, 95.

while Fillistorf agreed not to sell Grosfillex products outside Switzerland or to sell any competing products.   The only provision in the contract which might affect competition within the common market was that prohibiting Fillistorf from reselling the contract products outside Switzerland or from selling any competing products: for that prevented Fillistorf from selling these products within the common market.   The Commission concluded that this provision would not prevent, restrict or distort competition to any noticeable extent since: (a) Fillistorf was not in any case likely to resell Grosfillex products into the common market in competition with Grosfillex products sold there directly; the Fillistorf articles would have to cross a new customs barrier, and the Grosfillex prices in Switzerland were not noticeably lower than those in the common market; (b) there were already a large number of competing manufacturers of and traders in similar products within the common market.

**835    The Rieckermann case.**   The *Rieckermann* [93] decision involved the different situation which arises where the distributorship agreement concerns exports to a non-EEC country but both parties are situated within the common market.   In this case both were in Germany.   Under the agreement Rieckermann was made sole distributor in Japan of the highly complex and custom built heating installations manufactured by AEG-Elothem (AEG). Rieckermann undertook to sell these products only in Japan, and not to sell competing products.   The effect of the agreement was that Rieckermann was prevented:

(a) from selling AEG products in the common market, and

(b) from selling in Japan the products of AEG's competitors; while AEG was

(a) prevented from selling in Japan through itself or through any other undertaking (situated in the EEC or otherwise), and

(b) obliged to prevent its purchasers from reselling in Japan.

The Commission held there was no noticeable restriction or distortion of competition within the common market for three main reasons.   First, Rieckermann was an export agency specialising in the Far East.   It had no interest in selling within the common market, was not equipped to do so, and no change in this position was likely in the future.   Secondly, market

[ 191 ]

conditions and the technical nature of the installations meant that the restriction upon Rieckermann against buying competing products for resale in Japan, or the restriction upon AEG against selling to others for export to Japan, could not noticeably affect competition. Thirdly, the prohibition on AEG itself selling to Japan had no effect within the common market. Similar considerations applied to AEG's obligation to prevent its other purchasers from reselling in Japan.

## 4. REQUIREMENTS CONTRACTS

**836** **In general.** " Requirements " contracts are those contracts under which one party is obliged to obtain all his supplies of certain products exclusively from the other party to the agreement. By such an agreement the acquirer deprives himself of the freedom to obtain those goods elsewhere, while at the same time other suppliers are denied an outlet for their products. In principle Article 85 (1) may apply to such agreements. At present, the available authorities are largely concerned with agreements to obtain supplies for *resale* exclusively from one source. In certain circumstances such agreements may benefit from exemption under Regulation 67/67.

**837** **Application of Article 85 (1): Brasserie de Haecht.** In deciding whether any particular requirements contract falls within Article 85 (1), the agreement must be considered in its whole legal and economic context, taking into account the existence of other agreements of the same type. Thus in the *Brasserie de Haecht* [95] case the European Court considered the effect of a typical " tied-house " contract whereby a Belgian café proprietor bound himself to obtain his supplies of beer, drinks and lemonade exclusively from one supplier in return for a loan from the suppliers of 50,000 Belgian francs. Considered alone, the agreement concerned only a minute proportion of the whole Belgian market. However, it was only one of a large number of similar contracts in which the small number of Belgian breweries had agreed like terms in respect of a large number of licensed premises in Belgium. The European Court held [96] that the existence of those other agreements was one of the factors that required consideration

[95] (23/67) [1968] C.M.L.R. 26. See also *Brasserie de Haecht (No. 2)* 48/72), February 6, 1973.
[96] *Ibid.* at pp. 40, 41.

when deciding as to the application of Article 85 (1). The decision in the *Brasserie de Haecht* case has raised considerable doubt as to the effect of Article 85 (1) in relation to " solus " contracts, especially tied-house agreements,[97] even in cases where the operation of such agreements is limited to the national market. However, by reason of the provisions of Regulation 67/67 (in the case of inter-State agreements) and of the provisions of Article 4 (2) of Regulation 17 (in the case of domestic agreements), the problems raised by the *Brasserie de Haecht* case may often be avoided in practice.

**838**   **Regulation 67/67.** Article 1 (1) (*b*) of Regulation 67/67 exempts from the application of Article 85 (1) of the Treaty agreements to which only two undertakings are party whereby " one party agrees with the other to purchase only from that other certain goods for resale." Where a requirements contract is bilateral and the parties concerned are situated in different Member States,[98] the agreement may therefore benefit from Regulation 67/67 provided that the other requirements of the Regulation are satisfied.[99] In certain cases exemption may also be obtained where the exclusive purchasing obligation is part of a reciprocal exclusive supply and purchasing arrangement.[1]

**839**   **Article 4 (2) of Regulation 17.** Where the parties are situated in the same Member State Regulation 67/67 has no application.[98] However, as has been seen,[2] Article 4 (2) (i) of Regulation 17 exempts from notification agreements to which only undertakings situated in the same Member State are party and which do not " involve imports or exports."[3] In *Bilger* [4] the European Court held that a requirements contract, the execution of which did not involve the goods in question crossing any national frontiers, fall within Article 4 (2). Agreements falling within Article 4 (2) may obtain " provisional validity " unless and until the competent authorities rule to the contrary.[5] It follows that many

---

[97] The Commission is at present conducting a general enquiry into the brewery sector under Art. 12 of Reg. 17. See *post*, § 1215.
[98] See Art. 1 (2) of Reg. 67/67.       [99] See *ante*, §§ 818–825.
[1] Art. 1 (1) (c) of Reg. 67/67. See also individual exemptions relating to specialisation agreements: §§ 1005 *et seq.*
[2] § 831, *ante*.       [3] See *ante*, §§ 528 *et seq.*
[4] (43/69) 8 C.M.L.Rev. 1971, 241; and see *ante*, § 529.
[5] *Ibid.* at pp. 243, 244. But see now *Brasserie de Haecht (No. 2)* (48/72), February 6, 1973, and the decisions discussed *ante*, §§ 410 *et seq.*

" domestic " requirements contracts may be enforceable by
virtue of Article 4 (2) of Regulation 17 and the various decisions [6]
of the European Court, irrespective of whether they in fact fall
within Article 85 (1) of the Treaty, a question which remains to
be finally decided.

### 5. SELECTIVE DISTRIBUTION

**840     In general.** One common distributive arrangement which
requires separate consideration is that of selective distribution. A
system of selective distribution occurs where a manufacturer
imposes on his distributors restrictions as to the persons to whom
they may resell the contract products. Such a system may fall
within Article 85 (1) if it has the effect of depriving a large number
of retailers of the opportunity to resell the contract products. The
application of Article 85 (1) to such agreements and the possibility
of obtaining exemption under Article 85 (3) may be illustrated by
the Commission's decision in *Re Omega*.[7]

**841     Re Omega.** Omega, a Swiss undertaking, granted to undertakings situated in each Member State the exclusive right to sell
Omega watches in their respective territories. Each of these
undertakings (known as the Omega general agents) distributed
the watches through a selective distribution network of retailers
(known as " the concessionaires "). These retailers were selected
not only on the basis of their professional competence, but also
quantitatively, each general agent limiting the number of concessionaires in each region to an optimum number depending on
local population and the presumed wealth of the area. Broadly,
the general agents and the concessionaires respectively undertook
only to supply for resale to other general agents or concessionaires,
and the concessionaires further undertook only to obtain supplies
from general agents or other concessionaires.

**842     Re Omega: the Commission's decision.** The Commission
held that Article 85 (1) applied to the Omega agreements for
two main reasons. First, the appointment of one exclusive
general agent in each Member State was likely to lead to a division
of the market along national boundaries. Secondly, the limitation
as to the number of concessionaires restricted competition, not

---

[6] See *ante*, § 410 *et seq.*
[7] J.O. 1970 L242/22, [1970] C.M.L.R. D49.

because the concessionaires were limited to persons of proper
technical qualifications and standing, but also because they were
limited to a number fixed by the general agent according to the
presumed purchasing power of the relevant area.    This latter
restriction prevented many technically qualified retailers from
stocking the contract products.    However, the Commission were
able to grant an exemption under Article 85 (3).[8]    The system of
general agents was found to improve distribution and to pass on
to the consumers a fair share of the resulting benefit, and there
was plenty of competition from other watchmakers.    The only
substantial question was whether the quantitative limitation
upon the number of concessionaires was a restriction indispensable
to obtaining the benefits of the agreement.    The Commission
found that where the products were expensive and of high quality
it was necessary to limit the number of outlets in this way; only
by restricting the number of concessionaires could the authorised
concessionaires obtain sufficient turnover to justify them stocking
a full range of products and providing after-sales and guarantee
services.    Accordingly, the Commission held the restriction
to be indispensable.    Before granting an exemption, however,
the Commission insisted upon the parties abandoning restrictions
which prevented the general agents from exporting outside their
own territories and also bound the concessionaires to obtain
supplies only from the general agent within their territory and
not to export outside it.

**843**        **Result of Re Omega.**    It may be inferred from *Re Omega* that
restrictions limiting the resale of technical and high quality
products only to qualified persons will generally fall outside
Article 85 (1).[9]    Other systems of selective distribution may
be justified under Article 85 (3) in appropriate cases.[10]    In such
cases, however, the Commission will be careful to insist upon the
removal of all the provisions which might restrict imports or
exports between Member States.[11]

**[The next paragraph is 901.]**

[8] *Ibid.* at p. D57.
[9] See also *Re Kodak*, J.O. 1970 L147/24, [1970] C.M.L.R. D19, D23.  *Cf. Re
NCH*, J.O. 1972 L22/16.
[10] See the Commission's announcement under Art. 19 (3) of Reg. 17.  *Re Saba*,
J.O. 1972 C116/4.
[11] See also, as to conditions of sale, *ante*, §§ 322 *et seq.*

CHAPTER 9

# INDUSTRIAL PROPERTY

## 1. INTRODUCTION

**901**  **In general.** The existence of industrial or commercial property rights[1] which are protected under the national laws of individual Member States raises difficult problems in the Community law of competition. First, there is the ever present conflict between, on the one hand, systems which confer legal monopolies and, on the other hand, systems which are intended to preserve and encourage the free play of competition. Thus, for example, the owner of a patent has, for a period of years, the right to exclude others from making use of his invention or marketing the products thereby manufactured. He also has the power to dispose of his right to others, either by assigning it outright to third parties or by licensing them to make, use or sell his product, usually upon payment of royalties and observance of other conditions. This right may be exercised in many different ways. The patentee may confer on the licensee an exclusive licence, which excludes even the patentee from exercising the rights subject to the licence, or a sole licence, which excludes every one except the patentee, or a non-exclusive licence, which permits the patentee himself to compete with the licensee and also to grant licences to others. Further the patentee may license one person to make or sell only in a defined territory while licensing others for other territories. Similarly, the owners of trademarks, copyrights, designs and secret processes may authorise others to make use of them. Clearly, the existence and exercise of such industrial property rights may restrict competition in respect of the products to which they relate. In systems of competition law generally, difficulties arise in defining the extent to which industrial property

---

[1] *i.e.* rights in patents, trademarks, registered designs, copyright and " know-how," in so far as such rights are protected under the municipal laws of Member States and other similar rights protected under those laws. For a general work on the patent laws of EEC countries see Alexander, *Brevets d'invention et règles de concurrence du Traité CEE* (1971).

rights may legitimately be exercised without placing unjustifiable restrictions on free competitive activity.[2]

**902** These difficulties arise in a particularly acute form in the common market. In addition to overcoming the general difficulty of the *operation* of a system of industrial property rights within a system of competition law, the EEC faces the additional task of *establishing* a common market between Member States. The purpose of the common market is to reproduce the conditions of one national market on a Community-wide scale. The major characteristic of a national market as regards industrial property rights is that goods lawfully marketed in one part of the national territory cannot usually be prevented by the threat of infringement action from reaching other parts of the national territory in the course of trade.[3] Within the Community, however, the national character of industrial property rights can often create obstacles to the free movement of goods. Each Member State protects the particular right within its own territory and decides autonomously what acts constitute an infringement of that right. The owner of the right, within a particular national territory, will often be able to use the right conferred by national law to prevent imports into that territory of all products of a kind protected by the right.[4] If, for example, a patentee owns a patent in both Belgium and the United Kingdom, he will, by relying on his United Kingdom national patent rights, be able to prevent the import into the United Kingdom of the patented products made in Belgium.[5] Two common situations present particular difficulties under EEC law. The first is where the right concerned belongs to different persons in different Member States, usually as a result of assignments or licences. The second is where the right concerned may be protected in one Member State, but not in another.

[2] For English law see *Terrell on the Law of Patents*, 12th ed., Chap. 10, particularly pp. 642–655. See also s. 8 (4) of the Restrictive Trade Practices Act 1956; ss. 37, 43 (6) Patents Act 1949 (compulsory grant of licences after adverse report by Monopolies Commission); s. 1 (2) Resale Prices Act 1964; and see Clause 93 of the Fair Trading Bill. For the position of patents under American anti-trust law see Neale, *The Anti-Trust Laws of the U.S.A.*, 2nd ed., pp. 300 *et seq.*
[3] *Cf.* Trademarks Act 1938, s. 22 (6).
[4] See generally Alexander, " The establishment of the common market and the problem of parallel patents " (1969) 14 *Anti Trust Bulletin* 181–220, 185 *et seq.*, and " Industrial Property Rights and the Establishment of the European Common Market " 9 C.M.L.Rev. 1972, 35, 37.
[5] See *Société Anonyme des Manufactures de Glaces* v. *Tilghman's Patent Sand Blast Co.* (1883) 25 Ch.D. 1, 9; *cf. Betts* v. *Wilmot* (1871) L.R.6 Ch.App. 239.

For example, the latter state may not accord such protection (*e.g.* at present there is no patent protection for drugs in Italy [6]) or the owner may not have applied for protection, or the protection may have expired. In such situations, the owner of a national industrial property right in one Member State may, by exercising that right, be able to prevent imports into that Member State of products which have been lawfully marketed in another Member State, even if the products have been sold there by the owner of the right himself, or by an associated company, or by a licensee. Thus, by invoking the provisions of national law, the owner of the right may be able to prevent imports and to partition the common market along national boundaries.

**903**     **Approach of the European Court.** Article 222 of the Treaty expressly provides that the "Treaty shall in no way prejudice the rules in Member States governing the system of property ownership." [7] In four cases [8] the European Court has been faced with situations where national systems of "property ownership" (industrial property rights) have been invoked to prevent the free movement of goods between Member States. The Court has sought to resolve the problem thus posed by holding that, while the Treaty of Rome does not affect the existence of national industrial property rights *per se*, several provisions of the Treaty strike at the use of industrial property rights to prevent imports and exports between Member States. It must be remembered that Articles 85 and 86 are only one part of the Treaty, one principal purpose of which is to create a true common market in which there is free movement of goods between States. Hence, the Court has relied not only upon Article 85 (1) (which may be applicable where the industrial property right used to prevent imports and exports derives from, or is exercised as a result of, an agreement or concerted practice) and upon Article 86 (which prevents the abuse of a "dominant position" which may be conferred by an industrial property right) but also upon the general principles of the Treaty concerning the free movement of goods which are laid down in Articles 30 to 36. Through a robust interpretation of

[6] See *Parke, Davis & Co.* v. *Probel* (24/67) [1968] C.M.L.R. 47; *post,* § 925.
[7] See also Art. 36; *post,* §§ 912 *et seq.*
[8] *Consten and Grundig* v. *EEC Commission* (56/64, 58/64) [1966] C.M.L.R. 418; *Parke, Davis & Co.* v. *Probel* (24/67) [1968] C.M.L.R. 47; *Sirena* v. *Eda* (40/70) [1971] C.M.L.R. 260; *Deutsche Grammophon* v. *Metro* (78/70) [1971] C.M.L.R. 631.

the relevant Treaty provisions, the Court has in large measure prevented the holders of industrial property rights from exercising those rights for the purpose of obstructing imports and exports between Member States.

**904** **Plan of this chapter.** This chapter is now divided into two main sections. The first section [9] is concerned with the Court's decisions in relation to the exercise of industrial property rights in order to prevent the import and export between Member States of products falling within the scope of the right concerned. The problems discussed in this section relate primarily to the establishment of free movement of goods within the Community. In the second main section of this chapter [10] the topic discussed is how far Article 85 (1) applies in detail to particular provisions in licensing agreements. The question of how far restrictions upon the licensor and licensee may be included in licensing and similar agreements without falling within Article 85 (1) is considered specifically in respect of patent, trademark and know-how agreements in the light of the relevant decisions and announcements of the Commission. Notification of such agreements is also discussed together with the possibilities of exemption under Article 85 (3).

### 2. THE EXERCISE OF INDUSTRIAL PROPERTY RIGHTS TO RESTRICT IMPORTS AND EXPORTS BETWEEN MEMBER STATES

#### (a) *Generally*

**905** **The Court's decisions.**[11] Where an industrial property right is relied upon to prevent or obstruct imports and exports between Member States, it is necessary to investigate whether the Treaty has been contravened in any of three relevant respects. First it is necessary to consider whether the right is exercised in reliance upon an agreement to which Article 85 (1) applies. Next, it must be asked whether the exercise of the right is contrary to Articles 30 to 36 of the Treaty, and particularly Article 36 thereof. Finally, Article 86 of the Treaty must be considered. The principles laid down in the four decisions of the European Court may be summarised as follows:

[9] §§ 905–929, *post.*
[10] §§ 930 *et seq., post.*
[11] See also Korah (1972) 35 M.L.R. 634; Gardiner 88L. Q.R. 507; Koch and Froschmaier, *Idea*, Vol. 9, No. 2.

1. Where as a result of agreements or assignments, rights to use the same trademark have become vested in different persons in different Member States, Article 85 (1) applies to those agreements or assignments where they would otherwise enable the respective holders of the rights in each Member State, by relying on the provisions of national law, to prevent the import of products bearing the same trademark originating from the holders of the rights in other Member States.[12]   A similar principle is applicable where the right concerned is akin to copyright.[13]

2. If an exclusive right akin to copyright is exercised to prohibit in one Member State the marketing of goods covered by the right that have been put on to the market by the holder of the right or with his consent in the territory of another Member State, the provisions of the Treaty regarding the free movement of goods are contravened.[14]

3. The exercise of a patent, trademark or copyright may fall within Article 86 of the Treaty if (a) the undertaking concerned has a dominant position within the common market or a substantial part of it, and (b) the exercise of the right is an improper exploitation thereof, and (c) trade between Member States is liable to be affected thereby.[15]

4. The mere exercise of a patent right which derives from national law does not contravene Article 85 (1) in the absence of any relevant agreement, nor does the mere exercise of such a right necessarily constitute a breach of Article 86 or the Treaty provisions relating to the free movement of goods.[16]

**906**     **Exercise of rights for proper purpose unaffected.** Although the precise formulation of the above principles, and in particular the extent to which some of them are properly to be confined to industrial property rights of particular kinds, is a matter for debate, the European Court has consistently laid down the principle that industrial rights *in themselves* are not affected by

[12] *Consten and Grundig* v. *EEC Commission* (56/64, 58/64) [1966] C.M.L.R. 418 *Sirena* v. *Eda* (40/70) [1971] C.M.L.R. 260; *post*, §§ 908 *et seq.*
[13] *Deutsche Grammophon* (78/70) [1971] C.M.L.R. 631.  The right concerned in that case was a statutory protection right in sound recordings equivalent to copyright.  See *note* 50, *post.*
[14] *Deutsche Grammophon* (78/70) [1971] C.M.L.R. 631; *post*, § 912.
[15] *Parke, Davis* (24/67) [1968] C.M.L.R. 47; *Sirena* (40/70) [1971] C.M.L.R. 260; *Deutsche Grammophon* (78/70) [1971] C.M.L.R. 631; *ante*, § 726.
[16] *Parke, Davis* (24/67) [1968] C.M.L.R. 47.

the Treaty.[17]  It should not be thought that the Treaty has
interfered with the right to protect industrial property where a
third party has unlawfully manufactured or made use of the
subject matter of the right without the consent of the owner or
anyone deriving title through him.

907    **Plan of this section.**  In this section the application of the
principle relating to Article 85 (1) set out above is considered
first, with particular reference to the decisions of the European
Court in *Grundig-Consten*[18] and *Sirena.*[19] The operation, in
relation to the laws of industrial property rights, of Articles 30 to
36 of the Treaty are next considered, with particular reference to
the European Court's decision in *Deutsche Grammophon.*[20]  The
application of Article 86 in this field, which may in practice be
limited, is considered in Chapter 7.[21]

### (b) *The application of Article 85 (1)*

908    **In general.**  The result of the Court's decisions relating to
Article 85 (1) of the Treaty is that, broadly speaking, it is not
possible to achieve a division of the common market between
various suppliers of products by means of an agreement
relating to the use of industrial property rights as a substitute for
a directly restrictive agreement which would fall under Article
85 (1).  In essence, the European Court has held that where, by
virtue of an agreement, a party obtains an industrial property
right which under the provisions of national law, enables that
party to prevent the importation of products covered by the right
which have been lawfully marketed in the territory of another
Member State, Article 85 (1) applies to the agreement in
question.[22]  As has been seen[23] an agreement falling under
Article 85 is not only void and unenforceable as between the
parties but may not be relied upon as against third parties.[24]

---

[17] *Ibid.* at p. 58.  *Consten and Grundig* v. *EEC Commission* [1966] C.M.L.R. 418
   475, 476.
[18] (56/64, 58/64) [1966] C.M.L.R. 418.
[19] (40/70) [1971] C.M.L.R. 260.
[20] (78/70) [1971] C.M.L.R. 631.
[21] *Ante*, § 726.
[22] *Sirena* (40/70) [1971] C.M.L.R. 260.  *Consten and Grundig* v. *EEC Commission*
   (56/64, 58/64) [1966] C.M.L.R. 418.
[23] *Ante*, § 408.
[24] *Béguelin* (22/71) [1972] C.M.L.R. 81.

Hence, the owners of industrial property rights may be enjoined from exercising them against third parties where the right to do so derives from an agreement which falls within Article 85 (1). The operation of this principle may first be illustrated by reference to two decided cases relating to trade marks, *Grundig-Consten* [22] and *Sirena*.[22] Then it is necessary to consider how far the principle extends to other industrial property rights. It should be noted that the rules discussed in the next section, in relation to Articles 30 to 36 of the Treaty, may also apply in cases where Article 85 (1) is infringed.[25]

**909** **Grundig-Consten.** As has been seen,[26] in *Grundig-Consten*, Consten was appointed Grundig's exclusive distributor in France, " absolute territorial protection" [27] being ensured by a system of export and import restrictions accepted by Grundig itself and also imposed by Grundig upon its other concessionaires and on German wholesalers. Additionally, Consten was authorised by Grundig under an agreement to register in France the trademark " GINT " (Grundig International), Consten agreeing to transfer or cancel the registration upon the expiry of the distribution agreement. The " GINT " mark appeared on Grundig products in addition to the " GRUNDIG " mark. It was the "GRUNDIG" mark which primarily associated the goods with Grundig while the " GINT " mark could be used by Consten as a means of preventing parallel imports [27] of Grundig products. If a third party obtained and imported Grundig products into France, Consten could sue for infringement in reliance upon the French registration of the " GINT " mark. The Commission found [28] that both the distribution agreement and the agreement relating to the " GINT " mark, which was ancillary thereto, fell under Article 85 (1), and it " required the parties to refrain from any measure " tending to obstruct the importation of the contract products into France by third parties. This order, under Article 3 (1) of Regulation 17,[29] had the effect of preventing Consten from exercising its French national trade

[25] *Post*, §§ 912 *et seq.*
[26] For fuller summaries of the facts of this case see *ante*, §§ 216 *et seq.*, and §§ 811 *et seq.*
[27] For " absolute territorial protection " and " parallel imports " see *ante*, §§ 812, 813.
[28] J.O. 1964 2545/64, [1964] C.M.L.R. 489.
[29] See *post*, §§ 1201 *et seq.*

mark rights in order to obstruct parallel imports. On appeal, the
Court of Justice substantially upheld the Commission's ruling.[30]
In essence, the Court held [31] that an agreement whereby one
party authorises the other to register the former's trademark in
the name of the latter in a Member State, thereby enabling the
latter, by relying on the registration and the national trademark
law, to prevent imports into that State of products manufactured
by the former and bearing the same mark, is restrictive of competition and falls within Article 85 (1). The operation of the
principle established in *Grundig-Consten* is reflected in the
Commission's decision in *Re Transocean Marine Paint Association* [32] and in Article 3 (*b*) (i) of Regulation 67/67.[33]

**910**    **Sirena.** In *Sirena* [34] the European Court went further than
it had in *Grundig-Consten*. It held that Article 85 (1) applied to
an agreement (in *Sirena* an assignment) as a result of which a
trademark was owned by one person in one Member State and by
another person in another Member State, so that the import into
the one Member State of trademarked products originating in the
other Member State could be prevented by the owner of the trademark in the first Member State. The facts were that in 1937 the
American company, Mark Allen, licensed to Sirena, an independent Italian firm, its Italian rights to the trademark " Prep " for
shaving cream. Sirena used the trademark for its own products
and subsequently renewed the trademark registration on its own
behalf. Mark Allen had similarly assigned its German rights in
the " Prep " trademark to a German company. When the
German manufactured products were sold in Italy under the
" Prep " mark, at a much lower price than Sirena's, Sirena
brought proceedings against both the importer, Novimpex, and
the retailers for infringement. On request from the Milan court
for an interpretative judgment the European Court held that the
exercise of trademark rights may come within the Treaty where
that exercise is " the object, the means or the consequence, of an
agreement." [35] The Court said [36]: " Such situations may arise

[30] (56/64, 58/64) [1966] C.M.L.R. 418.
[31] *Ibid.* at pp. 475, 476.
[32] J.O. 1967 163/10, [1967] C.M.L.R. D9.
[33] See *ante*, §§ 819 *et seq.*
[34] (40/70) [1971] C.M.L.R. 260.
[35] *Ibid.* at p. 274.
[36] *Ibid.*

in particular from agreements between trademark owners or their assignees, agreements intended to prevent imports from other Member States. The simultaneous assignment to several concessionaires of national trade mark rights for the same product, if it has the effect of re-establishing rigid frontiers between Member States, may prejudice trade between Member States and distort competition within the common market. The situation would be different if, in order to avoid sub-divisions into closed markets, agreements covering the use of national rights relating to the same trade mark took into account the necessity to moderate the general exercise of trade mark rights with regard to competition and the unity of the market, which are so important for the common market that Article 85 (1) protects them with absolute nullity.

" Article 85 therefore applies where, by virtue of trademark rights, imports of products originating in other Member States, bearing the same trademark because the owners have acquired the trademark itself or the right to use it through agreements with one another and with third parties, are prevented. The fact that national legislation makes the trademark rights dependent on circumstances of law and fact other than the aforementioned agreements, such as the registration of the trademark, or its undisturbed use, does not prevent the application of Article 85."

The Court also held that although the agreement had been concluded before the entry into force of the Treaty, it was necessary and sufficient that its effects continued after that date.[37]

**911      Extent of the principle in Sirena.** It follows directly from *Sirena* that assignments of and agreements concerning the use of national trademark rights may be within Article 85 unless qualified in such a way that the grantee is not put into a position to use his trademark right to prevent imports of products which lawfully bear the same trademark.[38] Such agreements are accordingly

---

[37] *Ibid.*
[38] Mégret, Waelbroeck and others, *Editions de l'Université de Bruxelles* (1972), p. 221 criticise *Sirena* on the ground that it was wrong to regard an executed assignment as falling within Art. 85 (1). It has been suggested that in reaching its decision in *Sirena* the Court may have been influenced by evidence on the file which indicated the existence of some continuing understanding between the parties. See Alexander, 9 C.M.L.Rev. 1972, 35, 43. Submissions of the Advocate-General [1971] C.M.L.R. 260, 267, 268.

notifiable unless they fall under Article 4 (2) of Regulation 17.[39] The first question that arises is whether the principle of *Sirena* extends to patents and other industrial property rights. In *Deutsche Grammophon*,[40] it appears that the European Court was prepared to extend the principle to an agreement relating to an exclusive copyright under German law, where such agreement enabled the right to be exercised " to effect a division of the common market by prohibiting imports from other Member States of products duly brought into the market in those states."[41] It is not yet decided whether the *Sirena* principle extends to patents. A number of distinctions can be drawn between trademarks and patent rights, and the Court itself drew such a distinction in *Sirena*.[42] It may well be that the decision in *Sirena* exemplifies a general rule that industrial property rights of all kinds, including patents, deriving from agreements, may not be exercised to prevent imports of products covered by the right lawfully marketed in another Member State because such agreements enable legal proceedings to be brought to prevent such imports, and are therefore void under Article 85 (1).[43] On the other hand the rule in *Sirena* must have certain limitations. Clearly, it would have no application where the imported products were merely imitations, *e.g.* where the mark had been unlawfully affixed in the exporting country. Whether *Sirena* applies where products lawfully bearing a mark in one country are inferior in quality to those bearing the same mark in another country remains to be decided.[44] Probably, *Sirena* would not apply to an agreement between parent and subsidiary,[45] although in such a case the principles discussed in *Deutsche Grammophon* would be applicable.[46] Also the rule would presumably not apply where the right in question had been vested in different parties otherwise than by a consensual arrangement (*e.g.* war time confiscation); whether it would apply in the case of a compulsory licence must remain doubtful.

[39] See *post*, § 957.    [40] (78/70) [1971] C.M.L.R. 631.
[41] *Ibid.* at p. 656.
[42] [1971] C.M.L.R. 260, 273. See also the submissions of the Advocate-General, *ibid.*, pp. 264–266.
[43] *Cf.* Art 3 (*b*) of Reg. 67/67; and see *Re Transocean Marine Paint Association*, J.O. 1967 163/10, [1967] C.M.L.R. D9.
[44] *Cf.* Trade Descriptions Act 1972, s. 1 (2).
[45] Such agreements generally fall outside Art. 85 (1); see *ante*, §§ 250 *et seq.* But *cf.* the Commission's intervention in *Re Remington Rand Italia*, Press Release, June 11, 1969.    [46] *Post*, §§ 912 *et seq.*

## (c) *Provisions Regarding the Free Movement of Goods*

**912 Articles 30–36.** It has been seen [47] that Article 85 (1) is applicable to an agreement whereby one party is enabled, by the use of national industrial property rights,[48] to effect a division of the common market by prohibiting imports from other Member States of products lawfully brought on to the market in those States. Quite apart from the application of Article 85 (1), an attempt to prevent imports and exports between Member States may contravene the principles laid down by the Treaty under the title " The Free Movement of Goods." The relevant Articles of that Title are Articles 30 to 36. The provisions of those Articles will be important where there is no agreement or concerted practice which infringes Article 85 (1). Articles 30 to 34 provide for the progressive abolition as between Member States of quantitative restrictions on imports and exports and " all measures having equivalent effect." Article 36 then provides that Articles 30 to 34 " shall not preclude prohibitions or restrictions on imports, exports, or goods in transit justified on grounds of . . . the protection of industrial and commercial property. Such prohibitions or restrictions shall not, however, constitute a means of arbitrary discrimination or a disguised restriction on trade between Member States." Thus Article 36 preserves, within limits, the effectiveness of national industrial property laws—notwithstanding that their operation interferes with the free movement of goods within the Community. The question is: What are those limits? This question must be considered in the light of the European Court's decision in *Deutsche Grammophon.*

**913 The issues raised in Deutsche Grammophon.** In *Deutsche Grammophon* [49] the European Court held that the provisions in the Treaty regarding the free movement of goods prohibited the exercise of an exclusive right akin to copyright in Germany to prevent the import into Germany of products covered by the copyright which had been marketed in France by the owner of the right, or with his consent, where that right was exercised solely because the products in question had not previously been

[47] *Ante,* §§ 908 *et seq.*
[48] The decisions relate to copyright and trademarks: for the extent of the principle, see § 911, *ante.*
[49] (78/70) [1971] C.M.L.R. 631.

marketed in Germany. The decision thus expressed must be explained by more detailed reference to the facts of the case and the relevant provisions of the Treaty. But the question arises whether *Deutsche Grammophon* lays down a principle of general application, namely, that an infringement action does not lie at the suit of the owner of *any* industrial property right to prohibit the marketing in one Member State of products that have been sold by the *owner himself or with his consent* in another Member State.

914    **Plan of this subsection.** In this subsection, therefore, the facts of *Deutsche Grammophon* and the Court's decision are considered first. Then the extent of the principle laid down, and the meaning of the phrase " sold by the Plaintiff himself or with his consent," are discussed. Then the differences between an action which infringes Article 85 (1) and action which infringes the provisions relating to free movement of goods are considered. Finally, reference is made to the question whether the rule in *Deutsche Grammophon* is affected by the transitional provisions relating to the free movement of goods applicable in the period following accession.

915    **The facts.** Deutsche Grammophon G.m.b.H. (DG) sold records in Germany under the Polydor label. Pursuant to the German system of resale price maintenance, DG sold only to retailers who maintained DG's resale prices on DG records acquired from DG or imported from abroad. In France, where r.p.m. is illegal, DG records were marketed exclusively by DG's wholly owned subsidiary, Polydor S.A. (Polydor). In 1969, Metro-SB-Grossmarkte G.m.b.H. (Metro) bought Polydor records from DG but did not observe resale prices. DG, pursuant to the German system of r.p.m., cut off supplies. However, in 1970 Metro managed to obtain Polydor records from a Hamburg wholesaler. These records had originally been supplied by DG to Polydor, but they had reached Hamburg via a Swiss enterprise. Metro were still able however to sell them at a price well below that maintained by other DG retailers in Germany. DG sued Metro for an injunction to prevent the records being sold in

breach of the statutory copyright protection accorded to manufacturers of sound recordings.[50]

916      **Reference to the European Court.** The proceedings were
referred to the European Court by the German court. The
European Court was, in effect, asked to decide whether Community law is infringed if the exclusive right conferred on a
manufacturer of sound recordings by national legislation to
distribute the protected products can be used to prohibit the
domestic marketing of products that have been brought on to the
market in the territory of another Member State by the manufacturer himself or with his consent.[51]

917      **Decision of the European Court.** In so far as the Court
considered the application of Article 85 (1) and Article 86, the
Court laid down principles which were, in all relevant respects,
similar to those laid down in *Sirena*.[52]  However, in *Deutsche
Grammophon* there was almost certainly no relevant agreement to
which Article 85 (1) was applicable.  DG sought to exercise an
exclusive right which derived not from any agreement, but
directly from a German statute.  Nor was the agreement between
DG and Polydor relevant in this respect; being an agreement
between a parent and a wholly owned subsidiary it would fall
outside Article 85 (1) altogether.[53]  It was in these circumstances
that the Court held that apart from Article 85 (1) and Article 86
it was still necessary to consider whether the exercise of the right
was prohibited by the provisions in the Treaty relating to the
"Free Movement of Goods,"[54] including the provisions of Article
36.  The Court held [55]:

" Although Article 36 permits prohibitions or restrictions on
the free movement of goods that are justified for the protection

---

[50] Statute of September 9, 1965 concerning Copyright and Similar Protection
Rights.  An equivalent right in other EEC countries exists only in Italy but some
States have provisions which achieve the same effect.  Thus Polydor in France
would probably have been protected by the French law of unfair competition.
See [1971] C.M.L.R. 631, 635.  For the copyright of sound recordings in English
law see Copinger and Skone-James, *Copyright*, 11th ed., pp. 304 *et seq.*
[51] [1971] C.M.L.R. 631, 656.
[52] (40/70) [1971] C.M.L.R. 230; *ante,* §§ 910 *et seq.*
[53] *Ante,* § 250.
[54] Title I of the Treaty (Art. 9 *et  seq.*) is entitled " Free Movement of Goods."
The relevant provisions are Arts. 30–37 " Elimination of Quantitative
Restrictions as between Member States."
[55] [1971] C.M.L.R. 631, 657.

of industrial and commercial property, it only allows such restrictions on the freedom of trade to the extent that they are justified for the protection of the rights that form the specific object of this property.

" If a protection right analogous to copyright is used in order to prohibit in one Member State the marketing of goods that have been brought onto the market by the holder of the right or with his consent in the territory of another Member State solely because this marketing has not occurred in the domestic market, such a prohibition maintaining the isolation of the national markets conflicts with the essential aim of the Treaty, the integration of the national markets into one uniform market. This aim could not be achieved if by virtue of the various legal systems of the Member States private persons were able to divide the market and cause arbitrary discriminations or disguised restrictions in trade between the Member States.

" Accordingly it would conflict with the provisions regarding the free movement of goods in the common market if a manufacturer of recordings exercised the exclusive right granted to him by the legislation of a Member State to market the protected articles in order to prohibit the marketing in that Member State of products that had been sold by him himself or with his consent in another Member State solely because this marketing had not occurred in the territory of the first Member State."

**918**   **The reasoning in Deutsche Grammophon.**   The reasoning by which the Court reached its decision is not wholly clear from the judgment in *Deutsche Grammophon*. The Court said that the exercise of the industrial right concerned was contrary to the provisions regarding the free movement of goods generally, but the only one of those provisions which it specifically mentioned was Article 36. It must at least be assumed that the Court regarded the provisions relating to the free movement of goods as " directly applicable " *i.e.* capable of overriding national law and conferring rights upon individuals without specific incorporation into national law by municipal legislation.[56]   The underlying basis of the Court's conclusion may be expressed in at least two different ways. One alternative is as follows: to the extent that it could be used to prohibit imports of goods from other

[56] *Ante*, § 140; see also the references in the judgment to Arts. 3 (*f*) and 5 (2) of the Treaty.

Member States lawfully marketed there by the owner of a copyright or with his consent, the German Copyright Law relied on by Deutsche Grammophon was a measure having equivalent effect to a quantitative restriction upon imports. To that extent it contravened Article 30 *et seq.*, directly applicable provisions.[57] Hence it could not be relied upon for that purpose before a national court. The exception under Article 36 in favour of prohibitions or restrictions on imports justified on the grounds of the protection of industrial and commercial property could not be applied where there was an arbitrary discrimination or a disguised restriction on trade between Member States, namely the purported prohibition by Deutsche Grammophon of the import of goods which had been previously marketed with the consent of that company, in another Member State. The second alternative is that the Court considered Article 36 to be not merely a proviso to Article 30 *et seq.*, but an independent directly applicable provision to be read as follows: " prohibitions or restrictions [on imports justified on the grounds of the protection of industrial and commercial property] shall not constitute a means of arbitrary discrimination or a disguised restriction on trade between Member States." In many cases little will turn on which basis is the correct one; but in the period immediately following accession the issue may be important in relation to the impact upon the principle of *Deutsche Grammophon* of the transitional rules concerning the implementation in the acceding States of the provisions relating to the free movement of goods.[58]

**919**    **Other industrial property rights.** *Deutsche Grammophon* decided that it was contrary to the provisions regarding the free movement of goods for a party, in reliance upon his copyright, to seek to prohibit the marketing in one Member State of products which had been sold by that party himself or with his consent in another Member State. As a result of the *Deutsche Grammophon* case, the German Court declared that it would be contrary to the Treaty to permit DG to invoke the German Copyright Law to prevent resales by Metro of imported products.[59] The question

---

[57] The original transitional period for the implementation of these provisions was complete.
[58] See *post*, § 929.
[59] [1972] C.M.L.R. 107.

arises whether the decision, which concerned copyright, is equally applicable to other types of industrial property rights. There appears to be nothing in principle to prevent the application of the decision to trademarks. Difficulties have been suggested in applying the rule to patents, which have a more limited duration and are intended to protect invention and foster technical development.[60] The Commission's view,[61] however, is that the rule in *Deutsche Grammophon* applies to industrial and commercial property rights of all kinds. It is thought that in considering whether the exercise of any particular property right is contrary to the provisions relating to the free movement of goods one general test to apply is to ask: is this a *bona fide* and legitimate exercise of the right in question? or is this right being exercised pursuant to an arbitrary discrimination or a disguised restriction on trade between Member States?

**920 Conditions for application of rule.** Whatever the kinds of industrial property rights to which *Deutsche Grammophon* may apply, it is necessary to consider the circumstances in which the rule may come into operation. It appears from the Court's judgment [62] that for the rule to apply three conditions must be fulfilled: (i) the products the import of which it is sought to prevent must have been previously marketed in another Member State, (ii) that marketing must have been by the owner himself or with his consent and (iii) the right concerned must be exercised solely to prevent the sale in another Member State of products not previously marketed there. These requirements are considered in turn.

**921    Products sold in another Member State.** In *Deutsche Grammophon* the European Court expressly said that the rule was applicable where the goods concerned " have been brought into the market by the holder of the right or with his consent in

---

[60] See Korah (1972) 35 M.L.R. 634; Alexander, 9 C.M.L.Rev. 1972, 35. One particular problem relates to how far a patentee would have to keep out of markets where he had no patent protection *e.g.* because it had expired, in order to protect himself against imports from that market. *Cf. Betts* v. *Wilmot* (1870) L.R. 6 Ch.App. 239: the owner of a U.K. patent who, *by himself or his agent* sells the patented articles abroad without reservation or condition, cannot prevent the reimportation into the U.K. of the articles so sold.
[61] First Report on Competition Policy, para. 68.
[62] [1971] C.M.L.R. 631, 655–658.

the territory of another Member State."[63]  It appears, therefore,
that the goods concerned must have been marketed in another
Member State before the rule in *Deutsche Grammophon* may
apply.  Thus, if a licensee in one Member State seeks to sell
directly into the territory of his licensor goods that have not
been previously marketed on some other national territory (*e.g.*
goods that have been manufactured under licence by the licensee),
the rule in *Deutsche Grammophon* will not apply.  What constitutes " marketing " may in some cases be a difficult question;
but it appears that under the Treaty the licensor may protect
himself against *direct exports* by his licensee. On the other
hand once the products covered by the licence have been
marketed in another Member State, the licensor will not be able
to rely on his national industrial property rights to prevent
imports into his own national territory.

**922**  **Products sold by the owner or with his consent.**  Typically,
products will have been sold in another Member State with the
consent of the owner of a national industrial property right where
such products are sold by the owner's distributors or licensees.
In such cases, the rule in *Deutsche Grammophon* will prevent the
owner of a national industrial property right from preventing
imports into his own territory.  Of course, if the reverse situation
arises *i.e.* where it is the licensee or the distributor who wishes to
use industrial property rights derived from the licensor to prevent
parallel imports then in so far as the agreement conferring those
rights enables parallel imports to be prevented, that agreement
may be caught under Article 85 (1).[64]

**923**  **Products sold by assignees.**  Where a patentee holds patents
in two Member States (*e.g.* U.K. and France) and assigns his
rights in one Member State (*e.g.* France) to an assignee in that
State, the question arises as to whether the patentee may rely on
his English patent to prevent the import of products manufactured
under the French patent by the French assignee and lawfully
marketed in France.  In such circumstances have the goods been
sold in France " with the consent of " the patentee?  *Sirena* [65]

[63] *Ibid.* at p. 657.  See also Art. 3 (*b*) of Reg. 67/67.
[64] *Ante,* §§ 908 *et seq.*
[65] *Ante,* §§ 910, 911.

may suggest that such an assignment may amount to sufficient
" consent." The position may be more doubtful when the
assignment took place prior to the coming into force of the
Treaty.[66]

**924    Products sold by controlled companies.** *Deutsche Grammophon*
itself was a case where a parent company was seeking to prevent
the imports of goods marketed in another Member State by a
wholly owned subsidiary. Where a parent has control over a
subsidiary, *Deutsche Grammophon* will prevent the parent
invoking industrial property rights to prevent imports of goods
sold in another Member State by that subsidiary. In such cases
the sale by the subsidiary will have been made with the consent
of the parent. Cases may, however, arise where it is the *subsidiary*
which seeks to use industrial property rights to prevent the import
into its country of goods originally put on the market in another
Member State by the company controlling it or another company
under the control of the same controlling company. Article
85 (1) will probably not be applicable, since there is no agreement
between economically independent undertakings.[67] In such
circumstances however, it is thought that the rule in *Deutsche
Grammophon* would apply, the plaintiff subsidiary being treated
as the same economic person as the parent who consented to the
goods being first marketed in another Member State.

**925    Products sold without the consent of the owner.** In *Deutsche
Grammophon* the Court held [68] that under Article 36 the holder
of an industrial property right was entitled to protect the right
which was " the specific object of the property." Thus the
exercise of an industrial property right to protect in one Member
State goods coming from another which have been marketed
there without the consent of the owner or anyone deriving title
under him would not, it is submitted, fall within the principle of
the *Deutsche Grammophon* case. Thus, in *Parke, Davis* [69]
products made and marketed in Italy without the consent of the

---

[66] January 1, 1958; see note 38, *ante.*
[67] *Ante,* § 250; but *cf. Re Remington Rand Italia,* Press Release, June 11, 1969.
[68] [1971] C.M.L.R. 631, 657.
[69] (24/67) [1968] C.M.L.R. 47, 59. It has been suggested that in fact the drugs
were made originally under a " know-how " licence from Parke, Davis. See
Korah (1972) 35 M.L.R. 634.

Dutch patentee were subsequently imported into Holland; the exercise by the Dutch patentee of its industrial property rights was held not to constitute an arbitrary discrimination nor a disguised restriction on trade between Member States. It is also doubtful whether the rule in *Deutsche Grammophon* has any application to cases where one party has, *without* the consent of the other, acquired the right to use in certain Member States industrial property rights formerly belonging to the latter *e.g.* as a result of war-time confiscation (although the position might be different if there was some continuing collaboration between the parties *e.g.* as to standardisation).[70] The application of the rule in *Deutsche Grammophon* to compulsory patent licensees remains undecided.

**926    Exercise of right solely to prevent imports.** In *Deutsche Grammophon* the Court said [71] that the exercise of the right concerned to prevent imports of products marketed in another Member State by the owner of the right or with his consent was prohibited where the right was exercised " solely because this marketing has not occurred in the domestic market." It is thought that the Court added this proviso to indicate that the rule in *Deutsche Grammophon* applies where the plaintiff has no " legitimate " interest in preventing imports of the products. If, for example, goods marketed by the plaintiff or with his consent in another Member State were imported in a damaged condition, then it might be legitimate for the plaintiff to prevent their resale. In every case, it is submitted, the question will be whether the exercise of the right constitutes, under Article 36, a " means of arbitrary discrimination or a disguised restriction on trade between Member States."

**927    Deutsche Grammophon: a " de minimis " rule?** As has been seen, Article 85 (1) applies only where the agreement in question restricts competition and affects trade between Member States to a " noticeable extent. " Whether a similar rule would be appropriate under Articles 30 to 36 of the Treaty is undecided.

**928    Regulation 17 inapplicable to Articles 30 to 36.** It should be noted that under Articles 30 to 36 the sole " sanction " for a

---

[70] *Ante*, § 328.
[71] [1971] C.M.L.R. 631, 659.

breach of the Treaty is that a national court should dismiss the proceedings for infringement.[72]  This is in contrast to Article 85 (1) and Article 86, for contravention of which fines may be imposed under Regulation 17.[73]  Agreements relating to industrial property rights and falling within Article 85 (1) may require notification under that Regulation.[74]  There is no question of a fine or of notification under the provisions relating to the free movement of goods, to which Regulation 17 has no application.

**929**    **Deutsche Grammophon: transitional provisions.**  Under the transitional arrangements in force following the accession of the United Kingdom, Ireland and Denmark to the Community, it is provided [75] that quantitative restrictions on imports or exports shall, from the date of accession, be abolished between the Community as originally constituted and the new Member States and between the new Member States themselves.  It is further provided that " measures having equivalent effect to such restrictions shall be abolished by January 1st 1975 at the latest." The application of the rule in *Deutsche Grammophon* in respect of imports or exports between the Community as originally constituted and the new Member States and as between the new Member States themselves in the period prior to January 1, 1975 is uncertain.  The question may depend in part upon whether Article 36 contains an independent directly applicable prohibition against the use of industrial property rights as a means of arbitrary discrimination or a disguised restriction on trade, or whether Article 36 is merely a provision qualifying Articles 30 to 34.  If the former is the case, then the rule in *Deutsche Grammophon* may be applicable from the date of accession, if the latter then the position is more doubtful.[76]

### 3.  LICENSING: THE APPLICATION OF ARTICLE 85 (1)

#### (a) *Generally*

**930**    **Licensing.**  This section of this chapter deals in turn with the application of Article 85 (1) to patent licences and licensing

---

[72] See the references to Art. 5 (2) of the Treaty at [1971] C.M.L.R. 631, 656.
[73] *Post*, §§ 1201 *et seq.*
[74] See generally §§ 501 *et seq., ante*, and § 957, *post*.
[75] Act of Accession, Art. 42; Cmnd. 4862, Pt. I, p. 42.
[76] See generally *ante*, § 918.

agreements,[77] trademark licences, registered user agreements
and know-how agreements. Also considered are the rules relating
to the notification of such agreements [78] and the question of
exemption under Article 85 (3).[79] In considering the application
of Article 85 (1) to such agreements it is first necessary to bear in
mind the general principle already discussed [80] in the light of
*Grundig-Consten* [81] and *Sirena*, [82] namely that Article 85 (1)
may apply to an agreement whereby the licensee is enabled, by
relying on the agreement and his rights under national law, to
prevent the importation of products covered by the right which
have been lawfully marketed in other Member States.[83] It is also,
however, necessary to consider whether there are other provisions
in a particular licence or licensing agreement which may contravene Article 85 (1). In this context the normal principles should
be applied. In each case it must be ascertained whether the
licence or agreement may adversely affect trade between Member
States and prevent, restrict or distort competition within the
common market to a noticeable degree.[84] In this context regard
must be had to the restrictions accepted by the parties under the
agreement, irrespective of whether the effect of the agreement is to
increase competition within the common market.[85] Further, if
there is a noticeable effect upon competition and upon trade
between Member States, it is immaterial whether the parties to
the agreement are situated in one Member State or outside the
Community. If Article 85 (1) is applicable to the agreement,
there remains the possibility of obtaining exemption under
Article 85 (3). Even where the agreement in question falls
outside Article 85 (1) it must be remembered that the exercise of
industrial property rights to restrict imports and exports between
Member States may be contrary to Articles 30 to 36 of the
Treaty.[86]

[77] For the purposes of EEC law there are no relevant differences between licences
and licensing agreements, and no distinction is drawn between them in this
chapter.
[78] *Post*, § 957; see generally, *ante*, §§ 501 *et seq.*
[79] *Post*, § 959; see generally, *ante*, §§ 601 *et seq.*
[80] *Ante*, §§ 908–911.
[81] *Consten and Grundig* v. *EEC Commission* (56/64, 58/64) [1966] C.M.L.R. 418;
*ante*, §§ 908, 909.
[82] (40/70) [1971] C.M.L.R. 260; *ante*, §§ 910, 911.
[83] For the application of these principles to patents see *ante*, §§ 910, 911.
[84] See generally §§ 201 *et seq.*, *ante*.
[85] *Ante*, § 219.
[86] *Ante*, §§ 912 *et seq.*

### (b) *Patent Licences and Licensing Agreements*

**(i) Sources**

**931    Sources.** Guidance as to the application of Article 85 (1) to patent licences and agreements may be obtained from a number of sources. On December 24, 1962 the Commission issued a notice on patent licensing agreements (in this chapter referred to as " the Patent Notice ").[87]  In the Patent Notice the Commission indicated those restrictions which it considered might be imposed in a patent licence without bringing the licence within the ambit of Article 85 (1). The Patent Notice, however, may be regarded as applying only to simple licensing arrangements between a patent holder and a single licensee. The Notice expressly excluded joint patents, reciprocal cross licences and " multiple parallel licences." [88]  These latter are accordingly discussed separately in this section.[89]  Further assistance to those considering the application of Article 85 (1) is also provided by the Commission's *Guide Pratique* of 1962.[90]  The Patent Notice and *Guide Pratique* provide general guidance and are without prejudice to any decision of the courts. Guidance may also be obtained from subsequent statements and decisions of the Commission. Important in this context are the Commission's decisions in *Re Burroughs-Delplanque*,[91]  *Re Burroughs-Geha*,[92] *Re Raymond*,[93] and *Re Davidson Rubber*.[94]  In one important respect (the matter of exclusivity) these decisions have reversed the Patent Notice.[95]  The recent views of the Commission on the general subject of patent licensing are also to be found in the Commission's First Report on Competition Policy.[96]

**932    Plan of this subsection.** In the following discussion the application of Article 85 (1) is considered in relation to some of the more common restrictions found in patent licences. Considered first are those imposed on the licensee. Then the question of an

---

[87] App. 11, *post*. This Notice is almost universally known as " the Christmas Message."
[88] Patent Notice, II.
[89] *Post*, §§ 950 *et seq.*
[90] See *ante*, § 135.
[91] J.O. 1972 L13/50, [1972] C.M.L.R. D67.
[92] J.O. 1972 L13/53, [1972] C.M.L.R. D72.
[93] J.O. 1972 L143/39, [1972] C.M.L.R. D45.
[94] J.O. 1972 L143/31, [1972] C.M.L.R. D52.
[95] See *post*, §§ 944 *et seq.*
[96] (1972) at §§ 58 *et seq.*

" exclusive licence " granted by the licensor is considered, followed by a discussion of certain arrangements excluded from the Patent Notice. Finally, licences in respect of non-Member States are considered.

## (ii) Restrictions imposed on the licensee

933    **Restrictions on the licensee covered by the patent.** The first group of restrictions mentioned in the Patent Notice consists of restrictions on the licensee which, in the Commission's view, involve only the partial retention by the patentee of the exclusive right which he holds under the patent.[97] Broadly speaking, such restrictions do not fall under Article 85 (1).[98] Since the Notice itself is set out in Appendix 11 of this work, these restrictions may be shortly summarised. Briefly, the patentee may limit the licensee in respect of (i) the method of exploiting the patent (*i.e.* making, using or selling), (ii) the quantities in which the patented product may be manufactured, (iii) the method of exploiting the patent or the application of the patented process, (iv) the duration of the licence (*i.e.* a licence of shorter duration than the patent), (v) the geographical area in which the patent may be used (*i.e.* a regional licence for part of the territory for which the patent is granted, or a licence limited to one place of exploitation or a specific factory),[99] (vi) the circumstances in which the licensee may assign or sub-license.[1] The First Report on Competition Policy confirms that the Commission's present view in respect of many of the above restrictions is broadly the same as it was in 1962.[2]

934    **Limitation on manufacturing rights.** The *Burroughs*[3] and *Davidson Rubber*[4] decisions appear to confirm that a restriction upon a licensee to manufacture only in one Member State falls

[97] Patent Notice I/A.
[98] But see §§ 944 *et seq.*
[99] See § 935, *post.*
[1] See also the *Burroughs* cases [1972] C.M.L.R. D67 at D71 and D72 at D75; *Re Davidson Rubber* [1972] C.M.L.R. D52, D60.
[2] The First Report does not make express reference to (iii) above. In some circumstances limitations as to the technical applications of a patented process may be unduly restrictive. *Cf.* The U.S. experience explained in *Bloxham, Licensing Rights in Technology,* 1972, p. 112.
[3] J.O. 1972 L13/50, 53, [1972] C.M.L.R. D67, D72.
[4] J.O. 1972 L143/31, [1972] C.M.L.R. D52.

outside Article 85 (1), but in those cases the licensees were free to sell in other Member States outside their respective territories.

**935    Limitation on selling rights.**    In the Patent Notice the Commission said that the licensor was entitled to limit the licensee as to the method of exploiting the patent and as to the area in which the licensee might exploit the patent, provided that the limitations imposed were " within the scope of the patent " *i.e.* involve only the partial retention of the right of prohibition which the patentee has by virtue of his patent.[5]    It would appear to follow that a patentee who holds a patent in a given national territory may lawfully restrict the licensee to making or selling the patented products only within that national territory, even though the effect of such a licence is to prevent the licensee himself from exporting directly to other Member States.    On the other hand, there are a number of qualifications which must be made to the above proposition, and this important point cannot be regarded as free from doubt. First, the Patent Notice was expressed not to apply where there are " multiple parallel licences "[6] *e.g.* the licensor has granted other licences under patents held in other Member States to licensees in those States. It is not clear how far *de facto* restrictions on exports may be imposed upon the licensees in these circumstances.    It seems from the *Guide Pratique* that the Commission considers that an undertaking by a licensee not to export to other Member States may bring the licence under Article 85 (1) in some circumstances, but the circumstances in which that may occur are undefined.[7]    Secondly, it is probable that a territorial limitation on the selling rights of a licensee is only permissible in the cases of a non-exclusive licence.    Exclusive licences to make and sell may fall within Article 85 (1) by virtue of their exclusivity and have hitherto only received negative clearance where in fact the licensees were free to sell outside their national territories.[8] Thirdly, it is clear that a licensor may not impose on the licensee an obligation to impose on *his* customers restrictions on export— for this would be a restriction going beyond the scope of the patent.[9]

[5] But note the examples given by the Commission in the Patent Notice at I/A.
[6] Patent Notice, II; *post*, § 952.
[7] *Guide Pratique*, Part II, (III), (3).
[8] *Post*, §§ 944 *et seq.*  But see also Reg. 67/67, *ante*, §§ 811 *et seq.*
[9] See also *Guide Pratique*, Part II, (III), (3).

936    Subject to the doubt that exists in the case of multiple parallel licences, it is probable that the present position is that a licensor may restrict the selling rights of the *non-exclusive licensee* to a national territory, but once the licensee has lawfully marketed the goods, then neither the licensor nor other licensees or assignees can rely either upon contractual provisions or upon their industrial property rights to prevent imports and exports between Member States. In particular, in accordance with the principle of *Sirena* [10] other licensees or assignees will be unable to rely on their rights under the licence or assignment to prevent imports of patented products originally marketed elsewhere in the common market by other licensees or assignees. Nor, under the rule in *Deutsche Grammophon*,[11] will the licensor be able to rely on his own industrial property rights to prevent imports of products that have been lawfully marketed elsewhere by the licensor himself or by his licensee with his consent. But where a non-exclusive licensee seeks to sell *directly* outside the national territory to which his selling rights are confined, where no *marketing* of the products has taken place within that national territory, there does not at present appear to be anything in Article 85 (1) or in the rule in *Deutsche Grammophon* to prevent the licensor from seeking to restrain the licensee, at least in territories where the licensor has patent protection.[12] The whole question, however, remains open.

937    **Other restrictions falling outside Article 85 (1).** It is clear from the Commission's decisions, the Patent Notice and the First Report on Competition Policy that the following restrictions generally fall outside Article 85 (1): (i) the obligation to fix a distinctive sign of origin to the patented product, provided the licensee is not prevented from affixing his own mark,[13] (ii) the obligation to conform to the patentee's requirements as to quality and to his technical instructions,[14] and to quality control inspections,[15] (iii) the obligation to manufacture in sufficient quantity,[16] although possibly the obligation to manufacture in sufficient

[10] *Ante*, §§ 908–911.            [11] *Ante*, §§ 912–929.
[12] And see *ante*, § 921.
[13] Patent Notice I/B; *Re Burroughs-Delplanque* [1972] C.M.L.R. D67, D70. First Report on Competition Policy, para. 76.
[14] Patent Notice I/C; *Re Burroughs-Delplanque* [1972] C.M.L.R. D67, D70.
[15] *Re Raymond* [1972] C.M.L.R. D45, D50.
[16] *Re Burroughs-Delplanque* [1972] C.M.L.R. D67, D70.

quantity may fall within the Treaty if it would have the effect of preventing the licensee from manufacturing or selling competing products, and (iv) the obligation to submit disputes to arbitration.[17]

938    **Tying obligations.** In principle, tying obligations which require the patent licensee to obtain certain products only from the licensor, fall within the Treaty.[18] However, tying arrangements are, in the Commission's view, permissible if they are indispensable for a technically proper utilisation of the patent.[19] The Commission does not regard the licensee's obligation to observe quality requirements and technical directions laid down by the licensor as restrictive.[20] Accordingly, the licensor may impose on the licensee standards of quality in respect of semi-finished products, raw materials or components. Where it is not feasible to define the quality of these materials sufficiently objectively, the licensor may impose on the licensee an obligation to obtain them only from certain sources of supply in order to ensure the quality of the ultimate product.

939    **Improvements.** Patent licences commonly impose an obligation on the licensee to grant the licensor the exclusive right to any improvement the licensee may have made to the invention. Such clauses fall within Article 85 (1).[21] In order to fall outside Article 85 (1), the licensee should be obliged to licence the licensor only on a non-exclusive basis and such obligation should be balanced by reciprocal obligations entered into by the licensor. A mutual obligation to communicate improvements or new uses is not considered to be restrictive of competition.[22]

940    **Competing products.** An obligation imposed on the licensee not to acquire, manufacture or sell competing products may fall under Article 85 (1).[23]

[17] *Ibid.;* see also *Re Davidson Rubber* [1972] C.M.L.R. D52, D60.
[18] First Report on Competition Policy, para. 71. See also Bulletin of the European Communities, May 1966. *Cf.* Patents Act 1949, s. 57.
[19] Patent Notice I/C and IV, 3rd para. First Report on Competition Policy para. 71.
[20] *Ante,* § 937.
[21] Patent Notice I/D and IV, 1st para.; First Report on Competition Policy para. 77.
[22] *Re Davidson Rubber* [1972] C.M.L.R. D52, D60; *Re Raymond* [1972] C.M.L.R. D45, D51; *post,* § 954.
[23] *Guide Pratique,* Part II, (III), (3).

**941** **Conditions of sale.** A provision as to the terms on which the licensee shall sell to other persons may fall under Article 85 (1).[24] Such a restriction will usually fall outside the scope of the patent. Particularly prohibited by Article 85 (1) will be an obligation to impose an export ban upon subsequent purchasers.

**942** **"No-challenge" clause.** An obligation on the licensee not to challenge the validity of the patents covered by the licence may fall under Article 85 (1).[25] Such obligation prevents the licensee from obtaining release from the burdens of the licence by establishing the invalidity of the patent, and may have the effect of artificially prolonging the patent's duration.

**943** **Restrictions must not exceed duration of patent.** In so far as the licensor may validly impose restrictions upon his licensee, it is clear that he may only do so for the duration of the validity of the patent.[26] In *Re Gema*,[27] a decision under Article 86, the Commission struck down royalty payments in respect of copyright which had already expired, or did not belong, directly or indirectly, to Gema.

**(iii) Exclusive licences**
**944** **Exclusivity.** The clauses considered hitherto have been concerned with restrictions upon the licensee. If, however, the licensor grants the licensee an exclusive licence he deprives himself of the ability to grant any other licence to undertakings within the territory to which the licence relates. The question arises as to how far such exclusive licences may fall within Article 85 (1). In the Patent Notice the Commission said such licences fall outside Article 85 (1).[28] In more recent decisions, however, the Commission has held an exclusive licence to fall within Article 85 (1). In *Re Burroughs-Delplanque* the Commission said[29]: " A patent confers on its holder the exclusive rights to manufacture the products which are the subject of the invention. The holder may cede by licences for a given territory the use of rights

[24] *Ibid.*
[25] *Re Davidson Rubber* [1972] C.M.L.R. D52, D55. *Cf. Re Raymond* [1972] C.M.L.R. D45; §§ 953–954, *post. Cf. Terrell, op. cit.*, paras. 616 *et seq.*
[26] First Report on Competition Policy, para. 72; Patent Notice.
[27] J.O. 1971 L134/15, [1971] C.M.L.R. D35; *ante*, §§ 730 *et seq.*
[28] Patent Notice I/E.
[29] [1972] C.M.L.R. D67, D70.

derived from its patent. However if it undertakes to limit the exploitation of its exclusive right to a single undertaking in a territory and thus confers on that single undertaking the right to exploit the invention and to prevent other undertakings from using it, it thus loses the power to contract with other applicants for a licence. In certain cases such exclusive character of a manufacturing licence may restrict competition and be covered by the prohibition set out in Article 85 (1)."

**945**    **Circumstances in which Article 85 (1) applies.**    Accordingly it is necessary to examine the circumstances in which Article 85 (1) applies. At present it is difficult to do more than illustrate such circumstances by reference to the decisions of the Commission. In *Davidson Rubber* the Commission held,[30] on the facts, that the exclusivity clause did bring the licence within Article 85 (1). In the *Burroughs* decisions,[31] on the other hand, the Commission found that an exclusive licence did not noticeably restrict competition.

**946**    **Davidson Rubber.**[30]    The Davidson Rubber Company (Davidson), an American company, was the holder of two patents, one concerning a process for the manufacture of padded, seamless objects, especially elbow rests and seat cushions for motor vehicles, the other concerning the machinery for the carrying out of the process. Davidson had set up a network of exclusive licensees to manufacture and sell the patented articles in Europe. One exclusive licence had been granted for Germany, the Benelux countries, and a non-Member State, another had been given for Italy, and a third given for France. Each licensee was, however, free to sell the products throughout the common market including the territories of other licensees. Combined with the patent licences were know-how agreements. The Commission found as a fact [32] that Davidson would not have succeeded in having its new process used in Europe by third parties if it had not agreed to protect its licensees in Europe against competition from new licensees. Without " exclusivity " the licensees would not have agreed to make the investments necessary to develop the process and adapt it to the requirements of the European market.

[30] J.O. 1972 L143/31, [1972] C.M.L.R. D52.
[31] J.O. 1972 L13/50, 53, [1972] C.M.L.R. D67, D72; *post*, §§ 948 *et seq.*; *cf. Re Raymond*, J.O. 1972 L143/39, [1972] C.M.L.R. D45; *post*, § 953.
[32] [1972] C.M.L.R. D52, D62.

947      However, despite these findings, the Commission considered
that the exclusive character of the licence rendered Article 85 (1)
applicable.[33]  The Commission found that the Davidson process
is the most important process for manufacture of elbow-rests for
cars.  The number of competing processes is limited and the
Davidson licensees held a considerable share of the market in
those articles in the Community.  The production of the German
licensee represented 20 per cent. of the total production of those
articles in Germany.  The equivalent figures for the French and
Italian licensees were 40 per cent. and 8 per cent. respectively.
Although there were no restrictions upon the sale of the contract
articles as made between Member States, the Commission found
that the exclusivity conferred by Davidson on each of its licensees
materially restricted Davidson's commercial freedom by preventing the grant of further licences to other manufacturers who might
wish to use the process in question, thus preventing those
manufacturers from exploiting the process within the Community.
The Commission found that trade between Member States was
adversely affected because the exclusivity conferred by Davidson
on each of its licensees in a given territory prevented third parties
from exploiting the patents and know-how in those territories and
subsequently exporting the products in question to other parts of
the Community.[34]  The Commission did however grant the parties
an exemption under Article 85 (3) which is further considered
below.[35]

948      **The Burroughs decisions.**[36]  *Davidson Rubber* may be contrasted with the *Burroughs* decisions where two exclusive licences
were held to fall outside Article 85 (1).  In those cases the product
concerned was a plasticised carbon paper.  Burroughs, an
American company, had granted an exclusive licence for France
and another exclusive licence for Germany.  In each case the
licensee was given the exclusive right to manufacture the product
and a non-exclusive right to sell and distribute the products
throughout the territory of the common market.  The licensees
were permitted to use Burroughs' trademarks but were free to

[33] *Ibid.* at p. D59.
[34] See also § 235, *ante.*
[35] *Post,* § 959.
[36] J.O. 1972 L13/50, 53, [1972] C.M.L.R. D67, D72.

affix their own marks. The Commission held [37] that the restriction upon the licensor inherent in the exclusivity provision did not, in this case, noticeably restrict competition. The Commission accepted the parties' estimate that plasticised carbon paper represented less than 10 per cent. of the total consumption of carbon paper in France and Germany respectively. Further, plasticised carbon paper other than that made with the Burroughs process was available on the market. The Commission was also influenced by the fact that each licensee, as well as the licensor itself, had full freedom to sell plasticised carbon papers in the whole of the common market. The products concerned could be transported relatively easily and cheaply.

**949**   **Result of the decisions.** It will be seen that every exclusive licence needs to be considered carefully in the light of many factors before it can be decided whether Article 85 (1) is applicable. In *Burroughs*, however, there were two important factors: (i) the relevant market share of the parties did not exceed 10 per cent. within the total territory covered by the licences and (ii) the licensees and the licensor were free to sell without restriction throughout the common market. Where these factors are both present, it is probable that the licence falls outside Article 85 (1), at least where the products in question are easily transportable.[38] How far the Commission is prepared to grant negative clearance when these factors are not present remains to be seen.

**950**   **(iv) Other arrangements falling outside the Patent Notice.**[39]

**Joint patents.** Jointly owned patents are not covered by the Patent Notice. Such patents often come about as a result of joint research and development, or as a result of a patent pooling agreement. Agreements providing for joint research and development or the setting up of such pools may themselves fall under Article 85 (1) where the parties accept noticeable restrictions on their competitive freedom.[40] Where patents are jointly owned care should be taken to ensure that the granting of licences should not lead to a covert market sharing agreement.

---

[37] [1972] C.M.L.R. D67 at D70; D72 at D74.
[38] See also §§ 245 *et seq., ante.*
[39] See Patent Notice, II.
[40] See §§ 1104 *et seq., post. Cf.* Clause 93 of the Fair Trading Bill.

**951 Cross licences.** Cross licensing arrangements were also excluded from the Patent Notice. Cross licensing occurs where patentees of different patents cross license each other under these patents. Provided that each such cross licence conforms with the principles already discussed, a cross licensing scheme will not necessarily fall within Article 85 (1). Cross licensing, however, may result in a division of the market between the parties, each licensee keeping out of the other licensee's area. Where a market sharing agreement results, Article 85 (1) will be applicable.

**952 Multiple parallel licences.** " Multiple parallel licences " were expressed to fall outside the Patent Notice. It is not entirely clear what is meant by this phrase, but it almost certainly covers the situation that arises where the owner of parallel patents in several Member States grants a series of licences under those patents to licensees in different Member States. Examples of such situations are seen in the *Burroughs* decisions[41] and in *Davidson Rubber*.[42] It is submitted that provided each of the parallel licences observes the principles already discussed, a scheme of multiple parallel patent licences, of itself, will not fall under Article 85 (1). Following the *Sirena*[43] decision it is necessary for each licence to be qualified in such a way that the licensee is not put into a position where he may rely on the licence and his rights under national law to prevent the import of products lawfully marketed by other licences in other Member States.

**(v) Patent licences for non-member States**[44]

**953 Re Raymond.** One question that arises is how far a patent licence granted by an undertaking within the common market in respect of a territory outside the common market may be caught by Article 85 (1). This question may particularly arise if the licence is exclusive and contains a prohibition against exports to the EEC. On this problem guidance may be obtained from the Commission's decision in *Re Raymond*[45] where negative clearance was granted in respect of a licence granted by a German

---

[41] J.O. 1972 L13/50, 53, [1972] C.M.L.R. D67, D72; *ante*, §§ 948, 949.
[42] J.O. 1972 L143/31, [1972] C.M.L.R. D52; *ante*, §§ 946, 947.
[43] (40/70) [1971] C.M.L.R. 260; *ante*, §§ 910 *et seq.*
[44] See also §§ 240 *et seq.*, *ante*.
[45] J.O. 1972 L143/39, [1972] C.M.L.R. D45.

patentee, Raymond, to a Japanese company, Nagoya.  There Raymond licensed Nagoya to manufacture in Japan patented plastic attachment components used in the construction of cars. The licence was exclusive to certain countries in the Far East and contained a prohibition on exports to the common market. First, the Commission considered [46] the export prohibition and decided on the facts that it would not noticeably influence competition within the common market.  The Commission held it was extremely unlikely that the Japanese licensee would, apart from the prohibition, export the goods to the Community.  The products concerned could only be manufactured to special order and in close and constant collaboration with the manufacturer placing the order.  Such collaboration would be virtually impossible between the licensee in Japan and a manufacturer in the common market.  In addition the Commission found that the articles covered by the licence could be obtained in the Community without difficulty from Raymond and other manufacturers of similar items.  Next, the Commission considered the exclusivity provision which prevented Raymond from granting a licence to any other licensee in certain Far East countries.  The Commission held that this provision did not restrict competition within the common market since it only had the effect of eliminating potential competitors on the Far East market.  Those competitors would be just as unlikely as Nagoya to be able to supply the products in question to the EEC.

**4**    **Other restrictions in Re Raymond.**  The Commission also considered two other restrictions contained in the licence, a " no challenge " clause and a clause whereby Nagoya agreed to sub-licence Raymond in respect of improvements made. Although a " no challenge " clause will often fall within Article 85 (1),[47] in this case the Commission held the clause was not restrictive.  On the facts, Nagoya had no interest in challenging Raymond's patents in Europe and any restriction relating to the patents in the Far East did not affect competition within the common market.  As to the improvements clause,[48] the parties amended an earlier version which provided that all improvements

[46] *Ibid.* at p. D48.
[47] See *ante,* § 942.
[48] See *ante,* § 939.

made by Nagoya to the Raymond technique should become the property of Raymond, and substituted a clause whereby Nagoya agreed to grant Raymond a non-exclusive licence. The Commission, it appears, was concerned to ensure that in Europe Raymond would not get an exclusive right to use improvements or modifications made by Nagoya.

### (c) *Trademark and Know-how Licences*

**955     Trademark licences.** The Patent Notice did not apply to trademark licences or registered user agreements but it is submitted that, in so far as they are relevant, the principles there set out should apply, *mutatis mutandis*, to trademarks. Further, it should be remembered that trademark licences, etc. will be governed by the rules laid down in *Grundig-Consten*,[49] *Sirena*[50] and *Deutsche Grammophon*,[51] which have already been discussed.[52] Several decisions of the Commission also relate to the collective use of trademarks.[53]

**956     Know-how agreements.** The Commission's position in respect of know-how agreements is not yet fully developed. It is probable that the principles set out in the Patent Notice are broadly applicable to licences of know-how[54]. The Commission considers that an obligation in a know-how agreement not to disclose the know-how and not to use it after the end of the agreement does not fall under Article 85 (1), but a restriction on the use of the know-how should extend only for as long as the know-how has not become part of the public domain.[55]

### (d) *Notification*

**957     Article 4 (2) (ii) (b) of Regulation 17.** When a restriction imposed by, or resulting from, a licensing agreement falls or may fall within Article 85 (1), the question of notification for the

[49] (56/64, 58/64) [1966] C.M.L.R. 418.
[50] (40/70) [1971] C.M.L.R. 260.
[51] (78/70) [1971] C.M.L.R. 631.
[52] *Ante*, §§ 905–929.
[53] See *Re VVVF*, J.O. 1969 L168/22, [1970] C.M.L.R. D1; *Re Association pour la promotion du tube d'acier soudé électriquement*, J.O. 1970 L153/14, [1970] C.M.L.R. D31; *Re SAFCO*, J.O. 1972 L13/44, [1972] C.M.L.R. D83; *Re Transocean Marine Paint Association*, J.O. 1967 163/10, [1967] C.M.L.R. D9.
[54] First Report on Competition Policy, para. 79; but territorial restrictions are unlikely to be permitted: see Jaume, Revue du Marché Commun, October 1972.
[55] *Ibid.* See also *Re Burroughs-Delplanque* [1972] C.M.L.R. D67, D70–D71; *ACEC-Berliet*, J.O. 1968 L201/7, [1968] C.M.L.R. D35.

purpose of obtaining exemption under Article 85 (3) must be considered.[56] However, not all such agreements are fully subject to notification. Article 4 (2) (ii) of Regulation 17 provides that the requirements of notification are relaxed in respect of agreements where: " not more than two undertakings are party thereto, and the agreements only . . . (b) impose restrictions on the exercise of the rights of the assignee or user of industrial property rights—in particular patents, utility models, designs or trademarks—or of the person entitled under a contract to the assignment, or grant, of the right to use a method of manufacture or knowledge relating to the use and to the application of industrial processes." Assignment, licences and analogous agreements thus fall within Article 4 (2) (ii) where two conditions are met: (i) the agreement imposes no restrictions upon the rights of the licensor or assignor, and (ii) the restrictions imposed on the assignee or licensee are restrictions only " on the exercise of the rights of the assignee or user " *i.e.* upon the exercise of the industrial property rights which form the subject of the assignment or licence.

958    **Extent of the exemption from notification.**    It is not, however, clear how far an agreement which falls within Article 85 (1) (*e.g.* because it falls outside the strict terms of the Patent Notice) may benefit from the limited relief from notification provided by Article 4 (2) (ii) (*b*) of Regulation 17. Little official guidance has been given. In the *Guide Pratique* of 1962 the Commission stated [57] that a restraint falling outside Article 4 (2) might exist, for example, where the licensee (i) assumes commitments extending beyond the period of validity of the industrial property right; (ii) may not acquire, manufacture, or sell any competing product; (iii) undertakes not to export to another Member State; (iv) undertakes to impose competitive restrictions on his customers. In practice, few agreements are likely to benefit from the provisions of Article 4 (2) (ii) (*b*).

(e) *Exemption Under Article 85 (3)*

959    **Generally.**    A licensing agreement which falls under Article 85 (1) and is duly notified may benefit like any other type of

[56] See generally *ante*, §§ 501 *et seq.* As to Art. 4 (2) of Reg. 17, see §§ 527 *et seq.*, *ante*; for the civil validity of agreements within Art. 4 (2) see §§ 410 *et seq. ante.*
[57] Part II, (III), (3).

agreement from an exemption under Article 85 (3) if the requirements of that provision are satisfied. Hitherto, the Commission
has only granted exemption in respect of a licensing agreement in
one case (*Davidson Rubber*),[58] but it has said [59] that it proposes
shortly to give more such decisions in order to define the circumstances in which exemption may be obtained. It also proposes
to explore the possibilities of granting a block exemption for
certain agreements pursuant to its powers under Regulation
19/65.[60]

960      **Davidson Rubber.** In *Davidson Rubber* [61] an exemption under
Article 85 (3) was granted in respect of exclusive patent licences
and know-how agreements made between an American company
(Davidson) and three manufacturers in the common market. The
agreements were found to contribute to promoting economic
progress by permitting the exploitation of the Davidson process
for moulding elbow rests and cushions for motor cars. The
agreements were found also to contribute to promoting technical
progress, and to improving production, in that they permitted
a rational adaptation of the Davidson techniques to European
requirements. The users, namely the manufacturers of the cars
for which the components were made by the Davidson process,
derived a fair share of the profits resulting from the licences
because they had available components made by a new technique
and offering increased security and greater comfort. The
exclusivity was found to be indispensable since Davidson would
not have succeeded in having its new process used in Europe by
third parties if it had not agreed to give its European licensees
exclusive rights in their national territories. Finally, it was
found that the parties did not have the power to eliminate
competition in a substantial part of the products concerned since
there was considerable competition in the relevant market. On
these facts, the Commission granted an exemption under
Article 85 (3).

**[The next paragraph is 1001.]**

[58] J.O. 1972 L143/31, [1972] C.M.L.R. D52; § § 946, 947, *ante.*
[59] First Report on Competition Policy, para. 80.
[60] See App. 5, *post.*
[61] [1972] C.M.L.R. D52, D61. See also *Re Transocean Marine Paint Association,*
J.O. 1967 L63/10, [1967] C.M.L.R. D9; *Re ACEC-Berliet,* J.O. 1968 L201/7,
[1968] C.M.L.R. D35.

## CHAPTER 10

# SPECIALISATION AGREEMENTS

## 1. IN GENERAL

**Generally.** In this chapter the operation of Article 85 is considered in relation to those agreements known as specialisation agreements. Specialisation agreements are agreements under which two or more manufacturers in the same field agree that each party will specialise in the production of certain types of products to the exclusion of products manufactured by the other parties. Further, each party undertakes to supply to the others, sometimes exclusively, the products in the manufacture of which he has specialised under the agreement, and to obtain exclusively from the others the products which he has agreed not to manufacture. In this way the parties are usually able to rationalise their production while continuing to offer to third parties the same, or a wider, range of products. More complicated specialisation agreements may also contain provisions relating to joint research and development; but agreements where the parties collaborate only in research and development, without providing for specialisation in manufacture, and agreements where two manufacturers in entirely *different* fields agree to joint development of a common product are dealt with in the next chapter of this work. This chapter thereby follows the practice of the Commission in confining the term " specialisation agreements " to those agreements where the parties actually give up the manufacture of products.

**Application of Article 85 (1).** Whether a particular specialisation agreement falls within Article 85 (1) is to be determined on the facts of each individual case by the application of the general principles already discussed.[1] Broadly speaking, where competing or potentially competing [2] manufacturers renounce the possibility of manufacturing or developing certain items, competition between them is restricted; similarly, if the agreement

[1] See Chap. 2, *ante.*
[2] *e.g.* as in *Sopelem-Langen*, J.O. 1972 L13/47, [1972] C.M.L.R. D77.

contains provisions relating to exclusive distribution, the freedom
of purchasers to obtain supplies directly from the parties is
restricted.  Where the undertakings concerned are situated in
different Member States, or even where the undertakings are
situated in the same Member State,[3] a specialisation agreement
may alter the relevant pattern of inter-State trade in a manner
capable of harming the creation of a single common market.  If
the agreement both affects trade between Member States and
prevents, restricts or distorts competition to a noticeable extent,
Article 85 (1) will be applicable.[4]  But Article 85 (1) may not
apply if the " specialisation " takes place between undertakings
which are not in competition and are unlikely to compete with
each other in the future,[5] or if the undertakings concerned hold
only a small share of the market.[6]

**1003    Application of Article 85 (3).**  Specialisation agreements may
benefit from an individual exemption where the requirements of
Article 85 (3) are satisfied, *i.e.* if it can be shown that they contribute to improvements in production or distribution, or to
promoting economic or technical progress, while allowing consumers a fair share of the resulting benefit, and neither imposing
restrictions which are not indispensable to the achievement of
these objectives, nor affording the parties the possibility of
eliminating competition in respect of a substantial part of the
products in question.[7]  To date the Commission has found in
six cases [8] that the specialisation agreements concerned improved
production by greater rationalisation and more intensive use of
equipment.  In five [9] of those decisions the Commission also

[3] See *Lightweight Paper*, J.O. 1972 L182/24, [1972] C.M.L.R. D94.
[4] See the following decisions discussed in this chapter; *Re Clima Chappée*, J.O.
1969 L195/1, [1970] C.M.L.R. D7; *Re Jaz-Peter*, J.O. 1969 L195/5, [1970]
C.M.L.R. 129; *Re FN-CF*, J.O. 1971 L134/6; *Re Sopelem-Langen*, J.O. 1972
L13/47, [1972] C.M.L.R. D77; *Re MAN-SAVIEM*, J.O. 1972 L31/29; *Re
Lightweight Paper*, J.O. 1972 L182/24, [1972] C.M.L.R. D94.  See also
*Dunlop-Pirelli*, J.O. 1969 L323/21, a decision granting negative clearance in
unusual circumstances.  Criticised by Mégret, Waelbroeck and others, *Le droit
de la Communauté économique européenne* (1972), p. 282.
[5] *Re Alliance de Constructeurs français de Machines-Outils*, J.O. 1968 L201/1,
[1968] C.M.L.R. D23.  A slightly surprising decision since one party retained
the ability to manufacture competing products in the future.  See also Notice
on Cooperation agreements, para. 5, App. 12, *post*.
[6] *Re Alliance de Constructeurs français de Machines-Outils*, note 5, *supra*.  See
also Notice on Agreements of Minor Importance, May 27, 1970, App. 13, *post*.
Also *ante*, § 245.                              [7] See generally Chap. 6, *ante*.
[8] See note 4, *supra*.          [9] Not in *Lightweight Paper*, note 4, *supra*.

found that the agreement resulted in an improvement in distribution. Each party was able to offer a broader range of products than previously and was enabled to increase its sales in the territory of the other party because of the experience and reputation of its partner in that territory. Further, in all cases the Commission was able to find that technical progress was promoted, noticeably where economies in production made greater resources available for investment and where the agreement was likely to lead to more effective research and development.[10] The advantages of specialisation agreements have been recognised by the publication of Regulation 2779/72 under which the Commission has granted block exemption to a limited class of such agreements.[11]

**1004**    **Plan of this chapter.** In this chapter the operation of Article 85 in relation to specialisation agreements is illustrated by discussion of the six individual decisions where an exemption has been granted under Article 85 (3).[12]  It is convenient to deal first with four decisions which display certain common features, namely, those in the cases of *Re Jaz-Peter* (*Jaz*),[13] *Re Clima Chappée and Buderus* (*Clima Chappée*),[14] Ne *FN-CF* (*FN-CF*)[15] and *Re Sopelem-Langem* (*Sopelem*).[16]  Separate consideration is given to the decisions in *Re MAN-SAVIEM*[17] and in *Re Lightweight Paper*.[18]  The new Regulation providing for block exemption of specialisation agreements is then discussed in the light of the guidance which those decisions provide.  Finally, the provisions of Article 4 (2) of Regulation 17 relating to the notification of specialisation agreements are discussed.

## 2. Individual Decisions by the Commission

### (a) *Clima Chappée, Jaz, FN-CF, Sopelem*

**1005**    **Four decisions.** In *Jaz*[19] a French and a German clock manufacturer agreed to concentrate their principal manufactured

---

[10] The agreements also relating to research and development were those in *FN-CF*, J.O. 1971 L134/6 and in *MAN-SAVIEM*, J.O. 1972 L31/29.
[11] J.O. 1972 L292/23, made under powers contained in Reg. 2821/71. *Post,* §§ 1023 *et seq.*
[12] See note 4, *ante.*
[13] J.O. 1969 L195/5, [1970] C.M.L.R. 129.
[14] J.O. 1969 L195/1, [1970] C.M.L.R. D7.
[15] J.O. 1971 L134/6.
[16] J.O. 1972 L13/47, [1972] C.M.L.R. D77.
[17] J.O. 1972 L31/29.
[18] J.O. 1972 L182/24, [1972] C.M.L.R. 94.
[19] Note 13, *ante.*

lines, with the German party specialising in the manufacture of large mechanical alarm clocks and the French party specialising in the manufacture of electric clocks and electric alarm clocks; they also agreed to exchange know-how. In *Clima Chappée* [20] a French and a German manufacturer agreed that each would specialise in the manufacture of certain types of air-conditioning and associated equipment. In *FN-CF* [21] a French and a Belgian manufacturer of small arms agreed that each would specialise in the manufacture of certain types of ammunition and to engage in joint research and development. In *Sopelem*, [22] a French and a German manufacturer of highly technical servo-command equipment agreed that each would specialise in certain types of automatic hydraulic equipment. Each agreement fell within Article 85 (1).

**1006**    **Common features.** These agreements each involved two undertakings situated in different Member States. Each contained the following main provisions:

(a) each party undertook not to manufacture certain products which the other was " better able " to manufacture;

(b) each party undertook to obtain solely from the other party all his requirements for resale in his own territory of those products which he had agreed not to manufacture (exclusive purchase);

(c) each party undertook to supply the specialisation products only to the other party for resale within a defined territory (exclusive supply), although in *Sopelem* this provision was implicit rather than express.

**1007**    **Restriction on manufacture.** Clearly the essence of a specialisation agreement is that the parties restrict their manufacture to certain items. For the purposes of Article 85 (3), this fundamental restriction (accepted in all six decisions by the Commission) [23] will ordinarily be regarded as indispensable to achieving the objectives of the specialisation agreement. In each of the four cases under discussion the Commission noted that each party had been assigned the exclusive manufacture of products which it

[20] Note 14, *ante.*
[21] Note 15, *ante.*
[22] Note 16, *ante.*
[23] Note 4, *ante.*

was already well able and equipped to manufacture and which the other party was, generally, less able and equipped to manufacture. Article 1 of the new Regulation for block exemption [24] recognises that specialisation agreements will contain such a fundamental restriction on manufacture.

**008** **Exclusive purchasing.** In each of the four cases, the Commission approved a provision whereby each party agreed to purchase exclusively from the other, for resale within a defined area, those products which each had agreed not to manufacture. Indeed such a provision is often a necessary protection for parties who have concentrated their production on a small range of items. In *Clima Chappée*, however, the exclusive purchase obligation was to continue only so long as the goods concerned could be purchased from the other partner at competitive prices. Article 2 1 (*c*) of the new Regulation now requires such a limitation of the terms of the exclusive purchase obligation as a condition of obtaining the benefit of block exemption.[25] Article 2 (1) (*c*), however, does not limit the exclusive purchase obligation only to those products required for resale within a defined area.

**009** **Exclusive supply.** In each of the four cases the parties agreed not only to purchase exclusively from each other those products which each had agreed not to manufacture, but also to supply those products which they continued to manufacture exclusively to the other party for resale within a defined area of the common market. In *Jaz, Clima Chappée* and *Sopelem* the exclusive concession was limited to the national territory of the partner concerned *i.e.* Jaz was appointed exclusive distributor in France for the products in which Peter specialised, and Peter was appointed exclusive distributor in Germany for the like products of Jaz; and similarly in *Clima Chappée* and *Sopelem*. Outside those national territories each party was free to distribute its own goods. In *FN-CF*, FN and CF respectively each undertook the exclusive distribution of its partner's products in Benelux and France. For Germany and Italy distribution was to be carried out exclusively by the party whose distribution network was the better developed, which at the time of the agreement was FN.

[24] *Post*, §§ 1026 *et seq.*
[25] *Post*, § 1036.

**1010**    **Justification of exclusive supply.**  In each of the four decisions, the exclusive supply restriction was held to improve distribution, but the reasons for holding that the restriction was " indispensable " varied in each case. It is still instructive to consider the treatment in the Commission's individual decisions, of exclusive supply, although the Regulation relating to block exemption now extends to agreements containing an exclusive supply provision.[26] In *Jaz* the relevant clause included an obligation to supply under the other party's trade mark and in minimum quantities. It was held that without such a clause the parties could not reasonably be expected to take the risk of concentrating their manufacture. The clause provided the necessary guarantee that each party would " be able to take the whole benefit from the sale in its own country of the specialised articles of its partner." In *Clima Chappée* the reciprocal exclusive distribution was described as " indispensable " to the specialisation in manufacturing. But in that case the parties were bound by the exclusive concession only as long as the other party's products remained competitive. In both *Jaz* and *Clima Chappée* it was also found that there was no restriction on sales by the parties to other countries in the common market, nor were there any restrictions as to resale by third parties. In *Sopelem* it was said that reciprocal exclusive supplies " guaranteed " to each party the best conditions for distribution of its products in the territory of the other, particularly in the installation, demonstration and after sales service of highly specialised equipment. Indeed in *Sopelem* there was no express provision as to exclusive supply, but the highly technical nature of the equipment meant that, in practice, the agreement could be operated only on the basis of exclusive supply. In *FN-CF* the Commission justified the exclusive supply obligation particularly by reference to the joint research and development which the parties were also carrying on under the agreement.

**1011**    **Restriction on manufacture or marketing of new items.**  In *FN-CF* each party agreed not, without the consent of the other, to manufacture new items which at the time of the agreement were not manufactured by either of them. Although the Commission's

---

[26] *Post*, § 1032. *Cf.* the previous draft Regulation [1972] C.M.L.R. D90.

decision did not clearly distinguish this restriction from the exclusive arrangements for existing products, it was considered indispensable in circumstances where any new products were likely to have been developed as a result of a joint collaboration. Similarly in *Jaz* each party granted its partner a right of priority in the exclusive marketing of new products, whether or not they fell within the products covered by the specialisation.   In that decision this restriction was regarded as indispensable in the light of the provisions relating to the exchange of know-how contained in the agreement.   The new Regulation for block exemption, however, does not permit any restriction on the manufacture or marketing of new products not manufactured by the parties at the time of the agreement.[27]

**012**    **Restrictions relating to products not the subject of specialisation.** In *Clima Chappée* each party was obliged to give preference to the other partner in purchases of products not covered by the specialisation agreement, price and quality being otherwise equal. The Commission permitted this clause as one of certain " accessory clauses closely linked to the specialisation and reciprocal exclusive concession."   In *Jaz*, Peter additionally appointed Jaz exclusive distributor in France in respect of its stopwatches, which were not covered by the specialisation provisions.   These stop-watches did not compete with any items in the Jaz range, and the Commission found that the appointment of Jaz to sell the stop-watches in France through its numerous points of sale and under its own trade mark, permitted an improvement in distribution.   No ancillary provisions of this nature are permitted by the block exemption set out in the new Regulation.

**013**    **Position of parties on the market.**   In considering whether an individual exemption may be granted under Article 85 (3), it must also be remembered that the Commission must be satisfied that the parties are not in a position where they may eliminate competition in respect of a substantial part of the products in question.   In *Clima Chappée* the Commission held merely that there were sufficient other manufacturers to ensure lively competition.   Similar findings were made in *Jaz* (where the French

[27] *Post*, § 1035.

[ 237 ]

party had 5 per cent. of the market for all alarm clocks in the EEC and was the largest French manufacturer), and in *Sopelem* (where the French and German parties ranked fifth and eleventh respectively in their national markets). In *FN-CF* the parties held 25 per cent. of the relevant market in France and Benelux and FN was the largest producer in Benelux. The Commission took into account the existence of strong competitors within the common market. In all cases the Commission also stressed that, despite the provisions relating to reciprocal exclusive supply as between the parties, third parties obtaining supplies from either party were able to import and export freely between Member States. In the new Regulation providing for block exemption, the criteria to be adopted as to market share and turnover are set out in Articles 3 and 4 thereof.[28]

**1014**      **Conditions attached to exemption.** Only in *FN-CF* did the Commission exercise its power, under Article 8 of Regulation 17, to attach conditions to the grant of an exemption. There, because of the parties' market strength, the parties were obliged to make biennial reports as to the implementation of the agreement, its effects, their sales prices and discounts, and their market shares in each Member State.

### (b) *MAN-SAVIEM* [29]

**1015**      **Provisions relating to development and manufacture.** Under this agreement two vehicle manufacturers, one French and one German, agreed to collaborate in the development, production and distribution of a range of medium and heavy-weight lorries. Broadly, it was agreed that each party should manufacture all the vehicles in the common range. It was also agreed that there would be a reciprocal exclusive supply as between the parties of certain parts and sub-assemblies for use in manufacture. This interchange of parts and sub-assemblies was, under the terms of the agreement, to be intensified as a result of further research and development. The effect of this provision was that the medium and heavy-weight vehicles manufactured by both parties would increasingly contain the same parts and sub-assemblies. Moreover, the French party was to concentrate primarily on research

[28] *Post*, § 1038.
[29] J.O. 1972 L31/29.

and development in the field of medium-weight vehicles and the German party in the field of heavy-weight vehicles. All new developments by either party were to be incorporated into the vehicles of the common range. Little by little, therefore, as research and development progressed, the vehicles assembled by each party would come to be virtually identical.

**016**     **Provisions relating to distribution.** As to distribution, it was agreed that the heavy and medium range lorries for the French market would be assembled and supplied exclusively by the French party. The heavy and medium range lorries for the German market would be assembled and supplied exclusively by the German party. For markets outside France and Germany, the medium range of vehicles were to be assembled and supplied exclusively by the French party, while the heavy range were to be assembled and supplied exclusively by the German. In effect, therefore, the German party agreed, for the sale of medium-weight vehicles, to keep out of all markets except the German market while the French party similarly agreed, for the sale of heavy-weight vehicles, to keep out of all markets except the French market. As already explained, however, as the agreement took effect there would cease to be anything more than minor differences in vehicles of equivalent weight leaving the production line of either party.

**017**     **Exemption under Article 85 (3): improvements.** The Commission held that the restrictions on competition in the agreement, and its effect on inter-State trade, was such as to bring the agreement within Article 85 (1). In granting exemption under Article 85 (3) the Commission found that each party was assured greater production for its parts and sub-assemblies; that each party had specialised in the products it was best able to produce; that cost savings could be made allowing the parties to get nearer to a position of optimum unit cost. For these reasons production was improved. Technical progress was likely to result from the provisions for joint research and development. Distribution was improved because of the reduction in the number of types and the standardisation that the agreement brought about, and because each party was able to widen its distribution through having products of its own manufacture incorporated in the units sold by the other party. The restrictions accepted by the parties were, the Commission found, indispensable to the achievement of these improvements.

**1018**     **Article 85 (3): elimination of competition.** In deciding whether the parties would be enabled to eliminate competition in respect of a substantial part of the products in question, the Commission took into account the total production of commercial vehicle manufacturers in Western Europe who sold their products within the common market. The combined production of MAN and SAVIEM (including production of light-weight vehicles which did not fall under the agreement) amounted to only 7.4 per cent. of the market as defined by the Commission. In the circumstances the Commission was able to hold that the agreement did not substantially eliminate competition.

### (c) *Lightweight Paper* [30]

**1019**     **Generally.** *Lightweight Paper* is of significance because it involved five manufacturers of one country whose position on the national market was very strong. Until *Lightweight Paper* the Commission's decisions on specialisation agreements concerned only joint ventures between undertakings in different Member States, a form of co-operation which the Commission have always considered to be particularly valuable in bringing about the objectives of the common market. In *Lightweight Paper* the Commission approved a specialisation agreement which was intended to enable the parties in one Member State to maintain an already very substantial market share against fierce competition from within and without the common market.

**1020**     **Circumstances of the agreement.** The agreement was made between the principal French manufacturers of cigarette paper who were also manufacturers of other lightweight paper and replaced an earlier agreement relating to production quotas.[31] Under the agreement each party undertook " in principle " to limit its production to certain types and qualities of paper. The agreement contained no other restrictions of competition. In cigarette paper the parties held 80 per cent. of the market in

[30] J.O. 1972 L182/24, [1972] C.M.L.R. 94.
[31] See *ante*, §§ 325 *et seq.*

France and 70 per cent. in Benelux. In other types of lightweight paper the parties production was 15 per cent. of total common market production. The parties exported 13 per cent. of their total production to other Member States.

**1021**     **Article 85 (1).** The Commission held that Article 85 (1) was applicable in that the limitation on production restricted competition between the parties. Since the parties held a large share of the market in Member States other than France, consumers in those Member States were limited in their choice of supplier. In these circumstances trade between Member States was also likely to be adversely affected.

**1022**     **Article 85 (3).** The Commission found that production was improved and technical progress likely in that each manufacturer concentrated on his particular speciality and achieved economies of scale. Cost savings had already benefited the consumer. The Commission also accepted that the limitation on production was indispensable to the agreement to specialise, but held that, in view of the parties' market position, no other restrictions accepted by parties could have been regarded as indispensable. The main question, therefore related to the elimination of competition. The Commission found (i) there was strong competition in all lightweight papers within the common market, both from common market producers and other parties, (ii) demand for lightweight papers came from a small number of large undertakings who could exert considerable bargaining power, (iii) there was reason to suppose that a world market for the goods would be created and (iv) the restriction on competition as between the parties was not irreversible under the agreement. On the basis of these factors the Commission concluded that competition would not be eliminated for a substantial part of the products concerned. However the Commission imposed upon the parties, under Article 8 (1) of Regulation 17, obligations (i) to report all arbitral awards relating to the provisions of the agreement,[32] (ii) to render a report on the working of the agreement two years after the decision and (iii) to report any cross share-holding or exchanges of management personnel (*e.g.* interlocking directorships)

[32] For the reason why this condition was imposed, see [1972] C.M.L.R. D94 at D102.

between the participating undertakings, and any proposal for merger or takeover likely to occur between them or between one of them and a third party.

### 3. THE BLOCK EXEMPTION

#### (a) *Generally*

**1023**    **The new block exemption.**   The Commission's new Regulation providing for a block exemption for specialisation agreements has recently been enacted. Regulation 2779/72 supersedes a draft Regulation, previously published by the Commission, which was in several respects of more limited application. In particular, the new Regulation permits certain restrictions as to exclusive supply which were not permitted under the previous draft. The text of the new Regulation reproduced in Appendix 8 is taken from the official English translation.

**1024**    **Requirements for exemption.**   In order to benefit from the block exemption (a) the agreement must be of a kind described in Article 1 of the new Regulation, (b) the agreement must not contain any restrictions on competition other than those set out in Article 2 of the new Regulation, and (c) the products covered by the agreement, and the parties thereto, must fulfil the requirements of Articles 3 and 4 of the Regulation. All the provisions of the block exemption apply equally to concerted practices.[33]

**1025**    **Likely scope of block exemption.**   The new block exemption is likely to be of limited application, principally because the limits of market share and turnover which must be satisfied under Articles 3 and 4 are low, and the criteria there used may be difficult to apply in individual cases. On the other hand, the block exemption closely reflects the decisions discussed above relating to individual exemptions under Article 85 (3). A central feature in five of the six agreements individually exempted was the provision relating to the parties reciprocal obligations of exclusive supply and purchase in respect of the products mentioned in the agreement.[34] Exclusive supply obligations are still permitted under

[33] Art. 7.
[34] See *ante*, §§ 1001–1018; not including *Re Lightweight Paper*, J.O. 1972 L182/24, [1972] C.M.L.R. D94.

the new block exemption. In addition, the exclusive purchasing obligation permitted appears to be wider than that contained in any of the decisions relating to individual exemption.[35]

### (b) *Article 1*

**1026**    **Article 1.** Article 1 of the new Regulation provides that agreements to which the exemption relates are those in accordance with which undertakings agree with each other for the purposes of specialisation not to manufacture or have manufactured by other undertakings certain products so long as the agreement remains in force and to leave to the other parties to the agreement the task of manufacturing those products or of having them manufactured by other undertakings. Clearly a provision of the kind discussed in Article 1 is the fundamental clause upon which specialisation agreements are founded. It appears in all agreements which have been individually exempted by the Commission. It should be noted that Article 1 contains three basic elements: (i) the agreement must be " for the purposes of specialisation "; (ii) the undertakings concerned must agree not to manufacture, or have manufactured for them, certain products, but only for so long as the agreement remains in force; and (iii) the manufacture of those products which one party has agreed not to produce must be undertaken by the other party. The following additional comments may be made.

**1027**    **Number of parties.** The exemption is not restricted to agreements between two undertakings. The number of parties to the agreement is not relevant, provided the parties satisfy the provisions as to combined market share and turnover set out in Articles 3 and 4.[36]

**1028**    **No requirement that one party " better able " to produce.** In each of the individual exemptions discussed above the Commission approved the restriction upon manufacture where one party was " better able " than the other party to manufacture the products covered by the agreement. There is no similar requirement under Article 1. Presumably, the Commission considers that

[35] Art. 2 (c); *post,* § 1036.
[36] *Post,* § 1038.

parties taking advantage of the block exemption will allocate
responsibilities so as to make the best use of their resources; but
the Commission retains reserve powers to withdraw the benefit
of the block exemption in the event of abuse.[37]

**1029**    **Restrictions on manufacturing new products.** In *FN-CF*[38]
each party agreed not to manufacture, without the consent of the
other, new products which were not being manufactured by
either party at the time of the agreement. This agreement,
however, also provided for joint research and development, and
the Commission permitted this restriction in a context where any
new products were likely to be developed only in the course of a
joint collaboration. Article 1 does not, so it appears, con-
template a prohibition against manufacturing goods not previously manufactured by the parties. For such a restriction it
appears that individual exemption is likely to continue to be
required.

### (c) *Article 2*

**1030**    **Article 2 (1) (a).** Under Article 2 (1) (*a*) of the Regulation the
parties are permitted to accept an obligation not to conclude,
without consent of the other parties, specialisation agreements
with other undertakings concerning identical products or products
which must be considered by the user to be similar by reason of
their properties, their price or their use. An obligation to this
effect was found in *MAN-SAVIEM*,[39] although it was not found
in other agreements.

**1031**    **Article 2 (1) (b): supply.** Article 2 (1) (*b*) of the Regulation
permits the imposition of an obligation to deliver to the other
parties the products which are covered by the specialisation and
to conform in this respect with minimum standards. Clearly,
if one party agrees not to manufacture certain products, he may
need to be able to impose on the other parties an obligation to
deliver those products to him. This may be achieved under
Article 2 (1) (*b*) which also permits the party supplied to insist on
certain minimum standards.

[37] See § 1042, *post.*
[38] J.O. 1971 L134/6. See *ante*, §§ 1005 *et seq.* See also *Jaz*, J.O. 1969 L195/5,
[1970] C.M.L.R. 129; *ante*, §§ 1005 *et seq.*
[39] J.O. 1972 L31/29; *ante*, § 1015.

**1032**     **Exclusive supply permitted.** In many of the cases discussed above,[40] each party agreed to deliver relevant products only to the other party within a particular area *i.e.* each party appointed the other his exclusive dealer in a particular territory. Under Article 2 (1) (*d*) an obligation to grant the other contracting parties the exclusive distribution of the specialisation products is permitted, but only in so far as the other contracting parties do not restrict the possibility of traders and consumers obtaining those products elsewhere in the common market. The proviso to Article 2 (1) (*d*) is similar to that found in Regulation 67/67 [41]; it is clear that the parties may not use direct export bans nor industrial property rights to protect the territory of the exclusive distributor.

**1033**     **Price of supply.** There is no provision that the obligation to deliver must be at competitive prices.[42]

**1034**     **Exclusion of third parties.** It appears from Article 2 (1) (*d*) of the new Regulation that the benefit of the block exemption is not lost even where one party appoints the other as his exclusive distributor in respect of the whole common market area; Article 2 (2) (*d*) does not restrict the permitted exclusive distributorship to any particular area within the Community. It would appear to follow that the Regulation will continue to apply even where the obligation to supply products covered by the specialisation agreement to the other party effectively results in the *de facto* exclusion of direct supplies to third parties. But no doubt the Commission would consider using its powers under Article 5 of the Regulation [43] if third parties in other parts of the common market in fact had difficulty in obtaining supplies from the exclusive distributor. In doubtful cases individual exemption may be applied for.[44]

**1035**     **Supply of products not covered by the specialisation agree-**

---

[40] *Ante,* §§ 1001–1018; all except *Lightweight Paper,* J.O. 1972 L182/24, [1972] C.M.L.R. D94; *ante,* § 1019.
[41] *Ante,* §§ 818 *et seq.*
[42] Contrast Art. 2 (*c*) of the new Regulation.
[43] § 1042, *post.*
[44] *Ante,* §§ 601 *et seq.*

**ment.**[45]  As has been seen,[46] the individual exemptions discussed above sometimes contained provisions relating to products which were not the subject of the specialisation agreement *e.g.* in *Jaz* the German partner appointed the French partner as exclusive dealer in France for its stop-watches. In *Jaz* too, each party was given the right to be supplied exclusively, within its own area, with any new products manufactured by the other party, whether or not they were specialisation products. Under Article 2 (1) (*b*) the obligation to supply may relate only to products covered by the specialisation agreement. If supply obligations are accepted in respect of products not so covered, the benefit of the block exemption will be lost.

**1036**     **Article 2 (1) (c): exclusive purchasing.**  Article 2 (1) (*c*) provides that an obligation may be imposed on the parties to the agreement to obtain solely from the other parties their requirements of the products which are covered by the specialisation agreement. That obligation is however subject to the proviso that each party is to be released from its obligations where more favourable conditions of supply are found. Clearly, an exclusive purchasing obligation of the same kind is necessary in order to protect all the parties where they have each restricted their range of production. But it should be noted that the obligation imposed may not be absolute; the parties must remain free to purchase elsewhere if similar products are available at more competitive prices. A provision to this effect was found in *Clima Chappée*.[47] Secondly, the exclusive purchase obligation may not extend to other products not covered by the specialisation agreement. An obligation, such as that also found in *Clima Chappée*, to favour the other party in respect of unrelated products would also fall outside the block exemption. In one respect, however, Article 2 (1) (*c*) is wider than the exclusive purchasing provision found in individual decisions by the Commission. In several of these decisions [48] one party undertook to obtain exclusively from the other party all his requirements of the products covered by the

---

[45] *i.e.* any products other than those which either party has agreed not to manufacture.
[46] *Ante*, § 1012.
[47] *Ante*, § 1008.
[48] *Ante*, §§ 1001–1018.

specialisation, for resale within a defined territory. The new
Regulation appears to permit an obligation to obtain from the
other party all requirements of products covered by the specialisation, irrespective of where they are to be sold.

**1037** **Article 2 (2) (a) and (b).** Article 2 (2) (*a*) of the Regulation
provides that each party may impose on the others obligations to
provide after-sales and guarantee services in respect of those
products which he has delivered to them pursuant to the agreement. Obligations to hold stocks and parts are also permitted
under Article 2 (2) (*b*) of the new Regulation. It may be doubted
whether any such provisions fall under Article 85 (1) at all;
clearly they are included in the new block exemption for the
avoidance of doubt. Unlike Regulation 67/67,[49] which relates to
distribution agreements, the new block exemption does not
specifically provide for an obligation upon one party to promote
the goods of the others [50]; but it may be doubted whether Article
85 (1) would apply to this provision either.

### (d) *Articles 3 and 4*

**1038** **Market share and turnover.** The new Regulation imposes
very narrow limits in respect of the market position of the parties
whose agreements may benefit therefrom. Under Article 3 of
the new Regulation the block exemption is only applicable where
two conditions are satisfied. First, the products which are covered
by the specialisation agreement must not represent, in any
Member State [51] of the common market, more than 10 per cent.
of the volume of business carried out in identical products or
products considered similar by the user by reason of their properties, their price or their use. Secondly the total turnover of the
undertakings concerned in products of all descriptions during the
preceding accounting year must not exceed 150 million units of
account. Article 3 (3) provides a kind of marginal relief. In the
event that over two consecutive accounting years the market
share and turnover should exceed the figures mentioned by not
more than 10 per cent., then the exemption may nonetheless be
applicable.

[49] *Ante*, § 818.
[50] as occurred *e.g.* in *Sopelem*; *ante*, §§ 1001–1018.
[51] *Cf.* Art. 4 (2) (iii) (*c*) of Reg. 17 which refers to " a substantial part of the common market ", § 1047, *post*.

**1039**     **Calculation of market share and turnover.** Article 4 lays down conditions for determining market share and turnover similar in all respects to those provided in the Commission's Notice of May 1970 concerning agreements of minor importance.[52]

### (e) *Other Provisions Relating to Block Exemption*

**1040**     **Duration.** Article 1 of the new Regulation provides that the block exemption is to be applicable until December 31, 1977.

**1041**     **Retrospective effect.** Article 6 provides that Regulation 2779/72 has retroactive effect to the date when the conditions of that Regulation were fulfilled. However, such date may not be earlier than the date of notification of those agreements which were subject to notification prior to January 18, 1972.[53] Thus, the only agreements which benefit from the retroactive effect of the Regulation are those which (i) were subject to notification and have been duly notified; or (ii) were exempt from notification under Article 4 (2) of Regulation 17, as amended.[54]

**1042**     **Revocation.** Article 5 of the new Regulation provides that the Commission may examine whether a particular agreement, decision or concerted practice otherwise falling under the block exemption is nonetheless incompatible with Article 85 (3). The Commission is to watch out particularly for situations where there is reason to suppose that the rationalisation does not provide substantial results or that it leads to prejudicial effects for users. If the agreement is found to be incompatible with Article 85 (3), the Commission has power, under Article 7 of Regulation 2822/71 to revoke the benefit of the block exemption in respect of that agreement, possibly with retroactive effect.

### 4.   NOTIFICATION OF SPECIALISATION AGREEMENTS

**1043**     **Article 4 (2) (iii) (c) of Regulation 17.** Under Article 4 (2) (iii) (c) of Regulation 17[55] certain specialisation agreements,

---

[52] *Ante*, § 245.
[53] The date of coming into force of Reg. 2822/71, amending Reg. 17.  See Art. 191 of the Treaty.
[54] *Post*, § 1043.
[55] As amended by Reg. 2822/71.

decisions and concerted practices are specifically exempted from the requirement of notification.  That provision is applicable to agreements " which have as their sole object specialisation in the manufacture of products, including the agreements necessary for its attainment, when the products which are the object of specialisation do not represent in a substantial part of the common market more than 15 per cent. of the total turnover realised in products which are identical or are considered similar by the consumer by reason of their properties, price and use, and when the total annual turnover realised by the participating undertakings does not exceed 200 million units of account."  Regulation 17 provides that such agreements, decisions and concerted practices may be notified to the Commission.

**1044**    **Sole object.**  The requirement that agreements must have as their " sole object " specialisation in order to benefit from Article 4 (2) (iii) (c) undoubtedly restricts the scope of that provision.  Of the agreements discussed hitherto, it is probably only *Lightweight Paper* [56] that could confidently be regarded as having specialisation as its sole object.  In that agreement the only restriction accepted by the parties was a limitation on manufacture, for the purposes of specialisation.  The question that arises is whether specialisation agreements which also contain wider provisions, relating *e.g.* to exclusive supply and purchase and/or to joint collaboration in research and development, can properly be regarded as being agreements having specialisation as their *sole* object.  One approach to this question is to ask in each case whether such provisions can properly be described as " necessary for the attainment of specialisation in manufacture."  If the answer to this question is in the negative, then it may be doubted whether specialisation is the *sole* object of the agreement.

**045**    **Provisions necessary for the attainment of specialisation.**  The alternative requirement contained in Article 4 (2) (iii) (c) that the agreement shall be necessary for the attainment of the specialisation in manufacture, may also be difficult to apply in practice.  Whether any provision can be described as " necessary " in any particular agreement may, for example, depend on the position of the parties in the market.  Thus in *Lightweight Paper*,[57] where

[56] J.O. 1972 L182/24, [1972] C.M.L.R. D94; *ante*, § 1019.
[57] See note 56.

the parties had a strong position, the Commission would not
have regarded any restriction other than the restriction on
manufacture as " indispensable " to the achievement of specialisation. In *Clima Chappée* [58] and *Jaz*,[59] on the other hand,
the Commission regarded the obligations relating to reciprocal
exclusive supply and purchase as not only permissible but
indissolubly linked with the specialisation agreements. Under
Article 4 (2) (iii) (*c*), however, the question as to what is " necessary " for attaining the specialisation, arises only where the
market strength of the parties is sufficiently modest to fulfil the
criteria as to market share and turnover set out in that Article.
It is thought that, while some guidance as to the meaning of
" necessary " may be obtained from the restrictions found in the
agreements exempted by the Commission in *Clima Chappée, Jaz*
and *Sopelem*,[60] the only provisions that can with reasonable
safety be regarded as " necessary " are those that the Commission
has felt able to authorise under the new Regulation providing
for block exemption. Thus, Article 4 (2) (iii) (*c*) can probably
be safely acted upon only by undertakings whose agreements
would benefit from the block exemption, but for the fact that
their market shares exceeded 10 per cent. (though by not more than
5 per cent.) and that their turnovers exceeded 150 million units
of account (though by not more than 50 million units of account).

**1046**    **Standardisation and research and development provisions.** It
is thought that specialisation agreements which also have as their
object joint research and development (*e.g. FN-CF*[61] and
*MAN-SAVIEM*[62]) or standardisation of types cannot be
regarded as agreements having specialisation as their *sole* object.
However Articles 4 (2) (iii) (*a*) and 4 (2) (iii) (*b*) of Regulation 17
respectively provide that agreements having as their sole object
" development or uniform application of standards and types "
and " joint research and development " are also exempt from
notification. Can Articles 4 (2) (iii) (*a*) (*b*) and (*c*) be read
together so as to exempt an agreement where it has as its only
objects research, standardisation and development *and* specialisation in the manufacture of products, including the agreements

[58] J.O. 1969 L195/1, [1970] C.M.L.R. D7.
[59] J.O. 1969 L195/5, [1970] C.M.L.R. 129.
[60] J.O. 1972 L13/47, [1972] C.M.L.R. D77.          [61] J.O. 1971 L134/6.
[62] J.O. 1972 L31/29.

necessary for its attainment? While in many cases there may be no good reason to deprive an agreement of the benefit of Article 4 (2) where the sole objects of the agreement are limited to those set out in Article 4 (2) (iii) (*a*) to (*c*), it may also be true that the competitive effects of *e.g.* a specialisation agreement differ as to whether it also contains additional provisions relating to R. & D. or standardisation. Accordingly, if a specialisation agreement otherwise satisfies Article 4 (2) (iii) (*c*) it is doubtful whether it is exempt from notification where it contains further provisions, the sole object of which is research and development and/or standardisation.[63]

**1047**    **Market position and turnover.** The requirements of Article 4 (2) (iii) (*c*) relating to market share and turnover are cumulative. In practice, it may be very difficult to ascertain whether the products which are the object of the specialisation (*i.e.* those in which one or other of the parties has agreed to specialise) represent more than 15 per cent. of the volume of business done in identical products, or those " considered by consumers " to be " similar " by reason of their " characteristics " " price " and " use," in a " substantial part " of the common market. As to the meaning of the phrase " a substantial part of the common market," [64] some guidance may be obtained from the Commission's original draft of the Regulation which amended Regulation 17 to include Article 4 (2) (iii) (*c*).[65] That provided that on the one hand the territory formed by Belgium, Luxembourg and Holland and on the other hand the territory of one of the other Member States (West Germany, Italy or France) constituted a substantial part of the common market. That definition was omitted from the Regulation [66] as finally published, presumably to retain flexibility. In calculating the relevant turnover of the participating undertakings, it may be advisable to take into account the criteria laid down in Article 4 of the new Regulation relating to block exemption of specialisation agreements and in the Commission's Notice of May 27, 1970,[67] although these criteria are not specifically set out in the amendment to Regulation 17.

**[The next paragraph is 1101.]**

[63] *Cf.*, see *Re Schweppes Agreement* (*No. 2*) [1971] 2 All E.R. 1473.
[64] See also *ante*, § 710.        [65] J.O. 1970 C 92/16, [1970] C.M.L.R. D40.
[66] Reg. 2822/71.                                        [67] *Ante*, § 247.

## CHAPTER 11

## RESEARCH AND DEVELOPMENT AGREEMENTS

### 1. INTRODUCTION

**1101**    **Generally.** In this chapter the application of Article 85 is considered in relation to research and development agreements *i.e.* agreements relating to the joint execution of research or the joint development of the results of research up to the stage of industrial application. Such agreements may fall under Article 85 (1) if the parties accept restrictions as to the exploitation of their joint work, or as to the carrying on of individual research, particularly where the parties are actual or potential competitors. On the other hand research and development agreements may encourage technical progress and bring about improvements in production. Thus, if the other conditions of Article 85 (3) are fulfilled, a research and development agreement falling within Article 85 (1) may benefit from exemption.

**1102**    **Approach adopted by the Commission.** The Commission has sought both to define situations in which a research and development agreement can fall outside Article 85 (1) and to determine, by means of individual decisions, the application of Article 85 (3).[1] Moreover, certain agreements having research and development as their sole object, have been exempted from notification.[2] Power has been granted by the Council [3] for the Commission to issue a block exemption, but as yet no draft has been published.

**1103**    **Plan of this chapter.** In this chapter the application of Article 85 (1) to research and development is considered first. Then the application of Article 85 (3) is discussed with particular reference to the decisions in *Henkel-Colgate*,[4] involving two major detergent manufacturers and in *Re the Agreement ACEC-Berliet*,[5]

---

[1] For the application of Art. 85 (3), see generally §§ 601 *et seq., ante.*
[2] Reg. 17 as amended by Reg. 2822/71.
[3] Reg. 2821/71.
[4] J.O. 1972 L14/14; *post*, §§ 1107 *et seq.*
[5] J.O. 1968 L201/7, [1968] C.M.L.R. D35; *post*, §§ 1110 *et seq.*

an agreement involving the joint development of a particular type of bus. Finally, notification is dealt with. The research and development aspects of *Re FN-CF*[6] have already been considered in Chapter 10.[7]

## 2. ARTICLE 85 (1)

**1104**     **Notice of July 28, 1968.** In the Notice concerning Co-operation Agreements of July 28, 1968 [8] the Commission stated [9] that, except in certain defined circumstances, Article 85 (1) did not apply to agreements having as their sole object the joint implementation of research and development projects; or the joint placing of research and development contracts; or the sharing out of research and development projects among the participating enterprises; or the mere exchange of experience and results in the field of research. The circumstances in which the Commission considered that Article 85 (1) might apply were (i) if the parties agreed to refrain from research work of their own in some or all of the fields covered by the agreement, (ii) if the parties accepted restraints as to the exploitation of their joint work, (iii) if the parties did not have access to the results of the joint work at least in proportion to their participation, (iv) if the granting of licences to third parties, was expressly or tacitly excluded.[10] The Commission's Notice was addressed to all undertakings irrespective of size, but it must now be read in the light of the Commission's decision in *Henkel-Colgate*,[11] where Article 85 (1) was held to be applicable to an agreement which had the *effect* of excluding independent research as between competing parties, even though there was no express prohibition against such research in the agreement. It is convenient to illustrate the operation of the principles set out in the Notice by

---

[6] J.O. 1971 L134/6.
[7] *Ante,* §§ 1005 *et seq.*
[8] App. 12, *post;* [1968] C.M.L.R. D5 and see *ante,* § 229.
[9] Para. 3; see App. 12, *post.*
[10] But the Commission considers that arrangements where the granting of licences required the consent of the parties or " majority approval " may be " justified " in joint R & D agreements. It is not clear whether such a provision falls outside Art. 85 (1) or requires exemption under Art. 85 (3). See also joint patents, *ante,* § 950.
[11] J.O. 1972 L14/14; *post,* §§ 1107 *et seq.*

reference to that decision, and to two earlier decisions of the Commission, *Re Eurogypsum* [12] and *Re Research and Development*. [13]

**1105**    **Re Eurogypsum.** [14]    In this decision, which shortly preceded the Notice of July 28, 1968, the Commission found that Article 85 (1) was not applicable to the articles and regulations of the Eurogypsum Association.    The sole aim of the association was found to be the organisation, carrying out and exploitation of research for the benefit of the plaster and gypsum industry.    The association did not place any restriction on the carrying out of independent research by individua. parties.    Nothing in the constitution of the association discriminated between the members, who were established in different Member States.    Each member of the association had equal access to the association's work.    *A fortiori* the decision in *Eurogypsum* should be applicable where the undertakings concerned are situated in the same Member State. [15]

**1106**    **Re Research and Development.** [16]    In this decision, which concerned two unnamed parties, the Commission found Article 85 (1) applicable to an agreement because the parties did not have equal access to the results of the joint research and development. [17]    The parties had agreed that each, in his primary marketing territory, should have access to the results of their joint research royalty free whereas the other party would be required to pay a royalty not exceeding 2 per cent.    This preference, given to each party in its own marketing territory, was likely to lead to market sharing.    Although a small preference, it was sufficient to bring the agreement within Article 85 (1) in circumstances where the parties occupied positions of importance in a situation of oligopoly.    In *Henkel-Colgate* [18] the Commission stated that an

---

[12] J.O. 1968 L57/9, [1968] C.M.L.R. D1.
[13] [1971] C.M.L.R. D31.
[14] Note 12, *supra.*
[15] If a national association discriminates against nationals of other Member States, Art. 86 may be infringed.    See § 723, *ante.*
[16] Note 13, *supra.*
[17] Although the terms of the agreement and the descriptions of the parties as set out in the decision bear striking resemblances to the *Henkel-Colgate* agreement; *post*, §§ 1107 *et seq.*
[18] J.O. 1972 L14/14.

identical preference was found in that agreement when first notified. The parties were required to delete it before the Commission gave a favourable decision under Article 85 (3).

**1107**    **Henkel-Colgate** [18]**: the facts.** Henkel and Colgate manufacture detergents in competition with each other. In 1971, Henkel, Colgate, Unilever and Proctor and Gamble, held in the aggregate 80 per cent. of the detergents market within the Community. Figures published independently [19] of the Commission's decision indicate that Henkel controlled 27 per cent. of the detergent market within the EEC while Colgate held 10 per cent. However in Belgium and Luxembourg Henkel held 75 per cent. of the market while in France Colgate held 65 per cent. Under the agreement between the parties, Henkel and Colgate proposed to set up a joint subsidiary in order to carry out research relating to detergents. The sole aim of the agreement was to carry out research and development. Each party had equal access to the results on payment of royalties. The agreement did not prevent either party from carrying out independent research and development in the field assigned to the joint company, but it did provide that each party would make available the results of any such independent work to the joint company and therefore to the other party. Although not a restriction on carrying out individual research, this provision seriously diminished the competitive advantage which one party might obtain over the other by carrying out such research. In the Commission's view, another important feature of the situation was that, as a result of the agreement, both parties were in fact extremely unlikely in the future to carry out any independent research in the field assigned to the joint company. Prior to the agreement, the parties had already carried out a considerable amount of such research, without success, and the failure of that research was the reason for setting up the joint company. The Commission found that although the agreement did not expressly prevent the parties from carrying out independent research, the setting up of the joint company nonetheless had this effect.

**108**    **Henkel-Colgate: Article 85 (1).** In the oligopolistic market for detergents, independent research and development is

[19] *Business Europe*, October 29, 1972, p. 347.

extremely important. Because independent research and development was, in fact, excluded and because of the importance of research and development to these two substantial companies, the Commission considered that Article 85 (1) was applicable. Thus an agreement falling within the terms of the Notice on Co-operation Agreements [20] was found to fall under Article 85 (1) where it had the effect of excluding independent research; and in this respect the Notice is demonstrated to be only a general guide and not a comprehensive and definitive statement of the position of research and development agreements. In *Henkel-Colgate* the Commission made it clear that the fact that the parties had a very substantial market share was vital to the Commission's conclusion that Article 85 (1) was applicable. But even where the parties to an agreement are relatively small a situation could arise where a joint research agreement has the effect, even without the object, of excluding independent research. In such circumstances the application of Article 85 (1) would require careful consideration.

### 3. ARTICLE 85 (3)

**1109**     **Henkel-Colgate: Article 85 (3).**[21] Since the agreement had as its object the carrying out of research and development it was clearly of a type likely to bring about technical progress. Further, the Commission considered that competition would ensure that consumers received a fair share of the benefits. The Commission also held that the agreement did not contain any unnecessary restrictions. In particular, it should be noted (i) that the area for research was limited and clearly defined; therefore the research activities of the parties in other areas would not be affected by the agreement; (ii) that the obligation to pay royalties to the joint company for use of the results did not exceed, in each country and in respect of each licence, the period of the patent; (iii) that each party was to have equal access to the results of the research and development; and (iv) that the provision enabling each party to make royalty free sales in his prime marketing area had been deleted. Finally, although the parties held very substantial shares of the market, the Commission was able to find that the agreement

---

[20] *Ante,* § 1104; App. 12, *post.*
[21] For the application of Art. 85 (3) generally see *ante,* §§ 601 *et seq.*

did not give the parties the possibility of eliminating competition for a substantial part of the products concerned. The Commission held that although the parties held substantial market shares, they were not together occupying "a dominant position," for the products concerned, in any market in the Community. Nonetheless, the *Henkel-Colgate* decision is very significant of the extent to which the Commission is willing to go in authorising this type of agreement, even where the parties are in a very strong position. The strong position of the parties explains the conditions which the Commission attached to its decision. As already explained, the agreement was required to be amended; in order to prevent the danger of market sharing, the Commission required that it be notified of all licences granted by the joint subsidiary; lastly the parties were obliged to render detailed reports as to the operation of the agreement and to report any interchanges of executive staff or " interlocking directorships."

**1110    ACEC-Berliet [22]: the facts.** The agreement between ACEC and Berliet related primarily to development. ACEC had invented a type of electrical transmission for use in commercial vehicles, of which Berliet was a prominent manufacturer. Under the agreement ACEC agreed to study the adaptation of that transmission to vehicles manufactured by Berliet. Berliet agreed in return to study the possibility of developing and producing a bus using the ACEC transmission. The agreements contained restrictions as to competition in that (i) ACEC agreed to supply its transmission only to Berliet in France and, further, only to one manufacturer in each Member State and to a limited number of manufacturers in third countries and (ii) Berliet agreed to buy electric transmissions only from ACEC. Accordingly, the Commission held that the agreement fell within Article 85 (1). ACEC and Berliet did not compete in the same manufacturing field and were not likely to do so. Thus the agreement was not of the type described by the Commission as a specialisation agreement.[23] There was " specialisation " but this existed quite independently of the agreement.

[22] J.O. 1968 L201/7, [1968] C.M.L.R. D35.
[23] For specialisation agreements see *ante*, §§ 1001 *et seq.*

**1111**     **Application of Article 85 (3).**[24]   The Commission found that
the agreement promoted technical progress and was likely to lead
to improvements in production such as more effective development work, and the emergence of a new and improved product.
Consumers were to be expected to be allowed a fair share of the
benefit, assuming that the agreement led to production, since the
new vehicles were expected to be subject to strong competition
from buses equipped with conventional transmissions.   Even if
the buses with electric transmissions turned out to be much better
than other buses, protection for consumers was provided by the
fact that ACEC would still be able to sell its transmissions to a
limited number of other manufacturers both in the common
market and outside.   Nor did the agreement place any restriction
on competition between those manufacturers using the ACEC
system.   Under the agreement as originally drafted ACEC undertook to deliver its transmissions only to Berliet, to certain Belgian
users and to two other manufacturers in France and Italy.
Before granting exemption under Article 85 (3), the Commission
required that this restriction be varied to permit ACEC to deliver
its transmissions to one manufacturer in each Member State
and also to a few manufacturers in third countries.   The Commission therefore required an increase in the number of bus
manufacturers to whom ACEC should be free to sell its transmissions as a condition of finding the requirements of Article
85 (3) satisfied.

**1112**     **Indispensable nature of the restrictions.**   The restrictions on the
persons to whom ACEC might sell electric transmissions and
from whom Berliet might acquire electric transmissions were of
importance to the Commission in deciding whether the agreement
imposed on the undertakings in question restrictions which were
indispensable to the obtaining of the objectives of improvement
of production and promotion of technical progress.   The Commission found that the restriction whereby ACEC undertook to
deliver in France its transmission only to Berliet and to co-operate
in joint development only with the latter, as well as the restriction
whereby Berliet undertook to purchase electric transmissions only
from ACEC gave each party the necessary protection to enable
them to bear the burden of the development of the new product

[24] For the application of Art. 85 (3) generally see *ante*, §§ 601 *et seq.*

with the high costs involved. However the limitation on ACEC as to the persons to whom it sold the transmissions outside France were found to be indispensable for different reasons. The aim of that restriction was to concentrate production of buses with electric transmissions in the hands of a limited number of manufacturers. The Commission felt that if, during the initial launching period, production had been dispersed among a large number of manufacturers, none of them would have succeeded in producing a run of a size sufficient for profitability, and the whole economic success of the new product might be compromised. Hence the justification of this restriction had nothing to do with whether it was indispensable to bringing about the co-ordination between ACEC and Berliet. The Commission wished to ensure that once Berliet began manufacture and sale of buses equipped with ACEC transmission, the agreement between ACEC and Berliet would not rule out the possibility of competition between Berliet and other manufacturers using ACEC transmission.

### 4. Notification and Block Exemption

**113**    **Article 4 (2) of Regulation 17.**[25]   Under Article 4 (2) (iii) (*b*) of Regulation 17, as amended, an agreement does not require to be notified if it has as its " sole object joint research and development." Until amended by Regulation 2821/71 this provision applied to an agreement which had as its " sole object joint research for improvement of techniques, provided the results are accessible to all parties thereto and may be used by each of them."

**114**    **Sole object.**   In determining whether an agreement may benefit from Article 4 (2), as amended, the only consideration is whether the agreement has research and development as its *sole* object. Thus the agreement must be carefully scrutinised lest it should contain provisions which could be said to have other objects *e.g.* market sharing. Strictly it is necessary to consider only the object of the agreement rather than its effects. Even if the objects of the agreement also relate to standardisation of types, or to specialisation in manufacture, which fall within

---

[25] See, generally §§ 413–414, 528 *et seq., ante.*

Article 4 (2) (iii) (*a*) and 4 (2) (iii) (*c*) respectively, and it has no other objects, it is doubtful whether the agreement is exempt from notification.[26]

**1115**    It may be doubted whether there is significance in the recent amendment to Regulation 17 which deleted the proviso that research and development agreements were exempt from notification only provided that the results were accessible to all parties. If in any given case the results are not equally available to each party, then it would be necessary to consider carefully the agreement to see whether it had objects other than research and development *e.g.* a division of markets.  Perhaps the Commission, in amending Regulation 17, had in mind those agreements where the access of the parties to the results is proportionate to their contribution to the work done.

**1116**    **Block exemption.**  The Council has issued a Regulation [27] permitting the Commission to issue a block exemption for agreements which have as their object: " the research and development of products or processes up to the stage of industrial application, as well as making use of the results, including provisions regarding industrial property rights and confidential technical knowledge."  The Commission has not yet taken any steps to exercise its powers to issue such a block exemption.

[The next paragraph is 1201.]

---

[26] See *ante,* § 533; see also *ante,* § 1046.
[27] Reg. 2821/71.

CHAPTER 12

## ENFORCEMENT

### 1. THE COMMISSION'S POWERS TO TERMINATE INFRINGEMENTS AND IMPOSE FINES

**201    Generally.** This section is concerned with the powers of the Commission under Regulation 17 to terminate infringements of the Treaty and to impose fines. Under Article 3 of that Regulation the Commission may by decision require an undertaking or an association of undertakings to bring an infringement of Article 85 (1) or Article 86 of the Treaty to an end. Under Article 16 of that Regulation the Commission may enforce its requirements by imposing upon undertakings daily default fines (called periodic penalty payments). Under Article 15 of Regulation 17 the Commission may also impose heavy fines in respect of infringements of Articles 85 and 86. Ancillary to these powers, the Commission has wide powers to make investigations and require information which are discussed in the next section of this chapter.[1]

**202    Power to terminate infringements.** The Commission may, by a decision, require an undertaking or association of undertakings to terminate an infringement.[2] In accordance with the Treaty [3] a decision is binding in its entirety upon those to whom it is addressed. A decision requiring the termination of an infringement brings to an end the provisional validity of a duly notified agreement.[4] In most cases, moreover, the Commission will order the parties to terminate an infringement forthwith. Thus in *Re Gema* [5] the Commission directed the undertaking

---

[1] *Post*, §§ 1213 *et seq.*
[2] Art. 3 of Reg. 17.
[3] Art. 189.
[4] See *Re Van Katwijk*, J.O. 1970 L242/18, [1972] C.M.L.R. D43; *ante*, § 326. *Re German Ceramic Tiles*, J.O. 1971 L10/15, [1972] C.M.L.R. D6; *ante*, § 308. See also *Re Grundig-Consten*, J.O. 1964 2545/64; *ante*, §§ 811 *et seq.* See also *ante*, § 410. Under Art. 9 (2) of Reg. 17 the Commission has power to apply Art. 85 (1) notwithstanding that the time for notification has not yet expired.
[5] J.O. 1971 L134/15, [1971] C.M.L.R. D35.

concerned to amend various provisions of its constitution and regulations within six months, but first it also ordered that the relevant infringements be terminated forthwith  In *Re Continental Can Co.*[6] the Commission required the company to put an end to its violation of Article 86, and to that end required that the company present its proposals to the Commission within six months of the decision.  Decisions of the Commission ordering the termination of an infringement must be published.[7]  Such publication must include the main contents of the decision and the names of the parties, but must have regard to the legitimate business interests of the undertakings concerned.[8]

**1203**  **Recommendations to terminate infringements.** Instead of issuing a decision requiring the termination of an infringement the Commission is permitted, at its own discretion, to issue a recommendation to that effect.[9]  Unlike a decision, a recommendation does not require to be published and is of no binding force.[10]  If the parties comply with a recommendation then the Commission has no need to take or publish a formal decision.

**1204**  **Periodic penalty payments.** The Commission may by decision impose on undertakings default fines, called periodic penalty payments [11] in order to enforce a requirement that they put an end to an infringement of Article 85 or Article 86 of the Treaty.  The default fine may be from 50 to 1,000 units of account [12] per day, calculated from the date appointed by the decision.  A decision to impose such penalties can only be taken following a decision under Article 3 of Regulation 17 requiring the termination of an infringement.[13]  A mere recommendation under Article 3 (3) will not suffice.  It is submitted that a decision to impose a default fine cannot take effect any earlier than the date of that decision itself.  The Commission also has power to impose default fines

---

[6] J.O. 1972 L7/25, [1972] C.M.L.R. D11.  But see *Europemballage and Continental Can Co. Inc.* v. *EC Commission* (6/72), *The Times*, February 26, 1973.
[7] Art. 21 (1) of Reg. 17.
[8] Art. 21 (2) of Reg. 17.
[9] Art. 3 (3) of Reg. 17.
[10] See Arts. 189 and 191 of the Treaty.
[11] Art. 16 of Reg. 17.  See *CSC–ZOJA*, J.O. 1972 L299/51.
[12] The unit of account is fixed in terms of gold (see Art. 18 of Reg. 17).  Prior to the devaluation of the U.S. dollar in 1972, one unit of account was equal to one U.S. dollar.
[13] Art. 16 (1) (a) of Reg. 17.

to compel the parties to comply with directions of the Commission under Article 8 (3) of Regulation 17,[14] which relates to the revocation or amendment of a decision granting exemption under Article 85 (3) of the Treaty.[15] If the parties subsequently comply with the Commission's requirements, the Commission may reduce the amount of the penalties.[16]

**1205** **Fines in respect of infringements.** The Commission is empowered to impose fines where undertakings intentionally or neligently infringe Article 85 (1) or Article 86 of the Treaty.[17] There are at present no decisions as to the meaning of the phrase " intentionally or negligently." In addition to imposing fines for breaches of Article 85 (1) and Article 86 the Commission may impose fines for the wilful or negligent commission of a breach of any obligation imposed as a condition of obtaining exemption under Article 85 (3).[18] Decisions imposing fines are expressed not to be of a criminal law nature.[19] There is no power to fine individual directors or employees of undertakings.

**1206** **Amount of fines for infringements.** The Commission has power to impose fines ranging from 1,000 to one million units of account,[20] but the Commission may impose greater fines not exceeding 10 per cent. of the total turnover in the preceding business year of each of the undertakings participating in the infringement. In fixing the amount of the fine, regard is to be had both to the gravity and to the duration of the infringement.[21] Where more than one party is to be fined, the Commission's practice has been to have regard to the gravity of the infringement, and then to determine the individual liability of the parties in the light of the market share, the individual conduct and the importance of the role within the agreement or practice of each offender.[22]

[14] Art. 16 (1) (*b*) of Reg. 17.
[15] See *ante*, §§ 633 *et seq.*
[16] Art. 16 (2) of Reg. 17.
[17] Art. 15 (2) (*a*) of Reg. 17. For the Commission's powers to impose fines for providing incorrect information etc. see *post*, § 1219.
[18] Art. 15 (2) (*b*) of Reg. 17. See also Art. 8 (1) of Reg. 17 and §§ 601 *et seq., ante.*
[19] Art. 15 (4) of Reg. 17.
[20] Art. 15 (2) of Reg. 17. For units of account see note 12, *ante.*
[21] Art. 15 (2) of Reg. 17.
[22] *Boehringer Mannheim* v. *EC Commission* (45/69) 16 Rec. 769; CCH CMR, § 8085, noted at 8 C.M.L.Rev. 1971, 86. See also *Re Sugar Cartel* (Commission decision), January 2, 1973.

For some years no fines were imposed. In 1969 and thereafter fines were imposed in the *Dyestuffs* [23] decision (40,000 to 50,000 u.a.); the *Quinine* [24] decision (65,000 to 210,000 u.a.); the *Pittsburg Corning* decision (100,000 u.a.); the *CSC-ZOJA* decision (200,000 u.a.); the *Sugar Cartel* decision (100,000 to 1,500,000 u.a.); and in *WEA-Filipacchi* (60,000 u.a.). [25]

**1207** **Double jeopardy.** It may happen that conduct constituting an infringement of Article 85 (1) or Article 86 is also an infringement of the competition law of a Member State. [26] Where fines are imposed under the law of a Member State in respect of conduct which is also an infringement of Treaty provisions, the Commission, in imposing fines, is obliged to take account of fines already imposed in a Member State. [27] The position may be different where fines are imposed under the law of a non-Member State. In the *Quinine* case the Commission refused to take account of a fine imposed in the United States upon one member of the cartel. [28] The point is not however finally decided since in that case the Commission also found that the conduct for which the fines had been imposed in the United States was not the same conduct as led to the fine under Community law.

**1208** **Notified agreements.** The power of the Commission to impose fines for infringements is suspended by notification of an agreement. Provided that the parties do not go beyond the agreement that has been notified, fines may not be imposed for the operation of that agreement during the period before the Commission takes a decision. [29] When the Commission issues a formal decision

---

[23] J.O. 1969 L195/11, [1969] C.M.L.R. D23. One fine of 40,000 u.a. was reduced to 30,000 u.a. on appeal. See cases (48/69, 49/69, 51–56/59) [1972] C.M.L.R. 557; for the facts see *ante*, §§ 210 *et seq.*

[24] J.O. 1969 L192/5, [1969] C.M.L.R. D41; certain fines were reduced on appeal by 10,000 u.a. See cases (41/69) (44/69) (45/69) 16 Rec. 661 *et seq.*; CCH, CMR §§ 8083 *et seq.* noted at 8 C.M.L.Rev. 1971, 86; for the facts see *ante*, § 305.

[25] *Re Pittsburgh Corning Europe*, J.O. 1972 L272/35, [1973] C.M.L.R. D2; *Re CSC–ZOJA*, J.O. 1972 L299/51; *Re Sugar Cartel*, decision of January 2, 1973; *Re WEA–Fillipacchi*, J.O. 1972 L303/52.

[26] For the relationship between Community and national competition law see *ante*, § 142.

[27] *Walt Wilhelm* v. *Bundeskartellamt* (14/68) 15 Rec. 1; [1969] C.M.L.R. 100, 120–121.

[28] *Re Boehringer Mannheim G.m.b.H.*, J.O. 1971 L282/46 [1972] C.M.L.R. D121, confirmed on appeal (Case 7/72), December 14, 1972.

[29] Art. 15 (5) of Reg. 17; and see *Re Pittsburgh Corning Europe*, note 25, *supra*.

refusing to apply Article 85 (3), such decision brings to an end the period in which the parties are protected against fines and the period in which the agreement has provisional validity.[30] Article 15 (6) of Regulation 17 provides that the Commission may inform the parties that after a preliminary examination it feels that the application of Article 85 (3) is not justified. As explained above, this procedure is rarely used.[31]

09      **Pre-Accession agreements.**   Agreements which were in existence on January 1, 1973 and which fall under the prohibition of Article 85 (1) solely by reason of the enlargement of the Communities, (Accession agreements) are exempt from fines in respect of acts done during the period between January 1, 1973 and June 30, 1973, provided such agreements are notified before that date.[32]   United Kingdom undertakings may, however, be party to unnotified agreements made before January 1, 1973 which in the Commission's view fell under Article 85 (1) even before the enlargement of the Communities.  Such would be the case where the agreement affected trade between Member States and restricted competition within the common market, notwithstanding that the parties were situated outside the Community *e.g.* a market sharing agreement between two United Kingdom parties providing for a division of markets within the Six.[33]   In respect of such agreements, it cannot be assumed that the Commission will not attempt to impose fines in respect of infringements committed prior to Accession.[34]   Notification prior to July 1, 1973 would not affect the Commission's powers to impose such fines, but whether the Commission possesses any such power remains an open question.  In the *ICI* case [35] the Court of Justice said [36] that the Commission's jurisdiction to impose fines was based not merely on the effects of actions committed inside the Community, but also upon activities *directly* carried on by the undertaking itself within the common market area (*e.g.* by a subsidiary).

[30] See also § 1202, *ante* and §§ 410, 504–505, *ante*.     [31] *Ante*, § 513.
[32] See *ante*, § 207, and §§ 517 *et seq.*     [33] See *ante*, §§ 240–241.
[34] But see *The Financial Times*, October 6, 1972, report of a conference on EEC and the Law held at the Royal Institute of International Affairs; and see *The Financial Times*, February 1, 1973.
[35] *ICI and others* v. *EC Commission* (48, 49/69) (51–57/69) [1972] C.M.L.R. 557.
[36] [1972] C.M.L.R. 557, 628–630, 640.  See also the submissions of the Advocate General, *ibid.* at pp. 640 *et seq.*  And as to extra territorial jurisdiction in restrictive practices legislation, see *ante*, §§ 240 *et seq.* and notes thereto.

**1210**    **Successors in title.** It may occur that by the time the
Commission seeks to impose fines for past conduct, an undertaking against which an infringement is alleged, has disposed of
all or part of its assets to another company. A passage in the
*Quinine* decision [37] may suggest that the company acquiring the
assets might be held responsible for the infringement committed
by its predecessor in title. In that decision the Commission found
that the infringements committed by a French undertaking were
almost exclusively committed at the time when the company was
a *société à responsibilité limitée.* It had been transformed
subsequently into a *societé anonyme* and had merged with
another company.[38] The Commission considered that a fine
might be imposed on the successor undertaking because it carried
on the same business as the previous s.à.r.l. and because it
received the assets held by the latter for the production and sale of
quinine. It is clear therefore that the mere transformation of a
company for example from a limited to an unlimited company or
from a private to a public company would not remove the liability
of the company for previous infringements. The position is not
so clear where the business and assets of the company have been
transferred to another company altogether. It is very doubtful
whether the acquiring company could be held liable for infringements committed by its predecessor in title.

**1211**    **Limitation period.** In the appeals to the European Court of
Justice from the *Quinine* decisions, the Court held that there is
no period of limitation with regard to an action by the Commission
against violation of the rules of competition.[39] There is, however,
a draft Council regulation [40] laying down a period of five years
after which the power of the Commission to impose fines for
infringement of Article 85 (1) or Article 86 is excluded.[41] Under
the draft the limitation period runs from the day on which the
infringement is brought to an end.[42] The running of time for

[37] *Re Quinine Cartel,* J.O. 1969 L192/5, [1969] C.M.L.R. D41, D74.
[38] Very broadly, the difference between an s.à.r.l. and an S.A. is equivalent to that
between a private and a public limited company.
[39] *e.g. Boehringer Mannheim G.m.b.H.* v. *Commission* (45/69) 16 Rec. 769, 798;
CMR § 8085 noted at 8 C.M.L.Rev. 1971, 86.
[40] App. 9, *post.*
[41] Art. 1 (1).
[42] Art. 1 (2).

limitation purposes is interrupted by any measure taken by the Commission, or by a Member State at the request of the Commission which is ·aimed at proving the infringement.[43] The running of time is also interrupted by, *inter alia*, the dispatch of a request for information by the Commission and the communication in writing of the commencement of proceedings by the Commission.[44] Under the draft, a measure taken against one party prevents the running of time not only as regards that party but also as regards all the undertakings participating in the infringement concerned.[45]

**12** **Enforcement of penalties.** Under Article 192 of the Treaty, decisions of the Commission which impose a pecuniary obligation on individuals and companies are enforceable. Enforcement is governed by the rules of civil procedure in force in the Member State where enforcement is carried out. In the United Kingdom the Commission may cause a decision under Article 192 of the Treaty to be registered with the High Court or Court of Session in Scotland whereupon it is to have the same force and effects as if it were a judgment or order given or made by that Court on the date of registration.[46] No such decision may be registered unless an order for enforcement has been appended by the Secretary of State. Under Article 192 of the Treaty such order is to be appended by the Secretary without any formality other than verification of the authenticity of the decision. Provision is made in the draft Council Regulation concerning periods of limitation for enforcement to become time-barred after a period of three years from the date of the decision.[47]

## 2. INVESTIGATION BY THE COMMISSION

**13** **Generally.** Much of the Commission's information with regard to competition matters comes from notifications and applications for negative clearance.[48] In addition, there are

---

[43] Art. 2 (1).
[44] *Ibid.*
[45] Art. 2 (2).
[46] The European Communities (Enforcement of Community Judgements) Order, 1972 S.I. 1590.
[47] [1972] C.M.L.R. D40. This may be changed to five years.
[48] *Ante,* §§ 501 *et seq.* Under Art. 15 (1) of Reg. 17 fines may be imposed for the provision of incorrect or misleading information supplied in applications for negative clearance and notifications.

several means by which the Commission may investigate possible infringements of the Treaty provisions. First, third parties may make complaints to the Commission, and the Commission must examine the circumstances which give rise to those complaints.[49] Secondly, the Commission may conduct general enquiries of its own into particular sectors of the Community economy.[50] Further, in order to carry out its functions, the Commission has wide powers to require information from Member States and from individual undertakings, including the power to investigate the books of an undertaking.[51] All these matters are discussed in this section. Throughout this investigation procedure the Commission collaborates closely with the authorities of Member States, with whom information is exchanged at various stages in the proceedings.[52] In addition the Commission keeps itself informed through press reports and other information coming to its attention.

**1214** **Complaints.** As has been seen,[53] Article 3 (1) of Regulation 17 provides that the Commission may by decision require undertakings to terminate an infringement where the Commission, upon application or upon its own initiative finds that an infringement exists. Article 3 (2) provides that those entitled to make application are (a) Member States; and (b) natural or legal persons who claim a legitimate interest. Any complaint and the supporting documents must be submitted to the Commission in seven copies.[54] Supporting documents should be either originals or duly certified copies.[55] The complaint must be in one of the Community languages, translations of any official documents not in an official language being supplied.[56] No particular form is required although the Commission has, as a matter of convenience, made available Form C for these purposes.[57] The Commission, having received a complaint, is to inform the complainant if it considers that on the basis of the information in

[49] *Post*, § 1214.
[50] *Post*, § 1215.
[51] *Post*, §§ 1216–1219.
[52] See Reg. 17, Arts. 10 (1), 10 (2), 11 (2) and 11 (6); also Art. 8 (2) of Reg. 99/63.
[53] *Ante*, § 1202.
[54] Art. 2 (1) of Reg. 27. A complaint led to the decision in *Re CSC–ZOJA*, J.O. 1972 L299/51.
[55] Art. 2 (2) of Reg. 27.
[56] Art. 2 (3) of Reg. 27.
[57] Available from the addresses set out at § 536, *ante*.

its possession there are insufficient grounds for issuing a decision requiring the termination of the alleged infringement.[58]   When informing the complainant the Commission is to give its reasons and to fix a time limit for the complainant to submit any further comments in writing.[59]   Where the Commission has failed to take any action on the basis of a complaint and has not fulfilled its obligation to notify the complainant, the complainant may have a right to take proceedings before the European Court in order to require the Commission to act.[60]

**1215**  **Inquiries into sectors of the economy.**   The Commission has power to conduct a general inquiry into any economic sector in which it has cause to believe that competition is being restricted or distorted within the common market.[61]   In the course of such inquiry, undertakings in the sector concerned may be required to supply information required by the Commission in its tasks.[62] The procedure by which undertakings may be compelled to provide information is governed by Article 11 of Regulation 17.[63]   Failure to supply such information may result in a fine.[64]   The Commission may, in particular, require undertakings or associations of undertakings in the relevant sector to communicate to it all agreements, decisions and concerted practices which are exempt from notification by virtue of Article 4 (2) and Article 5 (2).[65] When making inquiries into sectors of the economy the Commission may also request undertakings or groups of undertakings whose size suggests that they occupy a dominant position within the common market or a substantial part of it to supply particulars of their structure and of their behaviour in the market.[66]   Such information permits the Commission to consider the possible application of Article 86.   Under the power to carry out inquiries into economic sectors the Commission has carried out a three

---

[58] Art. 6 of Commission Reg. 99/63.
[59] *Ibid.*
[60] See *post*, § 1230.
[61] Art. 12 of Reg. 17.
[62] Art. 12 (1) of Reg. 17.
[63] See § 1217 *post*, and in particular the decisions set out in note 81 thereto.  As to the secrecy of the information supplied see § 1226, *post*.
[64] *Post*, § 1219.
[65] Art. 12 (2) of Reg. 17.  For Art. 4 (2) and Art. 5 (2) agreements see *ante*, §§ 528 *et seq.*
[66] Art. 12 (3) of Reg. 17.

year enquiry into the margarine industry. During that inquiry an undertaking which was in a dominant position abandoned its " loyalty rebates " practice.[67] An inquiry into the tied-house system in the brewery industry [68] is currently in progress.

**1216** **Power to require information from Member States.** Article 11 (1) of Regulation 17 provides that, in carrying out its duties, the Commission may obtain all necessary information from the governments and competent authorities of the Member States.[69] However, the authorities [70] should supply information only where the Commission has requested specific information in a particular case; a general fishing expedition should not be allowed.[71] Subject to that, Article 11 (1) empowers the Commission to call upon the Registrar of Restrictive Trading Agreements to furnish information from the Register of Restrictive Trading Agreements (including information in the special section) [72] and also to supply information obtained under sections 14 and 15 of the Restrictive Trade Practices Act 1956.[73] Further, the Commission will have access to particulars furnished to the Department of Trade and Industry in respect of export agreements under section 31 (1) of that Act.[74] Under section 10 (3) of the European Communities Act 1972 information which has been obtained under or by virtue of the Restrictive Trade Practices Acts may be disclosed where such disclosure is made in pursuance of a Community obligation.[75] Section 10 (3) of the European Communities Act 1972 is to be replaced by clause 116 of the Fair Trading Bill. Clause 116 (1) restricts, subject to penalties, the disclosure of information with respect to any particular business obtained

[67] First Report on Competition (1972), para. 124.
[68] *Ibid.*; and for decisions requiring information in the course of that inquiry see *post*, § 1217, n. 81.
[69] For power to request information from undertakings see § 1217, *post*.
[70] In the U.K. presumably the Registrar of Restrictive Trading Agreements (see clause 89 of the Fair Trading Bill ("the Bill"); the DTI; and the Monopolies Commission.
[71] Up to March 1, 1973 no legislation had designated any "competent authorities." *Cf.* Denmark [1972] C.M.L.R. D129.
[72] The Register is maintained under s. 11 of the Restrictive Trade Practices Act 1956. The special section is not open to the public in accordance with s. 11 (3).
[73] Power to obtain information (s. 14); power of High Court to examine on oath (s. 15).
[74] But see now clause 94 of the Bill.
[75] Restrictive Trade Practices Act 1956, s. 33 (1) as amended by s. 10 (3) of the European Communities Act. For " community obligations " see Sched. I, Pt. II of the latter Act.

under the Restrictive Trade Practices Acts of 1956 and 1968, or under the Fair Trading Bill. Clause 116 (2) (*b*) provides that clause 116 (1) does not apply to a disclosure made in pursuance of a Community obligation within the meaning of the European Communities Act 1972. Under this clause the Director General of Fair Competition and the Monopolies and Mergers Commission will have power to supply information lawfully requested by the Commission. The secrecy of such information is protected under Article 20 of Regulation 17.[76]

**217**     **Power to request information from undertakings.** The Commission also has wide powers to compel undertakings and associations of undertakings directly to provide information, upon penalty of a fine.[77] When requesting information from an undertaking or association of undertakings, the Commission must send a copy of the request to the competent authority of the relevant Member State.[78] The Commission must state the legal basis upon which the request is made, and indicate the penalties for supplying incorrect information.[79] The appropriate representatives of the undertaking concerned are under an obligation to furnish the information requested.[80] If the information is not supplied within the time limit fixed by the Commission, then the Commission may by decision require the information to be supplied.[81] If the undertaking further defaults in the supply of information, then the Commission may impose penalties.[82]

**218**     **Power of investigation.** Article 14 empowers the Commission, in carrying out its duties, to undertake all necessary investigations into undertakings and associations of undertakings. Article 14 (1) specifies that the power extends to the examination of

[76] *Post*, § 1226. Such protection is not always effective.
[77] Art. 11 (1) of Reg. 17; for penalties see § 1219, *post*.
[78] Art. 11 (2) of Reg. 17.
[79] Art. 11 (3) of Reg. 17.
[80] Art. 11 (4) of Reg. 17.
[81] Art. 11 (5) of Reg. 17. For examples of such decisions see *Re Brasserie Esperance*, J.O. 1971 L161/2; *Re Union des Brasseries*, J.O. 1971 L161/6; *Re Brasserie Maes*, J.O. 1971 L161/10 (requests for information in the course of a sector inquiry, § 1215, *ante*); *Re CICG-ZVEI-ZPU*, J.O. 1971 L34/13 (request for information following a complaint); *Re S.I.A.E.*, J.O. 1971 L254/15, [1972] C.M.L.R. D112 (request for information in the course of an investigation under Art. 86). The inevitable delay before such decisions are taken lessens the Commission's effectiveness.
[82] *Post*, § 1219.

books and other business records, the taking of copies of or extracts from the books and business records, a request for oral explanations " on the spot " and entrance on to premises, land or vehicles.  The officials of the Commission carrying out the investigation are required to produce to the undertaking concerned the necessary authorisation in the form specified.[83]  Such officials may be assisted by officials of the competent authorities of the Member State concerned.[84]  If an undertaking refuses to submit voluntarily to such an investigation, then the Commission may take a decision requiring the undertaking to submit to such an investigation.[85]  Before taking a decision to make such an investigation, the Commission is to consult with the competent authority of the Member State in whose territory the investigation is to be made.[86]  Failure to comply with such a decision renders the undertaking concerned liable to penalties.[87]  Further, where an undertaking refuses to submit to an investigation, Member States are required to afford the Commission the necessary assistance in procuring the carrying out of their duties.[88]  For this purpose the United Kingdom is required to introduce legislation within six months of accession.[89]  Under Article 13 of Regulation 17 the Commission may call upon the competent authorities of a Member State to undertake the investigations which the Commission might otherwise undertake under Article 14.  The secrecy of information obtained under Articles 13 and 14 of Regulation 17 is protected under Article 20 thereof.[90]

**1219**    **Penalties.**  Article 15 (1) of Regulation 17 provides for fines of from 100 to 5,000 units of account [91] where undertakings or associations of undertakings intentionally or negligently supply incorrect or incomplete information in response to a request lawfully made by the Commission or where during an investigation they produce books or other business records in incomplete

---

[83] Art. 14 (2) of Reg. 17.
[84] Art. 14 (5) of Reg. 17.  No competent authorities had been appointed in the U.K. up to March 1, 1973; *cf* Denmark [1972] C.M.L.R. 129.
[85] Art. 14 (3) of Reg. 17.                [86] Art. 14 (4) of Reg. 17.
[87] *Post*, § 1219.                        [88] Art. 14 (6) of Reg. 17.
[89] Art. 25 (4) of Reg. 17.  Not all of the original Six complied with their obligations within the time limit provided.  See Second General Report of the activities of the Communities (1968), para. 32.  It is thought that all of the Six have now complied or are in the process of doing so.  And see note 84, *supra*.
[90] *Post*, § 1226.
[91] One unit of account equals slightly more than US $1.  See *ante*, note 12.

form. One such fine, amounting to 4,000 units of account, has so far been imposed.[92] Fines may similarly be imposed where an undertaking refuses to supply information.[93] Such fines may not, however, be imposed unless the Commission having once asked for and failed to receive information has subsequently taken a formal decision requiring information to be supplied.[94] Fines may only be imposed where that decision is disobeyed.[95] Fines of a similar amount may be imposed for refusal to submit to an investigation ordered by formal decision of the Commission under Article 14 (3) of Regulation 17.[96] Under Article 16 of Regulation 17 the Commission may by decision impose daily default fines in respect of each day that an undertaking fails to supply complete and correct information or to submit to an investigation.[97] Such fines may be of an amount of from 50 to 1,000 units of account per day.[98]

**1220**    **Authorities in Member States.** Although Article 9 (3) of Regulation 17 provides that the competent authorities[99] in the Member States may in certain very limited circumstances " apply Article 85 (1) and Article 86 " in accordance with Article 88 of the Treaty,[1] there are no competent authorities within the United Kingdom who have any independent power (whether under the Treaty, under Regulation 17 or under U.K. domestic law) to impose fines, make investigations or require information relating to the enforcement of Articles 85 (1) and Article 86.

### 3. PROCEDURE PRIOR TO A DECISION

**1221**    **Generally.** This section is concerned with the procedure which the Commission must follow before delivering a decision in the exercise of its powers under Regulation 17. Briefly, the Commission must give the undertakings concerned the opportunity of making submissions to it[2] before reaching a decision

[92] *S.A. Raffinerie Tirlemontoise,* Bulletin 11/1971, Chap. I, para. 5.
[93] Art. 15 (1) (*b*) of Reg. 17.
[94] See *ante,* § 1217.
[95] Art. 15 (1) (*b*) and Art. 11 (5) of Reg. 17.
[96] Art. 15 (1) (*c*) of Reg. 17. For Art. 14 (3) of Reg. 17 see *ante,* § 1218.
[97] Art. 16 (1) (*c*) and (*d*) of Reg. 17.
[98] Art. 16 (1) of Reg. 17. For units of account see note 12 *ante.*
[99] For an interpretation of the term " competent authorities " to include national courts see *ante,* § 421.
[1] See also *ante,* § 421; for Art. 88 of the Treaty see *ante,* § 117.
[2] *Post,* § 1223.

relating to the grant or refusal of negative clearance,[3] or of exemption under Article 85 (3),[4] before taking a formal decision requiring the termination of an infringement,[5] and before imposing fines or periodic penalty payments.[6] The Commission may also give other persons an opportunity to make submissions to it and must do so if such persons show " a sufficient interest." [7] Before a decision is given relating to negative clearance or exemption under Article 85 (3), the main terms of the decision must be published in the Official Journal of the Communities.[8] Finally, before reaching any of the above decisions, and before taking a decision to begin a sector enquiry [9] the Commission must consult with, and receive the opinion of, a body called the Advisory Committee on Restrictive Practices and Monopolies.[10] All these matters are discussed in this section.

**1222    Informal negotiation.** Although this section is primarily concerned with formal procedural matters, it must be emphasised at the outset that there is considerable scope for informal negotiation with the Commission, particularly in the case of applications for negative clearance or requests for exemption under Article 85 (3). Thus, upon the Commission making its views known to the parties, it is open to them to propose amendments to their agreements, and to discuss the issues raised on an informal basis with the Commission. In this way many matters may often be amicably resolved without the need to resort to the formal procedure or the taking and publication of a formal decision.

**1223    The right to make submissions.** Before the Commission takes a decision the parties have certain fundamental rights to make submissions to the Commission in answer to the objections which the Commission raises against them.[11] Accordingly, before reaching a decision the Commission must give the parties notice

---

[3] *Ante,* §§ 501–503.
[4] *Ante,* §§ 601 *et seq.*
[5] Art. 3 (1) of Reg. 17; *ante,* § 1202.
[6] Under Arts. 15 and 16 of Reg. 17; *ante,* §§ 1204 *et seq.* and § 1219.
[7] Art. 19 (2) of Reg. 17; *post,* § 1223.
[8] Art. 19 (3) of Reg. 17; *post,* § 1225.
[9] *Ante,* § 1215.
[10] *Post,* § 1224.
[11] See generally Reg. 99/63; App. 4, *post.*

in writing of such objections.[12]   The communication by the Commission of these objections is the first formal stage of the hearing of the parties and other interested persons.   These objections must be addressed directly to each of the parties or to their joint agent.[13]   They may be sent to an address outside the territory of the Communities.[14]   The parties must have at least two weeks in which to reply, a period which may be extended.[15] As an alternative to direct communication, the Commission may inform the parties by giving notice in the Official Journal of the Communities if the circumstances appear appropriate, in particular where notice is to be given to a number of undertakings but no joint agent has been appointed.[16]   No fines or periodic penalty payments may be imposed if the objections have only been notified by publication in the Official Journal.[17]   Only the objections raised against undertakings on which they have been afforded the opportunity of making known their views may be the subject of the Commission's decision.[18]   Only the main evidence against the parties need be made known to them.[19] Any natural or legal persons showing a sufficient interest must be given the opportunity to make known their views in writing to the Commission.[20]   Further, any party which the Commission proposes to fine or to penalise or which otherwise shows a sufficient interest may require the holding of an oral hearing.[21] The Commission may also afford any other person the opportunity of orally expressing his views.[22]   The Commission may summon the parties to the hearing on the day it appoints,[23] and the Member States may send representatives.[24]   At such hearings companies should appear by duly authorised representatives, who

---

[12] Article 2 (1) of Reg. 99/63.
[13] *Ibid.*
[14] *ICI and others* v. *EC Commission* (52, 53/69) [1972] C.M.L.R. 557, 637.
[15] Art. 11 of Reg. 99/63: see this Article generally for time limits.
[16] Art. 2 (2) of Reg. 99/63.
[17] Art. 2 (3) of Reg. 99/63.
[18] Art. 4 of Reg. 99/63.
[19] *Consten and Grundig* v. *EEC Commission* (56/64, 58/64) [1966] C.M.L.R. 418, 469.
[20] Art. 5 of Reg. 99/63.
[21] Art. 7 (1) of Reg. 99/63.
[22] Art. 7 (2) of Reg. 99/63.
[23] Art. 8 (1) of Reg. 99/63.   Twelve days' notice of the date of the hearing is not unreasonably short provided the parties have in fact had adequate time to prepare their case.   *ICI and others* v. *EC Commission* (55, 56/69) [1972] C.M.L.R. 557, 644.
[24] Art. 8 (2) of Reg. 99/63.

may be assisted by advocates or by other qualified persons.[25] Hearings are held in private.[26] Persons are to be heard separately or in the presence of the other persons summoned to attend. The choice would appear to depend on whether any one party has a legitimate interest in keeping information secret from other parties.[27]

**1224 Consultation.** After hearing the views of the parties and before taking its decision the Commission must consult with the Advisory Committee on Restrictive Practices and Monopolies.[28] The Advisory Committee is composed of officials competent in the matter of restrictive practices and monopolies. Each Member State is to appoint an official to represent it.[29] Consultation with the Advisory Committee is to take place at a joint meeting convened by the Commission on at least fourteen days' notice.[30] The Advisory Committee may deliver an opinion but it is not made public.[31]

**1225 Publicity.** Before a decision is taken granting negative clearance or in application of Article 85 (3), the gist of the notification or of the request for negative clearance must be published in the Official Journal.[32] In publishing such notice account is to be taken of the legitimate interest of undertakings in the protection of their business secrets.[32] The Commission is further obliged to publish decisions taken by it granting negative clearance, granting revoking or amending an exemption under Article 85 (3) or ordering the termination of an infringement,[33] but such publications must respect the legitimate business secrets of the undertakings concerned.[34] The obligation imposed on the Commission to publish decisions does not extend to decisions

---

[25] Art. 9 (2) of Reg. 99/63. See also *ICI and others* v. *EC Commission* (49/69) [1972] C.M.L.R. 557, 630.
[26] Art. 9 (3) of Reg. 99/63.
[27] *Ibid.*
[28] Art. 10 of Reg. 17 and Art. 1 of Reg. 99/63. See also § 1221, *ante.*
[29] Art. 10 (4) of Reg. 17.
[30] Art. 10 (5) of Reg. 17.
[31] Art. 10 (6) of Reg. 17.
[32] Art. 19 (3) of Reg. 17.
[33] Art. 21 (1) of Reg. 17.
[34] Art. 21 (2) of Reg. 17.

imposing fines or periodic penalty payments. The European Court has however commended the Commission for publishing such decisions.[35]

**1226** **Secrecy.** Article 20 (1) of Regulation 17 provides that information acquired as a result of inquiries and investigations by the Commission is to be used only for the purpose of the relevant request or investigation. Further, the Commission and the competent authorities of the Member States, their officials and servants must not disclose information acquired by them as a result of the application of Regulation 17 and of " the kind covered by the obligation of professional secrecy " *i.e.* legitimate business secrets.[36] Community officials and servants who breach that provision risk disciplinary proceedings. The Community is liable in damages to the party concerned.[37] The Commission may however publish general information or surveys which do not contain information relating to particular undertakings.[38]

### 4. CONTROL OVER THE COMMISSION BY THE EUROPEAN COURT OF JUSTICE

**1227** **Generally.** The European Court has three distinct types of jurisdiction in exercising control over the Commission in relation to Articles 85 and 86 of the Treaty. These are (i) unlimited jurisdiction to review decisions whereby the Commission has fixed a fine or period penalty payment; (ii) power to review the legality of formal decisions taken by the Commission; and (iii) jurisdiction to declare that the Commission has failed to take action required to be taken under the Treaty. This latter jurisdiction may constitute a means whereby a person who has made a complaint to the Commission,[39] including possibly a party to a notified agreement,[40] may require the Commission to take a decision. All these matters are discussed in this section. This section is not concerned with the provisions of Article 177

---

[35] (41/69) *ACF Chemiefarma*, 16 Rec. 661, 694, 695; CCH, CMR § 8032. Noted at 8 C.M.L.Rev. 1971, 86.
[36] Art. 20 (2) of Reg. 17; but such protection in not always effective.
[37] Art. 215 of the Treaty.
[38] Art. 20 (3) of Reg. 17.
[39] See *ante*, § 1214.
[40] *Post*, § 1230.

of the Treaty whereby preliminary rulings on points of Community law appearing in national courts may be referred to the European Court of Justice.[41]

1228      **Appeal against decisions imposing fines.**    The European Court of Justice has unlimited jurisdiction, under Article 17 of Regulation 17, to review decisions whereby the Commission has fixed a fine or periodic penalty payment.    The Court may cancel, reduce or increase the fine or periodic penalty payment imposed. In the *Quinine* cases fines imposed by the Commission were reduced since it was found that not all of the allegations made by the Commission were substantiated.[42]    The Court reduced the fine imposed on one of the parties in the *Dyestuffs* case,[43] but dismissed the appeals of the other parties.

1229      **Review of other decisions.**    Under Article 173 of the Treaty appeals lie to the Court against decisions of the Commission " on grounds of lack of competence, infringement of an essential procedural requirement, infringement of the Treaty or of any rule of law relating to its application, or misuse of powers."    A detailed discussion of this provision is outside the scope of this work, but under this limited jurisdiction the Court may review decisions relating to (i) negative clearance,[44] (ii) orders to terminate infringements,[45] (iii) the grant, withdrawal or variation of an exemption under Article 85 (3),[46] (iv) a requirement that information be provided,[47] (v) an order to submit to an investigation,[48] and (vi) notices under Article 15 (6) of Regulation 17 stating that after preliminary examination the Commission is of the opinion that exemption cannot be granted to an agreement falling under Article 85 (1).[49]    A case may be brought under Article 173 of the Treaty by any natural or legal person against

---

[41] See *ante*, § 409.  See Mathijsen, *A Guide to European Community Law*, Sweet & Maxwell/Mathew Bender (1972), paras. 3–59 *et seq.*

[42] (41/69) (44/69) (45/69) 8 C.M.L. Rev. 1971, 86; these three cases are reported in CCH; CMR para. 8083 *et seq.*

[43] *ICI and others* v. *EC Commission* (48, 49/69, 51–57/69) [1972] C.M.L.R. 557, esp. at p. 650.

[44] *Ante*, §§ 501–505.

[45] *Ante*, § 1202.

[46] *Ante*, §§ 601 *et seq.* and §§ 631 *et seq.*

[47] *Ante*, § 1217.

[48] *Ante*, § 1218.

[49] *Ante*, §§ 513, 1208.

whom a decision has been addressed.  It may also be brought by any natural or legal person against a decision which, although addressed to another person, is of direct and individual concern to the claimant.  Few decisions of the Commission have hitherto been appealed to the Court.[50]  In the case of a decision granting or refusing exemption under Article 85 (3) the European Court has said [51] that the exercise of the Commission's powers necessarily implies complex economic judgments, and the Court must be prepared to respect the character of those judgments. Provided the Commission has properly interpreted the Treaty and complied with essential procedural requirements and " natural justice " the Court will not generally interfere with the Commission's conclusions on economic matters.

**1230**      **The Commission's failure to act.**   Under Article 175 of the Treaty an action may be brought for a declaration that the Commission has failed to act, where action is required by the Treaty.  The action is admissible only if the Commission has first been called upon to act and if within two months of being so called upon, no action has been taken.  Proceedings under Article 175 may be brought by a Member State.  They may also be brought by any natural or legal person but only if that person's complaint is that the Commission has failed to address to him an act, other than a recommendation or an opinion.  It is not clear whether delay in dealing with an application for negative clearance or for exemption under Article 85 (3) is an infringement of the Treaty sufficient to give the applicant a claim under Article 175.  On the other hand a person who has made a complaint may be able to require the Commission to act.  If, on the basis of the complaint, the Commission does not order the termination of an infringement, it is required to inform the complainant of the reasons why it considers that on the basis of the information in its possession there are insufficient grounds for issuing the order.[52]  Failure to inform the complainant in this

---

[50] See *e.g. Consten and Grundig* v. *EEC Commission* (56/64, 58/64) [1966] C.M.L.R. 418; *Re Noordwijks Cement Accoord* (8–11/66) [1967] C.M.L.R. 77; *Dyestuffs case,* note 23, *supra*; *VCH* v. *EC Commission* (8/72) [1973] C.M.L.R. 7; *Boehringer Mannheim* v. *EC Commission (No. 2)* (7/72), December 14, 1972; *Europemballage Corporation and Continental Can Co. Inc.* v. *EC Commission* (6/72), *The Times,* February 26, 1973.
[51] *Consten and Grundig* v. *EEC Commission* (56/64, 58/64) [1966] C.M.L.R. 418, 477.                                                [52] Art. 6 of Reg. 99/63

way within two months of being called upon to act, may entitle the complainant to bring proceedings under Article 175. A party to a notified agreement who wishes to speed the consideration of that agreement might be able to do so by using the complaint procedure, particularly if that party wanted to free itself from restrictions imposed by the agreement which were provisionally valid by virtue of notification.[53]

**1231**    **Period for bringing actions.** Proceedings provided for in Article 173 are to be instituted within two months of the publication of the measure against which action is taken or, if later, within two months of its notification to the plaintiff.[54] If it was not notified to the plaintiff then proceedings are to be instituted within two months of the date when it came to the knowledge of the plaintiff. The European Court has held that the same provisions apply to proceedings brought in respect of decisions imposing fines or periodic penalty payments.[55] Proceedings under Article 175 [56] are to be brought within four months of the date when the plaintiff first called upon the Commission to act.[57]

**1232**    **Stay of execution pending Court's decision.** Under Article 185 of the Treaty actions brought before the European Court are not to have suspensory effects. The Court is, however, empowered to order a stay of execution. In *Europemballage* v. *EC Commission*[58] the Court refused to order a stay of execution on the grounds that the order did not require the termination of the infringement but merely that Continental Can should make proposals to the Commission with a view to terminating the infringement. In interlocutory proceedings in connection with the appeal against the Commission's decision in *Gema* [59] the Court stated that a stay of execution may be granted in exceptional

---

[53] For provisional validity and notification see *ante*, §§ 410 *et seq.*, 501 *et seq.* respectively.
[54] As to whether notification to a subsidiary is good notification to a parent, see *ICI* v. *EC Commission* (48/69) [1972] C.M.L.R. 557, 620.
[55] *ICI* v. *EC Commission* (48/69) [1972] C.M.L.R. 557, 620.
[56] *Ante*, § 1230.
[57] Art. 175 of the Treaty.
[58] *Europemballage Corporation and Continental Can Co. Inc.* v. *EC Commission* (6/72) [1972] C.M.L.R. 690, 692; see *ante*, § 739; for further proceedings see *The Times*, February 26, 1973.
[59] *Gema* v. *EC Commission* (45/71) [1972] C.M.L.R. 694, 697.

circumstances for example where the execution of the Commission's decision was capable of seriously disturbing the activities of the applicant. Where execution of the decision would merely constitute " a nuisance " without paralysing the activities of the applicant irretrievably, a stay of execution would not normally be given.[60]

---

[60] See *ante*, § 731.

# TREATY ESTABLISHING THE EUROPEAN ECONOMIC COMMUNITY

## RULES ON COMPETITION

### *Rules Applying to Undertakings*

## Article 85

(1) The following shall be prohibited as incompatible with the common market: all agreements between undertakings, decisions by associations of undertakings and concerted practices which may affect trade between Member States and which have as their object or effect the prevention, restriction or distortion of competition within the common market, and in particular those which:

(a) directly or indirectly fix purchase or selling prices or any other trading conditions;

(b) limit or control production, markets, technical development, or investment;

(c) share markets or sources of supply;

(d) apply dissimilar conditions to equivalent transactions with other trading parties, thereby placing them at a competitive disadvantage;

(e) make the conclusion of contracts subject to acceptance by the other parties of supplementary obligations which, by their nature or according to commercial usage, have no connection with the subject of such contracts.

(2) Any agreements or decisions prohibited pursuant to this Article shall be automatically void.

(3) The provisions of paragraph (1) may, however, be declared inapplicable in the case of:

—any agreement or category of agreements between undertakings;

—any decision or category of decisions by associations of under-takings;

—any concerted practice or category of concerted practices;

which contributes to improving the production or distribution of goods or to promoting technical or economic progress, while allowing consumers a fair share of the resulting benefit, and which does not:

(a) impose on the undertakings concerned restrictions which are not indispensable to the attainment of these objectives;

(b) afford such undertakings the possibility of eliminating competition in respect of a substantial part of the products in question.

## Article 86

Any abuse by one or more undertakings of a dominant position within the common market or in a substantial part of it shall be prohibited as incompatible with the common market in so far as it may affect trade between Member States. Such abuse may, in particular, consist in:

(a) directly or indirectly imposing unfair purchase or selling prices or other unfair trading conditions;

(b) limiting production, markets or technical development to the prejudice of consumers;

(c) applying dissimilar conditions to equivalent transactions with other trading parties, thereby placing them at a competitive disadvantage;

(d) making the conclusion of contracts subject to acceptance by the other parties of supplementary obligations which, by their nature or according to commercial usage, have no connection with the subject of such contracts.

## Article 87

(1) Within three years of the entry into force of this Treaty the Council shall, acting unanimously on a proposal from the Commission and after consulting the Assembly, adopt any appropriate regulations or directives to give effect to the principles set out in Articles 85 and 86.

If such provisions have not been adopted within the period mentioned, they shall be laid down by the Council, acting by a qualified majority on a proposal from the Commission and after consulting the Assembly.

(2) The regulations or directives referred to in paragraph (1) shall be designed, in particular:

(a) to ensure compliance with the prohibitions laid down in Article 85 (1) and in Article 86 by making provision for fines and periodic penalty payments;

(b) to lay down detailed rules for the application of Article 85 (3), taking into account the need to ensure effective supervision on the one hand, and to simplify administration to the greatest possible extent on the other;

(c) to define, if need be, in the various branches of the economy, the scope of the provisions of Articles 85 and 86;

(d) to define the respective functions of the Commission and of the Court of Justice in applying the provisions laid down in this paragraph;

(*e*) to determine the relationship between national laws and the provisions contained in this Section or adopted pursuant to this Article.

## Article 88

Until the entry into force of the provisions adopted in pursuance of Article 87, the authorities in Member States shall rule on the admissibility of agreements, decisions and concerted practices and on abuse of a dominant position in the common market in accordance with the law of their country and with the provisions of Article 85, in particular paragraph (3), and of Article 86.

## Article 89

(1) Without prejudice to Article 88, the Commission shall, as soon as it takes up its duties, ensure the application of the principles laid down in Articles 85 and 86. On application by a Member State or on its own initiative, and in cooperation with the competent authorities in the Member States, who shall give it their assistance, the Commission shall investigate cases of suspected infringement of these principles. If it finds that there has been an infringement, it shall propose appropriate measures to bring it to an end.

(2) If the infringement is not brought to an end, the Commission shall record such infringement of the principles in a reasoned decision. The Commission may publish its decision and authorise Member States to take the measures, the conditions and details of which it shall determine, needed to remedy the situation.

## Article 90

(1) In the case of public undertakings and undertakings to which Member States grant special or exclusive rights, Member States shall neither enact nor maintain in force any measure contrary to the rules contained in this Treaty, in particular to those rules provided for in Article 7 and Articles 85 to 94.

(2) Undertakings entrusted with the operation of services of general economic interest or having the character of a revenue-producing monopoly shall be subject to the rules contained in this Treaty, in particular to the rules on competition, in so far as the application of such rules does not obstruct the performance, in law or in fact, of the particular tasks assigned to them. The development of trade must not be affected to such an extent as would be contrary to the interests of the Community.

(3) The Commission shall ensure the application of the provisions of this Article and shall, where necessary, address appropriate directives or decisions to Member States.

\*      \*      \*      \*      \*

## ELIMINATION OF QUANTITATIVE RESTRICTIONS BETWEEN MEMBER STATES[1]

### Article 30

Quantitative restrictions on imports and all measures having equivalent effect shall, without prejudice to the following provisions, be prohibited between Member States.

### Article 31

Member States shall refrain from introducing between themselves any new quantitative restrictions or measures having equivalent effect.

This obligation shall, however, relate only to the degree of liberalisation attained in pursuance of the decisions of the Council of the Organisation for European Economic Co-operation of January 14, 1955. Member States shall supply the Commission, not later than six months after the entry into force of this Treaty, with lists of the products liberalised by them in pursuance of these decisions. These lists shall be consolidated between Member States.

### Article 32

In their trade with one another Member States shall refrain from making more restrictive the quotas and measures having equivalent effect existing at the date of the entry into force of this Treaty.

These quotas shall be abolished by the end of the transitional period at the latest. During that period, they shall be progressively abolished in accordance with the following provisions.

### Article 33

(1) One year after the entry into force of this Treaty, each Member State shall convert any bilateral quotas open to any other Member States into global quotas open without discrimination to all other Member States.

On the same date, Member States shall increase the aggregate of the global quotas so established in such a manner as to bring about an increase of not less than 20 per cent. in their total value as compared with the preceding year. The global quota for each product, however, shall be increased by not less than 10 per cent.

The quotas shall be increased annually in accordance with the same rules and in the same proportions in relation to the preceding year.

The fourth increase shall take place at the end of the fourth year after the entry into force of this Treaty; the fifth, one year after the beginning of the second stage.

(2) Where, in the case of a product which has not been liberalised, the global quota does not amount to 3 per cent. of the national production of the State concerned, a quota equal to not less than 3 per cent. of such national production shall be introduced not later than

[1] For transitional provisions see p. 288, *post.*

one year after the entry into force of this Treaty. This quota shall be raised to 4 per cent. at the end of the second year, and to 5 per cent. at the end of the third. Thereafter, the Member State concerned shall increase the quota by not less than 15 per cent. annually.

Where there is no such national production, the Commission shall take a decision establishing an appropriate quota.

(3) At the end of the tenth year, each quota shall be equal to not less than 20 per cent. of the national production.

(4) If the Commission finds by means of a decision that during two successive years the imports of any products have been below the level of the quota opened, this global quota shall not be taken into account in calculating the total value of the global quotas. In such case, the Member State shall abolish quota restrictions on the product concerned.

(5) In the case of quotas representing more than 20 per cent. of the national production of the product concerned, the Council may, acting by a qualified majority on a proposal from the Commission, reduce the minimum percentage of 10 per cent. laid down in paragraph (1). This alteration shall not, however, affect the obligation to increase the total value of global quotas by 20 per cent. annually.

(6) Member States which have exceeded their obligations as regards the degree of liberalisation attained in pursuance of the decisions of the Council of the Organisation for European Economic Cooperation of January 14, 1955 shall be entitled, when calculating the annual total increase of 20 per cent. provided for in paragraph (1), to take into account the amount of imports liberalised by autonomous action. Such calculation shall be submitted to the Commission for its prior approval.

(7) The Commission shall issue directives establishing the procedure and timetable in accordance with which Member States shall abolish, as between themselves, any measures in existence when this Treaty enters into force which have an effect equivalent to quotas.

(8) If the Commission finds that the application of the provisions of this Article, and in particular of the provisions concerning percentages, makes it impossible to ensure that the abolition of quotas provided for in the second paragraph of Article 32 is carried out progressively, the Council may, on a proposal from the Commission, acting unanimously during the first stage and by a qualified majority thereafter, amend the procedure laid down in this Article and may, in particular, increase the percentages fixed.

## Article 34

(1) Quantitative restrictions on exports, and all measures having equivalent effect, shall be prohibited between Member States.

APPENDIX 1

(2) Member States shall, by the end of the first stage at the latest, abolish all quantitative restrictions on exports and any measures having equivalent effect which are in existence when this Treaty enters into force.

### Article 35

The Member States declare their readiness to abolish quantitative restrictions on imports from and exports to other Member States more rapidly than is provided for in the preceding Articles, if their general economic situation and the situation of the economic sector concerned so permit.

To this end, the Commission shall make recommendations to the States concerned.

### Article 36

The provisions of Articles 30 to 34 shall not preclude prohibitions or restrictions on imports, exports or goods in transit justified on grounds of public morality, public policy or public security; the protection of health and life of humans, animals or plants; the protection of national treasures possessing artistic, historic or archaeological value; or the protection of industrial and commercial property. Such prohibitions or restrictions shall not, however, constitute a means of arbitrary discrimination or a disguised restriction on trade between Member States.

## TRANSITIONAL PROVISIONS

*Treaty of Accession: Act concerning the*
*Conditions of Accession and the Adjustments to the Treaties*

### ELIMINATION OF QUANTITATIVE RESTRICTIONS

### Article 42

Quantitative restrictions on imports and exports shall, from the date of accession, be abolished between the Community as originally constituted and the new Member States and between the new Member States themselves.

Measures having equivalent effect to such restrictions shall be abolished by January 1, 1975 at the latest.

# REGULATION 17 [1]

*First Regulation Implementing Articles 85 and 86 of the Treaty*

THE COUNCIL OF THE EUROPEAN ECONOMIC COMMUNITY,

HAVING REGARD to the Treaty establishing the European Economic Community, and in particular Article 87 thereof;

HAVING REGARD to the proposal from the Commission;

HAVING REGARD to the Opinion of the Economic and Social Committee;

HAVING REGARD to the Opinion of the European Parliament;

WHEREAS in order to establish a system ensuring that competition shall not be distorted in the common market, it is necessary to provide for balanced application of Articles 85 and 86 in a uniform manner in the Member States;

WHEREAS in establishing the rules for applying Article 85 (3) account must be taken of the need to ensure effective supervision and to simplify administration to the greatest possible extent;

WHEREAS it is accordingly necessary to make it obligatory, as a general principle, for undertakings which seek application of Article 85 (3) to notify to the Commission their agreements, decisions and concerted practices;

WHEREAS, on the one hand, such agreements, decisions and concerted practices are probably very numerous and cannot therefore all be examined at the same time and, on the other hand, some of them have special features which may make them less prejudicial to the development of the common market;

WHEREAS there is consequently a need to make more flexible arrangements for the time being in respect of certain categories of agreements, decisions and concerted practices without prejudging their validity under Article 85;

WHEREAS it may be in the interest of undertakings to know whether any agreements, decisions or practices to which they are party, or propose to become party, may lead to action on the part of the Commission pursuant to Article 85 (1) or Article 86;

WHEREAS, in order to secure uniform application of Articles 85 and 86 in the common market, rules must be made under which the Commission, acting in close and constant liaison with the competent authorities of the Member States, may take the requisite measures for applying those Articles;

[1] J.O. 1962 13/204; came into force March 13, 1962.

WHEREAS for this purpose the Commission must have the cooperation of the competent authorities of the Member States and be empowered, throughout the common market, to require such information to be supplied and to undertake such investigations as are necessary to bring to light any agreement, decision or concerted practice prohibited by Article 85 (1) or any abuse of a dominant position prohibited by Article 86;

WHEREAS in order to carry out its duty of ensuring that the provisions of the Treaty are applied the Commission must be empowered to address to undertakings or associations of undertakings recommendations and decisions for the purpose of bringing to an end infringements of Articles 85 and 86;

WHEREAS compliance with Articles 85 and 86 and the fulfilment of obligations imposed on undertakings and associations of undertakings under this Regulation must be enforceable by means of fines and periodic penalty payments;

WHEREAS undertakings concerned must be accorded the right to be heard by the Commission, third parties whose interests may be affected by a decision must be given the opportunity of submitting their comments beforehand, and it must be ensured that wide publicity is given to decisions taken;

WHEREAS all decisions taken by the Commission under this Regulation are subject to review by the Court of Justice under the conditions specified in the Treaty; whereas it is moreover desirable to confer upon the Court of Justice, pursuant to Article 172, unlimited jurisdiction in respect of decisions under which the Commission imposes fines or periodic penalty payments;

WHEREAS this Regulation may enter into force without prejudice to any other provisions that may hereafter be adopted pursuant to Article 87;

HAS ADOPTED THIS REGULATION:

## Article 1
*Basic provision*

Without prejudice to Articles 6, 7 and 23 of this Regulation, agreements, decisions and concerted practices of the kind described in Article 85 (1) of the Treaty and the abuse of a dominant position in the market, within the meaning of Article 86 of the Treaty, shall be prohibited, no prior decision to that effect being required.

## Article 2
*Negative clearance*

Upon application by the undertakings or associations of undertakings concerned, the Commission may certify that, on the basis of the facts in its possession, there are no grounds under Article 85 (1) or Article 86 of the Treaty for action on its part in respect of an agreement, decision or practice.

## Article 3

*Termination of infringements*

(1) Where the Commission, upon application or upon its own initiative, finds that there is infringement of Article 85 or Article 86 of the Treaty, it may by decision require the undertakings or associations of undertakings concerned to bring such infringement to an end.

(2) Those entitled to make application are:

(*a*) Member States;

(*b*) natural or legal persons who claim a legitimate interest.

(3) Without prejudice to the other provisions of this Regulation, the Commission may, before taking a decision under paragraph (1), address to the undertakings or associations of undertakings concerned recommendations for termination of the infringement.

## Article 4

*Notification of new agreements, decisions and practices*

(1) Agreements, decisions and concerted practices of the kind described in Article 85 (1) of the Treaty which come into existence after the entry into force of this Regulation and in respect of which the parties seek application of Article 85 (3) must be notified to the Commission. Until they have been notified, no decision in application of Article 85 (3) may be taken.

(2) Paragraph (1) shall not apply to agreements, decisions or concerted practices where:

(i) the only parties thereto are undertakings from one Member State and the agreements, decisions or practices do not relate either to imports or to exports between Member States;

(ii) not more than two undertakings are party thereto, and the agreements only:

(*a*) restrict the freedom of one party to the contract in determining the prices for or conditions of business on which the goods which he has obtained from the other party to the contract may be resold; or

(*b*) impose restrictions on the exercise of the rights of the assignee or user of industrial property rights—in particular patents, utility models, designs or trade marks—or of the person entitled under a contract to the assignment, or grant, of the right to use a method of manufacture or knowledge relating to the use and to the application of industrial processes;

(iii) they have as their sole object:

(*a*) the development or uniform application of standards or types;

[ 291 ]

APPENDIX 2

[(*b*) joint research and development;

(*c*) specialisation in the manufacture of products, including agreements necessary for the achievement thereof;

—where the products which are the object of specialisation do not, in a substantial part of the common market, represent more than 15 per cent. of the volume of business done in identical products or those considered by the consumers to be similar by reason of their characteristics, price and use, and

—where the total annual turnover of the participating undertakings does not exceed 200 million units of account.

These agreements, decisions and concerted practices may be notified to the Commission].[2]

## Article 5

*Notification of existing agreements, decisions and practices*

(1) Agreements, decisions and concerted practices of the kind described in Article 85 (1) of the Treaty which are in existence at the date of entry into force of this Regulation and in respect of which the parties seek application of Article 85 (3) shall be notified to the Commission [before November 1, 1962].[3] [However, notwithstanding the foregoing provisions, any agreements, decisions and concerted practices to which not more than two undertakings are party shall be notified before February 1, 1963].[4]

(2) Paragraph (1) shall not apply to agreements, decisions or concerted practices falling within Article 4 (2); these may be notified to the Commission.

## Article 6

*Decisions pursuant to Article 85 (3)*

(1) Whenever the Commission takes a decision pursuant to Article 85 (3) of the Treaty, it shall specify therein the date from which the decision shall take effect. Such date shall not be earlier than the date of notification.

(2) The second sentence of paragraph (1) shall not apply to agreements, decisions or concerted practices falling within Article 4 (2) and Article 5 (2), nor to those falling within Article 5 (1) which have been notified within the time limit specified in Article 5 (1).

[2] Amended by Reg. 2822/71.
[3] Substituted by Reg. 59, Art. 1 (1). For transitional provisions see also Art. 25, *post*, p. 301.
[4] Added by Reg. 59, Art. 1.

[ 292 ]

## Article 7

*Special provisions for existing agreements, decisions and practices*

(1) Where agreements, decisions and concerted practices in existence at the date of entry into force of this Regulation and notified [within the time limits specified in Article 5 (1)] [4] do not satisfy the requirements of Article 85 (3) of the Treaty and the undertakings or associations of undertakings concerned cease to give effect to them or modify them in such manner that they no longer fall within the prohibition contained in Article 85 (1) or that they satisfy the requirements of Article 85 (3), the prohibition contained in Article 85 (1) shall apply only for a period fixed by the Commission. A decision by the Commission pursuant to the foregoing sentence shall not apply as against undertakings and associations of undertakings which did not expressly consent to the notification.

(2) Paragraph (1) shall apply to agreements, decisions and concerted practices falling within Article 4 (2) which are in existence at the date of entry into force of this Regulation if they are notified [before January 1, 1967]. [5]

## Article 8

*Duration and revocation of decisions under Article 85 (3)*

(1) A decision in application of Article 85 (3) of the Treaty shall be issued for a specified period and conditions and obligations may be attached thereto.

(2) A decision may on application be renewed if the requirements of Article 85 (3) of the Treaty continue to be satisfied.

(3) The Commission may revoke or amend its decision or prohibit specified acts by the parties:

(*a*) where there has been a change in any of the facts which were fundamental in the making of the decision;

(*b*) where the parties commit a breach of any obligation attached to the decision;

(*c*) where the decision is based on incorrect information or was induced by deceit;

(*d*) where the parties abuse the exemption from the provisions of Article 85 (1) of the Treaty granted to them by the decision.

In cases to which subparagraphs (*b*), (*c*) or (*d*) apply, the decision may be revoked with retroactive effect.

---

[5] Substituted by Reg. 118/63, Art. 1. And see Art. 25, *post*, p. 301.

**Article 9**

*Powers*

(1) Subject to review of its decision by the Court of Justice, the Commission shall have sole power to declare Article 85 (1) inapplicable pursuant to Article 85 (3) of the Treaty.

(2) The Commission shall have power to apply Article 85 (1) and Article 86 of the Treaty; this power may be exercised notwithstanding that the time limits specified in Article 5 (1) and in Article 7 (2) relating to notification have not expired.

(3) As long as the Commission has not initiated any procedure under Articles 2, 3 or 6, the authorities of the Member States shall remain competent to apply Article 85 (1) and Article 86, in accordance with Article 88 of the Treaty; they shall remain competent in this respect notwithstanding that the time limits specified in Article 5 (1) and in Article 7 (2) relating to notification have not expired.

**Article 10**

*Liaison with the authorities of the Member States*

(1) The Commission shall forthwith transmit to the competent authorities of the Member States a copy of the applications and notifications together with copies of the most important documents lodged with the Commission for the purpose of establishing the existence of infringements of Articles 85 or 86 of the Treaty or of obtaining negative clearance or a decision in application of Article 85 (3).

(2) The Commission shall carry out the procedure set out in paragraph (1) in close and constant liaison with the competent authorities of the Member States; such authorities shall have the right to express their views on that procedure.

(3) An Advisory Committee on Restrictive Practices and Monopolies shall be consulted prior to the taking of any decision following upon a procedure under paragraph (1), and of any decision concerning the renewal, amendment or revocation of a decision pursuant to Article 85 (3) of the Treaty.

(4) The Advisory Committee shall be composed of officials competent in the matter of restrictive practices and monopolies. Each Member State shall appoint an official to represent it who, if prevented from attending, may be replaced by another official.

(5) The consultation shall take place at a joint meeting convened by the Commission; such meeting shall be held not earlier than fourteen days after dispatch of the notice convening it. The notice shall, in respect of each case to be examined, be accompanied by a summary of the case together with an indication of the most important documents, and a preliminary draft decision.

(6) The Advisory Committee may deliver an opinion notwithstanding that some of its members or their alternates are not present. A report of the outcome of the consultative proceedings shall be annexed to the draft decision. It shall not be made public.

## Article 11

*Requests for information*

(1) In carrying out the duties assigned to it by Article 89 and by provisions adopted under Article 87 of the Treaty, the Commission may obtain all necessary information from the Governments and competent authorities of the Member States and from undertakings and associations of undertakings.

(2) When sending a request for information to an undertaking or association of undertakings, the Commission shall at the same time forward a copy of the request to the competent authority of the Member State in whose territory the seat of the undertaking or association of undertakings is situated.

(3) In its request the Commission shall state the legal basis and the purpose of the request and also the penalties provided for in Article 15 (1) (*b*) for supplying incorrect information.

(4) The owners of the undertakings or their representatives and, in the case of legal persons, companies or firms, or of associations having no legal personality, the persons authorised to represent them by law or by their constitution, shall supply the information requested.

(5) Where an undertaking or association of undertakings does not supply the information requested within the time limit fixed by the Commission, or supplies incomplete information, the Commission shall by decision require the information to be supplied. The decision shall specify what information is required, fix an appropriate time limit within which it is to be supplied and indicate the penalties provided for by Article 15 (1) (*b*) and Article 16 (1) (*c*) and the right to have the decision reviewed by the Court of Justice.

(6) The Commission shall at the same time forward a copy of its decision to the competent authority of the Member State in whose territory the seat of the undertaking or association of undertakings is situated.

## Article 12

*Inquiry into sectors of the economy*

(1) If in any sector of the economy the trend of trade between Member States, price movements, inflexibility of prices or other circumstances suggest that in the economic sector concerned competition is being restricted or distorted within the common market,

the Commission may decide to conduct a general inquiry into that economic sector and in the course thereof may request undertakings in the sector concerned to supply the information necessary for giving effect to the principles formulated in Articles 85 and 86 of the Treaty and for carrying out the duties entrusted to the Commission.

(2) The Commission may in particular request every undertaking or association of undertakings in the economic sector concerned to communicate to it all agreements, decisions and concerted practices which are exempt from notification by virtue of Article 4 (2) and Article 5 (2).

(3) When making inquiries pursuant to paragraph (2), the Commission shall also request undertakings or groups of undertakings whose size suggests that they occupy a dominant position within the common market or a substantial part thereof to supply to the Commission such particulars of the structure of the undertakings and of their behaviour as are requisite to an appraisal of their position in the light of Article 86 of the Treaty.

(4) Article 10 (3) to (6) and Articles 11, 13 and 14 shall apply correspondingly.

### Article 13

*Investigations by the authorities of the Member States*

(1) At the request of the Commission, the competent authorities of the Member States shall undertake the investigations which the Commission considers to be necessary under Article 14 (1), or which it has ordered by decision pursuant to Article 14 (3). The officials of the competent authorities of the Member States responsible for conducting these investigations shall exercise their powers upon production of an authorisation in writing issued by the competent authority of the Member State in whose territory the investigation is to be made. Such authorisation shall specify the subject matter and purpose of the investigation.

(2) If so requested by the Commission or by the competent authority of the Member State in whose territory the investigation is to be made, the officials of the Commission may assist the officials of such authority in carrying out their duties.

### Article 14

*Investigating powers of the Commission*

(1) In carrying out the duties assigned to it by Article 89 and by provisions adopted under Article 87 of the Treaty, the Commission may undertake all necessary investigations into undertakings and associations of undertakings. To this end the officials authorised by the Commission are empowered:

(*a*) to examine the books and other business records;

(*b*) to take copies of or extracts from the books and business records;

(*c*) to ask for oral explanations on the spot;

(*d*) to enter any premises, land and means of transport of under-takings.

(2) The officials of the Commission authorised for the purpose of these investigations shall exercise their powers upon production of an authorisation in writing specifying the subject matter and purpose of the investigation and the penalties provided for in Article 15 (1) (*c*) in cases where production of the required books or other business records is incomplete. In good time before the investigation, the Commission shall inform the competent authority of the Member State in whose territory the same is to be made, of the investigation and of the identity of the authorised officials.

(3) Undertakings and associations of undertakings shall submit to investigations ordered by decision of the Commission. The decision shall specify the subject matter and purpose of the investigation, appoint the date on which it is to begin and indicate the penalties provided for in Article 15 (1) (*c*) and Article 16 (1) (*d*) and the right to have the decision reviewed by the Court of Justice.

(4) The Commission shall take the decisions referred to in para-graph 3 after consultation with the competent authority of the Member State in whose territory the investigation is to be made.

(5) Officials of the competent authority of the Member State in whose territory the investigation is to be made may, at the request of such authority or of the Commission, assist the officials of the Com-mission in carrying out their duties.

(6) Where an undertaking opposes an investigation ordered pur-suant to this Article, the Member State concerned shall afford the necessary assistance to the officials authorised by the Commission to enable them to make their investigation. Member States shall, after consultation with the Commission, take the necessary measures to this end before October 1, 1962.[5a]

## Article 15
*Fines*

(1) The Commission may by decision impose on undertakings or associations of undertakings fines of from one hundred to five thousand units of account where, intentionally or negligently:

(*a*) they supply incorrect or misleading information in an appli-cation pursuant to Article 2 or in a notification pursuant to Articles 4 or 5; or

[5a] See *post*, Art 25.

11*

(*b*) they supply incorrect information in response to a request made pursuant to Article 11 (3) or (5) or to Article 12, or do not supply information within the time limit fixed by a decision taken under Article 11 (5); or

(*c*) they produce the required books or other business records in incomplete form during investigations under Article 13 or 14, or refuse to submit to an investigation ordered by decision issued in implementation of Article 14 (3).

(2) The Commission may by decision impose on undertakings or associations of undertakings fines of from one thousand to one million units of account, or a sum in excess thereof but not exceeding 10 per cent. of the turnover in the preceding business year of each of the undertakings participating in the infringement where, either intentionally or negligently:

(*a*) they infringe Article 85 (1) or Article 86 of the Treaty; or

(*b*) they commit a breach of any obligation imposed pursuant to Article 8 (1).

In fixing the amount of the fine, regard shall be had both to the gravity and to the duration of the infringement.

(3) Article 10 (3) to (6) shall apply.

(4) Decisions taken pursuant to paragraphs (1) and (2) shall not be of a criminal law nature.

(5) The fines provided for in paragraph (2) (*a*) shall not be imposed in respect of acts taking place:

(*a*) after notification to the Commission and before its decision in application of Article 85 (3) of the Treaty, provided they fall within the limits of the activity described in the notification;

(*b*) before notification and in the course of agreements, decisions or concerted practices in existence at the date of entry into force of this Regulation, provided that notification was effected within the time limits specified in Article 5 (1) and Article 7 (2).

(6) Paragraph (5) shall not have effect where the Commission has informed the undertakings concerned that after preliminary examination it is of opinion that Article 85 (1) of the Treaty applies and that application of Article 85 (3) is not justified.

## Article 16
*Periodic penalty payments*

(1) The Commission may by decision impose on undertakings or associations of undertakings periodic penalty payments of from fifty to one thousand units of account per day, calculated from the date appointed by the decision, in order to compel them:

(*a*) to put an end to an infringement of Article 85 or 86 of the Treaty, in accordance with a decision taken pursuant to Article 3 of this Regulation;

(*b*) to refrain from any act prohibited under Article 8 (3);

(*c*) to supply complete and correct information which it has requested by decision taken pursuant to Article 11 (5);

(*d*) to submit to an investigation which it has ordered by decision taken pursuant to Article 14 (3).

(2) Where the undertakings or associations of undertakings have satisfied the obligation which it was the purpose of the periodic penalty payment to enforce, the Commission may fix the total amount of the periodic penalty payment at a lower figure than that which would arise under the original decision.

(3) Article 10 (3) to (6) shall apply.


## Article 17
*Review by the Court of Justice*

The Court of Justice shall have unlimited jurisdiction within the meaning of Article 172 of the Treaty to review decisions whereby the Commission has fixed a fine or periodic penalty; it may cancel, reduce or increase the fine or periodic penalty payment imposed.


## Article 18
*Unit of account*

For the purposes of applying Articles 15 to 17 the unit of account shall be that adopted in drawing up the budget of the Community in accordance with Articles 207 and 209 of the Treaty.


## Article 19
*Hearing of the parties and of third persons*

(1) Before taking decisions as provided for in Articles 2, 3, 6, 7, 8, 15 and 16, the Commission shall give the undertakings or associations of undertakings concerned the opportunity of being heard on the matters to which the Commission has taken objection.

(2) If the Commission or the competent authorities of the Member States consider it necessary, they may also hear other natural or legal persons. Applications to be heard on the part of such persons shall, where they show a sufficient interest, be granted.

(3) Where the Commission intends to give negative clearance pursuant to Article 2 or take a decision in application of Article 85 (3) of the Treaty, it shall publish a summary of the relevant application or notification and invite all interested third parties to submit their

observations within a time limit which it shall fix being not less than one month. Publication shall have regard to the legitimate interest of undertakings in the protection of their business secrets.

## Article 20
*Professional secrecy*

(1) Information acquired as a result of the application of Articles 11, 12, 13 and 14 shall be used only for the purpose of the relevant request or investigation.

(2) Without prejudice to the provisions of Articles 19 and 21, the Commission and the competent authorities of the Member States, their officials and other servants shall not disclose information acquired by them as a result of the application of this Regulation and of the kind covered by the obligation of professional secrecy.

(3) The provisions of paragraphs (1) and (2) shall not prevent publication of general information or surveys which do not contain information relating to particular undertakings or associations of undertakings.

## Article 21
*Publication of decisions*

(1) The Commission shall publish the decisions which it takes pursuant to Articles 2, 3, 6, 7 and 8.

(2) The publication shall state the names of the parties and the main content of the decision; it shall have regard to the legitimate interest of undertakings in the protection of their business secrets.

## Article 22
*Special provisions*

(1) The Commission shall submit to the Council proposals for making certain categories of agreement, decision and concerted practice falling within Article 4 (2) or Article 5 (2) compulsorily notifiable under Article 4 or 5.

(2) Within one year from the date of entry into force of this Regulation, the Council shall examine, on a proposal from the Commission, what special provisions might be made for exempting from the provisions of this Regulation agreements, decisions and concerted practices falling within Article 4 (2) or Article 5 (2).

## Article 23
*Transitional provisions applicable to decisions of authorities of the Member States*

(1) Agreements, decisions and concerted practices of the kind described in Article 85 (1) of the Treaty to which, before entry into

force of this Regulation, the competent authority of a Member State has declared Article 85 (1) to be inapplicable pursuant to Article 85 (3) shall not be subject to compulsory notification under Article 5. The decision of the competent authority of the Member State shall be deemed to be a decision within the meaning of Article 6; it shall cease to be valid upon expiration of the period fixed by such authority but in any event not more than three years after the entry into force of this Regulation.
Article 8 (3) shall apply.

(2) Applications for renewal of decisions of the kind described in paragraph (1) shall be decided upon by the Commission in accordance with Article 8 (2).

## Article 24

*Implementing provisions*

The Commission shall have the power to adopt implementing provisions concerning the form, content and other details of applications pursuant to Articles 2 and 3, and of notifications pursuant to Articles 4 and 5, and concerning hearings pursuant to Article 19 (1) and (2).

## [Article 25

(1) As regards agreements, decisions and concerted practices to which Article 85 of the Treaty applies by virtue of accession, the date of accession shall be substituted for the date of entry into force of this Regulation in every place where reference is made in this Regulation to this latter date.

(2) Agreements, decisions and concerted practices existing at the date of accession to which Article 85 of the Treaty applies by virtue of accession shall be notified pursuant to Article 5 (1) or Article 7 (1) and (2) within six months from the date of accession.

(3) Fines under Article 15 (2) (*a*) shall not be imposed in respect of any act prior to notification of the agreements, decisions and practices to which paragraph (2) applies and which have been notified within the period therein specified.

(4) New Member States shall take the measures referred to in Article 14 (6) within six months from the date of accession after consulting the Commission.][6]
This Regulation shall be binding in its entirety and directly applicable in all Member States.

Done at Brussels, February 6, 1962.

[6] Added by the Act concerning the conditions of Accession and the Adjustments to the Treaty, Annex 1 (Cmnd. 4862, II, p. 74).

## REGULATION 27 [1]

FIRST REGULATION IMPLEMENTING COUNCIL REGULATION NO. 17

*Form, Content and other Details concerning Applications
and Notifications*

THE COMMISSION OF THE EUROPEAN ECONOMIC COMMUNITY,

HAVING REGARD to the provisions of the Treaty establishing the European Economic Community, and in particular Articles 87 and 155 thereof;

HAVING REGARD to Article 24 of Council Regulation No. 17 of February 6, 1962 (First Regulation implementing Articles 85 and 86 of the Treaty);

WHEREAS under Article 24 of Council Regulation No. 17 the Commission is authorised to adopt implementing provisions concerning the form, content and other details of applications under Articles 2 and 3 and of notifications under Articles 4 and 5 of that Regulation;

WHEREAS the submission of such applications and notifications may have important legal consequences for each of the undertakings which is party to an agreement, decision or concerted practice; whereas every undertaking should accordingly have the right to submit an application or a notification to the Commission; whereas, furthermore, an undertaking exercising this right must inform the other undertakings which are parties to the agreement, decision or concerted practice, in order to enable them to protect their interests;

WHEREAS it is for the undertakings and associations of undertakings to transmit to the Commission information as to facts and circumstances in support of applications under Article 2 and of notifications under Articles 4 and 5;

WHEREAS it is desirable to prescribe forms for use in applications for negative clearance relating to implementation of Article 85 (1) and for notifications relating to implementation of Article 85 (3) of the Treaty, in order to simplify and accelerate consideration by the competent departments, in the interests of all concerned;

HAS ADOPTED THIS REGULATION:

### Article 1

*Persons entitled to submit applications and notifications*

(1) Any undertaking which is party to agreements, decisions or practices of the kind described in Articles 85 and 86 of the Treaty may

[1] J.O. 1962 35/1118.

submit an application under Article 2 or a notification under Articles 4 and 5 of Regulation No. 17. Where the application or notification is submitted by some, but not all, of the undertakings concerned, they shall give notice to the others.

(2) Where applications and notifications under Articles 2, 3 (1), 3 (2) (*b*), 4 and 5 of Regulation No. 17 are signed by representatives of undertakings, or associations of undertakings, or natural or legal persons such representatives shall produce written proof that they are authorised to act.

(3) Where a joint application or notification is submitted a joint representative should be appointed.

## Article 2
*Submission of applications and notifications*

(1) Seven copies of each application and notification and of the supporting documents shall be submitted to the Commission.

(2) The supporting documents shall be either originals or copies; copies must be certified as true copies of the original.

(3) Applications and notifications shall be in one of the official languages of the Community. Supporting documents shall be submitted in their original language. Where the original language is not one of the official languages, a translation in one of the official languages shall be attached.

## Article 3
*Effective date of submission of applications and registrations*

The date of submission of an application or notification shall be the date on which it is received by the Commission. Where, however, the application or notification is sent by registered post, it shall be deemed to have been received on the date shown on the postmark of the place of posting.

## Article 4
[ *Content of applications and notifications*

(1) Applications under Article 2 of Regulation No. 17 relating to the applicability of Article 85 (1) of the Treaty and notifications under Article 4 or Article 5 (2) of Regulation No. 17 shall be submitted on Form A/B as shown in the Annex to this Regulation.

(2) Applications and notifications shall contain the information asked for in Form A/B.

(3) Several participating undertakings may submit an application or notification on a single form.

(4) Applications under Article 2 of Regulation No. 17 relating to the applicability of Article 86 of the Treaty shall contain a full statement of the facts, specifying, in particular, the practice concerned and the position of the undertaking or undertakings within the common market or a substantial part thereof in regard to products or services to which the practice relates.][2]

## Article 5

*Transitional provisions*

(1) Applications and notifications submitted prior to the date of entry into force of this Regulation otherwise than on the prescribed forms shall be deemed to comply with Article 4 of this Regulation.

(2) The Commission may require a duly completed form to be submitted to it within such time as it shall appoint. In that event, applications and notifications shall be treated as properly made only if the forms are submitted within the prescribed period and in accordance with the provisions of this Regulation.

## Article 6

This Regulation shall enter into force on the day following its publication in the *Official Journal of the European Communities*.

This Regulation shall be binding in its entirety and directly applicable in all Member States.

Done at Brussels, May 3, 1962.

### FORM A/B [3]

This form and the supporting documents should be forwarded in seven copies together with proof in duplicate of the representative's authority to act.

If the space opposite each question is insufficient, please use extra pages, specifying to which item on the form they relate.

TO THE COMMISSION OF THE EUROPEAN COMMUNITIES
Directorate General for Competition
170, rue de la Loi, Brussels 4[4]

A. Application for negative clearance pursuant to Article 2 of Council Regulation No. 17 of February 6, 1962 relating to implementation of Article 85 (1) of the Treaty.

B. Notification of an agreement, decision or concerted practice under Articles 4 and 5 of Council Regulation No. 17 of February 6, 1962.

[2] Amended by Reg. 1133/68.
[3] Substituted by Reg. 1133/68.
[4] The present address is 200, rue de la Loi, 1040 Brussels.

REGULATION 27

I. Information regarding parties.

1. Name, forenames and address of person submitting the application or notification. If such
person is acting as representative, state also the
name and address of the undertaking or association of undertakings represented and the name,
forenames and address of the proprietors or
partners or, in the case of legal persons, of their
legal representatives.

Proof of representative's authority to act must
be supplied.

If the application or notification is submitted
by a number of persons or on behalf of a number
of undertakings, the information must be given
in respect of each person or undertaking.

2. Name and address of the undertakings which are
parties to the agreement, decision or concerted
practice and name, forenames and address of the
proprietors or partners or, in the case of legal
persons, of their legal representatives (unless this
information has been given under I (1)).

If the undertakings which are parties to the
agreement are not all associated in submitting
the application or notification, state what steps
have been taken to inform the other undertakings.

This information is not necessary in respect of
standard contracts (see Section II 1 (b) below).

3. If a firm or joint agency has been formed in
pursuance of the agreement, state the name and
address of such firm or agency and the names,
forenames and addresses of its legal or other
representatives.

4. If a firm or joint agency is responsible for operating the agreement, state the name and address
of such firm or agency and the names, forenames
and addresses of its legal or other representatives.

Attach a copy of the statutes.

5. In the case of a decision of an association of
undertakings, state the name and address of the
association and the names, forenames and
addresses of its legal representatives.

Attach a copy of the statutes.

6. If the undertakings are established or have their seat outside the territory of the common market (Article 227 (1) and (2) of the Treaty), state the name and address of a representative or branch established in the territory of the common market.

II. Information regarding contents of agreement, decision or concerted practice:

1. If the contents were reduced to writing, attach a copy of the full text unless (a), (b) or (c) below provides otherwise.

    (a) Is there only an outline agreement or outline decision?

    If so, attach also copy of the full text of the individual agreements and implementing provisions.

    (b) Is there a standard contract, *i.e.* a contract which the undertaking submitting the notification regularly concludes with particular persons or groups of persons (*e.g.* a contract restricting the freedom of action of one of the contracting parties in respect of resale prices or terms of business for goods supplied by the other contracting party)?

    If so, only the text of the standard contract need be attached.

    (c) If there is a licensing agreement of the type covered by Article 4 (2) (ii) (*b*) of Regulation No. 17, it is not necessary to submit those clauses of the contract which only describe a technical manufacturing process and have no connection with the restriction of competition; in such cases, however, an indication of the parts omitted from the text must be given.

2. If the contents were not, or were only partially, reduced to writing, state the contents in the space opposite.

3. In all cases give the following additional information:

    (a) Date of agreement, decision or concerted practice.

    (b) Date when it came into force and, where applicable, proposed period of validity.

(c) Subject: exact description of the goods or services involved.
(d) Aims of the agreement, decision or concerted practice.
(e) Terms of adherence, termination or withdrawal.
(f) Sanctions which may be taken against participating undertakings (penalty clause, expulsion, withholding of supplies, etc.).

III. Means of achieving the aims of the agreement, decision or concerted practice:
1. State whether and how far the agreement, decision or concerted practice relates to:
   —adherence to certain buying or selling prices, discounts or other trading conditions
   —restriction or control of production, technical development or investment
   —sharing of markets or sources of supply
   —restrictions on freedom to purchase from, or resell to, third parties (exclusive contracts)
   —application of different terms for supply of equivalent goods or services

2. Is the agreement, decision or concerted practice concerned with supply of goods or services:
   (a) within one Member State only?
   (b) between a Member State and third States?
   (c) between Member States?

IV. If you consider Article 85 (1) to be inapplicable and are notifying the agreement, decision or concerted practice as a precaution only:
(a) Please attach a statement of the relevant facts and reasons as to why you consider Article 85 (1) to be inapplicable, e.g. that the agreement, decision or concerted practice:
   1. does not have the object or effect of preventing, restricting or distorting competition; or
   2. is not one which may affect trade between Member States.
(b) Are you asking for a negative clearance pursuant to Article 2 of Regulation No. 17?

# APPENDIX 3

V. Are you notifying the agreement, decision or concerted practice, even if only as a precaution, in order to obtain a declaration of inapplicability under Article 85 (3)?

If so, explain to what extent:

---

1. the agreement, decision or concerted practice contributes towards
   —improving production or distribution, or
   —promoting technical or economic progress;

---

2. a proper share of the benefits arising from such improvement or progress accrues to the consumers;

---

3. the agreement, decision or concerted practice is essential for realising the aims set out under 1 above; and

---

4. the agreement, decision or concerted practice does not eliminate competition in respect of a substantial part of the goods concerned.

---

VI. State whether you intend to produce further supporting arguments and, if so, on which points.

---

The undersigned declare that the information given above and in the annexes attached hereto is correct. They are aware of the provisions of Article 15 (1) (*a*) of Regulation No. 17.

[Date]

[Signatures]

---

EUROPEAN COMMUNITIES COMMISSION  Brussels, [date]
170, rue de la Loi[4]

Directorate General
for Competition

To

Acknowledgement of receipt

(This form will be returned to the address inserted above if completed in a single copy by the person lodging it).

Your application for negative clearance dated————————

Your notification dated——————————concerning:

(a) Parties:
1.————————

2.————————and others.

(There is no need to name the other undertakings party to
the arrangement)

(b) Subject————————

(Brief description of the restriction on competition)

was received on——————————and registered under No. IV

————————————

*Please quote the above number in all correspondence*

## APPENDIX 4

## REGULATION 99/63 [1]

### On the Hearings Provided for in Article 19 (1) and (2) of Council Regulation No. 17

THE COMMISSION OF THE EUROPEAN ECONOMIC COMMUNITY,

HAVING REGARD to the Treaty establishing the European Economic Community, and in particular Article 87 and 155 thereof;

HAVING REGARD to Article 24 of Council Regulation No. 17 of February 6, 1962 (First Regulation implementing Articles 85 and 86 of the Treaty);

WHEREAS the Commission has power under Article 24 of Council Regulation No. 17 to lay down implementing provisions concerning the hearings provided for in Article 19 (1) and (2) of that Regulation;

WHEREAS in most cases the Commission will in the course of its inquiries already be in close touch with the undertakings or associations of undertakings which are the subject thereof and they will accordingly have the opportunity of making known their views regarding the objections raised against them;

WHEREAS, however, in accordance with Article 19 (1) of Regulation No. 17 and with the rights of defence, the undertakings and associations of undertakings concerned must have the right on conclusion of the inquiry to submit their comments on the whole of the objections raised against them which the Commission proposes to deal with in its decisions;

WHEREAS persons other than the undertakings or associations of undertakings which are the subject of the inquiry may have an interest in being heard; whereas, by the second sentence of Article 19 (2) of Regulation No. 17, such persons must have the opportunity of being heard if they apply and show that they have a sufficient interest;

WHEREAS it is desirable to enable persons who pursuant to Article 3 (2) of Regulation No. 17 have applied for an infringement to be terminated to submit their comments where the Commission considers that on the basis of the information in its possession there are insufficient grounds for granting the application;

WHEREAS the various persons entitled to submit comments must do so in writing, both in their own interest and in the interests of good administration, without prejudice to oral procedure where appropriate to supplement the written evidence;

[1] J.O. 1963 No. 127/2268.

WHEREAS it is necessary to define the rights of persons who are to be heard, and in particular the conditions upon which they may be represented or assisted and the setting and calculation of time limits;

WHEREAS the Advisory Committee on Restrictive Practices and Monopolies delivers its Opinion on the basis of a preliminary draft decision; whereas it must therefore be consulted concerning a case after the inquiry in respect thereof has been completed; whereas such consultation does not prevent the Commission from reopening an inquiry if need be;

HAS ADOPTED THIS REGULATION:

## Article 1

Before consulting the Advisory Committee on Restrictive Practices and Monopolies, the Commission shall hold a hearing pursuant to Article 19 (1) of Regulation No. 17.

## Article 2

(1) The Commission shall inform undertakings and associations of undertakings in writing of the objections raised against them. The communication shall be addressed to each of them or to a joint agent appointed by them.

(2) The Commission may inform the parties by giving notice in the *Official Journal of the European Communities*, if from the circumstances of the case this appears appropriate, in particular where notice is to be given to a number of undertakings but no joint agent has been appointed. The notice shall have regard to the legitimate interest of the undertakings in the protection of their business secrets.

(3) A fine or a periodic penalty payment may be imposed on an undertaking or association or undertakings only if the objections were notified in the manner provided for in paragraph (1).

(4) The Commission shall when giving notice of objections fix a time limit up to which the undertakings and associations of undertakings may inform the Commission of their views.

## Article 3

(1) Undertakings and associations of undertakings shall, within the appointed time limit, make known in writing their views concerning the objections raised against them.

(2) They may in their written comments set out all matters relevant to their defence.

(3) They may attach any relevant documents in proof of the facts set out. They may also propose that the Commission hear persons who may corroborate those facts.

## Article 4

The Commission shall in its decisions deal only with those objections raised against undertakings and associations of undertakings in respect of which they have been afforded the opportunity of making known their views.

## Article 5

If natural or legal persons showing a sufficient interest apply to be heard pursuant to Article 19 (2) of Regulation No. 17, the Commission shall afford them the opportunity of making known their views in writing within such time limit as it shall fix.

## Article 6

Where the Commission, having received an application pursuant to Article 3 (2) of Regulation No. 17, considers that on the basis of the information in its possession there are insufficient grounds for granting the application, it shall inform the applicants of its reasons and fix a time limit for them to submit any further comments in writing.

## Article 7

(1) The Commission shall afford to persons who have so requested in their written comments the opportunity to put forward their arguments orally, if those persons show a sufficient interest or if the Commission proposes to impose on them a fine or periodic penalty payment.

(2) The Commission may likewise afford to any other person the opportunity of orally expressing his views.

## Article 8

(1) The Commission shall summon the persons to be heard to attend on such date as it shall appoint.

(2) It shall forthwith transmit a copy of the summons to the competent authorities of the Member States, who may appoint an official to take part in the hearing.

## Article 9

(1) Hearings shall be conducted by the persons appointed by the Commission for that purpose.

(2) Persons summoned to attend shall appear either in person or be represented by legal representatives or by representatives authorised by their constitution. Undertakings and associations of undertakings may moreover be represented by a duly authorised agent appointed from among their permanent staff.

Persons heard by the Commission may be assisted by lawyers or university teachers who are entitled to plead before the Court of Justice of the European Communities in accordance with Article 17 of the Protocol on the Statute of the Court, or by other qualified persons.

(3) Hearings shall not be public. Persons shall be heard separately or in the presence of other persons summoned to attend. In the latter case, regard shall be had to the legitimate interest of the undertakings in the protection of their business secrets.

(4) The essential content of the statements made by each person heard shall be recorded in minutes which shall be read and approved by him.

### Article 10

Without prejudice to Article 2 (2), information and summonses from the Commission shall be sent to the addressees by registered letter with acknowledgement of receipt, or shall be delivered by hand against receipt.

### Article 11

(1) In fixing the time limits provided for in Articles 2, 5 and 6, the Commission shall have regard both to the time required for preparation of comments and to the urgency of the case. The time limit shall be not less than two weeks; it may be extended.

(2) Time limits shall run from the day following receipt of a communication or delivery thereof by hand.

(3) Written comments must reach the Commission or be dispatched by registered letter before expiry of the time limit. Where the time limit would expire on a Sunday or public holiday, it shall be extended up to the end of the next following working day. For the purpose of calculating this extension, public holidays shall, in cases where the relevant date is the date of receipt of written comments, be those set out in the Annex to this Regulation, and in cases where the relevant date is the date of dispatch, those appointed by law in the country of dispatch.

This Regulation shall be binding in its entirety and directly applicable in all Member States.

Done at Brussels, July 25, 1963.

### Annex

Referred to in the third sentence of Article 11 (3).
(List of public holidays)

| | | | |
|---|---|---|---|
| New year | 1 Jan. | Belgian National Day | 21 July |
| Good Friday | | Assumption | 15 Aug. |
| Easter Saturday | | All Saints | 1 Nov. |
| Easter Monday | | All Souls | 2 Nov. |
| Labour Day | 1 May | Christmas Eve | 24 Dec. |
| Schuman Plan Day | 9 May | Christmas Day | 25 Dec. |
| Ascension Day | | Boxing Day | 26 Dec. |
| Whit Monday | | New Year's Eve | 31 Dec. |

# REGULATION 19/65 [1]

*On Applying Article 85 (3) of the Treaty to Categories of*
*Agreements and of Concerted Practices*

THE COUNCIL OF THE EUROPEAN ECONOMIC COMMUNITY,

HAVING REGARD to the Treaty setting up the European Economic Community, and in particular Article 87 thereof;

HAVING REGARD to the proposal of the Commission;

HAVING REGARD to the Opinion of the Assembly;

HAVING REGARD to the Opinion of the Economic and Social Committee;

WHEREAS the declaration of inapplicability of the provisions of Article 85 (1) of the Treaty may, in accordance with the provisions of paragraph 3 of the same Article, relate to categories of agreements, of decisions and of concerted practices which fulfil the conditions required by those provisions;

WHEREAS procedures for applying Article 85 (3) must be adopted by way of a Regulation, laid down on the basis of Article 87;

WHEREAS in view of the large number of notifications lodged in pursuance of Regulation No. 17 it is advisable that the Commission be enabled, in order to facilitate its task, to declare by way of a Regulation that the provisions of Article 85 (1) are inapplicable to certain categories of agreements and of concerted practices;

WHEREAS it should be laid down under what conditions the Commission, in close and constant liaison with the competent authorities of the Member States, may exercise such power when sufficient experience has been gained in the light of individual decisions and when it becomes possible to specify those categories of agreements and concerted practices in respect of which the conditions of Article 85 (3) may be considered as being fulfilled;

WHEREAS the Commission, by its action and in particular by Regulation No. 153, indicated that there can be no question of easing the procedures stipulated by Regulation No. 17 in respect of certain types of agreements or concerted practices which are particularly liable to distort competition in the common market;

WHEREAS by virtue of Article 6 of Regulation No. 17 the Commission may stipulate that a decision taken in accordance with Article 85 (3) of the Treaty shall apply with retroactive effect; whereas the Commission should also be empowered to lay down such provision by way of a Regulation;

[1] J.O. 1965 36/533.

WHEREAS by virtue of Article 7 of Regulation No. 17, agreements, decisions and concerted practices may be exempted from prohibition by decision of the Commission, particularly if they are so altered as to fulfil the requirements for applying Article 85 (3); whereas it is advisable that the Commission be enabled to grant the same benefit, by means of a regulation, to such agreements and concerted practices if they are so altered as to fall within a category defined in an exempting regulation;

WHEREAS, since there can be no exemption save when all the conditions set out in Article 85 (3) are present, the Commission must have the power to prescribe, by decision, the requirements to be fulfilled by an agreement or concerted practice which owing to special circumstances has certain effects incompatible with Article 85 (3);

HAS ADOPTED THIS REGULATION:

### Article 1

(1) Without prejudice to the application of the Council's Regulation No. 17, the Commission may declare by means of a Regulation and in accordance with Article 85 (3) of the Treaty, that Article 85 (1) shall not apply to categories of agreements to which only two undertakings are parties and by which

(a) —one undertakes to supply the other alone with certain products with a view to their resale within a specified part of the common market territory, or

—one undertakes to purchase from the other alone certain products with a view to their resale, or

—sole supply or purchase commitments in respect of certain products with a view to resale, of the type envisaged in the two preceding sub-paragraphs, have been entered into by the two undertakings, or which

(b) include limitations imposed in relation to the acquisition or use of industrial property rights—in particular of patents, utility models, industrial designs and models or trade marks—or to the rights arising out of contracts which include transfer of, or licence to use, manufacturing processes or knowledge relating to the use or application of industrial techniques.

(2) The regulation shall define those categories of agreements to which it applies, and shall specify in particular:

(a) the restrictions or clauses which may not be included in the agreements;

(b) the clauses which must be included in the agreements, or other requirements which must be fulfilled.

(3) Paragraphs (1) and (2) of this Article shall apply *mutatis mutandis* to categories of concerted practices to which only two undertakings are parties.

[ 315 ]

APPENDIX 5

## Article 2

(1) A regulation in pursuance of Article 1 shall be adopted for a limited period.

(2) It may be revoked or amended where circumstances have altered with respect to a factor essential in its adoption; in such case, a period of adaptation shall be laid down for the agreements and concerted practices referred to in the earlier regulation.

## Article 3

A regulation laid down in accordance with Article 1 may stipulate that it shall apply with retroactive effect to agreements and concerted practices which could, at the date of its entry into force, have benefited by a decision issued with retroactive effect in pursuance of Regulation No. 17, Article 6.

## Article 4

(1) A regulation laid down in accordance with Article 1 may stipulate that the prohibition laid down in Article 85 (1) of the Treaty shall not apply, for the period fixed by such regulation, to agreements and concerted practices which were already in existence at March 13, 1962, and which do not fulfil the requirements of Article 85 (3) [; or]

A regulation pursuant to Article 1 may stipulate that the prohibition contained in Article 85 (1) of the Treaty shall not apply, for such period as shall be fixed by that regulation, to agreements and concerted practices already in existence at the date of accession to which Article 85 applies by virtue of accession and which do not satisfy the conditions of Article 85 (3), where:[2]

—such agreements and concerted practices are so amended, within three months from the coming into force of the regulation, that they fulfil the said requirements in accordance with the provisions of the regulation, and

—the amendments are brought to the notice of the Commission within the time-limit fixed by the regulation.

(2) Paragraph (1) of this Article shall only apply to agreements and concerted practices which had to be notified before February 1, 1963, in accordance with Article 5 of Regulation No. 17, if they have been so notified before such date.

[Paragraph (1) shall not apply to agreements and concerted practices to which Article 85 (1) of the Treaty applies by virtue of accession and which must be notified before July 1, 1973, in accordance with Articles 5 and 25 of Regulation No. 17, unless they have been so notified before that date.][2]

[2] Added by the Act concerning the conditions of Accession and Adjustments to the Treaties, Annex I, V. Competition.

(3) The benefit of the provisions laid down pursuant to paragraph (1) of this Article may not be invoked in cases pending at the date of entry into force of a regulation adopted pursuant to Article 1; neither may such benefit be invoked in support of a claim for damages against third parties.

**Article 5**

When the Commission intends to adopt a regulation, it shall publish the draft thereof and shall invite all persons concerned to submit their comments within a time-limit which shall be fixed by the Commission and shall in no case be less than one month.

**Article 6**

(1) The Commission shall consult the Consultative Committee on matters relating to cartels and monopolies:

(*a*) before publishing a draft regulation.

(*b*) before adopting a regulation.

(2) Article 10 (5) and (6) of Regulation No. 17, relating to consultation with the Consultative Committee, shall apply *mutatis mutandis*, it being understood that the joint meetings with the Commission shall take place at the earliest one month after despatch of the notice convening them.

**Article 7**

Should the Commission, either on its own initiative or at the request of a Member State or of natural or legal persons establishing the fact of a legitimate interest, ascertain that in a given case agreements or concerted practices dealt with by a regulation laid down pursuant to Article 1 of this Regulation have nevertheless certain effects which are incompatible with the requirements laid down in Article 85 (3) of the Treaty, it may withdraw the benefit of application of that regulation and may issue a decision, in accordance with Articles 6 and 8 of Regulation No. 17, without the notification referred to in Article 4 (1) of Regulation No. 17 being required.

**Article 8**

The Commission shall, before January 1, 1970, submit to the Council a draft regulation designed to amend this Regulation as shall appear necessary in the light of experience.

This Regulation shall be binding in all its parts and directly applicable in all Member States.

Done at Brussels, March 2, 1965.

# REGULATION 67/67[1]

*On the Application of Article 85 (3) of the Treaty to Certain Categories of Exclusive Dealing Agreements*

THE COMMISSION OF THE EUROPEAN ECONOMIC COMMUNITY,

HAVING REGARD to the Treaty establishing the European Economic Community, and in particular Articles 87 and 155 thereof;

HAVING REGARD to Article 24 of Regulation No. 17 of February 6, 1962;

HAVING REGARD to Regulation No. 19/65/EEC of March 2, 1965 on the application of Article 85 (3) of the Treaty to certain categories of agreements and concerted practices;

HAVING REGARD to the Opinions delivered by the Advisory Committee on Restrictive Practices and Monopolies in accordance with Article 6 of Regulation No. 19/65/EEC;

WHEREAS under Regulation No. 19/65/EEC the Commission has power to apply Article 85 (3) of the Treaty by regulation to certain categories of bilateral exclusive dealing agreements and concerted practices coming within Article 85;

WHEREAS the experience gained up to now, on the basis of individual decisions, makes it possible to define a first category of agreements and concerted practices which can be accepted as normally satisfying the conditions laid down in Article 85 (3);

WHEREAS since adoption of such a regulation would not conflict with the application of Regulation No. 17 the right of undertakings to request the Commission, on an individual basis, for a declaration under Article 85 (3) of the Treaty would not be affected;

WHEREAS exclusive dealing agreements of the category defined in Article 1 of this Regulation may fall within the prohibition contained in Article 85 (1) of the Treaty; whereas since it is only in exceptional cases that exclusive dealing agreements concluded within a Member State affect trade between Member States, there is not need to include them in this Regulation;

WHEREAS it is not necessary expressly to exclude from the category as defined those agreements which do not fulfil the conditions of Article 85 (1) of the Treaty;

WHEREAS in the present state of trade exclusive dealing agreements relating to international trade lead in general to an improvement in

[1] J.O. 1967 57/849.

distributing because the entrepreneur is able to consolidate his sales activities; whereas he is not obliged to maintain numerous business contracts with a large number of dealers, and whereas the fact of maintaining contacts with only one dealer makes it easier to overcome sales difficulties resulting from linguistic, legal, and other differences; whereas exclusive dealing agreements facilitate the promotion of the sale of a product and make it possible to carry out more intensive marketing and to ensure continuity of supplies, while at the same time rationalising distribution; whereas, moreover, the appointment of an exclusive distributor or of an exclusive purchaser who will take over, in place of the manufacturer, sales promotion, after-sales service and carrying of stocks, is often the sole means whereby small and medium-size undertakings can compete in the market; whereas it should be left to the contracting parties to decide whether and to what extent they consider it desirable to incorporate in the agreements terms designed to promote sales; whereas there can only be an improvement in distribution if dealing is not entrusted to a competitor;

WHEREAS as a rule such exclusive dealing agreements also help to give consumers a proper share of the resulting benefit as they gain directly from the improvement in distribution, and their economic or supply position is thereby improved as they can obtain products manufactured in other countries more quickly and more easily;

WHEREAS this Regulation must determine the obligations restricting competition which may be included in an exclusive dealing agreement; whereas it may be left to the contracting parties to decide which of those obligations they include in exclusive dealing agreements in order to draw the maximum advantages from exclusive dealing;

WHEREAS any exemption must be subject to certain conditions; whereas it is in particular advisable to ensure through the possibility of parallel imports that consumers obtain a proper share of the advantages resulting from exclusive dealing; whereas it is therefore not possible to allow industrial property rights and other rights to be exercised in an abusive manner in order to create absolute territorial protection; whereas these considerations do not prejudice the relationship between the law of competition and industrial property rights, since the sole object here is to determine the condition for exemption of certain categories of agreements under this Regulation;

WHEREAS competition at the distribution stage is ensured by the possibility of parallel imports; whereas, therefore, the exclusive dealing agreements covered by this Regulation will not normally afford any possibility of preventing competition in respect of a substantial part of the products in question;

WHEREAS it is desirable to allow contracting parties a limited period of time within which they may, in accordance with Article 4 of Regulation No. 19/65/EEC, modify their agreements and practices so as to satisfy the conditions laid down in this Regulation, without it being possible, under Article 4 (3) of Regulation No. 19/65/EEC, to rely thereon in actions which are pending at the time of entry into force of this Regulation, or as grounds for claims for damages against third parties;

WHEREAS agreements and concerted practices which satisfy the conditions set out in this Regulation need no longer be notified; whereas Article 4 (2) (a) of Regulation No. 27, as amended by Regulation No. 153, can be repealed, since agreements which it was possible to notify on Form B1 would normally come within the scope of the exemption;

WHEREAS agreements notified on Form B1 and not amended so as to satisfy the conditions of this Regulation should be made subject to the normal notification procedure, in order that they may be examined individually;

HAS ADOPTED THIS REGULATION:

## Article 1

(1) Pursuant to Article 85 (3) of the Treaty and subject to the provisions of this Regulation it is hereby declared that until [December 31, 1982] [2] Article 85 (1) of the Treaty shall not apply to agreements to which only two undertakings are party and whereby

- (a) one party agrees with the other to supply only to that other certain goods for resale within a defined area of the common market; or
- (b) one party agrees with the other to purchase only from that other certain goods for resale; or
- (c) the two undertakings have entered into obligations, as in (a) and (b) above, with each other in respect of exclusive supply and purchase for resale.

(2) Paragraph (1) shall not apply to agreements to which undertakings from one Member State only are party and which concern the resale of goods within that Member State.

## Article 2

(1) Apart from an obligation falling within Article 1, no restriction on competition shall be imposed on the exclusive dealer other than:

- (a) the obligation not to manufacture or distribute, during the duration of the contract or until one year after its expiration, goods which compete with the goods to which the contract relates;
- (b) the obligation to refrain, outside the territory covered by the contract, from seeking customers for the goods to which the contract relates, from establishing any branch, or from maintaining any distribution depot.

[2] Substituted by Reg. 2591/72.

(2) Article 1 (1) shall apply notwithstanding that the exclusive dealer undertakes all or any of the following obligations:

(*a*) to purchase complete ranges of goods or minimum quantities;

(*b*) to sell the goods to which the contract relates under trade marks or packed and presented as specified by the manufacturer;

(*c*) to take measures for promotion of sales, in particular:

—to advertise,

—to maintain a sales network or stock of goods,

—to provide after-sale and guarantee services,

—to employ staff having specialised or technical training.

## Article 3

Article 1 (1) of this Regulation shall not apply where:

(*a*) manufacturers of competing goods entrust each other with exclusive dealing in those goods;

(*b*) the contracting parties make it difficult for intermediaries or consumers to obtain the goods to which the contract relates from other dealers within the common market, in particular where the contracting parties:

(i) exercise industrial property rights to prevent dealers or consumers from obtaining from other parts of the common market or from selling in the territory covered by the contract goods to which the contract relates which are properly marked or otherwise properly placed on the market;

(ii) exercise other rights or take other measures to prevent dealers or consumers from obtaining from elsewhere goods to which the contract relates or from selling them in the territory covered by the contract.

## Article 4

(1) As regards agreements which were in existence on March 13, 1962 and were notified before February 1, 1963, the declaration contained in Article 1 (1) of inapplicability of Article 85 (1) of the Treaty shall have retroactive effect from the time when the conditions of application of this Regulation were fulfilled.

(2) As regards all other agreements notified before the entry into force of this Regulation, the declaration contained in Article 1 (1) of inapplicability of Article 85 (1) of the Treaty shall have retroactive effect from the time when the conditions of application of this Regulation were fulfilled, but not earlier than the day of notification.

### Article 5

As regards agreements which were in existence on March 13, 1962, notified before February 1, 1963 and amended before August 2, 1967 so as to fulfil the conditions of application of this Regulation, the prohibition in Article 85 (1) of the Treaty shall not apply in respect of the period prior to the amendment, where such amendment is notified to the Commission before October 3, 1967. As regards agreements, decisions or concerted practices for exclusive dealing already in existence at the date of accession to which Article 85 (1) applies by virtue of accession, the prohibition in Article 85 (1) of the Treaty shall not apply where they are modified within six months from the date of accession so as to fulfil the conditions contained in this Regulation.[3] The notification shall take effect from the time of receipt thereof by the Commission. Where the notification is sent by registered post, it shall take effect from the date on the postmark of the place of dispatch.

### Article 6

The Commission shall examine whether Article 7 of Regulation No. 19/65/EEC applies in individual cases, in particular when there are grounds for believing that:

- (*a*) the goods to which the contract relates are not subject, in the territory covered by the contract, to competition from goods considered by the consumer as similar goods in view of their properties, price and intended use;
- (*b*) it is not possible for other manufacturers to sell, in the territory covered by the contract, similar goods at the same stage of distribution as that of the exclusive dealer;
- (*c*) the exclusive dealer has abused the exemption:
  - (i) by refusing, without objectively valid reasons, to supply in the territory covered by the contract categories of purchasers who cannot obtain supplies elsewhere, on suitable terms, of the goods to which the contract relates;
  - (ii) by selling the goods to which the contract relates at excessive prices.

### Article 7

(1) Article 4 (2) (*a*) of Regulation No. 27 of May 3, 1962, as amended by Regulation No. 153, is hereby repealed.

(2) Notification, on Form B1, of an exclusive dealing agreement which does not fulfil the conditions contained in Articles 1 to 3 of this Regulation shall, if such agreement is not amended so as to satisfy those conditions, be effected before October 3, 1967, by submission

---

[3] Added by the Act concerning the conditions of Accession and Adjustments to the Treaties, Annex I, V. Competition. On the third and fourth sentences of Art. 5, see § 824, note 68.

of Form B, with annexes, in accordance with the provisions of Regulation No. 27.

## Article 8

Articles 1 to 7 of this Regulation shall apply by analogy to the category of concerted practices defined in Article 1 (1).

## Article 9

This Regulation shall enter into force on May 1, 1967.

This Regulation shall be binding in its entirety and directly applicable in all Member States.

Done at Brussels, March 22, 1967.

# REGULATION 2821/71 [1]

*Concerning the Application of Article 85 (3) of the Treaty to Categories of Agreements, Decisions and Concerted Practices*

THE COUNCIL OF THE EUROPEAN COMMUNITIES,

HAVING REGARD to the Treaty establishing the European Economic Community, and in particular Article 87 thereof;

HAVING REGARD to the proposal from the Commission;

HAVING REGARD to the Opinion of the European Parliament;

HAVING REGARD to the Opinion of the Economic and Social Committee;

WHEREAS the provisions of Article 85 (1) of the Treaty may, in accordance with the provisions of paragraph (3) of that Article, be declared inapplicable to categories of agreements, decisions and concerted practices which fulfil the conditions of those provisions;

WHEREAS the procedure for application of Article 85 (3) must be adopted by a regulation based on Article 87;

WHEREAS the creation of a common market requires the adaptation of undertakings to the conditions of the enlarged market and whereas the cooperation of the undertakings can be a suitable means of achieving this;

WHEREAS agreements, decisions and concerted practices on cooperation between undertakings which allow the latter to work more rationally and adapt their productivity and competitiveness to the enlarged market may, in so far as they come under the prohibition in Article 85 (1), under certain conditions be exempted therefrom; whereas this measure is necessary in particular as regards agreements, decisions and concerted practices in the field of standards and types, research and development of products or of processes up to the stage of industrial application and of making use of the results as well as of specialisation;

WHEREAS it is appropriate to put the Commission in a position to declare by means of a regulation that the provisions of Article 85 (1) are inapplicable to those categories of agreements, decisions and concerted practices, in order to make it easier for undertakings to cooperate in ways which are economically desirable and without adverse effect from the point of view of competition policy;

[1] J.O. 1971 L285/46.

# Regulation 2821/71

WHEREAS, the conditions should be laid down under which the Commission can exercise this power in close and constant co-operation with the competent authorities of the Member States;

WHEREAS, pursuant to Article 6 of Regulation No. 17, the Commission may provide that a decision taken in accordance with Article 85 (3) of the Treaty shall apply retrospectively; whereas it is advisable that the Commission should be able to make such a provision also by regulation;

WHEREAS, pursuant to Article 7 of Regulation No. 17, agreements, decisions and concerted practices may be exempted from the prohibition by a decision of the Commission, in particular if they are amended in such a way that they fulfil the conditions for application of Article 85 (3); whereas it is appropriate that the Commission should, by means of a regulation, be able to grant the same benefits to those agreements, decisions and concerted practices if they are amended in such a way that they come within a category specified in an exempting regulation;

WHEREAS the possibility cannot be excluded that, in a specific case, the conditions set out in Article 85 (3) may not be fulfilled; whereas it must be possible for the Commission to regulate such a case in pursuance of Regulation No. 17 by means of a decision having future effect;

HAS ADOPTED THIS REGULATION:

### Article 1

(1) Without prejudice to the application of Regulation No. 17, the commission may declare, by means of a regulation and in accordance with Article 85 (3) of the Treaty, that Article 85 (1) is not applicable to categories of agreements between undertakings, decisions by associations of undertakings and concerted practices which have as their object:

(a) the application of standards and types;

(b) the research and development of products or processes up to the stage of industrial application, as well as making use of the results, including provisions regarding industrial property rights and confidential technical knowledge;

(c) specialisation, including the agreements necessary for the achievement thereof.

(2) The regulation must include a definition of the categories of agreements, decisions and concerted practices to which it applies and in particular specify:

(a) the restrictions and provisions which may or may not appear in the agreements, decisions and concerted practices;

[ 325 ]

(*b*) the provisions which must appear in the agreements, decisions and concerted practices or the other conditions which must be fulfilled.

## Article 2

(1) A regulation made pursuant to Article 1 shall be adopted for a limited period.

(2) It may be repealed or amended when there has been a change in any of the factors which were basic to its adoption; in that case a period shall be provided for the adaptation of the agreements, decisions and concerted practices coming under the previous regulation.

## Article 3

A regulation adopted pursuant to Article 1 may provide for its application with retrospective effect to the agreements, decisions and concerted practices which, on the day of its entry into force, would have been eligible for a decision with retrospective effect in accordance with Article 6 of Regulation No. 17.

## Article 4

(1) A regulation made pursuant to Article 1 may provide that the prohibition laid down in Article 85 (1) of the Treaty shall not apply, for the period determined in the regulation, to the agreements, decisions and concerted practices concerned which were in existence on March 13, 1962 and which do not fulfil the conditions of Article 85 (3):

—if they are amended within six months from the entry into force of the regulation, in such a way that they fulfil the conditions which are stated in the regulation, and

—if the amendments are notified to the Commission within the period determined in the regulation.

[A Regulation adopted pursuant to Article 1 may lay down that the prohibition referred to in Article 85 (1) of the Treaty shall not apply, for the period fixed in the same Regulation, to agreements and concerted practices which existed at the date of accession and which, by virtue of accession, come within the scope of Article 85 and do not fulfil the conditions set out in Article 85 (3).][2]

(2) Paragraph (1) shall apply to agreements, decisions and concerted practices which were notifiable before February 1, 1963, in accordance with Article 5 of Regulation No. 17, only if they were notified before that date.

[Paragraph (1) shall be applicable to those agreements and concerted practices which, by virtue of the accession, come within the scope of Article 85 (1) of the Treaty and for which notification before July 1, 1973 is mandatory, in accordance with Articles 5 and 25 of Regulation No. 17, only if notification was given before that date.][2]

[2] Added by Reg. 2743/72, Art. 1.

(3) Benefits arising from provisions made pursuant to paragraph (1) cannot be invoked in legal proceedings which have been commenced before the date of entry into force of a regulation adopted in pursuance of Article 1; neither can they be invoked as grounds for damages against third parties.

## Article 5

When the Commission proposes to adopt a regulation it shall publish the draft thereof to enable all interested parties and organisation to let it be informed of their comments within a period, which may not be less than one month, to be fixed by the Commission.

## Article 6

(1) The Commission shall consult the Advisory Committee on Restrictive Practices and Monopolies:

(a) before publishing a draft regulation;

(b) before adopting a regulation.

(2) Paragraphs (5) and (6) of Article 10 of Regulation No. 17 on consultation with the Advisory Committee shall apply by analogy, except that joint meetings with the Commission will take place at the earliest one month after dispatch of the notice convening them.

## Article 7

If the Commission ascertains, on its own initiative or at the request of a Member State or of natural or legal persons who show a legitimate interest, that in a specific case agreements, decisions or concerted practices covered by a regulation made pursuant to Article 1 have nevertheless certain effects which are incompatible with the conditions specified in Article 85 (3) of the Treaty, it may, in withdrawing the benefit of application of that regulation, take a decision in accordance with Articles 6 and 8 of Regulation No. 17 without the notification referred to in Article 4 (1) of Regulation No. 17 being required.

This Regulation shall be binding in its entirety and directly applicable in all Member States.

Done at Brussels, December 20, 1971.

## REGULATION 2779/72[1]

*on the Application of Article 85 (3) of the Treaty to Categories of Specialisation Agreements*

THE COMMISSION OF THE EUROPEAN COMMUNITIES,

HAVING REGARD to the Treaty establishing the European Economic Community, and in particular Articles 87 and 155 thereof;

HAVING REGARD to Council Regulation (EEC) No. 2821/71 of December 20, 1971 on application of Article 85 (3) of the Treaty to categories of agreements, decisions and concerted practices;

HAVING REGARD to the Opinions of the Advisory Committee on Restrictive Practices and Monopolies delivered pursuant to Article 6 of Regulation (EEC) No. 2821/71;

WHEREAS under Regulation (EEC) No. 2821/71 the Commission has power to apply Article 85 (3) of the Treaty by regulation to certain categories of agreements, decisions and concerted practices relating to specialisation, including agreements necessary for achieving the latter, which fall within Article 85 (1);

WHEREAS, since the adoption of such a Regulation would not conflict with the application of Regulation No. 17, the right of undertakings to apply in individual cases to the Commission for a declaration under Article 85 (3) of the Treaty would not thereby be affected;

WHEREAS agreements for the specialisation of production may fall within the prohibition contained in Article 85 (1);

WHEREAS agreements for the specialisation of production lead in general to an improvement in the production or distribution of goods, because the undertakings can concentrate on the manufacture of certain products, thus operate on a more rational basis and offer these products at more favourable prices; whereas it is to be anticipated that, with effective competition, users will receive a fair share of the profit resulting therefrom;

WHEREAS this Regulation must determine what restrictions on competition may be included in a specialisation agreement; whereas the restrictions on competition provided for in this Regulation are, in general, indispensable for the purpose of ensuring that the desired benefits accrue to undertakings and consumers; whereas it may be left to the contracting parties to decide which of these provisions they include in their agreements;

[1] J.O. 1972 L292/23.

WHEREAS in order to ensure that competition is not eliminated in respect of a substantial part of the goods in question, this Regulation applies only if the share of the market held by the participating undertakings and the size of the undertakings themselves do not exceed a specified limit;

WHEREAS this Regulation should also apply to specialisation agreements made prior to its entry into force;

HAS ADOPTED THIS REGULATION:

## Article 1

Pursuant to Article 85 (3) of the Treaty it is hereby declared that, subject as provided in this Regulation, until December 31, 1977 Article 85 (1) of the Treaty shall not apply to agreements whereby, with the object of specialisation, undertakings mutually bind themselves for the duration of the agreements not to manufacture certain products or cause them to be manufactured by other undertakings, and to leave it to the other contracting parties to manufacture such products or cause them to be manufactured by other undertakings.

## Article 2

(1) Apart from the obligation referred to in Article 1, no other restriction on competition shall be imposed on the contracting parties save the following:

(*a*) the obligation not to conclude with other undertakings specialisation agreements relating to identical products or to products considered by users to be similar by reason of their characteristics, price or use, except with the consent of the other contracting parties;

(*b*) the obligation to supply the other contracting parties with the products which are the subject of specialisation, and in so doing to observe minimum standards of quality;

(*c*) the obligation to purchase products which are the subject of specialisation solely from the other contracting parties, except where more favourable terms of purchase are available elsewhere and the other contracting parties are not prepared to offer the same terms;

(*d*) the obligation to grant to the other contracting parties the exclusive right to distribute the products which are the subject of specialisation so long as those parties do not—in particular by the exercise of industrial property rights or of other rights and measures—restrict the opportunities, for intermediaries or consumers, of purchasing the products to which the agreement relates from other dealers within the common market.

APPENDIX 8

(2) Article 1 shall apply notwithstanding that the following obligations are imposed:

 (*a*) the obligation to maintain minimum stocks of the products which are the subject of specialisation and of replacement parts for them;

 (*b*) the obligation to provide after-sale and guarantee services for the products which are the subject of specialisation.

**Article 3**

(1) Article 1 shall apply only:

 (*a*) if the products which are the subject of specialisation represent in any member country not more than 10 per cent. of the volume of business done in identical products or in products considered by consumers to be similar by reason of their characteristics, price or use; and

 (*b*) if the aggregate annual turnover of the participating undertakings does not exceed 150 million units of account.

(2) For purposes of applying paragraph (1) the unit of account shall be that adopted in drawing up the budget of the Community in accordance with Articles 207 and 209 of the Treaty.

(3) Article 1 of this Regulation shall continue to apply notwithstanding that in any two consecutive financial years the share of the market or the turnover is greater than as specified in paragraph 1, provided the excess is not more than 10 per cent.

**Article 4**

The aggregate turnover within the meaning of Article 3 (1) (*b*) shall be calculated by adding together the turnover achieved during the last financial year in respect of all products and services:

(1) by the undertakings which are parties to the agreement;

(2) by undertakings in respect of which the undertakings which are parties to the agreement hold:

 —at least 25 per cent. of the capital or of the working capital whether directly or indirectly; or

 —at least half the voting rights; or

 —the power to appoint at least half the members of the supervisory board, board of management or bodies legally representing the undertaking; or

 —the right to manage the affairs of the undertaking;

(3) by undertakings which hold in an undertaking, which is a party to the agreement:

[ 330 ]

—at least 25 per cent. of the capital or of the working capital whether directly or indirectly; or

—at least half the voting rights; or

—the power to appoint at least half the members of the supervisory board, board of management or bodies legally representing the undertaking; or

—the right to manage the affairs of the undertaking.

In calculating aggregate turnover no account shall be taken of dealings between the undertakings which are parties to the agreement.

## Article 5

The Commission shall examine whether Article 7 of Regulation (EEC) No. 2821/71 applies in any specific case, in particular where there is reason to believe that rationalisation is not yielding significant results or that consumers are not receiving a fair share of the resulting profit.

## Article 6

The non-applicability of Article 85 (1) provided for in Article 1 of this Regulation shall have retroactive effect from the time when the conditions requisite for the application of this Regulation were satisfied. In the case of agreements which prior to January 18, 1972 were compulsorily notifiable, the time aforesaid shall not be earlier than the day of notification.

## Article 7

Articles 1 to 6 of this Regulation shall apply by analogy to decisions by associations of undertakings and to concerted practices.

## Article 8

This Regulation shall enter into force on January 1, 1973.

This Regulation shall be binding in its entirety and directly applicable in all Member States.

Done at Brussels, December 21, 1972.

*For the Commission*
*The President*
S. L. MANSHOLT

# DRAFT REGULATION ON LIMITATION OF ACTIONS [1]

*Concerning Limitation of Actions in Cases of Prosecution and Execution of Judgment in the Fields of Transport Law and Competition Law of the European Economic Community*

The Council of the European Communities, in the light of the Treaty instituting the European Economic Community (especially Articles 75, 79 and 87), of the Commission's draft, of the opinions of the European Parliament and of the Economic and Social Committee, hereby promulgates the following Regulation.

## Preamble

WHEREAS,

(1) The provisions of the EEC transport law and competition law confer on the Commission the power to impose fines (sanctions) and penalties upon undertakings and associations of undertakings which violate the orders of the Commission relating to the supply of information or inspections or prohibitions of discrimination, cartels or abuse of dominant positions. But these provisions do not lay down any periods of limitation.

(2) It seems necessary, in order to provide legal certainty, to introduce the principle of limitation of actions and to govern its application. Rules to that effect, to be complete, should apply both to the power to impose fines (sanctions) and to the power to execute the decisions by which fines (sanctions) or penalties are imposed. Such a set of rules should fix the periods of limitation, the date from which the period of limitation runs and the measures whereby the period of limitation is interrupted or suspended.

(3) In that respect account should be taken both of the interests of undertakings and associations of undertakings and the requirements of the administrative practice of the Commission.

(4) As regards the power of the Commission to impose fines the periods of limitation should be fixed in relation to the nature of the infringement. The provisions governing the power of the Commission to impose fines (sanctions) lay down that the infringements of the orders of the Commission on the supply of information or inspections are less serious than violations of the prohibition of discrimination, cartels and abuse of dominant position. It is therefore justifiable to introduce the same distinction in the fixing of the limitation periods.

*Reprinted with permission from Common Market Law Reports Ltd., [1972] C.M.L.R D40.
[1] European Parliament, Session Papers 1971–72, Doc. 245/71.

In such circumstances it is expedient to lay down a limitation period of three years for violations of the orders of the Commission on the supply of information or inspections and of five years for all other infringements covered by the present regulation.

(5) As regards prosecutions, a prescription period cannot be given to the undertakings and associations of undertakings concerned while they are violating the provisions of the EEC transport law and competition law. Therefore it should be laid down that the limitation period runs only as from the day on which those concerned have put an end to the violation.

(6) Provision should be made for the possibility of interrupting the limitation period for prosecutions. The effects of the limitation period apply only in the case of inaction of the appropriate authority with regard to the violation within the period laid down. Undertakings and associations of undertakings should no longer benefit from the limitation period when such authority is, in accordance with the provisions in force, making formal inquiries [*procède à l'instruction*] or bringing proceedings for the infringement. It should therefore be provided that the limitation period be interrupted by any measure taken by the Commission or by a Member State at the request of the Commission, and which is aimed at proving such infringement. It should also be provided that such measures taken against an undertaking or association of undertakings concerned interrupt the limitation period with regard to all undertakings and associations of undertakings participating in the infringement.

(7) The decisions whereby the Commission imposes on undertakings or associations of undertakings fines (sanctions) or penalties are, in accordance with Article 192 of the Treaty instituting the European Economic Community, authority for their own execution [*forment titre exécutoire*]. It seems appropriate to subject the power of the Commission to execute such decisions to a limitation period of three years as from the day on which the decision acquired binding force.

(8) An interruption of the limitation period should, however, also be provided for in the case of execution. The limitation period does not run when the act upon which execution is to be levied is altered or a request to that effect is rejected. Nor may the undertakings or associations of undertakings which are subject to a pecuniary obligation benefit from limitation when the appropriate authority is engaging in distraint proceedings in accordance with the procedural provisions in force. It should therefore be provided that the limitation period is interrupted by a decision of the Commission altering the original amount of the fine (sanction) or penalty or rejecting a request to do so as well as by any measure taken by a Member State at the request of the Commission and aimed at the forcible recovery of the fine (sanction) or penalty.

(9) Finally, the limitation period should also be suspended when an arrangement for payment is granted.

BE IT THEREFORE ENACTED AS FOLLOWS:

### Article 1

*Limitations as regards prosecutions*

(1) The power of the Commission to impose fines (sanctions) for infringement of the provisions of the transport law or the competition law of the European Economic Community is subject to a period of limitation. The limitation period is

—three years in the case of infringement of the provisions relating to requests for information or to the carrying out of inspections,

—five years in the case of all other infringements covered by the present regulation.

(2) The limitation period runs from the day on which the infringement was brought to an end.

### Article 2

*Interruption of the limitation period as regards prosecutions*

(1) The limitation period is interrupted by any measure taken by the Commission or by a Member State at the request of the Commission and aimed at proving the infringement.

Measures interrupting the limitation period include:

(*a*) the despatch of a request for information by the Commission or by the appropriate authorities of a Member State at the request of the Commission, as well as the notification of a decision of the Commission requiring the information requested;

(*b*) the despatch or the production of an inspection warrant in writing by the Commission or by the appropriate authorities of a Member State at the request of the Commission, as well as the notification of a decision of the Commission ordering inspection;

(*c*) the communication in writing of the commencement of proceedings by the Commission;

(*d*) the communication in writing of the plaints alleged by the Commission.

(2) The measures referred to in paragraph (1) and taken in relation to an undertaking or association of undertakings concerned interrupt the limitation period with regard to all the undertakings or associations of undertakings, participating in the infringement.

(3) The limitation period begins again from each interruption.

### Article 3

*Limitation as regards execution*

(1) The power of the Commission to execute its decisions imposing fines (sanctions) or penalties for infringement of the provisions of the

transport law or the competition law of the European Economic Community is subject to a period of limitation. The limitation period is three years. The limitation period runs from the day on which the Commission's decision acquires binding force.

(2) The limitation period is interrupted:

(*a*) by notification of a decision of the Commission altering the original amount of the fine (sanction) or penalty or rejecting a request to do so;

(*b*) by any measure taken by a Member State at the request of the Commission and aimed at the forcible recovery of the fine (sanction) or penalty.

The limitation period begins again from each interruption.

(3) The limitation period is suspended for as long as an arrangement for payment is granted.

## Article 4

*Entry into force*

The present Regulation shall enter into force on——————.

The present Regulation shall be binding in its entirety and directly applicable in all Member States.

APPENDIX 10*

## ANNOUNCEMENT ON EXCLUSIVE AGENCY CONTRACTS MADE WITH COMMERCIAL AGENTS [1]

I. The Commission considers that contracts made with commercial agents, in which those agents undertake, for a specified part of the territory of the Common Market:

—to negotiate transactions on behalf of an enterprise, or

—to conclude transactions in the name and on behalf of an enterprise, or

—to conclude transactions in their own name and on behalf of this enterprise,

are not covered by the prohibition laid down in Article 85, paragraph (1) of the Treaty.

It is essential in this case that the contracting party, described as a commercial agent, should, in fact, be such, by the nature of his functions, and that he should neither undertake nor engage in activities proper to an independent trader in the course of commercial operations. The Commission regards as the decisive criterion, which distinguishes the commercial agent from the independent trader, the agreement—express or implied—which deals with responsibility for the financial risks bound up with the sale or with the performance of the contract. Thus the Commission's assessment is not governed by the way the " representative " is described. Except for the usual *del credere* guarantee, a commercial agent must not, by the nature of his functions, assume any risk resulting from the transaction. If he does assume such risks his function becomes economically akin to that of an independent trader and he must therefore be treated as such for the purposes of the rules of competition. In such circumstances exclusive agency contracts must be regarded as agreements made with independent traders.

The Commission considers that an " independent trader " is most likely to be involved where the contracting party described as a commercial agent:

—is required to keep or does in fact keep, as his own property, a considerable stock of the products covered by the contract, or

—is required to organise, maintain or ensure at his own expense a substantial service to customers free of charge, or does in fact organise, maintain or ensure such a service, or

—can determine or does in fact determine prices or terms of business.

* The Notices contained in Apps. 10–13 are reproduced by the kind permission of the Controller of Her Majesty's Stationery Office from *The Board of Trade Journal.*
[1] December 24, 1962.

II. In contrast to what is envisaged in this announcement about contracts made with commercial agents, the possibility that Article 85, paragraph (1), may be applicable to exclusive agency contracts with independent traders cannot be ruled out. In the case of such exclusive contracts the restriction of competition lies either in the limitation of supply, when the vendor undertakes to supply a given product only to one purchaser, or in the limitation of demand, when the purchaser undertakes to obtain a given product only from one vendor. In the case of reciprocal undertakings there will be such restrictions of competition on both sides. The question whether a restriction of competition of this nature is liable to affect trade between Member States depends on the circumstances of the case.

On the other hand, in the Commission's opinion, the conditions for the prohibition laid down in Article 85, paragraph (1), are not fulfilled by exclusive agency contracts made with commercial agents, since they have neither the object nor the effect of preventing, restricting or distorting competition within the common market. The commercial agent only performs an auxiliary function in the commodity market. In that market he acts on the instructions and in the interest of the enterprise on whose behalf he is operating. Unlike the independent trader, he himself is neither a purchaser nor a vendor, but seeks purchasers or vendors in the interest of the other party to the contract, who is the person doing the buying or selling. In this type of exclusive representation contract, the selling or buying enterprise does not cease to be a competitor; it merely uses an auxiliary, *i.e.* the commercial agent, to dispose of or acquire products on the market.

The legal status of commercial agents is determined, more or less uniformly, by statute in most of the member countries and by case law in others. The characteristic feature which all commercial agents have in common is their function as auxiliaries in the negotiation of business deals. The powers of commercial agents are subject to the rules laid down in civil law on " mandate" and "procuration." [2] Within the limits of those provisions the other party to the contract —who is the person selling or buying—is free to decide the product and the territory in respect of which he is willing to assign those functions to his agent.

Apart from the competitive situation on those markets where the commercial agent functions as an auxiliary to the other party to the contract, one has to consider the particular market on which commercial agents offer their services for the negotiation or conclusion of transactions. The obligation assumed by the agent—to work exclusively for one principal for a certain period of time—entails a limitation of supply on that market; the obligation assumed by the other party to the contract—to appoint him sole agent for a given territory— involves a limitation of demand on that market. Nevertheless, the Commission sees these restrictions as a result of the special obligation

---

[2] Perhaps better translated as " agency " and " delegation of powers."

to protect each other's interests which exists between the commercial agent and his principal. Thus the Commission does not consider that they involve any restriction of competition.

The object of this announcement is to give firms some indication of the considerations which will guide the Commission in interpreting Article 85, paragraph (1), of the Treaty, as it applies to exclusive distribution agreements made with commercial agents. Generally speaking, this explanation will remove the incentive for firms to obtain a negative clearance for the agreements in question, and will make it unnecessary to have the legal position established by an individual decision by the Commission; moreover there is no longer any need to notify agreements of this nature. This announcement is without prejudice to any interpretation that may be made by other competent authorities and in particular by the courts.

## ANNOUNCEMENT ON PATENT LICENCE AGREEMENTS [1]

I. On the basis of the facts known at present, the Commission considers that the following clauses in patent licence contracts are not covered by the prohibition laid down in Article 85, paragraph (1), of the Treaty:

A. Obligations imposed on the licensee which have as their object:

(1) the limitation to certain of the forms of exploitation of the invention which are provided for by patent law (manufacture, use, sale);

(2) the limitation:

(*a*) of the manufacture of the patented product,

(*b*) of the use of the patented process,
to certain technical applications;

(3) the limitation of the quantity of products to be manufactured or of the number of acts constituting exploitation;

(4) the limitation of exploitation:

(*a*) in time (a licence of shorter duration than the patent),

(*b*) in space (a regional licence for part of the territory for which the patent is granted, or a licence limited to one place of exploitation or to a specific factory),

(*c*) with regard to the person (limitation of the licensee's power of disposal, *e.g.* prohibiting him from assigning the licence or from granting sub-licences);

B. Obligations whereby the licensee has to mark the product with an indication of the patent;

C. Quality standards or obligations to procure supplies of certain products imposed on the licensee—in so far as they are indispensable for the technically perfect exploitation of the patent;

D. Undertakings concerning the disclosure of experience gained in exploiting the invention or the grant of licences for inventions in the field of perfection or application; this however applies to undertakings entered into by the licensee only if those undertakings are not exclusive and if the licensor has entered into similar undertakings;

[1] December 24, 1962.

[ 339 ]

E. Undertakings on the part of the licensor:

    (1)  not to authorise anyone else to exploit the invention;

    (2)  not to exploit the invention himself.

II. This announcement is without prejudice to the appraisal from a legal point of view of clauses other than those referred to at I(A) to (E).

Moreover a general appraisal does not appear possible for agreements relating to:

    (1)  joint ownership of patents,

    (2)  reciprocal licences,

    (3)  parallel multiple licences.

The appraisal of the clauses referred to at I(A) to (E) is confined to clauses of a duration not exceeding the period of validity of the patent.

III. The object of this announcement is to give enterprises some indication of the considerations by which the Commission will be guided in interpreting Article 85, paragraph (1), of the Treaty and in applying it to a number of clauses often found in certain patent licence contracts. So long as and in so far as such contracts do not contain restrictions other than those resulting from one or more of the clauses mentioned above, the Commission considers that they are not affected by the prohibition laid down in Article 85, paragraph (1). Generally speaking this specific information will remove the incentive for firms to obtain a negative clearance for the agreements in question, and will make it unnecessary to have the legal position established by an individual decision by the Commission; moreover there is no longer any need to notify agreements of this nature.

This announcement is without prejudice to any interpretation that may be made by other competent authorities and in particular by the courts.

A decision is to be made later on the question of the application of Article 85, paragraph (1), of the Treaty to clauses of the types mentioned above which are contained in contracts relating to joint ownership of patents, to the grant of reciprocal licences or parallel multiple licences, to agreements relating to the exploitation of other industrial property rights or of creative activities not protected by law and constituting technical improvements, and to any clauses other than those mentioned above.

This announcement is without prejudice to the interpretation of Article 4, paragraph (2), sub-paragraph (ii) (b) of Regulation No. 17.

IV. The undertakings listed at I(A) do not fall within the scope of the prohibition laid down in Article 85, paragraph (1), because they are covered by the patent. They only entail the partial maintenance of the right of prohibition contained in the patentee's exclusive right in relation to the licensee, who in other respects is authorised to exploit the invention. The list at I(A) is not an exhaustive definition of the rights conferred by the patent.

The obligation imposed on the licensee to mark the product with an indication of the patent (point I(B)) is in accordance with the patentee's legitimate interest in ensuring that the protected articles are clearly shown to owe their origin to the patented invention. Since the licensee may also make distinguishing marks of his own choice on the protected article, this provision has neither the object nor the effect of restricting competition.

The licensee's undertakings, mentioned at I(C), concerning the observance of certain quality standards for the protected products or for semi manufactures, raw materials or auxiliary materials, could not restrict competition which has to be protected (la concurrence à protéger) to the extent that they are intended to prevent the technically incorrect working of the invention. The undertaking to procure supplies of certain products can be left out of account, except when quality cannot be established by objective standards. In that case, such an undertaking has the same scope as quality standards.

The undertakings given by the licensee and mentioned at I(D) do not in any case have any restrictive effect on competition when the licensee retains the possibility of disclosing experience gained or of granting licences to third parties and is entitled to participate in the licensor's future acquisitions in the field of experience and inventions. With regard to undertakings given by the licensor concerning the disclosure of experience or the grant of a licence, as mentioned at I(D), these seem to be unexceptionable from the point of view of the law relating to competition, even without that limitation. Thus point I(D) only covers the obligation to disclose experience or to grant licences; this is without prejudice to the appraisal from a legal point of view of any restrictions imposed on the interested parties concerning the utilisation of such experience or inventions.

By the undertaking mentioned at I(E)—not to authorise the use of the invention by any other person—the licensor forfeits the right to make agreements with other applicants for a licence. Leaving out of account the controversial question whether such exclusive undertakings have the object or effect of restricting competition, they are not likely to affect trade between member states as things stand in the Community at present. The undertaking not to exploit the patented invention oneself is closely akin to an assignment of the right and accordingly does not seem to be open to objection.

## NOTICE ON CO-OPERATION AGREEMENTS [1]

Questions are frequently put to the Commission of the European Communities on the attitude it intends to take up, within the framework of the implementation of the competition rules contained in the Treaties of Rome and Paris, with regard to co-operation between enterprises. In this Notice, it endeavours to provide guidance which, though not exhaustive, could prove useful to enterprises in the correct interpretation of Article 85 (1) of the EEC Treaty and Article 65 (1) of the ECSC Treaty.

I. The Commission welcomes co-operation among small- and medium-sized enterprises where such co-operation enables them to work more rationally and increase their productivity and competitiveness on a larger market. The Commission considers that it is its task to facilitate co-operation among small- and medium-sized enterprises in particular. However, co-operation among large enterprises, too, can be economically justifiable without presenting difficulties from the angle of competition.

Article 85 (1) of the Treaty establishing the European Economic Community (EEC Treaty) and Article 65 (1) of the Treaty establishing the European Coal and Steel Community (ECSC Treaty) provide that all agreements, decisions and concerted practices (hereafter referred to as " agreements ") which have as their object or result the prevention, restriction or distortion of competition (hereafter referred to as " restraints of competition ") in the common market are incompatible with the common market and are forbidden; under Article 85 (1) of the EEC Treaty this applies, however, only if these agreements are liable to impair trade between the Member States.

The Commission feels that in the interests of the small and medium-sized enterprises in particular it should make known the considerations by which it will be guided when interpreting Article 85 (1) of the EEC Treaty and Article 65 (1) of the ECSC Treaty and applying them to certain co-operation arrangements between enterprises, and indicate which of these arrangements in its opinion do not come under these provisions. This notice applies to all enterprises, irrespective of their size.

There may also be forms of co-operation between enterprises other than the forms of co-operation listed below which are not prohibited by Article 85 (1) of the EEC Treaty or Article 65 (1) of the ECSC Treaty. This applies in particular if the market position of the enter-

[1] July 29, 1968.

prises co-operating with each other is in the aggregate too weak as to lead, through the agreement between them, to an appreciable restraint of competition in the common market and—for Article 85 of the EEC Treaty—impair trade between the Member States.

It is also pointed out, in respect of other forms of co-operation between enterprises or agreements containing additional clauses, that where the rules of competition of the Treaties apply, such forms of co-operation or agreements can be exempted by virtue of Article 85 (3) of the EEC Treaty or be authorised by virtue of Article 65 (2) of the ECSC Treaty.

The Commission intends to establish rapidly, by means of suitable decisions in individual cases or by general notices, the status of the various forms of co-operation in relation with the provisions of the Treaty.

No general statement can be made at this stage on the application of Article 86 of the EEC Treaty on the abuse of dominant positions within the common market or within a part of it. The same applies to Article 66 (7) of the ECSC Treaty.

As a result of this notice, as a general rule, it will no longer be useful for enterprises to obtain negative clearance, as defined by Article 2 of Regulation No. 17, for the agreements listed, nor should it be necessary for the legal situation to be clarified through a Commission decision on an individual case; this also means that notification will no longer be necessary for agreements of this type, However, if it is doubtful whether in an individual case an agreement between enterprises restricts competition or if other forms of co-operation between enterprises which in the view of the enterprises do not restrict competition are not listed here, the enterprises are free to apply, where the matter comes under Article 85 (1) of the EEC Treaty, for negative clearance, or to file as a precautionary measure, where Article 65 (1) of the ECSC Treaty is the relevant clause, an application on the basis of Article 65 (2) of the ECSC Treaty.

This Notice does not prejudice interpretation by the Court of Justice of the European Communities.

II. The Commission takes the view that the following agreements do not restrict competition.

   (1) *Agreements having as their sole object:*

      (a) *An exchange of opinion or experience,*

      (b) *Joint market research,*

      (c) *The joint carrying out of comparative studies of enterprises or industries,*

      (d) *The joint preparation of statistics and calculation models.*

Agreements whose sole purpose is the joint procurement of information which the various enterprises need to determine their future market behaviour freely and independently, or the use by each of the enterprises of a joint advisory body, do not have as their object or result the restriction of competition. But if the scope of action of the enterprises is limited or if the market behaviour is co-ordinated either expressly or through concerted practices, there may be restraint of competition. This is in particular the case where concrete recommendations are made or where conclusions are given such a form that they induce at least some of the participating enterprises to behave in an identical manner on the market.

The exchange of information can take place between the enterprises themselves or through a body acting as an intermediary. It is, however, particularly difficult to distinguish between information which has no bearing on competition on the one hand and behaviour in restraint of competition on the other, if there are special bodies which have to register orders, turnover figures, investment figures, and prices, so that it can as a rule not be automatically assumed that Article 85 (1) of the EEC Treaty or Article 65 (1) of the ECSC Treaty do not apply to them. A restraint of competition may occur in particular on an oligopolist market for homogeneous products.

In the absence of more far-reaching co-operation between the participating enterprises, joint market research and comparative studies of different enterprises and industries to collect information and ascertain facts and market conditions do not in themselves impair competition.

Other arrangements of this type, as for instance the joint establishment of economic and structural analyses, are so obviously not impairing competition that there is no need to mention them specifically.

Calculation models containing specified rates of calculations are to be regarded as recommendations that may lead to restraints of competition.

    (2) *Agreements having as their sole object:*

        (a) *Co-operation in accounting matters,*

        (b) *Joint provision of credit guarantees,*

        (c) *Joint debt-collecting associations,*

        (d) *Joint business or tax consultant agencies.*

These are cases of co-operation relating to fields that do not concern the supply of goods and services and the economic decisions of the enterprises involved, so that they cannot lead to restraints of competition.

Co-operating in accounting matters is neutral from the point of view of competition as it only serves for the technical handling of the accounting work. Nor is the creation of credit guarantee associations affected by the competition rules, since it does not modify the relationship between supply and demand.

Debt-collecting associations whose work is not confined to the collection of outstanding payments in line with the intentions and conditions of the participating enterprises, or which fix prices or exert in any other way an influence on price formation, may restrict competition. Application of uniform conditions by all participating firms may constitute a case of concerted practices, as may joint comparison of prices. In this connection, no objection can be raised against the use of standardised printed forms; their use must however not be combined with an understanding or tacit agreement on uniform prices, rebates or conditions of sale.

(3) *Agreements having as their sole object:*

   (a) *The joint implementation of research and development projects,*

   (b) *The joint placing of research and development contracts,*

   (c) *The sharing out of research and development projects among participating enterprises.*

In the field of research, too, the mere exchange of experience and results serves for information only and does not restrict competition. It therefore need not be mentioned expressly.

Agreements on the joint execution of research work or the joint development of the results of research up to the stage of industrial application do not affect the competitive position of the parties. This also applies to the sharing of research fields and development work if the results are available to all participating enterprises. However, if the enterprises enter into commitments which restrict their own research and development activity or the utilisation of the results of joint work so that they do not have a free hand with regard to their own research and development outside the joint projects, this can constitute an infringement of the rules of competition of the Treaties. Where firms do not carry out joint research work, contractual obligations or concerted practices binding them to refrain from research work of their own either completely or in certain sectors may result in a restraint of competition. The sharing out of sectors of research without an understanding providing for mutual access to the results is to be regarded as a case of specialisation that may restrict competition.

There may also be a restraint of competition if agreements are concluded or corresponding concerted practices applied with regard to the practical exploitation of the results of research and development work carried out jointly, particularly if the participating enterprises undertake or agree to manufacture only products or the types of products developed jointly or to share out future production among themselves.

It is of the essence of joint research that the results should be exploited by the participating enterprises in proportion to their participation. If the participation of certain enterprises is confined to a specific sector of the common research project or to the provision of only limited financial assistance, there is no restraint of competition so far as there has been any joint research at all—if the results of research are made available to these enterprises only in relation with the degree of their participation. There may, however, be a restraint of competition if certain participating enterprises are excluded from the exploitation of the results, either entirely or to an extent not commensurate with their participation.

If the granting of licences to third parties is expressly or tacitly excluded, there may be a restraint of competition; the fact that research is carried out jointly warrants, however, arrangements binding the enterprises to grant licences to third parties only by common agreement or by majority decision.

For the assessment of the compatibility of the agreement with the rules of competition, it does not matter what legal form the common research and development work takes.

(4) *Agreements which have as their only object the joint use of production facilities and storing and transport equipment.*

These forms of co-operation do not restrict competition because they are confined to organisational and technical arrangements for the use of the facilities. There may be a restraint of competition if the enterprises involved do not bear the cost of utilisation of the installation or equipment themselves or if agreements are concluded or concerted practices applied regarding joint production or the sharing out of production or the establishment or running of a joint enterprise.

(5) *Agreements having as their sole object the setting up of working partnerships for the common execution of orders, where the participating enterprises do not compete with each other as regards the work to be done or where each of them by itself is unable to execute the orders.*

Where enterprises do not compete with each other they cannot restrict competition by setting up associations. This applies in particular to enterprises belonging to different industries but also to firms of the same industry to the extent that their contribution under the working partnership consist only of goods or services which cannot be supplied by the other participating enterprises. It is not a question of whether the enterprises compete with each other in other industries so much as whether in the light of the concrete circumstances of a particular case there is a possibility that in the foreseeable future they may compete with each other with regard to the products or services involved. If the absence of competition between the enterprises and the maintenance of this situation are based on agreements or concerted practices, there may be a restraint of competition.

But even in the case of associations[2] formed by enterprises which compete with each other there is no restraint of competition if the participating enterprises cannot execute the specific order by themselves. This applies in particular if, for lack of experience, specialised knowledge, capacity of financial resources these enterprises, when working alone, have no chance of success or cannot finish the work within the required time-limit or cannot bear the financial risk. Nor

[2] For "associations" read "working partnerships." (amended by the Commission—see J.O. 1968, C84, August 28, 1968).

is there a restraint of competition if it is only by the setting up of an association that the enterprises are put in a position to make a promising offer. There may, however, be a restraint of competition if the enterprises undertake to work solely in the framework of an association.

(6) *Agreements having as their sole object:*

    (a) *Joint selling arrangements,*

    (b) *Joint after-sales and repair service, provided the participating enterprises are not competitors with regard to the products or services covered by the agreement.*

As already explained in detail under Section 5, co-operation between enterprises cannot restrict competition if the firms do not compete with each other.

Very often joint selling by small- or medium-sized enterprises— even if they are competing with each other—does not entail an appreciable restraint of competition; it is, however, impossible to establish in this Notice any general criteria or to specify what enterprises may be deemed " small or medium-sized."

There is no joint after-sales and repair service if several manufacturers, without acting in concert with each other, arrange for an after-sales and repair service for their product to be provided by an enterprise which is independent. In such a case there is no restraint of competition, even if the manufacturers are competitors.

(7) *Agreements having as their sole object joint advertising*

Joint advertising is designed to draw the buyers' attention to the products of an industry or to a common brand; as such it does not restrict competition between the participating enterprises. However, if the participating enterprises are partly or wholly prevented, by agreements or concerted practices, from themselves advertising or if they are subjected to other restrictions, there may be a restraint of competition.

(8) *Agreements having as their sole object the use of a common label to designate a certain quality, where the label is available to all competitors on the same conditions.*

Such associations for the joint use of a quality label do not restrict competition if other competitors, whose products objectively meet the stipulated quality requirements, can use the label on the same conditions as the members. Nor do the obligations to accept quality control of the products provided with the label, to issue uniform instructions for use, or to use the label for the products meeting the quality standards constitute restraints of competition. But there may be restraint of competition if the right to use the label is linked to obligations regarding production, marketing, price formation or obligations of any other type, as is for instance the case when the participating enterprises are obliged to manufacture or sell only products of guaranteed quality.

[ 347 ]

APPENDIX 13

## NOTICE CONCERNING MINOR AGREEMENTS [1]

The Commission considers, as it has already indicated on different occasions, that it is important to promote co-operation between undertakings in so far as it is economically desirable and does not raise any objections in respect of the policy of competition; it desires, in particular, to facilitate co-operation between small- and medium-sized undertakings. It was with this in mind that it published the " Announcement on agreements, decisions and concerted practices relating to co-operation between undertakings " [2]—hereinafter referred to as " agreements "—an announcement listing a series of agreements which, by their nature, do not restrict competition. With the present announcement, the Commission pursues its effort to define the field of application of Article 85 paragraph (1) of the Treaty establishing the European Economic Community with the aim of promoting co-operation between small- and medium-sized undertakings.

The Commission considers that the prohibition on agreements set down in Article 85 paragraph (1) of the Treaty of the European Economic Community does not cover those agreements which do not affect to a significant degree competition and trade between Member States. Only those agreements are prohibited which have an appreciable effect on market conditions, in other words, which appreciably modify the market position of non-participating undertakings and of consumers, that is, their outlets and sources of supply.

In the present announcement the Commission attaches a sufficiently concrete meaning to the term " appreciable " for undertakings to be able to decide for themselves whether agreements reached with other undertakings do not fall within the scope of Article 85 paragraph (1) on account of their minor importance. The quantitative definition of " appreciable " given by the Commission, does not however have an absolute value: it is quite possible that, in particular cases, agreements reached by undertakings which exceed the limits indicated below only affect competition and trade between Member States to an insignificant degree and consequently do not fall within the scope of Article 85 paragraph (1).

This announcement should eliminate the need to obtain negative clearance in the sense of Article 2 of Regulation 17 for the agreements envisaged. Nor should it any longer be necessary to seek to clarify the legal position by individual decisions of the Commission; there is therefore no need to notify such agreements for that purpose.

[1] May 27, 1970. J.O. 1970 C84/1.
[2] J.O. 1968 C75/3 corrected by J.O. 1968 C84.

[ 348 ]

However, when there is doubt in a particular case whether an agreement affects competition and trade between Member States to an appreciable degree, undertakings may request a negative clearance or may notify the agreement.

This announcement does not prejudice the interpretation of the Court of Justice of the European Communities.

The Commission considers that agreements between production or distribution undertakings are not covered by the prohibition of Article 85 paragraph (1) of the Treaty establishing the European Economic Community:

—when the products involved in the agreement represent, in the part of the common market where the agreement is effective, not more than 5 per cent. of the volume of business effected with identical products or products considered by consumers to be similar on account of their properties, price or use and

—when the aggregate annual turnover of the undertakings participating in the agreement does not exceed 15 million units of account or, in the case of agreements between commercial undertakings, 20 million units of account.

Furthermore, the Commission considers that the above agreements are not covered by the prohibition of Article 85 paragraph (1) if, in the course of two consecutive financial years, the market shares and the turnover thus fixed are exceeded by less than 10 per cent.

The aggregate turnover is derived from the sum of the turnovers of the last financial year comprising all products and services, achieved by:

1. undertakings taking part in the agreement;

2. undertakings in which the undertakings taking part in the agreement hold:
   —at least 25 per cent. of the capital or working capital, whether directly or indirectly,
   —or at least half the voting rights,
   —or the power to appoint at least half the members of the supervisory board or board of management, or of bodies legally representing the undertaking,
   —or the right to manage the undertaking's affairs;

3. Undertakings holding, in an undertaking which is taking part in the agreement:
   —at least 25 per cent. of the capital or working capital, whether directly or indirectly,
   —or at least half the voting rights,
   —or the power to appoint at least half the members of the supervisory board or board of management, or of bodies legally representing the undertaking,
   —or the right to manage the undertaking's affairs.

The aggregate turnover does not take into account transactions between undertakings taking part in the agreement.

# INDEX

Absolute territorial protection, 218,
626, 811–817, 822
  defined, 812
  exclusive dealing, 811–817, 822
    *See also* National markets, pro-
    tection of.
Abuse of dominant position generally. *See* Article 86.
Accession,
  pre-accession agreements, 1209
Accession agreements,
  defined, 207
  notification of, 411
  retroactive exemption, 632
  validity of, 208
    *See* Notification, provisional
    validity.
Accounting methods,
  standardisation of, 317
Advertising, joint, 351, 352
Advisory committee on restrictive
  practices and monopolies, 1224
Advocate-General, 111
After-sales service,
  joint, 346
Agent. *See* Sole agent; Sole agency
  agreements.
Agents and principals, 253
Aggregated rebates cartels, 334, 618
Agreements, Accession. *See* Ac-
  cession agreements.
Agreements,
  defined, 206
Agricultural products, 131
Aids granted by states, 119
Air conditioning equipment. *See*
  Table of Decisions: *Clima
  Chappée, Re.*
Aniline dyes. *See* Table of De-
  cisions: *ICI and others.*
Appeals against Commission's de-
  cisions, 1227–1232
Approximation of laws, 120
Article 4 (2) of Regulation 17,
  generally, 528–533
  information about agreements fall-
  ing under, 1215
Article 85, 113, 114, 715
  Article 86, relationship with, 715
  implementation generally, 116,
  121–138
  transitional provisions, 117, 118
Article 85 (1)
  (*a*)–(*e*), 201, 226, 301
  Accession agreements. *See* Accession agreements.
  accounting standardisation, 317

Article 85 (1)—*cont.*
  aggregated rebates cartel, 334
  common types of agreement, 301–
  353
  competition, prevention, distortion
  or restriction of, 215–229
  competition within common
  market, 227
  concerted practices, 211–214
  conditions of sale, 303–324
  conditions of trading, 343
  consultants, joint use of, 317
  controlled companies, 250–252
  credit guarantees, joint, 317
  debt-collecting, joint, 317
  decisions of associations of undertakings, 209-210
  definition of agreements, 206–208
  *de minimis* agreements, 245–249
  discounts, 308
  discrimination, 313, 323, 1105
  domestic agreements and, 236–237
  effect of agreement, 221–229
  exchange of opinions, experience,
  316
  exclusive dealing agreements, 801
  *et seq.*
  exclusive licences, 944
  export cartels, 306
  export prohibitions, 321–323, 343
  exports outside EEC, 243, 244
  extra-territorial effects of, 240–
  244, 833–835
  full line forcing, 314
  generally, 201–253, 301–353
  goodwill, sale of, 329
  imports into EEC, 242
  industrial property, 908–911, 930–
  958
  information agreements, 315, 316
  international price fixing cartels, 305
  investment, limitation on, 325
  joint advertising, 351, 352
  joint purchasing, 335
  joint selling, 337–346
  joint studies, 316
  market research, joint, 316
  market sharing, 325, 326, 330, 1331
  mergers and, 739
  national agreements, and, 236–237
  national export cartels, 306
  object of agreement, 221–225
  price agreements, 303–324
  production, limitation on, 325,
  327, 330
  quality control, 353
  quality labels, 353

[ 351 ]

Assembly, European, 108
Associations of undertakings,
  defined, 210
  discrimination in constitution of,
    1105
  recommendations of, 209
Authorities of Member States. *See*
  Member States.

Benefits, resulting from agreements.
  *See* Article 85 (3).
Block exemptions,
  generally, 127–129, 609
  exclusive dealing agreements, 127,
    128, 811, 818–828, *also see*
    Regulation 67/67.
  Research and development agree-
    ments, 129, 1102, 1116
  specialisation agreements, 1007,
    1008, 1010–1013
  standardisation agreements, 328
Books. *See* Resale price maintenance.
Brewery industry,
  enquiry into, 1215
British courts,
  agreements exempt from notifi-
    cation before, 422
  function of, generally, 139–153
  jurisdiction of, 409
  notified agreements before, 421
  unnotified agreements before, 401–
    409
British law,
  Community law, relationship with,
    139–153, 230
  conflict with Community law, 140,
    141
  European Communities Act, 149
  fair trading, 143–152
  mergers, 143, 145, 148, 149
  monopolies, 143, 145, 148, 149
  resale prices, 146, 149
  restraint of trade, 145, 149
  restrictive trade practices, 144,
    148–152

Carbon paper. *See* Table of
  Decisions: *Burroughs, Re.*
Cement industry. *See* Table of
  Decisions: *Limeburners, Re; NCH,
  Re; VCH, Re.*
Ceramic tiles. *See* Table of De-
  cisions: *German Ceramic Tiles, Re.*
Clocks and watches. *See* Table of
  Decisions: *Jaz-Peter, Re; Omega.*
Coal and steel, 106, 149
Commission,
  complaints to, 1214
  defined, 110

Commission—*contd.*
  duty to act, 1230
  enquiries by sector of economy,
    1215
  extra-territorial jurisdiction of,
    240–244
  informal negotiation with, 1222
  investigation by, 1213–1219
  Member States' authorities, col-
    laboration with, 1213, 1217, 1218
  notices of, 134, 135
  policy of, 132–135, 604–605
  power of investigation, 1218, 1219
  power to grant exemptions, 602,
    631–636
  power to obtain information,
    1215–1217, 1219
  territorial jurisdiction of, 1209
Commission of the European Communities. *See* Commission; Decisions of Commission.
Community law,
  national law, relationship with,
    139–153, 230
  " self executing " nature, 140
  superiority of, 140, 141
Complaints to Commission, 1214,
  1227, 1230
Concerted practices, 211–214
  conditions of trading, 303
  *Dyestuffs* case, 212–214
  evidence of, 212, 214
  *See also* Article 85 (1).
Conditions of purchase. *See* Conditions of trading.
Conditions of sale. *See* Conditions
  of trading.
Conditions of trading, 303–324, 343
  collectively agreed, 312
  horizontal agreements, as to, 304–
    317
  purchase terms, 309
  sales terms, 304–308, 310–314
  specialisation agreements, 626
  unfair,
    Article 86, 721
Consultants,
  joint use of, 317
Consumers,
  definition for Article 85 (3), 622
Co-operation agreements,
  Commission's encouragement of,
    605–608
  Commission Notice on, 229
  parties not in competition, 229
  permitted forms, 229
Copyright, 735, 905, 906, 913–929
  *See also* Industrial property.

Cosmetics and perfumes. *See* Table of Decisions: *Parfums Marcel Rochas, Re; ASPA, Re.*
Council of Ministers, 109
Courts. *See* British courts; European Court.
Courts of other Member States, decisions of, 137
Credit guarantees, joint, 317

Debt-collecting, joint, 317
Decisions of associations of undertakings, defined, 209
Decisions of Commission, 132, 133, 1201 *et seq.*
appeals against, 1227–1232
default fine, imposing, 1204
fines, imposing, 1205–1212
information, requiring, 1215, 1216
infringement, terminating, 1201–1212
investigation, requiring submission to, 1218
periodic penalty payment, imposing, 1204
procedure, 1221–1226
provisional validity, terminating, 1202, 1208
publicity of, 1202, 1225
stay of execution of, 1232
Decisions of courts. *See* British courts; European Court.
Declaration of inapplicability, Article 85 (1), of, 502
Delay by Commission, 504, 1230
*De minimis,*
Commission Notice on, 247, 248
*Deutsche Grammophon,* 927
joint purchasing, 335
joint selling, 340
price agreements, 308
*Volk* v. *Vervaecke,* 245
Department of Trade and Industry, Commission's power to obtain information from, 1216
Detergents. *See* Table of Decisions: *Henkel-Colgate, Re.*
*Deutsche Grammophon,*
assignee of right, products sold by, 923
conditions for application of rule, 920–929
controlled companies, sale by, 924
*de minimis,* 927
European Court, decision of, 917
European Court, reference to, 916
facts of, 915

*Deutsche Grammophon—contd.*
issues raised by, 913
other industrial property rights, 919
owner, sale by, 922
plaintiff's consent, sale with, 922
sale without, 925
products sold in another Member State, 921
reasoning in, 918
Regulation 17, application of, 928
" solely to prevent imports," 926
transitional provisions, 929
Director-General of Fair Trading, 144, 150–152, 1216
Discounts,
Article 85 (1), 303, 305, 308
aggregated rebates cartel, 334
Discrimination,
Article 85 (1), 313, 323
Article 86, 723, 732, 736
constitution of associations, in, 1105
nationality, on grounds of, 723, 732, 736
price, 323
terms of sale, in, 313
Distribution agreements, 801 *et seq.*
non-exclusive, 803
Distribution, selective,
Article 85 (3), 614, 625, 627
Domestic Agreements,
Article 85 (1) and, 236-237
exemption from notification, 529, 530
Dominant position, 630
call for evidence concerning, 1215
description of goods and services, 708, 709
*Henkel-Colgate,* 1109
*And see* Article 86.
Double jeopardy, 1207
Dumping, 119, 131
Dyestuffs. *See* Table of Decisions: *ICI and others.*

Economic Progress. *See* Article 85 (3).
Effect, doctrine of, 240–241
Electrical goods. *See* Table of Decisions: *Grundig-Consten, Re.*
Enforcement,
generally, 1201 *et seq.*
of Commission's orders by penalties, 1212
Enquiries by sector of economy, 1215
Equalisation, price, 339, 342
*See* Aggregated rebates cartel.

INDEX

European Coal and Steel Community, 106, 149
European Coal and Steel Treaty, undertakings, 201
European Communities Act 1972, general provisions, (ss. 2 and 3), 112, 140, 141, 149, 404, 407, 743
restrictive practices provisions, (s. 10), 149–153, 1216
European Court, Commission, control over, 1227–1232
function of, 111
generally, 111, 136
interpretative rulings, 409, 1227
jurisdiction of, 1227 et seq.
European Economic Community, purposes of, 101, 120
European Parliament, 108
Exclusive dealing agreements, 801 et seq.
absolute territorial protection, with, 811–817
absolute territorial protection, without, 815, 822
Article 85 (1), application of, 803, 808–817
Article 85 (3), application of, 811, 818–828
Article 86 and, 714
block exemption for, 811, 818–828
See also Regulation 67/67.
collective, 331–334, 714
de minimis, 816
domestic agreements, 529–530, 830, 831
exports from EEC, 833–835
function of, 808, 811
Grosfillex case, 834
Grundig-Consten, 812–814
imports into EEC, 832
inter-state, 811–829
joint sales agency, 337–346
obligation to import before resale, in, 827
Omega, Re, 841–843
protection of dealer, 809–814
Rieckermann case, 835
selective systems, 840–843
subsidiary and parent, between, 817
whole of common market, for, 829
See also Specialisation agreements.
Exclusive distributor. See Exclusive dealing agreements.
Exclusive licences, Article 85 (1), application of, 944–949
Article 85 (3), application of, 959, 960

Exclusive licences—contd.
Burroughs decisions, 948–949
Davidson-Rubber, 946–947, 960
Exemption under Article 85 (3). See Article 85 (3).
Exemption from Notification, domestic exclusive dealing agreements, 831
licensing agreements, 957-958
requirements contracts, 839
research and development, 1113–1115
specialisation agreements, 1043–1047
See also Article 4 (2) of Regulation 17.
Exhibitions, See Trade fairs.
Export agreements, British law, 148, 1216
See Article 85 (1).
Export cartels, 306, 338–340
Export restrictions, 321–323, 326, 330–332, 343
domestic exclusive dealing agreements, 831
Grundig-Consten, 234
outside EEC, 240–244, 338

Fair Trading, British law, 143–152
Director-General of, 144, 150–152
Fertilizers. See Table of Decisions: Belgaphos, Re; Cobelaz, Re, (No. 1) and (No. 2); Supexie, Re; Seifa, Re; CFA, Re.
Fines, amount of, 1206
double jeopardy, 1207
national legislation, under, 1207
notified agreements, in respect of, 1208
infringements, for, 1205–1212
pre-accession agreements, for, 1209
successors in title, liability of, 1210
See also Penalties.
Firearms. See Table of Decisions: FN-CF.
First Report on Competition Policy, 135
Fishery products, 131
Food products. See Table of Decisions: SOCEMAS, Re.
Form A/B, notification on, 535
Free movement of goods, Treaty provisions for, 120, 912, 917–929

[ 355 ]

Price discrimination,
Article 85 (1), 313, 323
Article 86, 723, 736
Price equalisation schemes, 339, 342
Price leaders,
Article 86, application to, 703
concerted practices and, 211
Prices, unfair,
Article 86, 721
Principals and agents, 253
Procedure,
initiation of, by Commission, 421
notification and negative clearance, for, 527 *et seq.*
prior to a decision, 1221
Production,
limitation on,
Article 85, 325–330
Article 86, 722
Production facilities,
joint use of, 229
Promotion, trade,
Article 85 (1) and, 347–353
Provisional validity, 403, 410–422
Accession agreements, 418
agreements for which exemption unlikely, 420
*Bilger* v. *Jehle*, 414
*Bosch* v. *de Geus*, 415, 417
*Brasserie de Haecht* (*No. 2*), 414–419
British courts, consequences for, 421, 422
decision of Commission terminating, 1202, 1208
new agreements, 419
old agreements, 415–417
*Portelange*, 415–417
Publicity,
decision of Commission, of, 1225
Purchasing,
joint, 335, 336
Purchasing terms. *See* Conditions of trading.

Quality control, 353
Quality improvement, 620
Quality labels, common, 353
Quinine. *See* Table of Decisions:
*ACF-Chemiefarma*; *Boehringer Mannheim*; *Buchler*.
Quotas,
Article 85 (1), 325, 327, 331
Article 85 (3), 608

Rationalisation agreements, 1001, 1003
*See also* Specialisation agreements generally.

Rebates,
aggregated, 618
*See also* Discounts.
Recommendation,
infringement, terminating, 1203, 1204
Recommended prices, 311, 620
Register of Restrictive Trading Agreements, 151, 1216
special section, 1216
Registrar of Restrictive Trading Agreements, 144, 150–152, 1216
Regulations,
generally, 121–131
*And see* Table of Regulations.
Regulation 17,
generally, 122–124
Regulation 67/67,
absolute territorial protection, 822
Accession agreements, 824
agreements to which applies, 819
competing manufacturers, 821
duration, 818
French law of unfair competition, 822
industrial property rights, use of, 822
non-qualifying agreements, 826–831
permitted restrictions, 820
requirements contracts, 838
revocation of benefit of, 623
transitional provisions, 825, 826
Requirements contracts, 801, 803, 836–839
Article 85 (1), application of, 837
*Brasserie de Haecht*, 837
exemption from notification, 839
Regulation 67/67, 838
Resale,
limitation on, in specialisation agreements, 626
*See also* Conditions of trading.
Resale prices,
collective recommendation of, 311
Resale price maintenance,
Article 85 (1), 303, 310, 311, 318–323, 333
collective enforcement, 310, 313
Commission's view, 319
exemption from notification, 530, 531
preservation of, 321
United Kingdom, in, 146, 149, 310
Research and development agreements, 1101–1116
*AC EC-Berliet*, 1110–1112
Article 85 (1), 1101–1108